Let only the eager, thoughtful and reverent enter here.

They only are loyal to this college
who departing bear their added riches in trust for mankind.

—PRESIDENT JAMES A. BLAISDELL
INSCRIPTIONS ON THE POMONA COLLEGE GATE

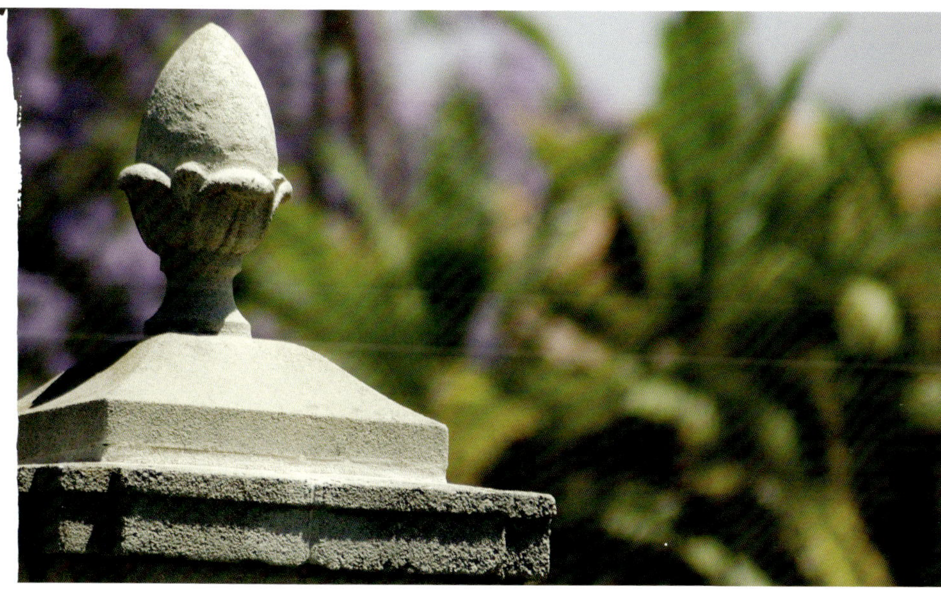

Mark Wood

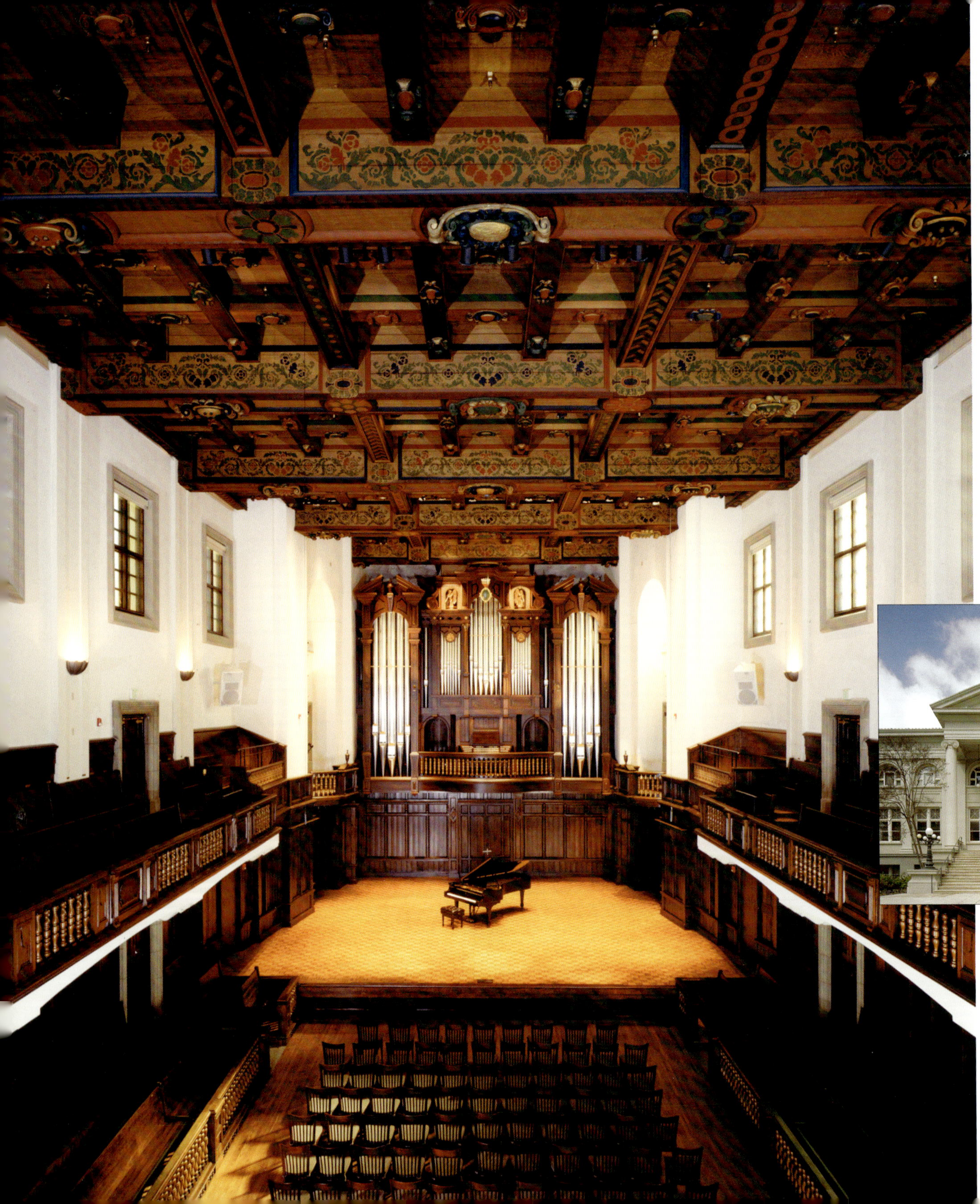

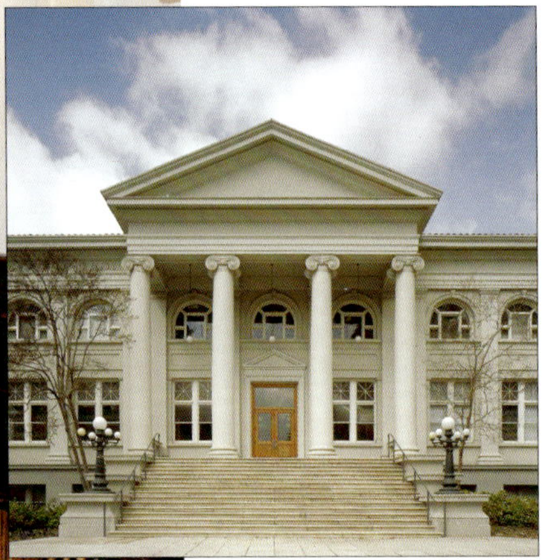

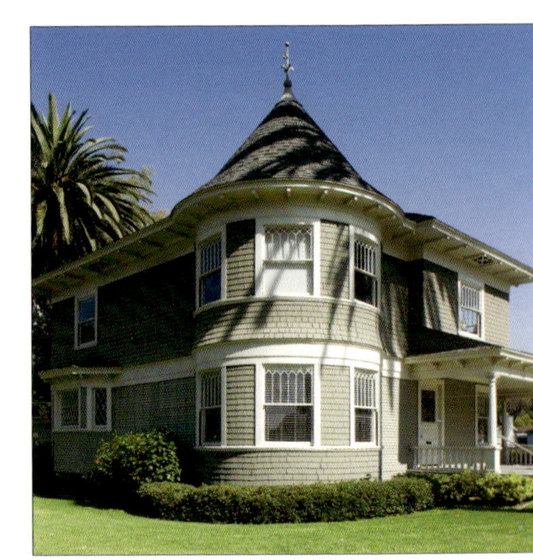

POMONA COLLEGE

Marjorie L. Harth

WITH ESSAYS BY Ronald Lee Fleming
George L. Gorse
Verlyn Klinkenborg
PRINCIPAL PHOTOGRAPHY BY Henry Cabala

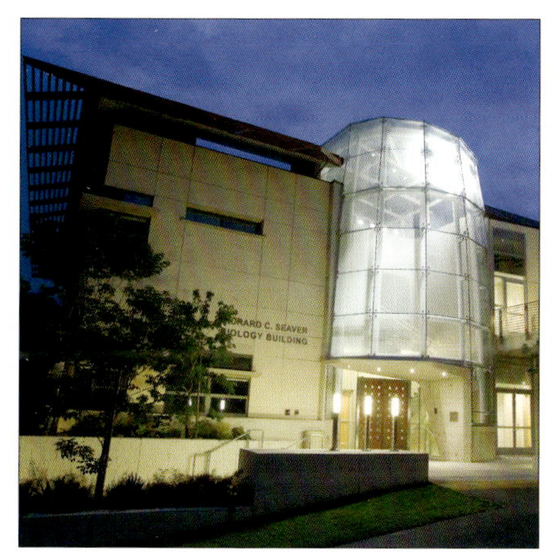

Pomona College

REFLECTIONS ON A CAMPUS

CLAREMONT, CALIFORNIA

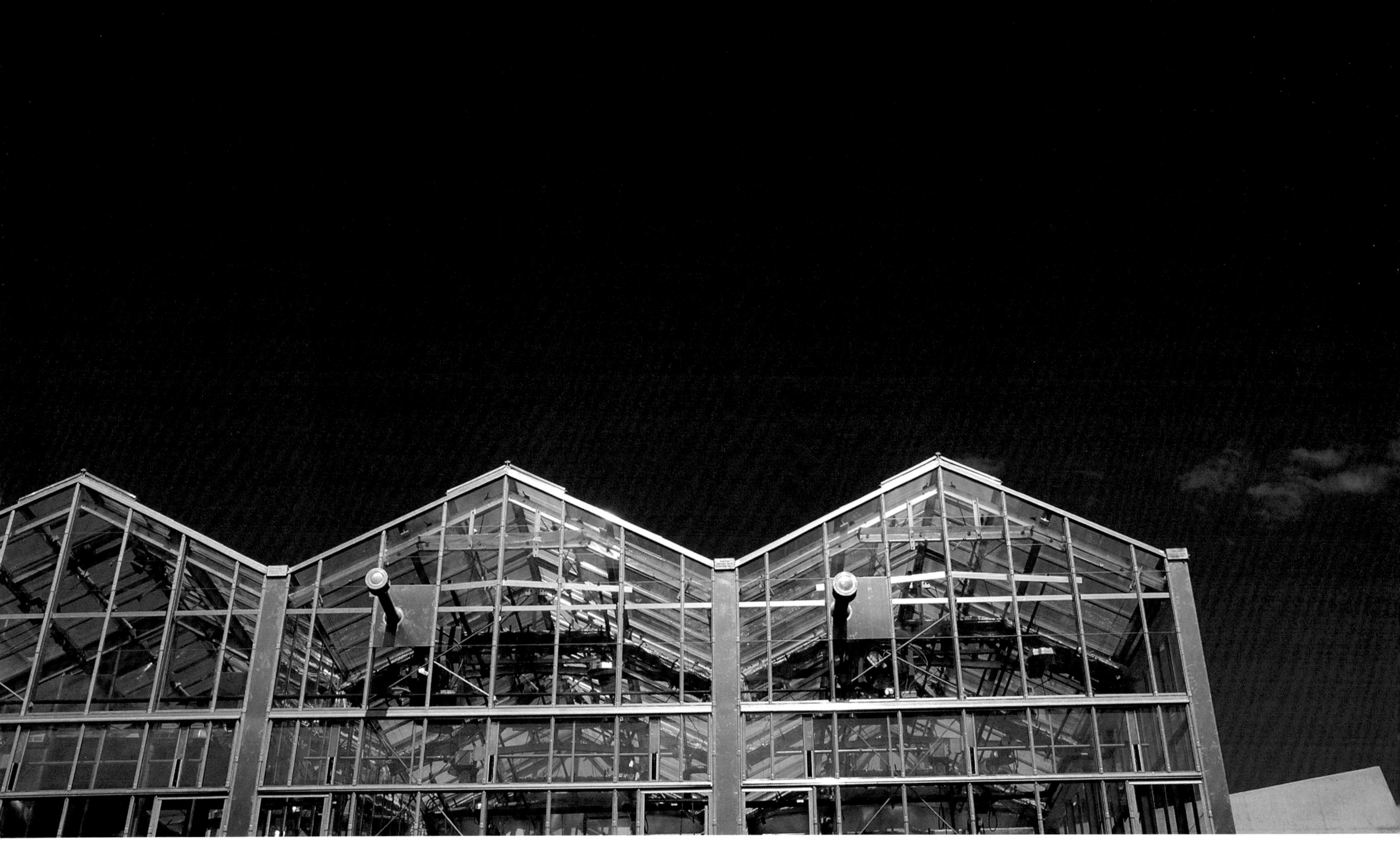

All unattributed photos courtesy of the Pomona College archives.

Library of Congress Control Number: 2007922099 ISBN: 978-0-9786996-5-9
Printed in Singapore
Designed by Lilli Colton

P. 1: College Gate (Mark Wood); P. 2, LEFT TO RIGHT: Mabel Shaw Bridges Hall of Music, interior after renovation of 2000–01 (Gene Sasse); Andrew Carnegie Building (Henry Cabala); Renwick House (Henry Cabala); Seaver Biology Building (Phil Channing); P. 7: Bridges Hall of Music (Mark Wood); PAGE 192: *Carnegie Building* (Henry Cabala); ABOVE: Seaver Biology Building (Gene Sasse)

Contents

This book is dedicated to the memory of Caroline Burtis Beatty (1912-2002), who served for decades as Pomona College's historical researcher, archivist, and guardian of institutional memory. Her love for the College—its people and its places, its history and its promise—has served as my inspiration and guide.

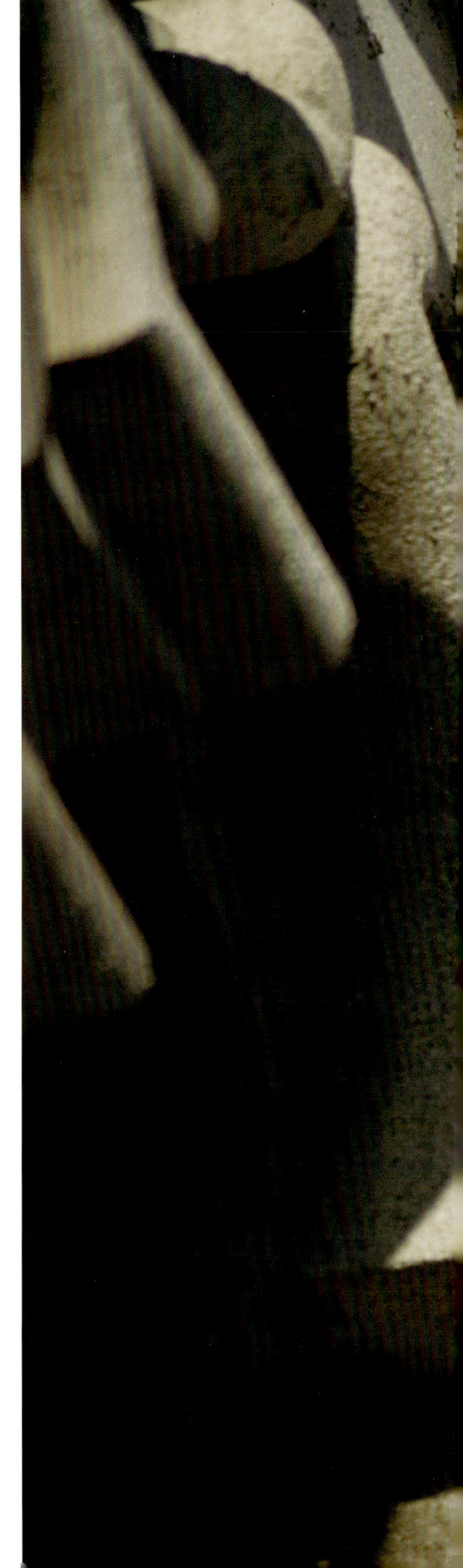

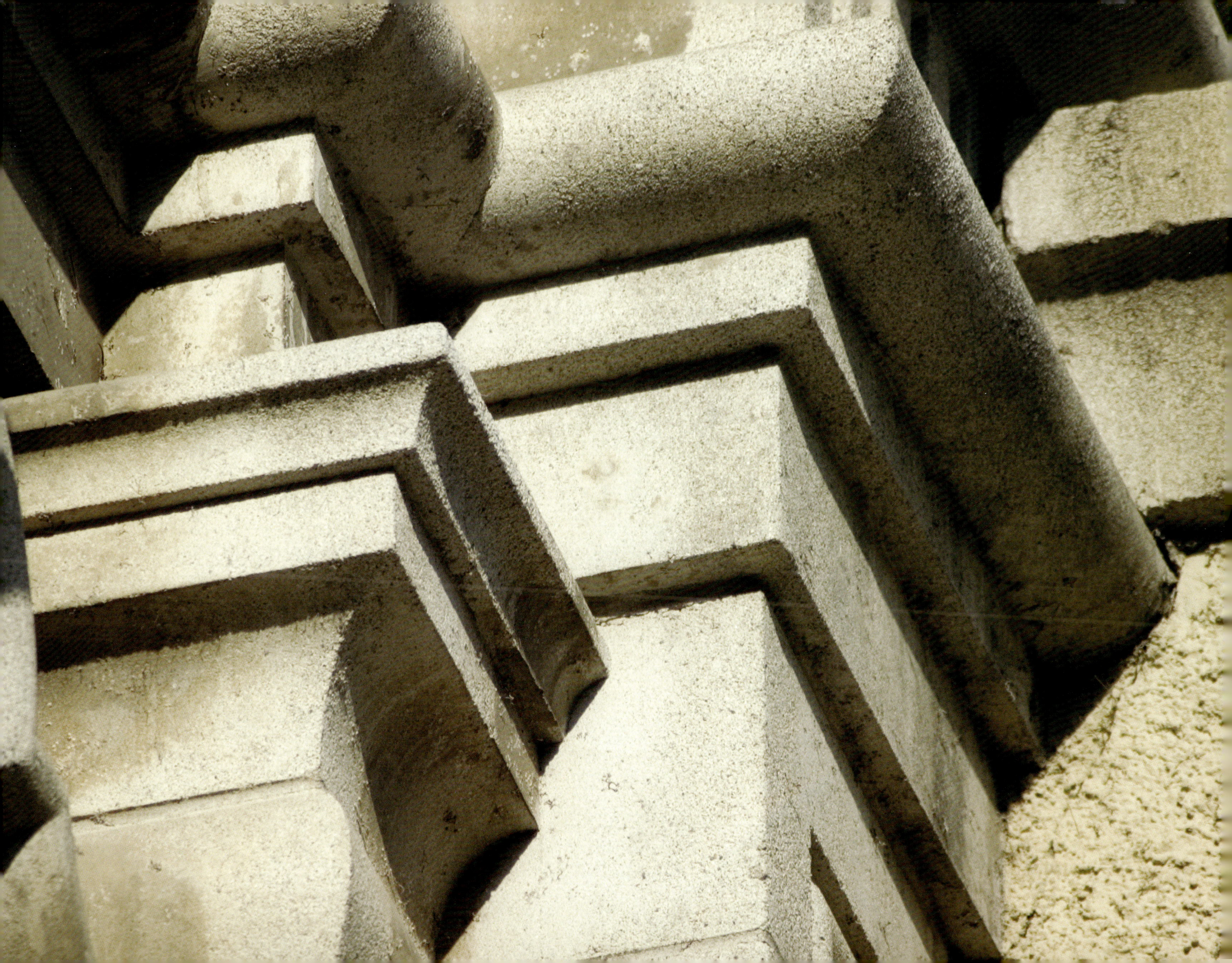

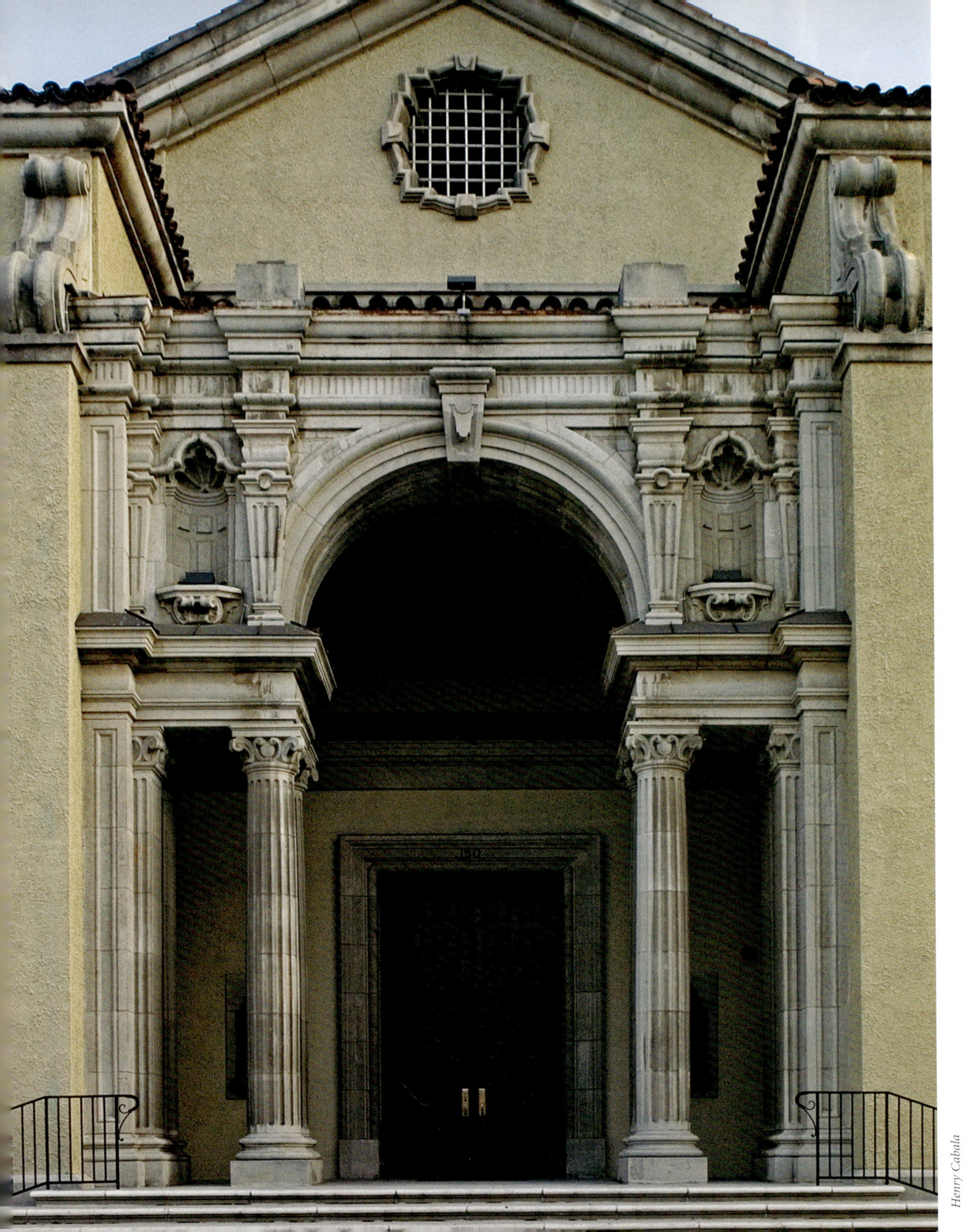

Henry Cabala

FOREWORD

Bridges Hall of Music

President's Foreword

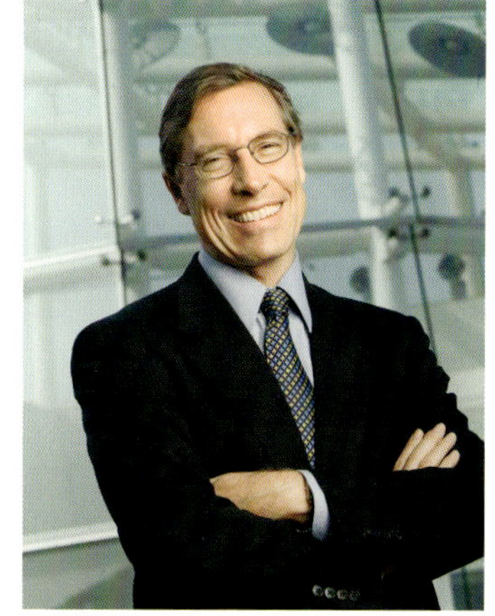

Phil Channing

President David W. Oxtoby

Pomona College is many things. It is an institution with the highest aspirations for undergraduate liberal arts education. It is the students, faculty, staff, and trustees who bring that mission to life. It is a unique set of traditions, values, and opportunities that frame the "Pomona experience." But before it can be any of those things, it is first of all a physical place—a campus.

In the late 1800s, the founders of Pomona College, looking out from a single wood-frame building onto an expanse of scrub desert some 35 miles east of Los Angeles, dared to imagine "a college in a garden." If you stroll this campus today—either on foot or through the pages of this book—I think you will agree that their unlikely dream has been fulfilled in an extraordinary fashion. From that audacious vision to the mature and beautiful campus of today has been a remarkable journey—a journey through a century of changing times, through hardship and prosperity, shifting architectural tastes and evolving educational philosophies.

That journey is what this book is all about. It is not a book about architecture or landscaping, per se, though many of its pages are filled with histories and images of buildings and gardens. This book is, first and foremost, an examination and celebration of Pomona College as a place—the aesthetics, traditions, priorities, needs, choices, and sacrifices that have shaped this campus over the past 120 years and continue to shape it today.

From my window in Alexander Hall, I look out onto one of the most beautiful garden spaces on any college campus—Marston Quadrangle. On an adjacent wall hangs a portrait of the man most responsible for bringing that space into being. It reminds me daily that the beauty of Pomona—like its other fine qualities—is due to visionary leaders like the man in that portrait, George Marston, one of the early chairs of the Buildings and Grounds Committee of the Board of Trustees. He and his successors —such people as Ranney C. Draper '25 and his son, Ranney E. Draper '60, Richard C. Seaver '43, and current chair A. Redmond Doms Jr. '62—have worked tirelessly to build and preserve all that is special about this place.

I would also like to express my gratitude to those who have helped to make this book a reality. We owe particular thanks to Ranney E. Draper, who has championed and supported this project from the beginning and who is largely responsible for bringing it to a successful conclusion, and to Marjorie L. Harth, who took on the challenge of researching and writing this volume following her retirement as director of the Pomona College Museum of Art two years ago.

As president, I spend a great deal of time thinking about the buildings and grounds that make up this campus. In most cases, the focus is on individual construction and renovation projects and the logistical demands inherent in them, but I am always aware that every project has ripple effects throughout the campus. I welcome the opportunity this book offers to step back and take a longer view, to consider the campus as an organic whole with a complex and significant history, and to enjoy reading the reflections of alumni who have known and loved Pomona for many years.

I hope this volume will serve as an invitation to those already familiar with this place to see the campus with fresh eyes. For those who have just made the College's acquaintance, I hope it will offer a glimpse of the rich architectural and institutional heritage that has given Pomona College one of the most beautiful campuses in America. ■ —David W. Oxtoby

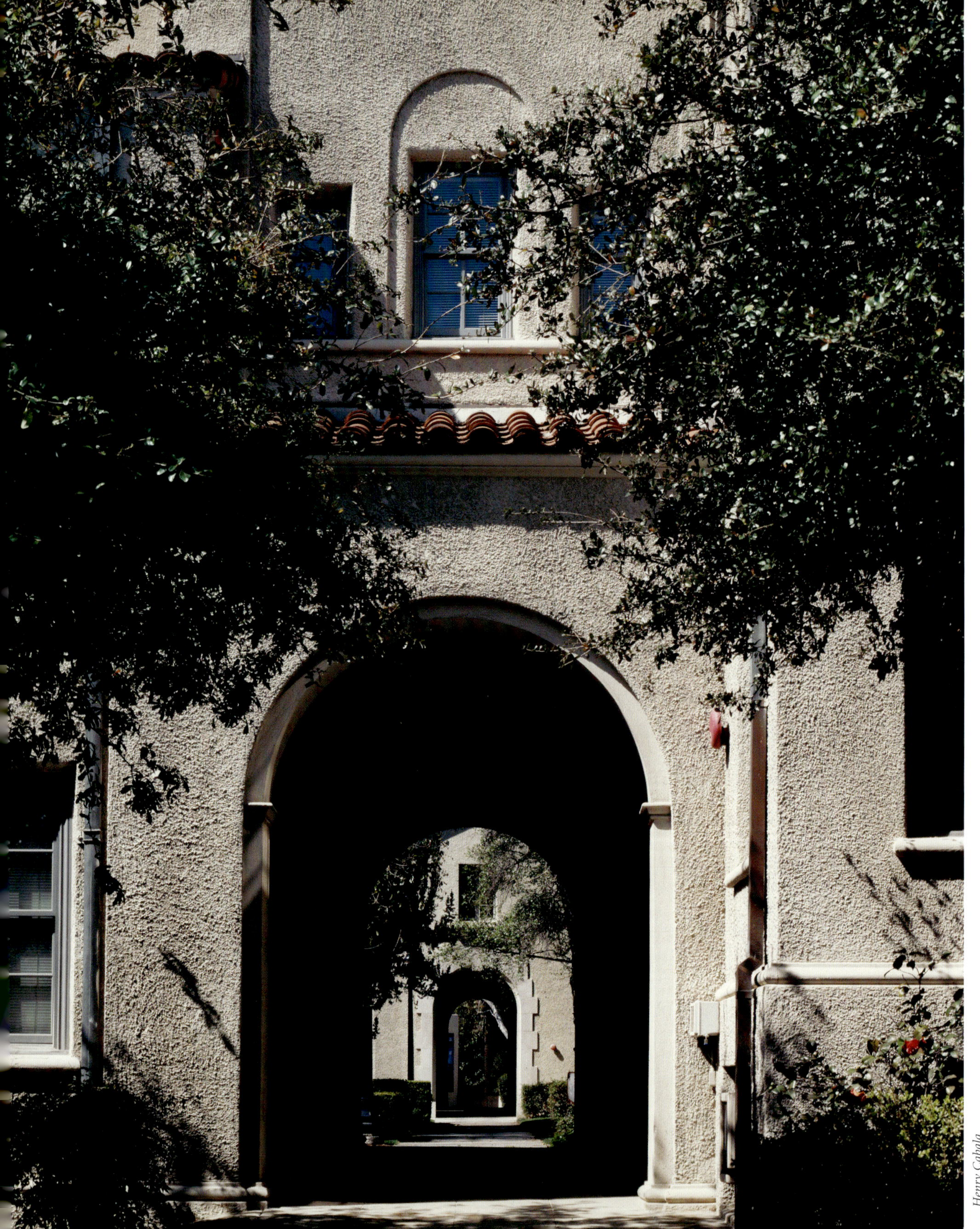

Henry Cabala

INTRODUCTION

Sumner Hall

Where We Started

We shall not cease from exploration
And the end of all our exploring
Will be to arrive where we started
And know the place for the first time.

—T.S. ELIOT, *LITTLE GIDDING*

IN JUNE 2005 WHILE RESEARCHING THIS BOOK, I heard a segment on National Public Radio about the "reinvention of the nursing home." Introduced—in that breathless manner indicating significant news—as an effort "to see if the way a nursing home looks can change the way people live," it reported promising findings that could influence the way future residences for seniors will be designed. What struck me, however, was the implication that the study's basic premise—that the design of the environment we inhabit affects the quality of our lives—was not only remarkable, but novel. Isn't that a given? True, those of us who aren't architects, designers, or otherwise required to be critically analytical of our physical surroundings, often become so only periodically—when we encounter a place for the first time, move into a new house, renovate a kitchen or bedroom, rearrange furniture. But even if we don't attach life-altering potential to such decisions, we know they matter, don't we? At the risk of making too much of an ostensibly unremarkable rhetorical question, it does seem relevant to this book and the premises on which it is based. I am as certain that "place" matters as I am hard-pressed to prove—indeed, even articulate—the concept. Nonetheless, this volume is, in part, an effort to reflect upon that notion as it applies to the campus of Pomona College, and to encourage others to do the same.

The Pomona College campus is widely acknowledged to be one of the most beautiful in the western United States, a physical place that supports and enhances an institution renowned for its academic excellence. The College has a distinguished architectural history, beginning with Myron Hunt's campus plan of 1908 and central buildings that have been preserved and have inspired later structures. But for College alumni, as for those who have taught and worked here, the campus is also more than a physical fact, more than a group of buildings and spaces with varying functions. It represents, for many, one of the most important and formative environments of their lives—the place for which they first left home, where they matured as students and as individuals, where lifelong friendships were forged, passion for learning ignited, career paths identified.

Pomona alumni are intensely loyal to the College. Many factors contribute to this, but one of these, surely, is the physical campus—the frame within which their experiences here took place. Alumni reminiscences often focus on particular events; when asked to reflect on the environment in which these occurred, it quickly becomes clear that the two are not only linked in memory but inextricable from one another. The effect of physical environment on our lives goes beyond the obvious realities of geography and climate to often overlooked minutiae—the quality of a particular space, a classroom, for example, in which we

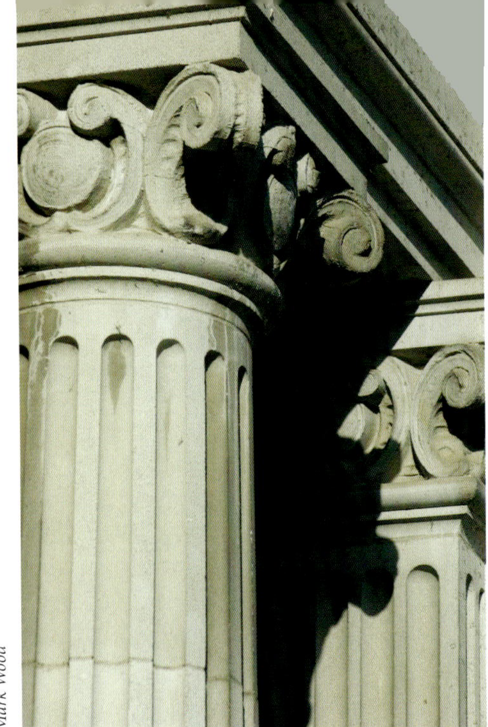
Mark Wood

Bridges Hall of Music

always felt intimidated; a favorite corner in the library that, for some reason, always made us feel intelligent, reassuring us that we belonged in academia. And the feelings and responses with which we invest the spaces we inhabit become integral to them, intertwined with their objective reality. As Verlyn Klinkenborg suggests in his lyrical preface to this volume, a college campus is, to a significant degree, a work of imagination—a product not only of the imaginings of those who visualized and took the lead in its physical realization, but also of those who have experienced it, who have frequented its buildings and trod its paths, who endlessly recreate it through the scrim of their perceptions. Hence the "reflections" of our title, to suggest that, alongside the fixed, factual and tangible, the notion of campus includes an elusive but nevertheless determining component of the subjective, of continuous becoming.

This book is also, of course, about the Pomona College campus seen objectively, as a complex assemblage of buildings and grounds with a history integral to the institution. It is a truism that we notice least what is under our noses, and even in an academic setting dedicated to critical awareness and analysis, our physical environment is often taken for granted. We tend to forget that the spaces we frequent as we go about our daily lives are not random but were consciously designed. One way to understand a campus is as a complex and evolving work of art. And if it is true that all art is to some degree self-portrait, then it is worth examining the campus as evidence of the individual and collective values it represents. Whether or not we are actively conscious of these—whether or not we stop to ask what a particular architectural style, configuration of buildings, or landscaping of a given area "says" about the College—these all convey meaning. As Pomona's eighth president, Peter W. Stanley (1991–2003), recently commented, "…at the end of the day, the College's identity and integrity are expressed visually in the shape and character of its house."

What is the nature of this "house"—of what does it consist? I have heard it said that the Pomona campus is difficult to represent visually because there is no single building, architectural style, or prospect that "stands for" the College, that encapsulates its essence. If this is so, and if it is frustrating for those responsible for presenting the College to the outside world, it is also telling and worth exploring as it reflects an institution that, like many, has grown over a sufficiently extended period of time that architectural and planning styles have changed along with the curriculum, student body, faculty and staff. Still, in reviewing the history of the College as a physical place, one finds a developmental tapestry that, while increasing in complexity over time, continually reveals the same interwoven threads: idealism, determination, curricular need, individual and collective philanthropy, astute financial management, and responsiveness to opportunity. Although the time line of campus development displays patterns that are, not surprisingly, tied in part to larger economic and political events, Pomona's growth has been remarkably consistent over its 120-year history. Crucial to this continuity is the fact that the College has consciously returned to its architectural roots in recent years, renovating older structures and designing new ones with attention to history and context. Ostensibly aesthetic in nature, this is a decision with complex logistical consequences, particularly as the technological sophistication of academic buildings increases and safety and accessibility concerns intensify. In telling the story of the Pomona College campus, this book endeavors to convey a sense of the complexity of the decisions that lie behind campus planning and growth, of the delicate balances that must be struck among conflicting, and often equally deserving, desiderata. Even brief exposure to the planning process leaves most with new respect for those who must make the decisions and the conviction that a truly successful campus project is little short of miraculous. Another of my several goals here is to honor those responsible for the campus we are privileged to enjoy.

In sum, then, this book is a celebration of Pomona College as a physical place; a tribute to those responsible for the form it has taken and the way it has developed; a gentle encouragement to look more closely, critically, and reflectively at our environment, both to enjoy it more fully and to refine our personal sensitivity to what draws us, as individuals, to certain spaces and leads us to avoid others; and an acknowledgement of the important role "place" plays in our lives. At the risk of presumption, it is my hope that, in a modest way, this book might do what good art does—make us more aware of ourselves, our world, and our place in it.

I frequently exhort students writing papers to articulate their goals clearly at the outset or risk being criticized for failing to do something they never intended. In that spirit, let me also say what this book is *not*. It is not a new history of Pomona College as an institution, nor is it an architectural history in the scholarly sense of that term. While as comprehensive as constraints of time and space have allowed, it offers, at best, a partial image of the campus. Even so, it is my hope that the picture that emerges here is both true and compelling, and that it will serve to remind those who know and love Pomona College and its campus of the extraordinary place it is and has been, and to introduce others to its riches.

The term "campus," derived from Latin for "field," is believed to have been used for the first time in this country at Princeton (founded 1746), where it referred to that university's grounds. Over time, the appellation came to refer to collegiate buildings as well (hence the later term "urban campus"), and, ultimately, extended to include the more abstract "spirit" of a place—its *genius loci*. It is the full extent of this definition—the inevitable interconnectedness of site, buildings, grounds and the values they reflect and experiences they frame—that this book proposes to address and celebrate.

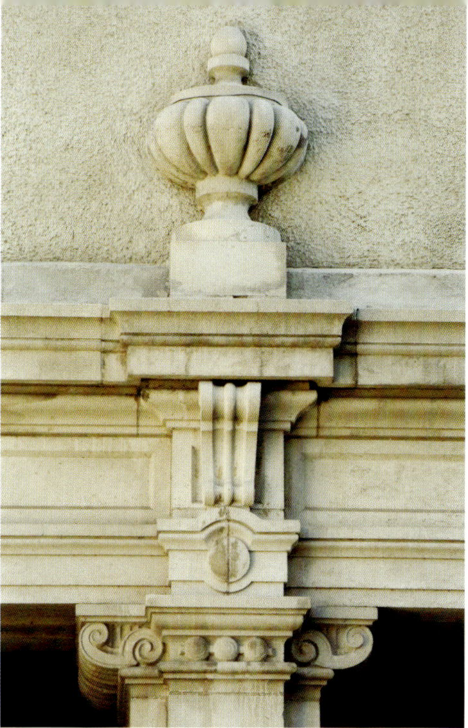

Henry Cabala

Bridges Hall of Music

Acknowledgements

Relatively little of a comprehensive nature has been written about the history and development of the American campus. Paul Venable Turner, whose *Campus: An American Planning Tradition* (1990) is the most notable exception, attributes this to the assumption that American campuses have, for the most part, developed in a haphazard fashion, their buildings reflecting the needs, economics, and taste of particular moments rather than coherent or comprehensive planning. In truth, evidence of campus planning in this country can be found from the earliest days of collegiate development. Furthermore, although early

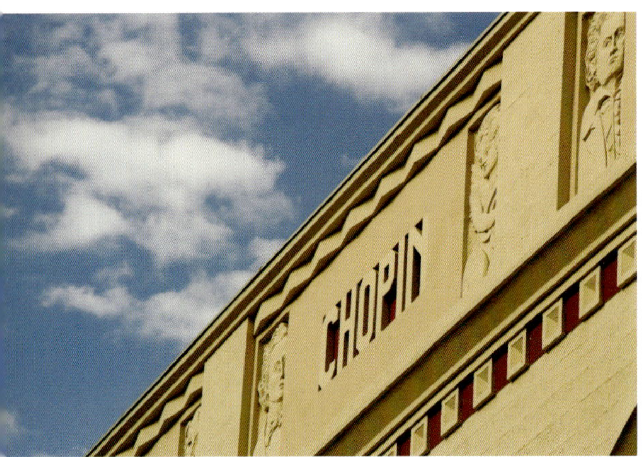

Henry Cabala

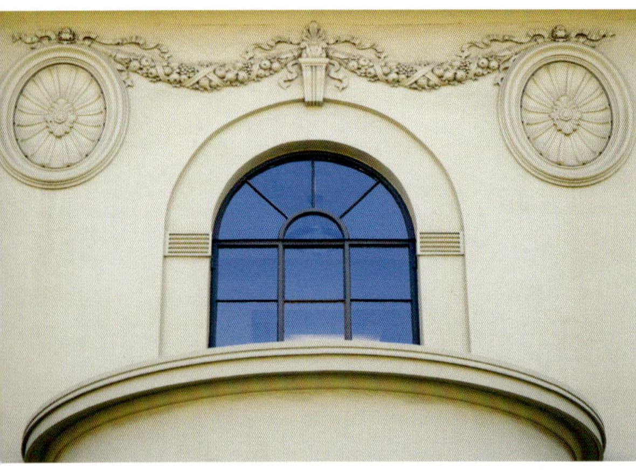

Henry Cabala

Bridges Auditorium

Mudd-Blaisdell Hall

American campus plans, particularly in the Colonial period, owed a debt to British universities, the physical development of the American college was largely independent, influenced primarily by local social, economic, and cultural forces, its development distinctly American in nature.

The history of Pomona College, including the development of its campus during its first 80 years, is admirably chronicled in President E. Wilson Lyon's *The History of Pomona College 1887–1969* (1977). Greatly indebted to Lyon's careful, chronological history, and also to those by Charles Burt Sumner and Frank Parkhurst Brackett, this volume deliberately sets a different course, focusing attention on the physical environment of the campus that reflects, and affects, the multi-faceted institution and the diverse community it embraces and serves. Other texts consulted are listed at the conclusion of the book.

A great deal of the factual information recorded here was gleaned from the Pomona College archives in the Office of Communications. The painstaking, ongoing task of collecting, maintaining, and providing materials from the College's history is the responsibility of Beverly-Jene Coffman, office manager and archivist in Communications. No researcher could be blessed with one more committed to the institution. For assistance in securing images, I am grateful to Kurt Helfrich, University Art Museum, University of California, Santa Barbara; Bonnie Ludt, Caltech Institute Archives; Carrie Marsh, Honnold Library of The Claremont Colleges; Bryan McDaniel, Chicago History Museum; and Edward Gaynor and Jeanne Pardee, University of Virginia Library.

Early in the research process, I was also fortunate to secure the assistance of Lori Kido DesRochers '06. A skillful writer, adept at selecting and summarizing diverse materials, Lori contributed significantly to the building texts that follow. As impressive as her tolerance for detail-oriented (and often mundane) tasks, has been her fascination with the process. Elected president of the Associated Students of Pomona College while engaged in this work, she based her Opening Convocation address in September 2005 on the experience, saying of her initial response to the archives: "Think what you could learn from spending a day, a week, a month just reading, consuming the history of our college in this way. The stories that would leap out, the patterns that would emerge, the images that would cling together like constellations forming the shape of our college's history—these were the things that fascinated me." Lori's enthusiastic participation in this project has been a true gift.

My work has also benefited enormously from alumni and from current and former members of the faculty and staff who graciously responded to my requests for reminiscences, many of which appear throughout the book. In this context I am particularly indebted to former presidents David Alexander and Peter Stanley for their thoughtful comments about the campus during their respective tenures, and to the late Carolyn Lyon, widow of the College's sixth president E. Wilson Lyon, who, with the assistance of her daughter Elizabeth Webb and son John Lyon, contributed favorite memories. Among the pleasures of this project for me has been the opportunity to work for the first time with talented photographer Henry Cabala and to collaborate again with graphic designer Lilli Colton, whom I met in 1981 and who designed the Museum's publications for many years. I am grateful for her artistry, which is apparent here, and equally for the tact, wit, and endless patience she has brought to the project.

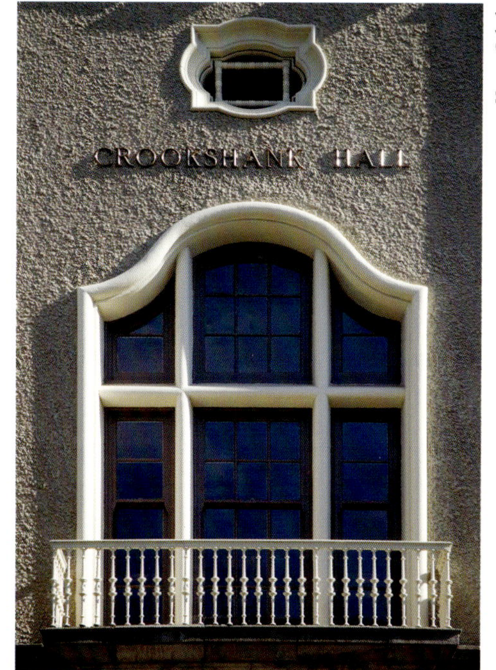

Henry Cabala

Crookshank Hall

This book is anchored by three key essays—Verlyn Klinkenborg's insightful introduction; George Gorse's text on Pomona's early architect Myron Hunt; and the reflections of Ronald Fleming that serve as a coda. The requests I made of these writers were challenging, requiring both sweeping and close-focus views of the College and the notion of campus. Together, they have responded to my inchoate musings about "place" with essays both enlightening and poetic.

If, as they say, the devil is in the details, it is editors who save writers from eternal damnation. I could not have been more fortunate in mine. Mark Wood, multi-talented overseer of Pomona's Communications department, and editor of the College's much-lauded magazine and of this project, has brought to it the full range of his skills, including primary responsibility for the selection of photographs. Distinguished architecture writer and editor Jayne S. Merkel, whom I am privileged also to call a friend, graciously agreed to comment upon (and save me from embarrassing errors within) those parts of the book that deal with the architectural context of Pomona's campus. My husband Norm Hines '61, whose love for Pomona College has enhanced my own, has patiently read drafts, made astute suggestions, and, as often as not, been inspired by the text to enlighten me about yet another Pomona legend.

Don Pattison, director of donor relations and, for many years, director of the College's Public Affairs Office and editor of *Pomona College Magazine*, has played so extensive and multi-faceted a role in making the dream of this book a reality that his name should, by rights, appear on the title page (an honor he has declined with a modesty that is altogether characteristic). To credit his editorial contributions, which have been extensive, is appropriate but wholly inadequate to express the gratitude I feel for the counsel he has provided. Don has fielded more questions, checked more facts, and responded to more whining pleas for moral support than should be required of anyone, let alone a volunteer, and has done so with a generosity approaching saintliness. As Pomona's historian, Don is successor to the legacy of Caroline Beatty, the College's remarkable researcher, archivist, and, from 1949 to 2002, fiercely committed conservator of its institutional history. Caroline had long hoped to see a publication about the campus; her lively spirit has informed my work and served as a continuing source of inspiration. While I cringe to think of the errors herein that she would have caught, I like to think she would be pleased with this book nonetheless.

It is customary for authors to credit at least one individual *without whose support this book would not have been possible.* Of all those to whom this admitted cliché properly applies here, one deserves particular mention. It was Ranney E. Draper '60, College trustee and extraordinarily generous patron, who first proposed the idea of publishing a book about Pomona's campus. Without his persistence and support, this project would, quite simply, never have been accomplished. ■

Marjorie L. Harth

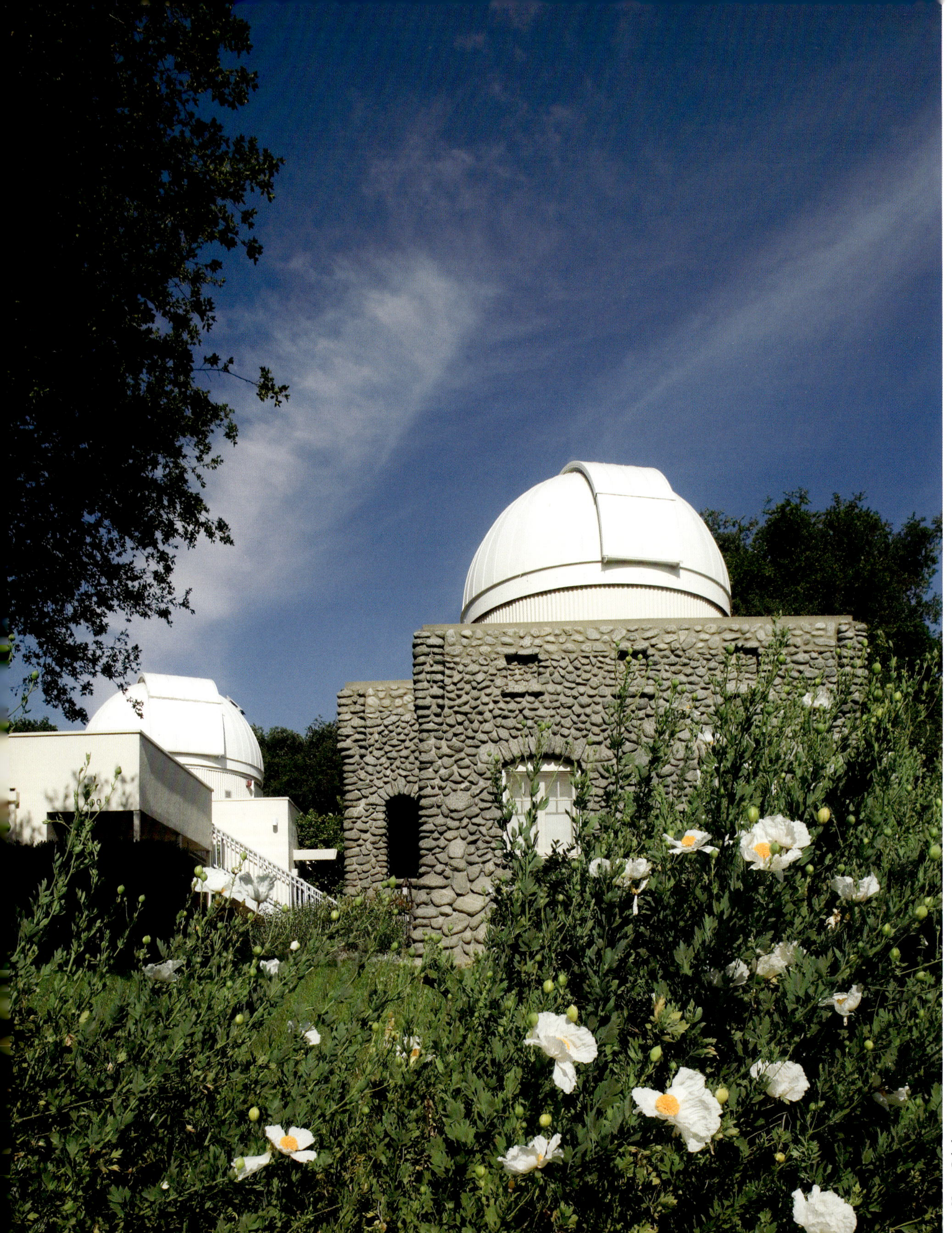

Henry Cabala

PREFACE

Brackett Observatory

Pomona as Place

I HAD FORGOTTEN THE SLOPE. Surely it was there when I was a student, thirty-some years ago. It underlies campus, Claremont, everything—an alluvial descent as gradual as a pigeon's glide-path from the mountains to the north, a geological absolute in a region where the absolutes are really only provisional. I had forgotten the hill in Indian Hill. I remembered the climb to Mount Baldy, the winding road, the glimpses, coming downhill, of the basin below. But the mountains and the fan of land beneath them seemed disconnected, as though the one were not the outwash of the other.

You cannot account for the place of Pomona College—where it is and what it is—without considering that slope, even though the fall from the north edge of campus to the south edge is just a few feet. And that only begins the list of things you must make sense of in order to account for Pomona. There is the altitude—always higher than you think—and the aridity. There is also what has been, through most of the College's existence, the steadily shifting character of its neighborhood—from open desert when it was founded to the present feeling that Claremont exists, more edgily defined somehow, in the midst of the filled-in crossword puzzle of suburbia. This was once a sleepy town at the forlorn eastern boundary of Los Angeles County. In those days all the development was yet to come, and everyone knew it would come from the west. That tidal wave has now passed onward to the east, cloistering the College, in a different sense than we usually mean, as it went.

All of these elements, and many more, define the place of Pomona College. Not to consider them is like not considering the psychological bracketing caused by the Foothill Freeway to the north and the San Bernardino Freeway to the south. You may be the kind of person who never loses the feel of that bracketing or who remains attuned to the sociological map of greater Los Angeles when you're on campus. But most of us forget. The campus is here to help us forget. Like any place, Pomona College holds certain physical possibilities open, while keeping all the others at bay. And yet, unlike most other kinds of places, it is also meant to help us keep certain possibilities open in ourselves.

That has always been the purpose of a college campus—to create a sense of protection, a sense of enclosure, and with it a sense of freedom. The architecture of the contemplative life has always run along certain lines, adjusted for local idioms. It is the architecture of communal privacy, where you are able to feel alone with your thoughts even in the presence of other people —who are alone with theirs. Usually, that means walls and courtyards, conspiratorial plantings in the borders and hedges, an array of buildings that resembles, in bad examples, a defensive huddle of musk-oxen. At its very worst, it means a complex of high rises that could pass for a Parisian suburb.

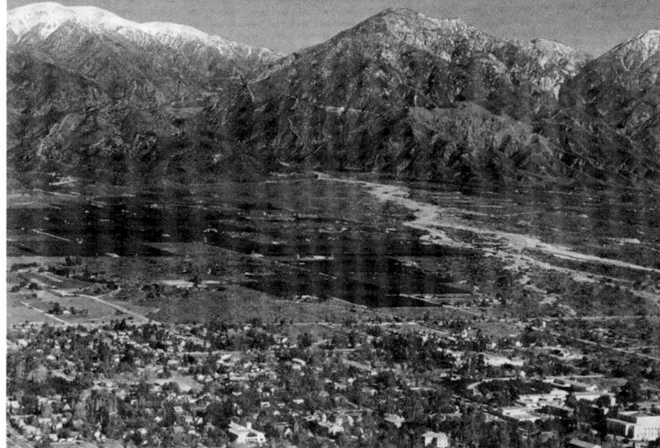

Robert Frampton

Aerial view of Claremont and mountains

OVERLEAF *Panoramic view of Claremont looking southeast (taken from current site of Sycamore School),* 1896

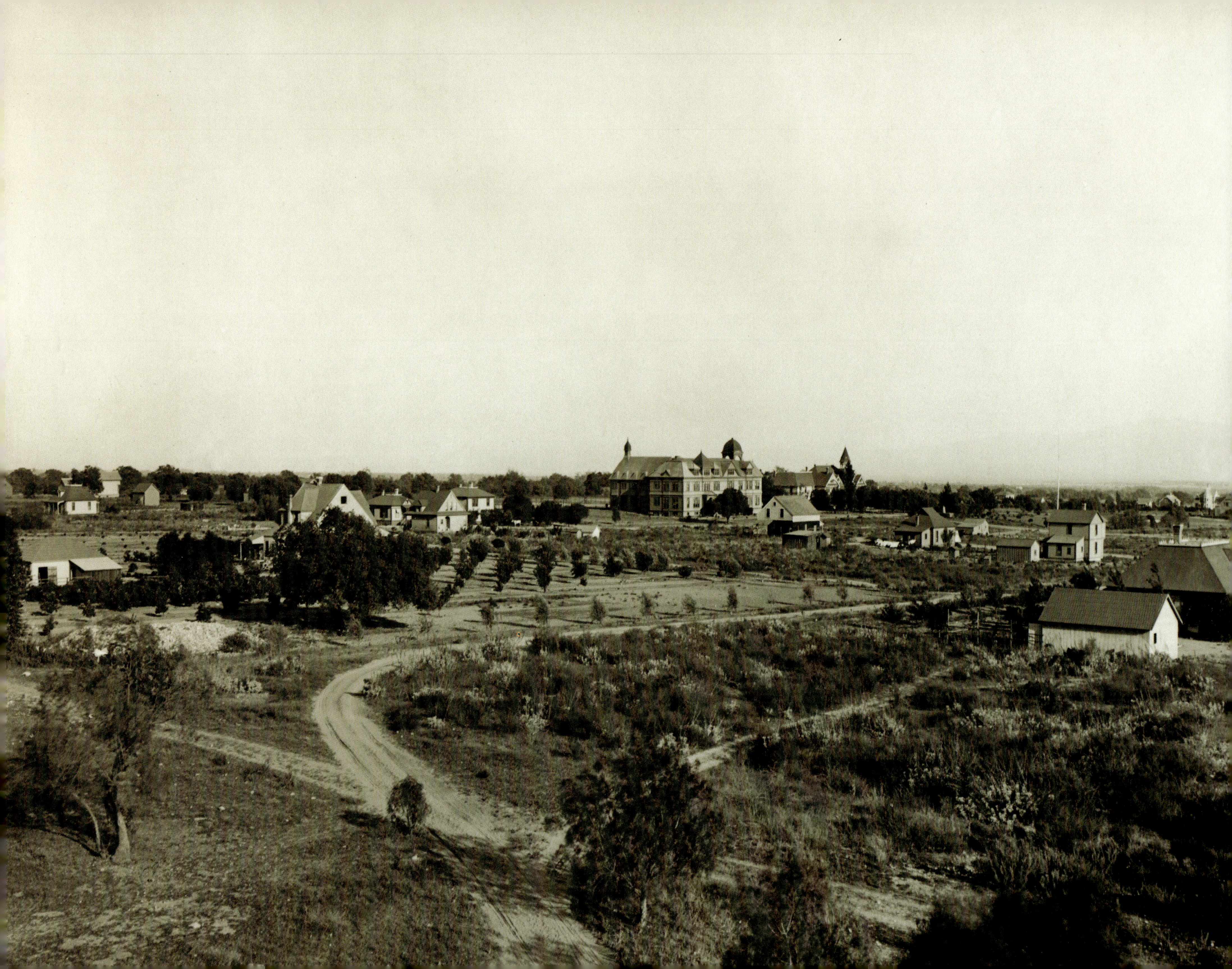

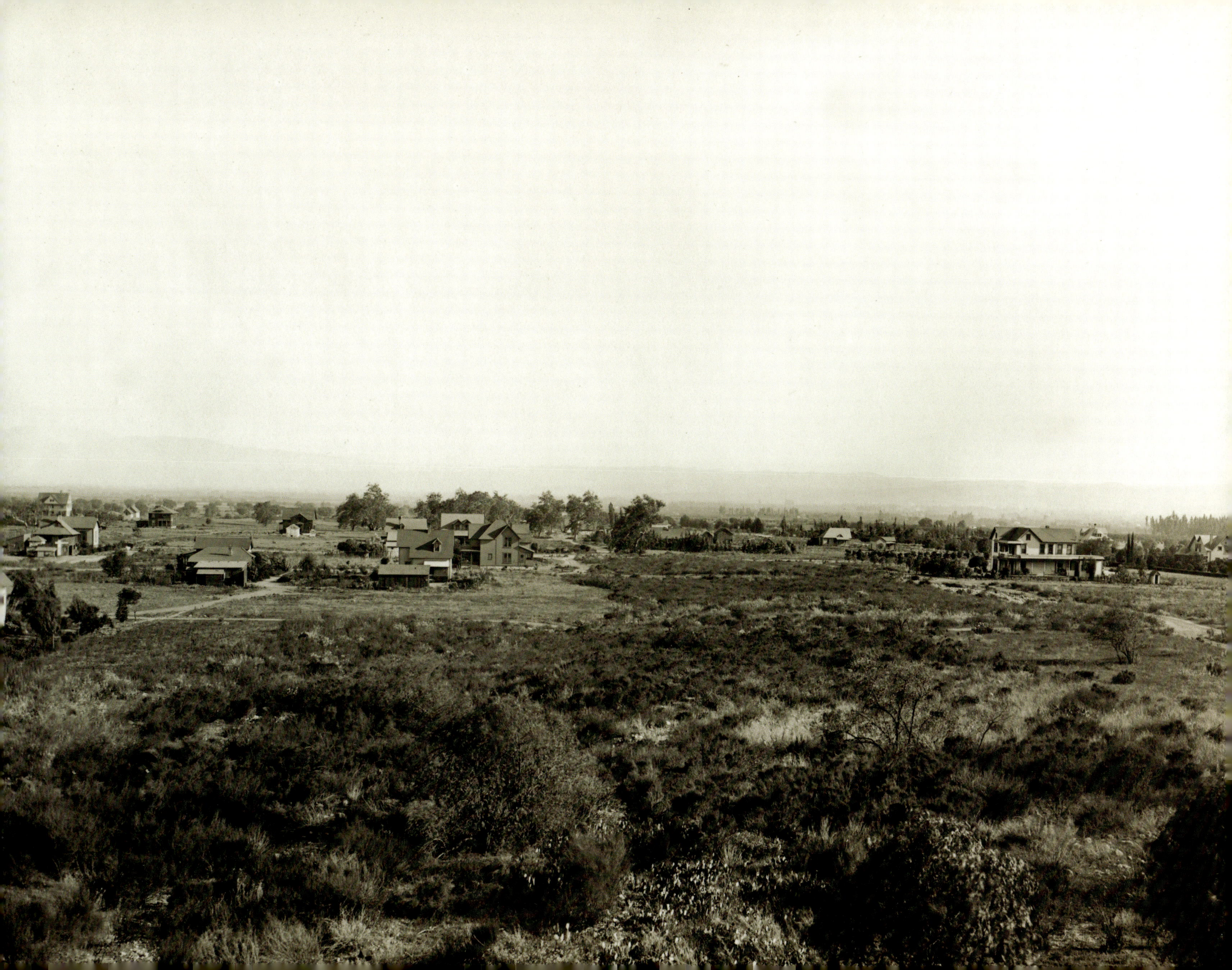

The feel of a college campus is rarely a very good metaphor for the kind of education to be found there. And yet nearly every student who passes through Pomona College finds that what he or she has learned here is utterly bound up with a sense of the campus itself, in ways that are more profound than seems possible at first. I'm still trying to decide, for instance, what it means that nearly the whole of my education at Pomona took place in a building—Holmes Hall—that has since been torn down. It has no real meaning—except in sentimental terms—and yet there is a meaning. In those days, the theater and English departments were closely intertwined. My sense of literature has always lingered on the edge of performance thanks to that fact. Now things are different. The two departments are no longer contiguous, and neither are the theatrical and literary enterprises. This is an artifact of place as much as philosophy.

Visitors, of course, are always struck by the beauty of Pomona College. But its real beauty isn't discernible to visitors. Small as the campus is, it has a surprising ability to withstand repetition, the repetition inherent in the four years that most students spend here, the narrow track they beat across campus day by day. From my own experience as a student here, I wonder how much I ever really noticed as I made my way to classes. I couldn't have named more than a few of the trees in Marston Quadrangle. The lawns would have been identifiable as "grass." I could not have said what was native in the Wash and what wasn't, nor did it occur to me at the time what a wash really was—that it was related in some way to the desert and the alluvial fan spreading outward from the mountains. The walk to class was never quite the same, not because of the change in season, but because of the change in text. One week it was Lear and the next week it was The Tempest. The variety of a physical campus is not infinite, but seen through the preoccupied haze of a good education it can come very close.

I now know vastly more about the plants that grow here. I can explicitly feel what I couldn't then—the way Pomona College alludes to a different world than southern California, to an academic world that has its roots much farther to the east. But no matter what I know now, no matter what I'm able to name and identify, I've lost the intimacy that every student has with this campus while going to college here. I don't imagine that the designers of Pomona College, as it has evolved over the years, have ever thought consciously about the nature of that intimacy, if only because it isn't something you can design for. Some students are engaged in a ruthless practicality from the moment they arrive at college, and others never lose their romanticism. And yet almost every senior feels that he or she is living in a place that has been many places in the time they've been here. Every day you walk by buildings and courtyards that belong to your past. And yet year by year the campus reconfigures itself in your own mind, so that when you walk past Wig Hall you're walking past the current crop of freshmen, not the place where you were a freshman.

What this means is that Pomona College—the campus itself—is always a work of imagination, the collaborative creation of everyone who wanders through it in search of an education. It is a figurative collaboration, since most of us aren't responsible for mowing the lawn or weeding the agapanthus and birds-of-paradise, or keeping the Wash under some kind of nominal

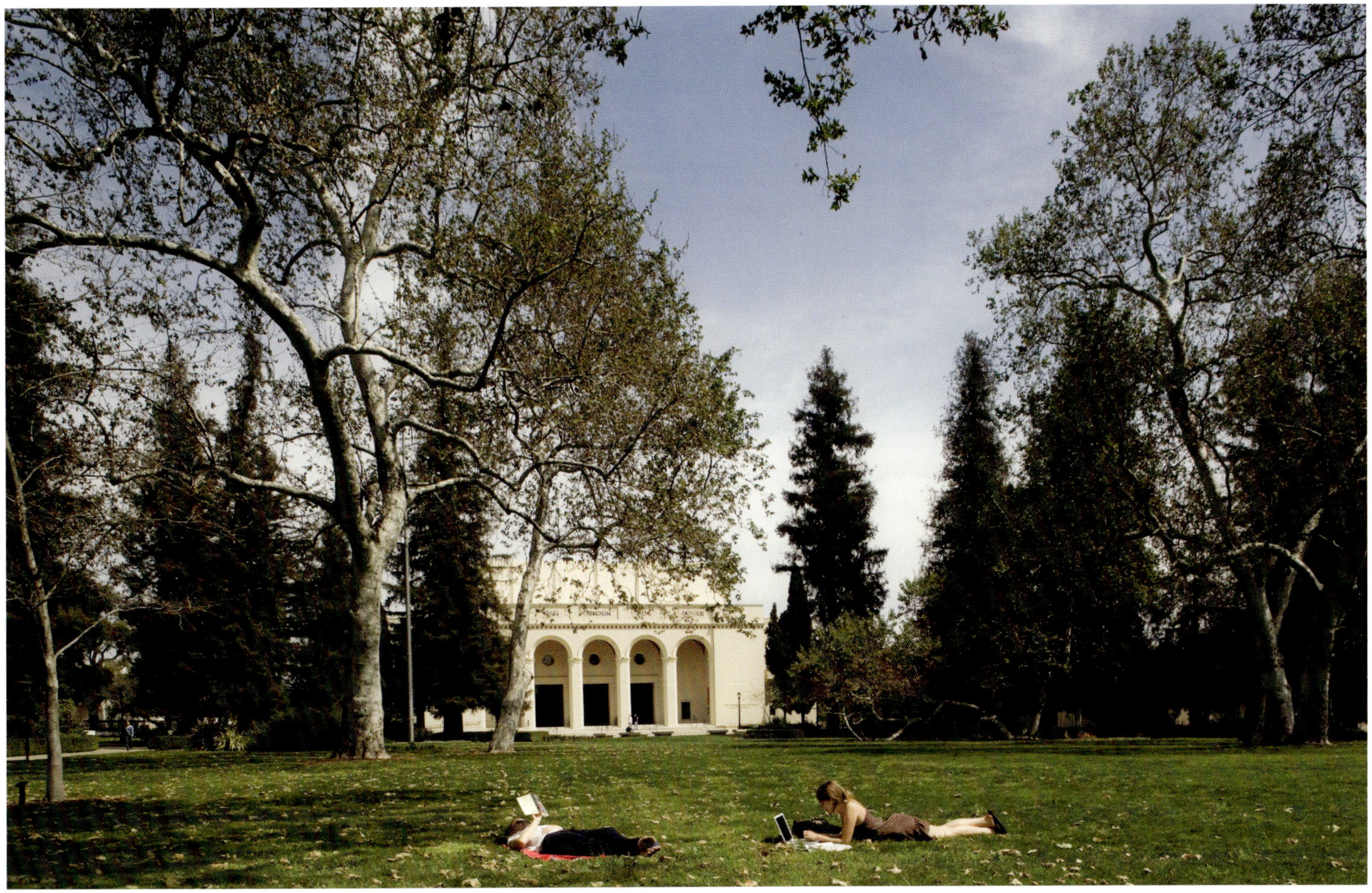

Henry Cabala

control. To a present-day visitor, it would appear as though the only students who are really reshaping this campus are the ones at work on the organic garden. But it isn't so. They are all reshaping the campus, according to their needs and their distractions and their affections, and if you were a student here, you did the same. It may sound like I'm exaggerating. But take a walk around campus. There will be places that feel almost neutral to you—impartial walks and disinterested gardens—but there will also be places that feel dense with memory, alive with the echo of your habitation. Those memories and echoes leave not even a vanishing trace on the actual substance of this college. They change nothing. But it's hard to think of them without admiring the laconic beauty of this place, its terseness, and discretion. ■

Verlyn Klinkenborg

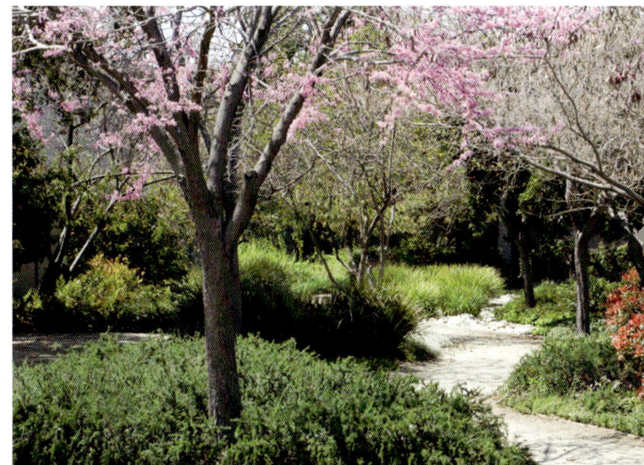

Henry Cabala

Marston Quadrangle and Bridges Auditorium

Garden behind Oldenborg Center

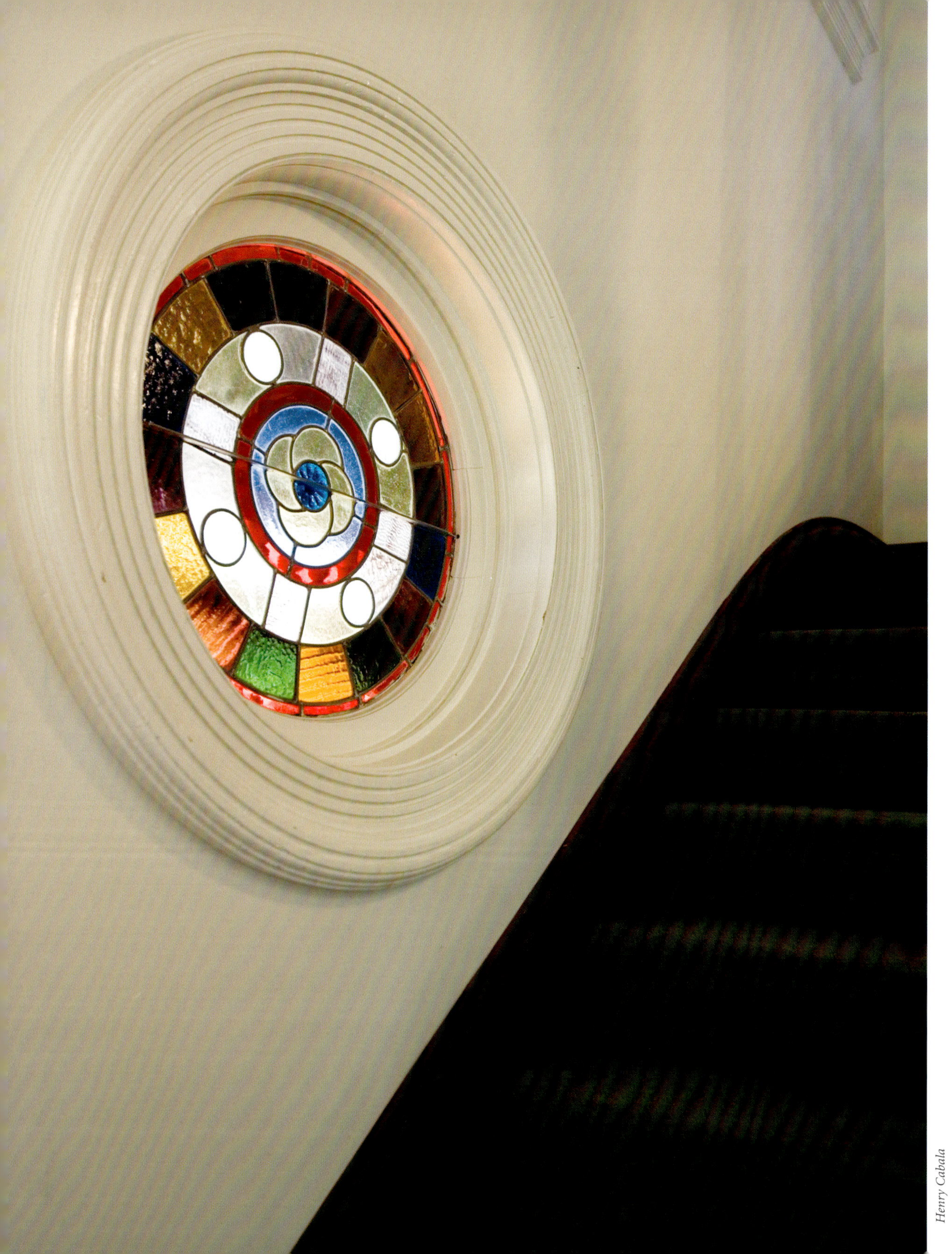

Henry Cabala

CHAPTER I *The* EARLY YEARS 1887–1908

Sumner House

The Early Years, 1887–1908

PRESIDENTS CYRUS BALDWIN, FRANKLIN FERGUSON, *and* GEORGE GATES

The American campus is a world in itself, a temporary paradise, a gracious stage of life.—LE CORBUSIER

THE FIRST TWENTY YEARS OF POMONA COLLEGE'S history were critical to its development not only as an institution, but also as a campus. To a remarkable degree, the College we see today was determined by decisions made in those years. That Pomona College took root in Claremont rather than on Piedmont Mesa in the City of Pomona, as originally anticipated, was the indirect result of the gift of one building—the Claremont Hotel (renamed Claremont Hall and, later, Sumner Hall)—and the trustees' subsequent vote to build another—Holmes Hall—just to its north. In short order, Pearsons, Smiley, and Carnegie followed, and although Sumner Hall was later relocated to make way for Marston Quadrangle, and Holmes Hall was ultimately replaced by Alexander Hall, today's central campus remains much as it was a century ago. The College's first two decades also saw the farsighted acquisition of more than sixty acres of undeveloped land (Blanchard Park, soon known as The Wash), establishing from the outset a recognition of the value of the natural environment in education and a commitment to preserve the beauty of what was then a remote site.

Reports of Pomona's early years by such authors as the Reverend Charles Burt Sumner (*The Story of Pomona College*, 1914) and Professor Frank Parkhurst Brackett (*Granite and Sagebrush*, 1944) make clear how daunting was the effort required to establish a college in this area, and accounts of the hardships endured by Pomona's first faculty, administrators, and students contrast poignantly with later idyllic images of the College's first brave buildings, splendidly isolated amidst the lemon and orange groves and against the spectacular backdrop of the mountains.

Beginnings

Nearly all of America's early academic institutions were founded by religious denominations and offered classics-based curricula with a religious, though not necessarily sectarian, orientation; the college was generally understood to be a "substitute for 'parental superintendance,'" a responsibility not taken lightly.[1] In these respects, Pomona fit the pattern. Pomona College was, as Frank Brackett wrote, "not a child of the boom…(but) in fact, a child of the churches," specifically the General Association of Congregational Churches of Southern California that had endeavored for twenty years to establish a Christian college in the

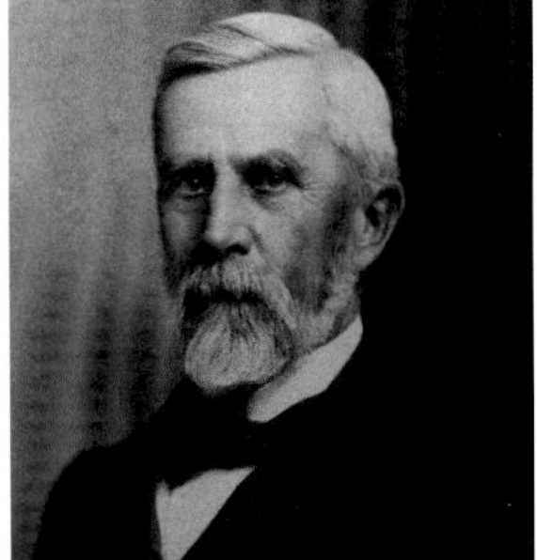

Charles Burt Sumner

state. The articles of incorporation of what was first referred to as "a college of the New England type," approved in Sacramento on October 14, 1887, stipulated that the "location of the College shall be near North Pomona, San Jose Township, Los Angeles, Co." The trustees first voted to name the College "Piedmont" after its anticipated site but later settled on "Pomona" in gratitude for the support of that city and for the Santa Fe Railroad station soon to be built in North Pomona, four miles south of the projected campus.

Leadership during the first two years after incorporation was provided by the Education Committee of the Association, which named the College's first fifteen trustees, and, most notably, by Charles Sumner. Newly appointed pastor of the Pilgrim Congregational Church in Pomona, he was persuaded to abandon his post in 1888 to become the fledgling college's "financial agent with supervisory authority." Sumner was to play a significant role in the development of the campus. It was he who persuaded Trustee and Board President Henry A. Palmer, who had just acquired land in an area known as Piedmont on Scanlon Mesa (later referred to as Piedmont Mesa), near the mouth of Live Oak Canyon, to donate 80 acres as a site for the College; to this an additional forty acres were given by the Misses Wheeler, two Boston ladies who were wintering in Pomona. Sumner was charged with constructing a central building and projecting the town that was expected to grow around the College as lots were sold. Even more pressing was his responsibility to insure that instruction could begin in September 1888. This it did, in Ayer Cottage, a five-room house on the corner of Fifth Street (now Mission) and White Avenue in Pomona that had been rented by the College. Meanwhile, on Piedmont Mesa, the cornerstone for the College's projected first building, an impressive brick edifice designed by Clinton Day, was laid in September 1888. Barely a month later, with classes under way in Pomona, Claremont entered the picture.

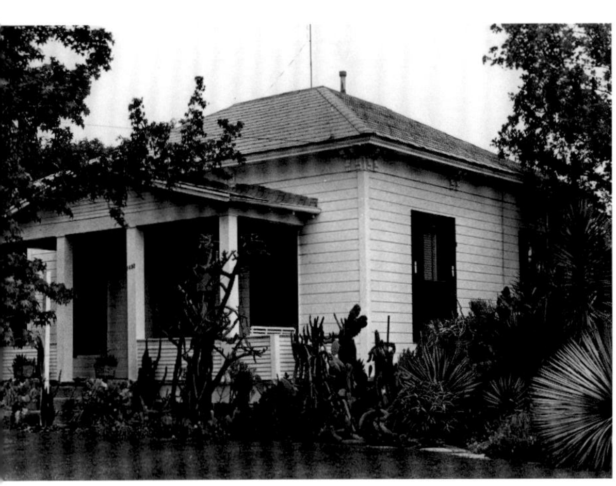

ABOVE *Ayer Cottage. Ayer Cottage still stands in Pomona but on a different site; a plaque marks its original location. In 1937, the College's 50th anniversary year, a replica was erected east of Sumner Hall (where Oldenborg now stands) and, for years, housed the radio station KSPC; in 1965 it was relocated and can now be seen (above) near the entrance to the Sontag Greek Theatre.*

OPPOSITE *Architect's sketch for College's first building (never built), Piedmont Mesa, 1888*

The founders' interest in Claremont was first occasioned by the availability of a completed, but not yet furnished hotel, built in 1887 by the Pacific Land Improvement Company in anticipation of an influx of investors to the area. The early 1870s had seen an unprecedented surge of investment in California land, with thousands flocking to the area and enthusiasm running high; "Claremont the Beautiful," as it was advertised to potential buyers, was considered a prime location. When the boom burst in 1888, the Claremont Hotel, suddenly rendered superfluous, was offered to the College along with 260 already-recorded lots that, it was understood, would be sold. Since the increasingly dire economic situation had also dimmed hopes for rapid campus expansion, the founders gratefully accepted. The building was signed over to the College on October 21 of that year and occupied in December. The move to Claremont was seen as temporary, however, and in 1891, when funds for a "recitation building" were offered by the Holmes family, it was assumed that this would be built on Piedmont Mesa and that the hotel (now Claremont Hall) would continue to house the "Preparatory Department" necessitated by the absence of adequate high school instruction in the area. In 1892, however, trustee concern about maintaining facilities in two locations ultimately led to the difficult (and less than unanimous) decision to abandon Piedmont Mesa in favor of Claremont and to return donated land and associated pledges.

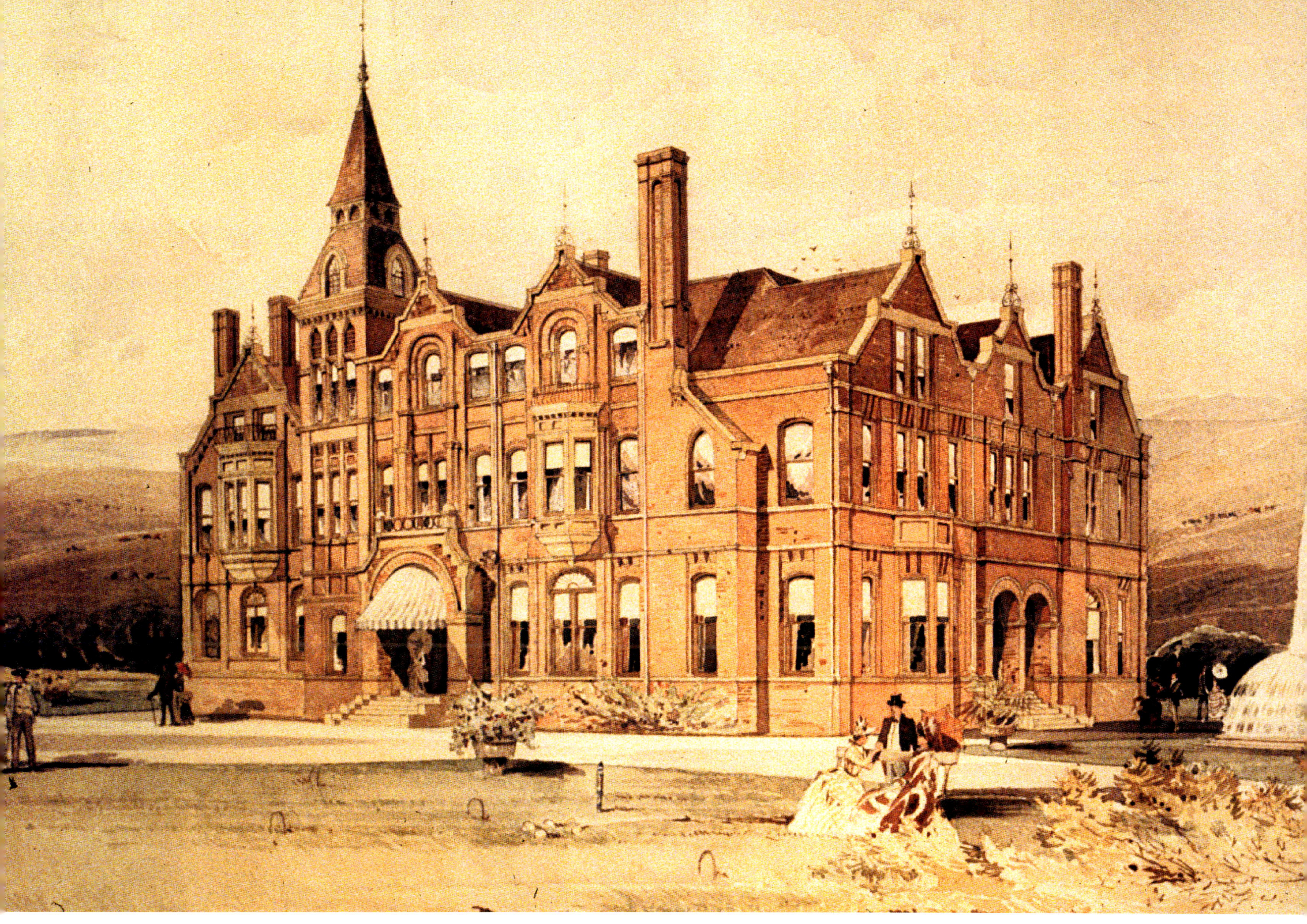

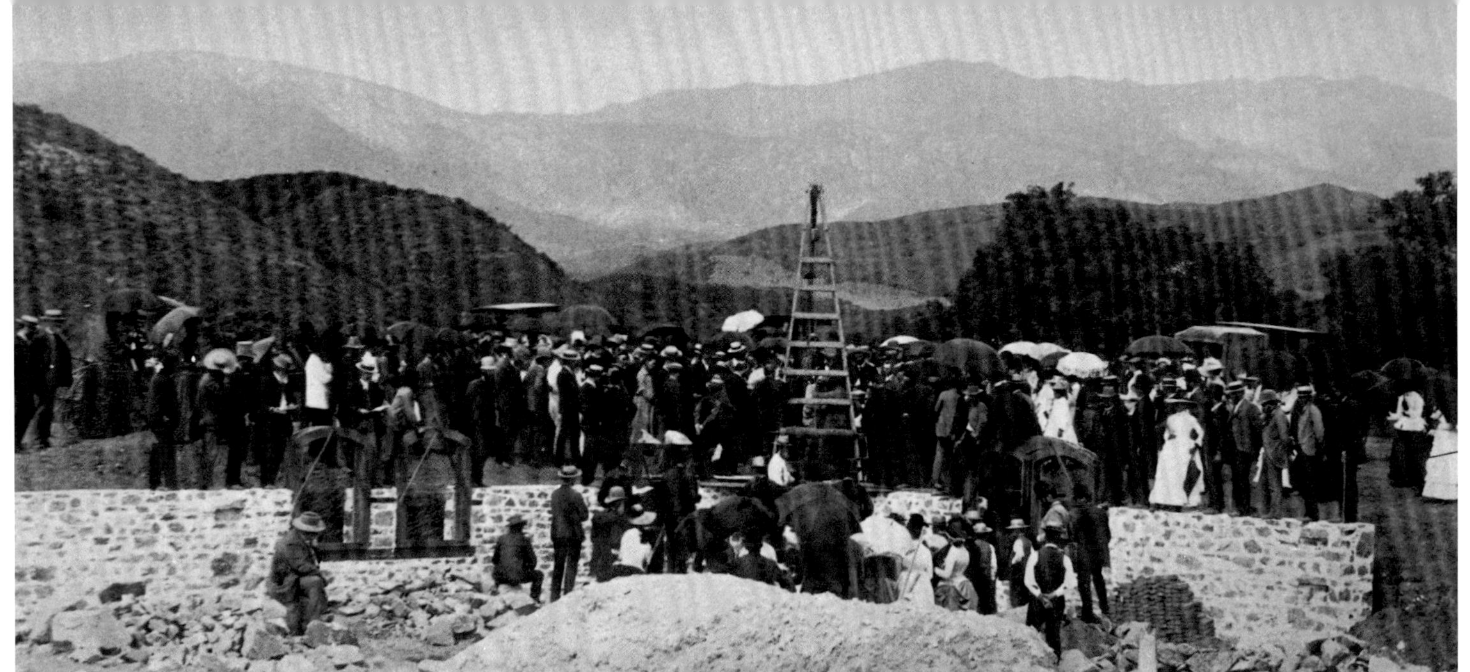

Laying the cornerstone, Piedmont Mesa, 1888

Three years later, the red sandstone cornerstone was moved to a site south of the present Carnegie Building by the Class of 1895 to mark their Class Day. As Wilson Lyon wrote: "In secret the class polished the stone, trimmed its edges, and prepared it for erection on a pedestal of seven stones, one for each member of the class. Upon the cornerstone they carved their class numerals and, in Greek, the class motto, which in translation reads 'Not to live but to live well.' Beneath the stone were placed duplicates of some of the papers laid under the stone originally in 1888."[2] The stone can be seen at that location today, a reminder of the College's beginnings. (According to Sumner, the papers originally placed under the Piedmont cornerstone were later buried under the Carnegie Building.)[3]

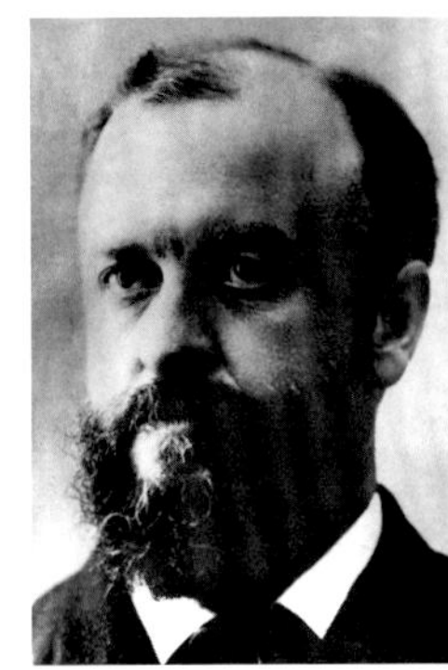

President Cyrus Grandison Baldwin

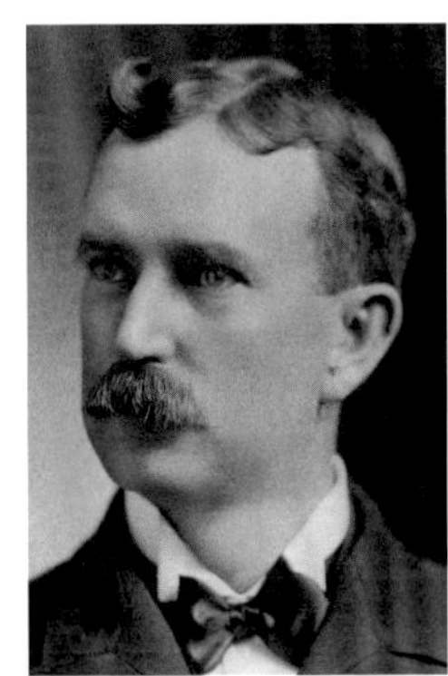

President Franklin La Du Ferguson

First Presidents

The period 1887–1908 also witnessed significant administrative change and development. The trustees had, from the outset, sought an individual qualified to become the College's first president, but it was only in 1890, three years after incorporation, that Cyrus Grandison Baldwin was identified and elected to the position. Baldwin came from a long line of college presidents—five uncles, two cousins, and one brother had held the office. After graduating from Oberlin (1873), he attended Andover Theological Seminary, taught Latin at Ripon College, was ordained in the Congregational Church, and, at the time of his appointment at Pomona, was working with the Iowa YMCA in Des Moines.

Baldwin came to Pomona well equipped for the job and was greatly loved and admired, enjoying a loyal following on campus and in the extended community in which he represented the College. During the seven years of his administration, enrollment grew from 116 (99 in the Preparatory Department, 17 collegians) to 250, of whom 80 were enrolled in the college course. It was under Baldwin that the decision was made to develop the campus in Claremont and that Holmes Hall was built.[4]

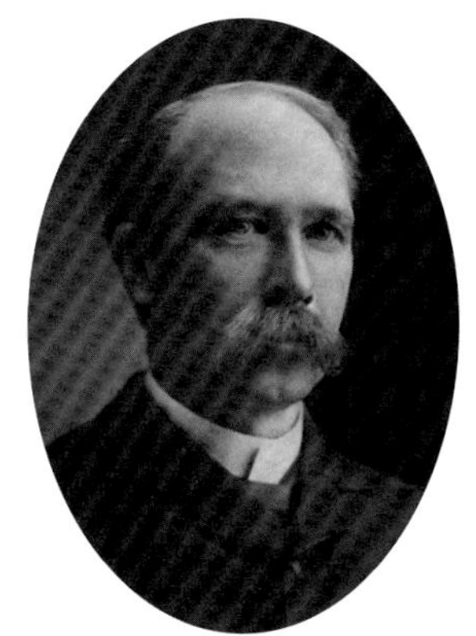

President George Augustus Gates

Despite such evidence of success, the College was sorely lacking in resources, and Baldwin found himself overwhelmed by the difficulties of raising desperately needed funds. Although the endowment grew by $100,000 under his supervision, he resigned in 1897, exhausted and discouraged. It is a measure of the high regard in which Baldwin was held that the Class of 1898 commissioned a portrait of him as a gift to the College, presenting it with appreciation for "his keen sense of justice, his insight into human nature, his scholarly attainments, his broad humanity and his liberal culture" and adding "but more than that, we love the man."[5]

Baldwin was followed by Franklin La Du Ferguson (1897–1901). As representative of the Congregational Education Society, Ferguson had approached donors, including D.K. Pearsons, on the College's behalf and was, therefore, already known to the trustees. Canadian by birth, Ferguson had been educated in Toronto and at Yale, where he studied for the ministry; he later held a pastorate in Connecticut and directed the Chadron Academy in Nebraska. Ferguson was confident, ambitious, and a tireless worker, and his previous success as a fund-raiser was certainly a factor in his selection. As president, he at first proved ingenious at securing funds for current expenses and endowment but, over time, his fondness for methods considered unduly risky and his business-based approach to academic administration led to a loss of confidence. At the end of his third year as president, his resignation was requested. Although Ferguson's tenure was brief and not without other controversies, it saw the addition of three important buildings: Pearsons Hall (1899), and, in 1900, The President's House and the first Renwick Gymnasium.

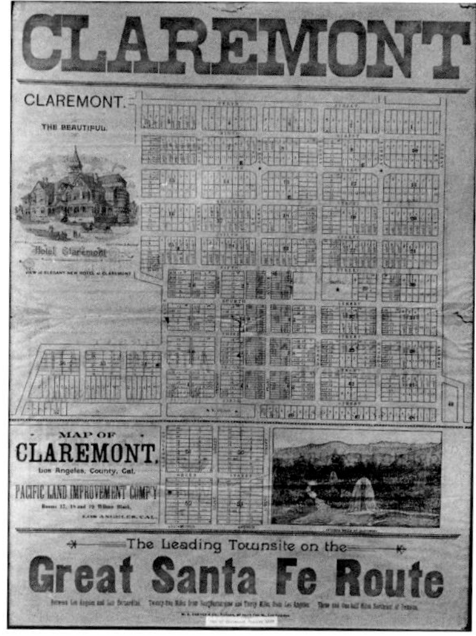

Map of Claremont "The Beautiful," 1887

Ferguson's presidency had convinced the trustees that the College needed an educator as president; their unanimous choice was George Augustus Gates (1902–09). Born in Vermont, he had attended Dartmouth College (Class of 1873), studied in Germany, and graduated in 1880 from Andover Theological Seminary. Before coming to Pomona he had held two pastorates and been president of Grinnell College in Iowa. Gates's academic experience, eloquence, and personal accessibility were welcome, and he was particularly close to the student body, which, he felt, was the College's greatest strength.[6] Despite notable success in strengthening the College's financial situation, Gates, like Baldwin before him, was debilitated and demoralized by the stresses of the task. In the fall of 1908, shortly after presiding over the dedication of Carnegie, Smiley, and Brackett Observatory, he offered his resignation.

Of the first three presidents, Gates had the most significant impact on the campus. His tenure saw the 1902 purchase of land north of Fourth Street for a library; the acquisition of Blanchard Park (The Wash) in 1905; the construction of the Claremont Inn (in collaboration with the City of Claremont, 1906); and the completion of three still-extant buildings—Carnegie Library, Smiley Hall, and Brackett Observatory (all 1908). Perhaps most important was the commissioning in 1908 of architect Myron Hunt to propose a campus plan that would guide future development, a farsighted decision on the part of the College that significantly affected its future.

OVERLEAF *Sumner and Holmes Halls, ca. 1893, from the south*

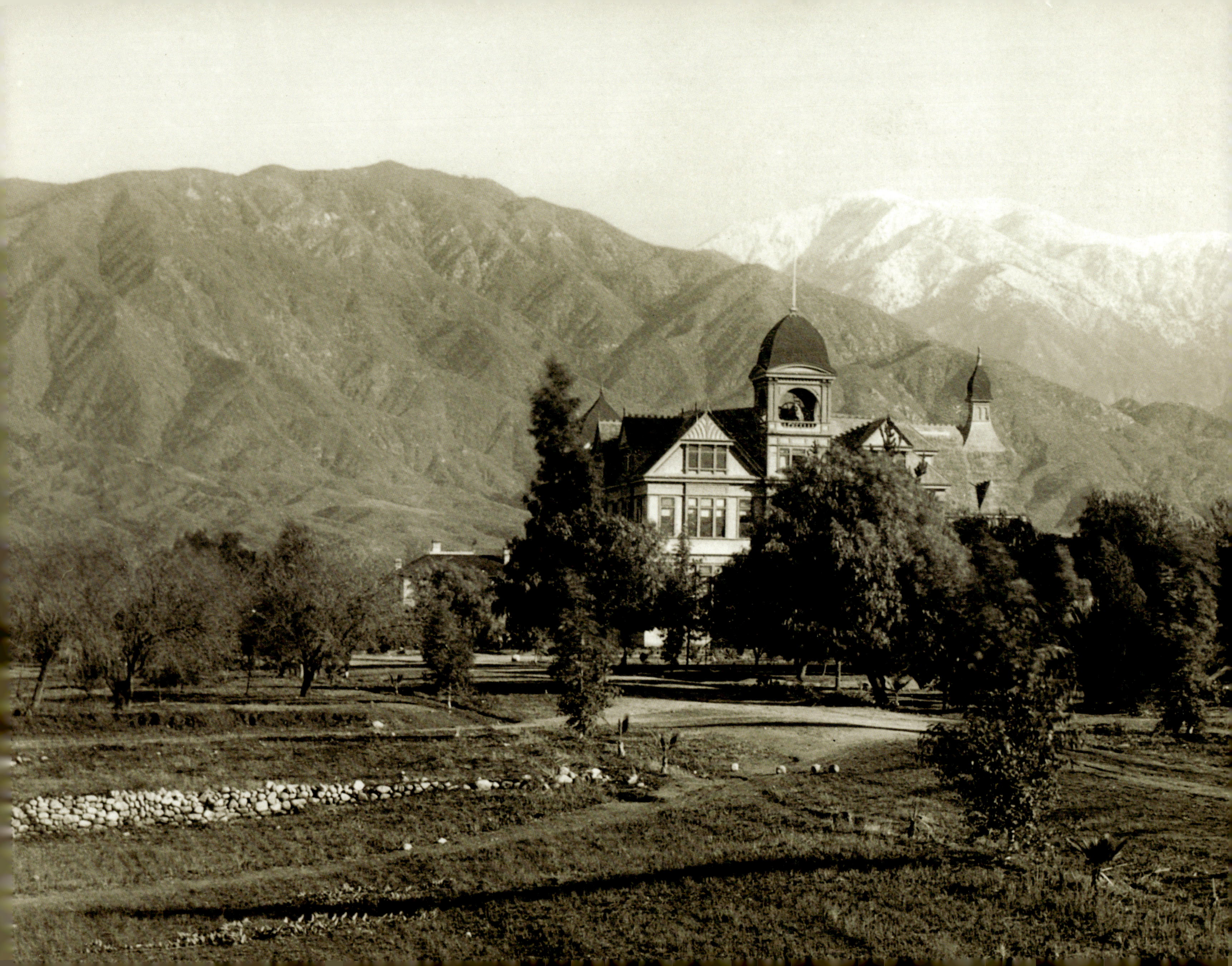

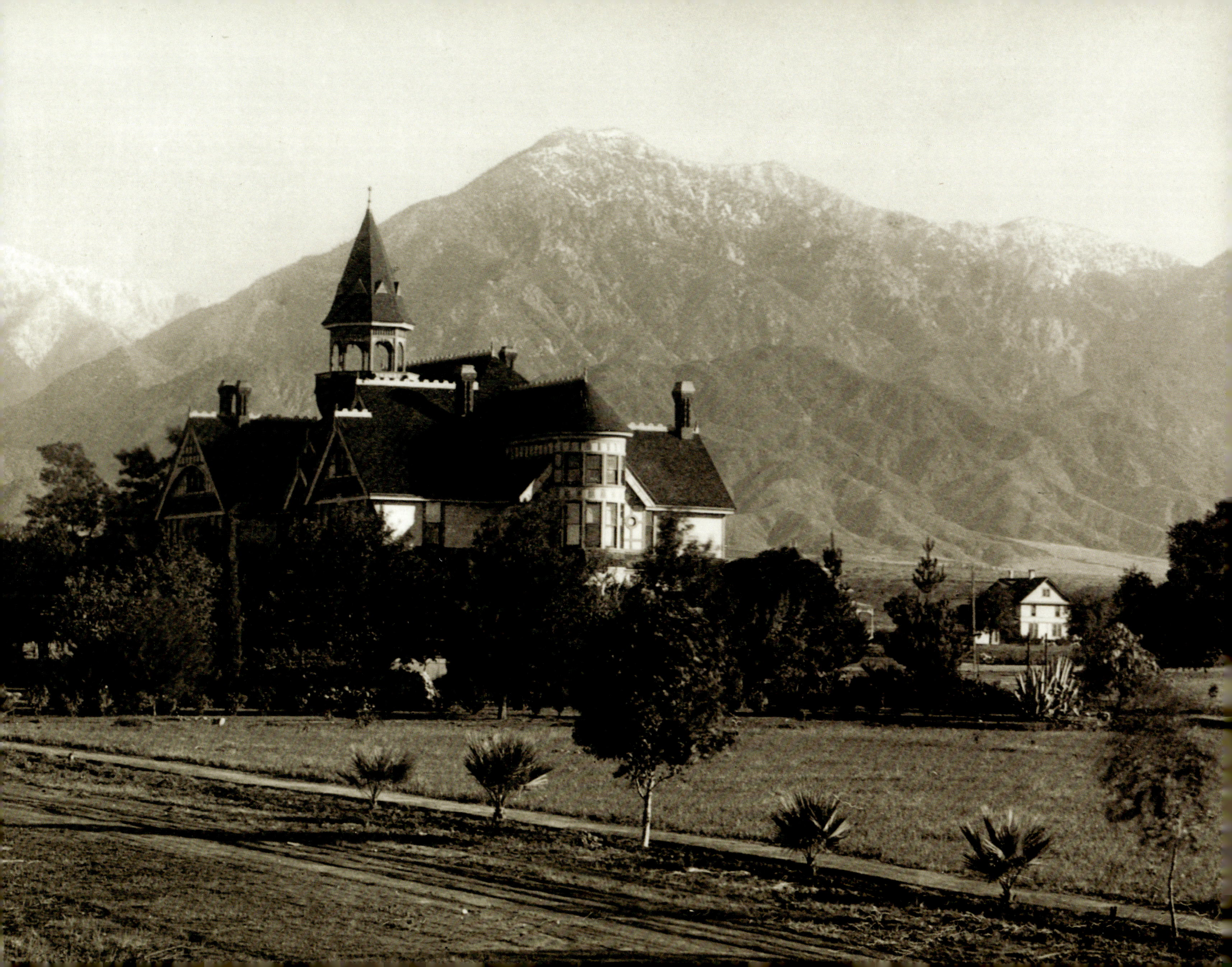

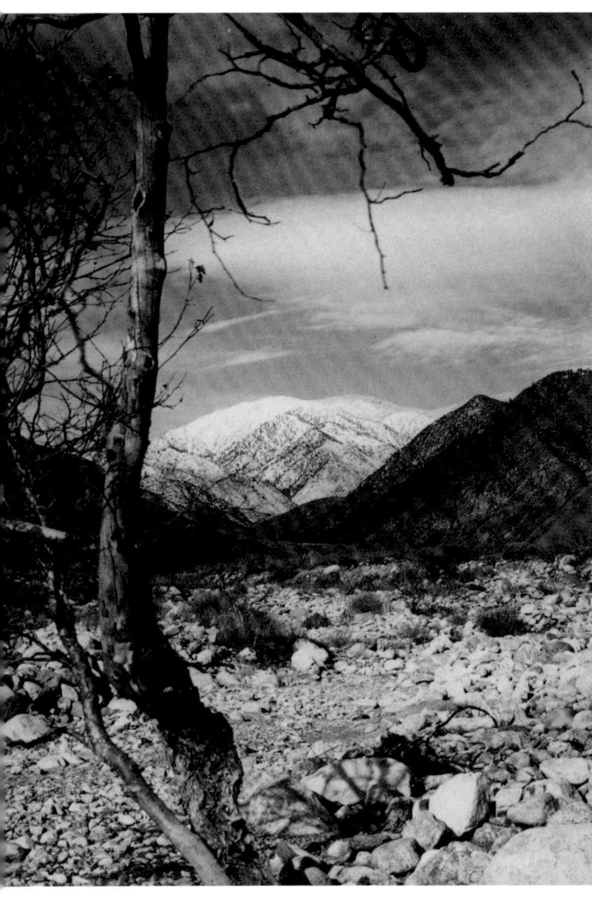

Blanchard Park (The Wash), acquired 1905, early view

Historical Context: The Early American Campus

Institutions of higher education had flourished in Europe since medieval times, and by the early 17th century, when America's first colleges were founded, the English collegiate system epitomized by Oxford and Cambridge was fully developed. The two universities had emerged from the religious chaos of the Protestant Reformation with newly strengthened curricula and high enrollments, and the popular enthusiasm for education reflected by their success was soon exported to the American colonies.[7]

Although the early American campus, particularly in the colonial period, owed a debt to British universities, the physical development of the American college was largely independent—influenced more by local social, economic, and cultural forces—and distinctly American in nature.[8] Education was considered a priority from this country's earliest days. The Massachusetts Colony had a college by 1640, a mere 10 years after its founding, and by 1776 there were nine degree-granting institutions in the country. Widely separated and responding to local needs, they followed a pattern, of which Pomona is an example, that came to distinguish American campuses from their urban-centered British forerunners. Particularly after the Revolution, there was a growing tendency to found colleges on remote frontiers. Initially, this was due to the desire to train American Indians for missionary work, but a certain distrust of cities and attraction to the idealized purity of nature became increasingly important factors. "The romantic ideal of the college in nature, removed from the distractions of civilization, has persisted up to the present time and has determined the location of countless institutions."[9] In the nineteenth century, nature was increasingly seen in transcendental terms, as possessing both aesthetic and moral value.[10] In selecting and developing a rural site for the College, Pomona's founders thus followed a pattern that distinguished American colleges from their European predecessors. In 1890, even before Claremont had been determined the College's permanent site, Board President H.A. Palmer and Professor Frank Brackett had planted *Eucalyptus viminalis* saplings along College Avenue; and the acquisition of The Wash (1905) and commitment of Trustee George W. Marston to landscaping assured both that the village surrounding the College would live up to the name "Claremont the Beautiful," as it had been dubbed by investors, and that Pomona students would always enjoy the benefits of a carefully developed natural environment.

The early Pomona College also reflected a national belief in the college campus as a community of scholars, a place where faculty and students lived and worked closely together. This is now so common that we forget that it was only in the nineteenth century that an American campus (Thomas Jefferson's University of Virginia, begun in 1817) was designed to accommodate living quarters for faculty and students. Before this, students lived off campus, responsible for their own lives outside highly individualized tutorial sessions. (Except for Pomona's first two years, when Claremont Hall served as a coeducational residence, male students in both the preparatory and college departments were boarded in local homes until Smiley Hall was completed in 1908.) Over time, the fear that dormitories would promote riotous behavior was replaced by the conviction that communal living would enhance an education that, it was recognized, should extend beyond the mastery of given academic fields and intellectual skills to an awareness of how to live responsibly and productively in the world.

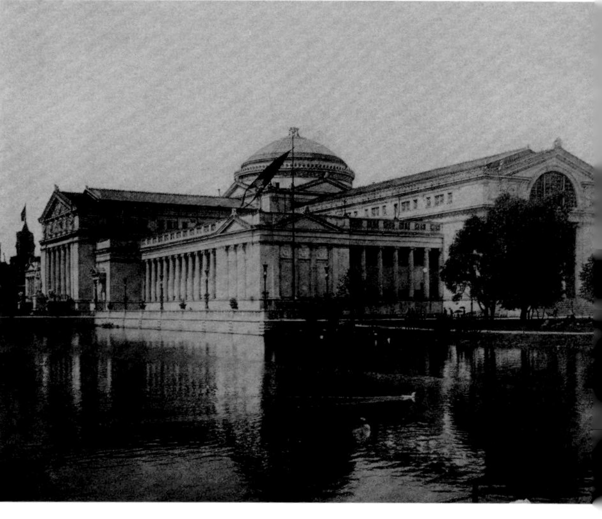

World's Columbian Exposition, View of the Palace of Fine Arts, Chicago, 1893, E.R. Walker, Chicago History Museum ICHi-39358

Pomona's Early Architecture

Pomona's first years coincided with a period of dramatic change in architectural fashion. The "central building" designed for Piedmont Mesa; the Claremont Hotel/Sumner Hall; and Holmes Hall were all Victorian in style, reflecting the prevailing taste throughout much of the nineteenth century for complex, highly ornamented structures that reflected the prosperity and optimism of America's "golden age." The 1893 World's Columbian Exposition in Chicago, an extravagantly ambitious undertaking popularly known as the White City, offered a new vision of architecture and city planning—classical in style but technologically advanced—and proved to be a watershed, inspiring the City Beautiful movement and, in a stroke, shifting architectural taste from idiosyncratic Victorian exuberance to a relatively restrained classicism. The contrast between the first Holmes Hall (1893)—with its varied facades broken by bays, and its complicated, sharply peaked, dormered roof topped by an ornate bell tower—and the simple, symmetrical block that was Pearsons (1899) demonstrates this shift. And, as architect Robert A.M. Stern has commented, architect F. P. Burnham's design for Carnegie (1908) would have been unimaginable without the example of the Chicago World's Fair. Although Carnegie, with its raised temple front and classical orders, remains the College's outstanding example of classical revival architecture, both Pearsons and Smiley (1908) reflect the taste for symmetry and restraint that was gaining favor among architects and their patrons—a style that, many felt, more appropriately expressed the values and aspiration of a humanistic education. When Holmes Hall was first renovated in 1916, and Sumner Hall in 1921, each was stripped of its third floor and Victorian gingerbread and encased (quite literally) in a greatly simplified stucco shell with a red tile roof—blending the influence of the regional Mission style with the new classical restraint.

In 1908, then, 20 years after the beginning of classes and with no fewer than nine campus buildings serving instruction, administration, housing, and athletics, and a substantial plot of undeveloped adjacent land acquired, the trustees wisely decided that a plan for future growth was needed. The commission to design a campus plan for Pomona was awarded to architect Myron Hunt (1862–1952). Born in Massachusetts and trained at MIT, Hunt first practiced in Chicago where he was associated with Boston-based architect H. H. Richardson, exposed to the work of Frank Lloyd Wright, and, like so many of his peers, profoundly influenced by the World's Columbian Exposition. Moving west in 1903, he established a practice in Pasadena that included private and institutional clients; his career ultimately included campus commissions from Caltech (then Throop Polytechnic) and Occidental College as well as Pomona. Hunt's arrival in Claremont marked the beginning of a period that would see the creation of some of the College's finest buildings and the development not only of an embracing vision for the campus but also of an architectural style that would distinguish and guide the College for years to come. ■

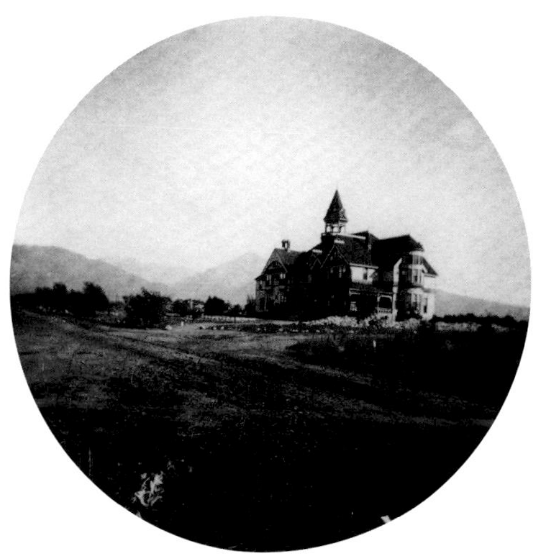

Claremont (later Mary L. Sumner) Hall, built 1887, before 1893

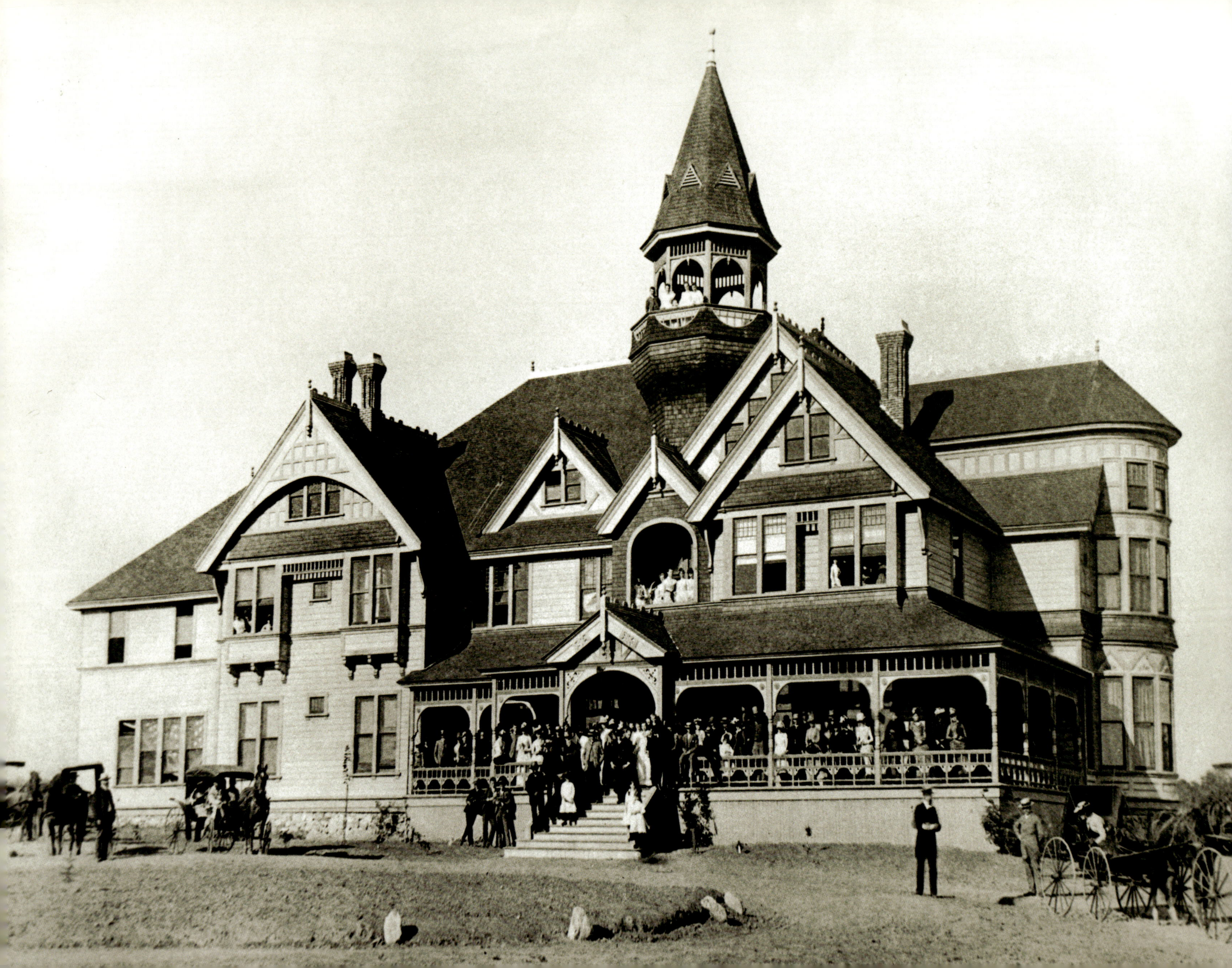

Mary L. Sumner Hall

Sumner Hall, which now houses Admissions, Campus Life, Study Abroad, and Mail Services, boasts the longest, most multi-faceted, and, arguably, most important history of any of Pomona's buildings. Its ultimate predecessor—the Hotel Claremont —was not only the College's first home in Claremont but also a factor in its location here, having been offered to the founders in 1888, less than a year after ground had been broken for a campus on Piedmont Mesa. Immediately renamed Claremont Hall, the spacious wood building, which had been built to attract investors to Claremont, was sited in splendid isolation on College (then Warren) Avenue. Its ground floor provided "recitation" rooms, an assembly room and parlor, a library, a dining room and a kitchen. Upstairs was an office suite for Pomona's first president, Cyrus Grandison Baldwin (1890–1898), along with rooms for students. Edwin Clarence Norton, Principal of the Preparatory Department and professor of Greek (and, from 1898–1926, dean of the College) roomed there with his family and presided over meals.

In 1893, when Holmes Hall was completed, Claremont Hall, rechristened Mary L. Sumner Hall in honor of the wife of the Reverend Charles Burt Sumner, founding trustee, became a dormitory for female students and the College's central dining hall. A third reincarnation occurred in 1921, when Sumner was dismantled and reconstructed in its present location east of Bridges Hall of Music in order to make way for the creation of the large central quadrangle anticipated in architect Myron Hunt's 1908 campus plan. That Sumner Hall was preserved reflected its importance to the early history of the College. In the move, the building was turned 180 degrees to face east, and one wing was removed and relocated to Dartmouth and Sixth Street where it served as a studio for art professor Hannah Tempest Jenkins. Once stripped of its Victorian gingerbread, the wood building was encased in a tile-roofed stucco shell, resulting in a building within a building. Parallel to Bridges Hall of Music across Memorial Court, Sumner became, once again, the College's central administration building, retaining this identity until the opening of Alexander Hall in 1991.

Carolyn Lyon, widow of the College's sixth president E. Wilson Lyon, recently recalled Sumner Hall in her day (Lyon was in office from 1941–69): "Everything was there…most of the administrators, all the facilities we normally associate with a college. The people in it worked so hard to create meaningful and valuable activities for generations of students. Nearly everything was concentrated in there at one time or another. So many important decisions were made in Sumner Hall, from the budget to the curriculum."[1] The Lyons' son John particularly remembers his father's office. "He had a bay window behind his desk, where the sun would filter in. And he had a long, long work table, a formal table, where people could have meetings with him. The office was lovely and filled with pictures and very nice furniture. There was also an alcove to the right of his office where I would often study. In 1964, I studied for the bar exam in that alcove office. Often on a Sunday, we would both go there for a couple of hours to catch up on things. While ostensibly 'catching up' on office work, he often read *The New York Times*."[2] ■

Mary L. Sumner Hall, built 1887, ca. 1896

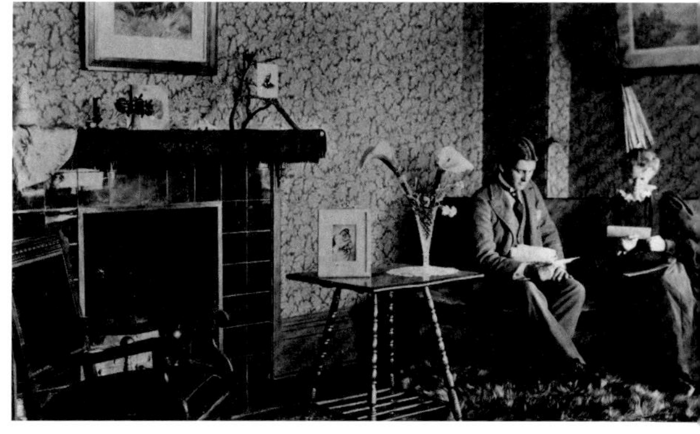

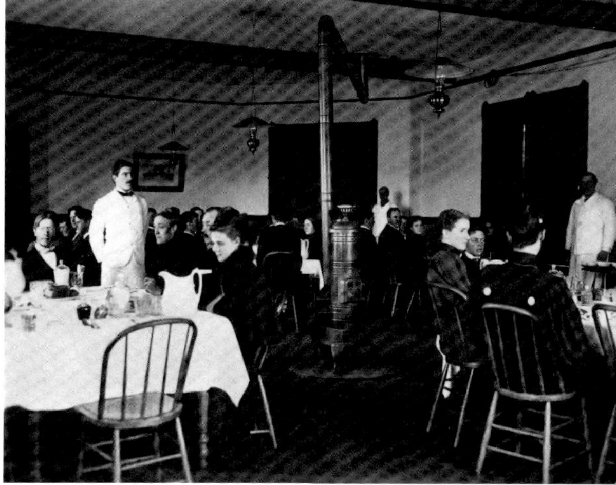

Sumner Hall, Parlor, 1890s

Sumner Hall, Dining Room

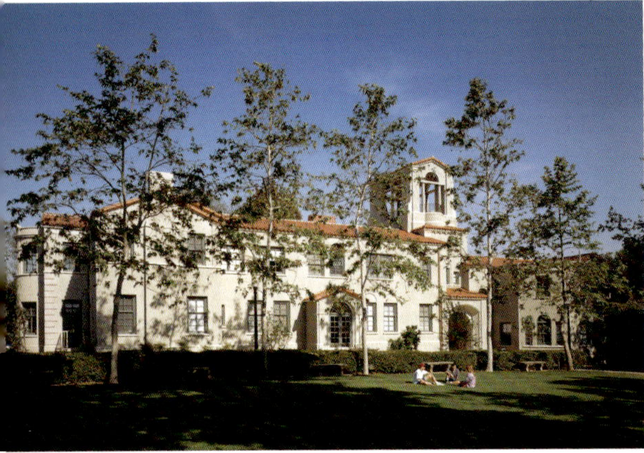

Mary L. Sumner Hall

BUILT 1887 as Hotel Claremont; deeded to the College and renamed Claremont Hall, 1888; renamed Mary L. Sumner Hall, 1893

LOCATION 333 North College Way

ARCHITECT John C. Pelton, Jr.

ORIGINAL LOCATION College (formerly Warren) Avenue between Fourth and Sixth Streets

ORIGINAL MATERIALS wood frame

DISMANTLED/MOVED/RECONSTRUCTED 1921, College Way, east of Bridges Hall of Music; re-dedicated 1923

RECONSTRUCTION ARCHITECTS Jamieson and Spearl

RECONSTRUCTION MATERIALS stucco shell enclosing original wood building, tile roof

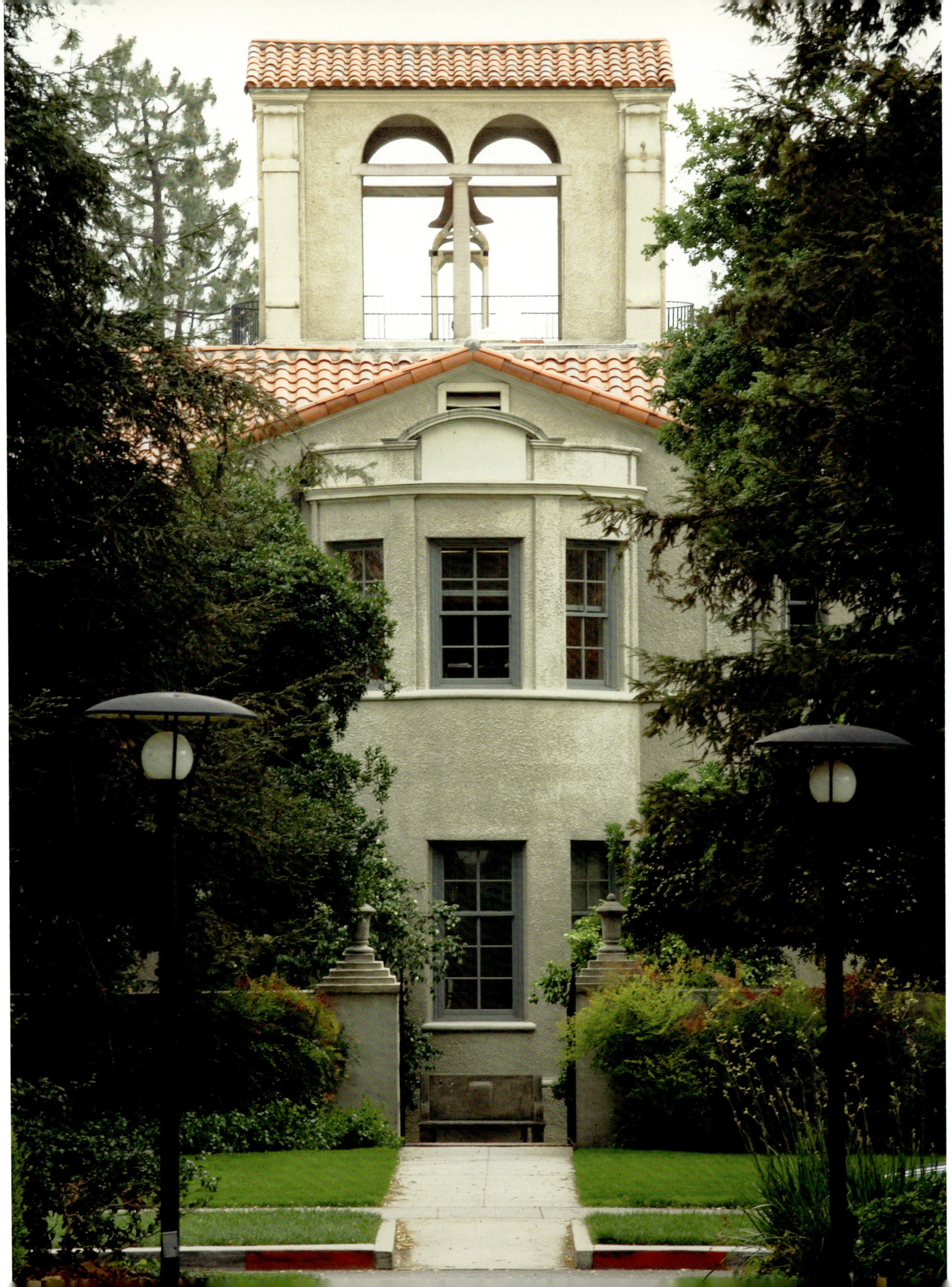

Henry Cabala

Cyrus W. Holmes, Jr. Hall

Holmes Hall was Pomona's second building and the first built by the College. The need for a "recitation building" was expressed in the College's first catalogue (1890–91), which suggested that "a memorial building would be a fitting gift from a Christian man or woman to a Christian College." In response, the widow and daughter of the late Cyrus W. Holmes, Jr., of Monson, Massachusetts, offered $25,000 over a period of five years. At the time (1891), it was still anticipated that Claremont Hall would house the "Preparatory Department" and that the College's campus would be built on Piedmont Mesa on land donated by Trustee and Board President Henry A. Palmer. The 1892 decision to site the College's first academic building in Claremont, thus grouping its facilities, was enormously significant for the future. The Holmes family agreed to pay for construction in Claremont, and Palmer's land was returned to him.

Located on the east side of College (then Warren) Avenue just south of Sixth Street, the original building was designed to be brick but ultimately constructed of less expensive redwood. Its rambling design and highly ornamented Queen Anne Victorian style matched that of Claremont Hall to its south. The main entrance, facing south, was flanked by two large palms that remain today. The building, lit by kerosene lamps, included two floors, each with seven recitation rooms and two offices; a basement containing a chemical laboratory and heating system; a chapel on the northeast that could seat 300; and a tower, complete with bell. Writing about the January, 1893, dedication of Holmes Hall, E. Wilson Lyon noted: "In the hearts and minds of all present that day Pomona College had moved from the provisional to the permanent."

Enrollment increases prompted a major building program in the first years of the new century that culminated in the remodeling of Holmes in 1916, supported in part by a further gift from Esther R. Holmes, during the tenure of President James Blaisdell. Although other buildings existed by now, Holmes remained the principal instructional facility, containing humanities and social science classrooms as well as administrative offices. The now-inadequate, original wood building was transformed, as Claremont (Sumner) Hall was soon to be, into a tile-roofed stucco structure, Mission Revival in style, that harmonized with its neighbors: Carnegie, Smiley, Rembrandt, and Little Bridges. The chapel, which continued to be used for student gatherings, was nearly doubled in size and given a stage and two music / dressing rooms. At the same time the entrance was moved to the west side (College Avenue), relating the building more effectively to the College's Gate at Sixth Street that had been installed in 1914. As reincarnated, Holmes lasted more than 70 years and proved so successful that architect James P. Jamieson and his associates, of St. Louis, became the College's supervising architects.

In the early days, Holmes served also as a social, religious, and civic center for the city, linking town and gown. By 1987, however, the structure had deteriorated. Deemed unsafe and impractical to renovate, it was closed to use and, in 1990, demolished, making room for Alexander Hall. The decision to replace Holmes with a new building met with opposition from Claremont preservation interests and led ultimately to important design decisions affecting its successor.

Holmes Hall is remembered by many. Emeritus Professor of Modern Languages Howard Young, whose office was once on the second floor ("with unbearable summer heat") and whose course load at the time was five classes per semester, including one that met at 8 a.m. on Saturday, recalls that "visitors, especially the Brits, remarked in unison that the acoustics of its stage had no par; across its proscenia walked

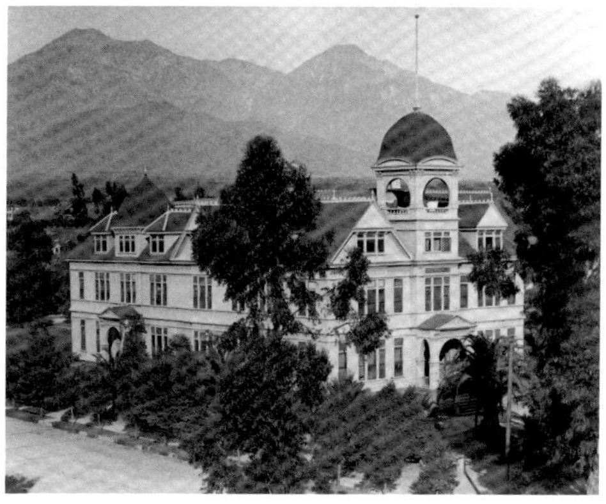

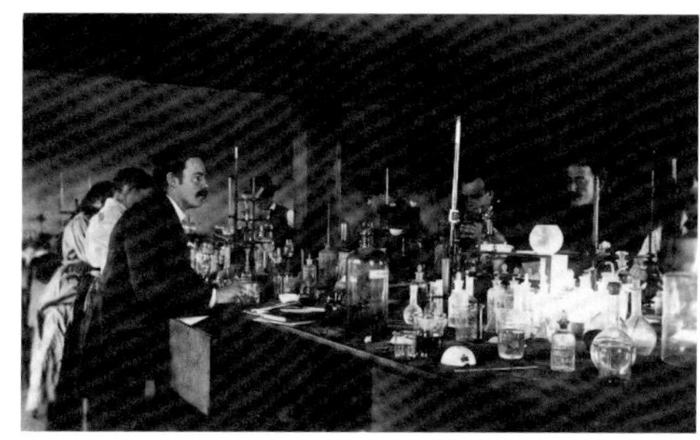

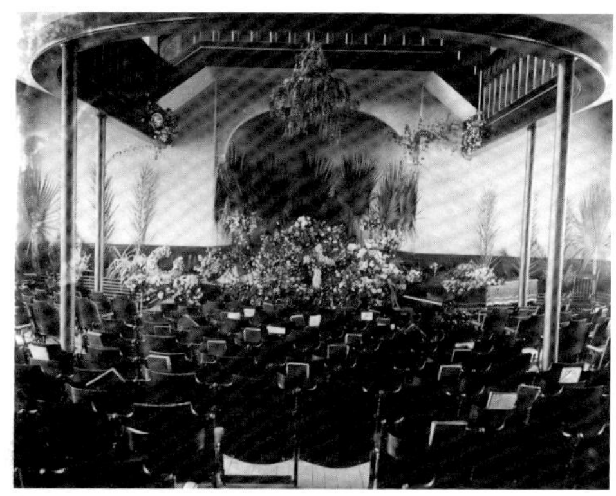

FROM TOP *Holmes Hall before reconstruction of 1916; Chemistry Laboratory; Auditorium*

OPPOSITE *Sumner Hall after reconstruction*

OVERLEAF *Holmes Hall, ca. 1893*

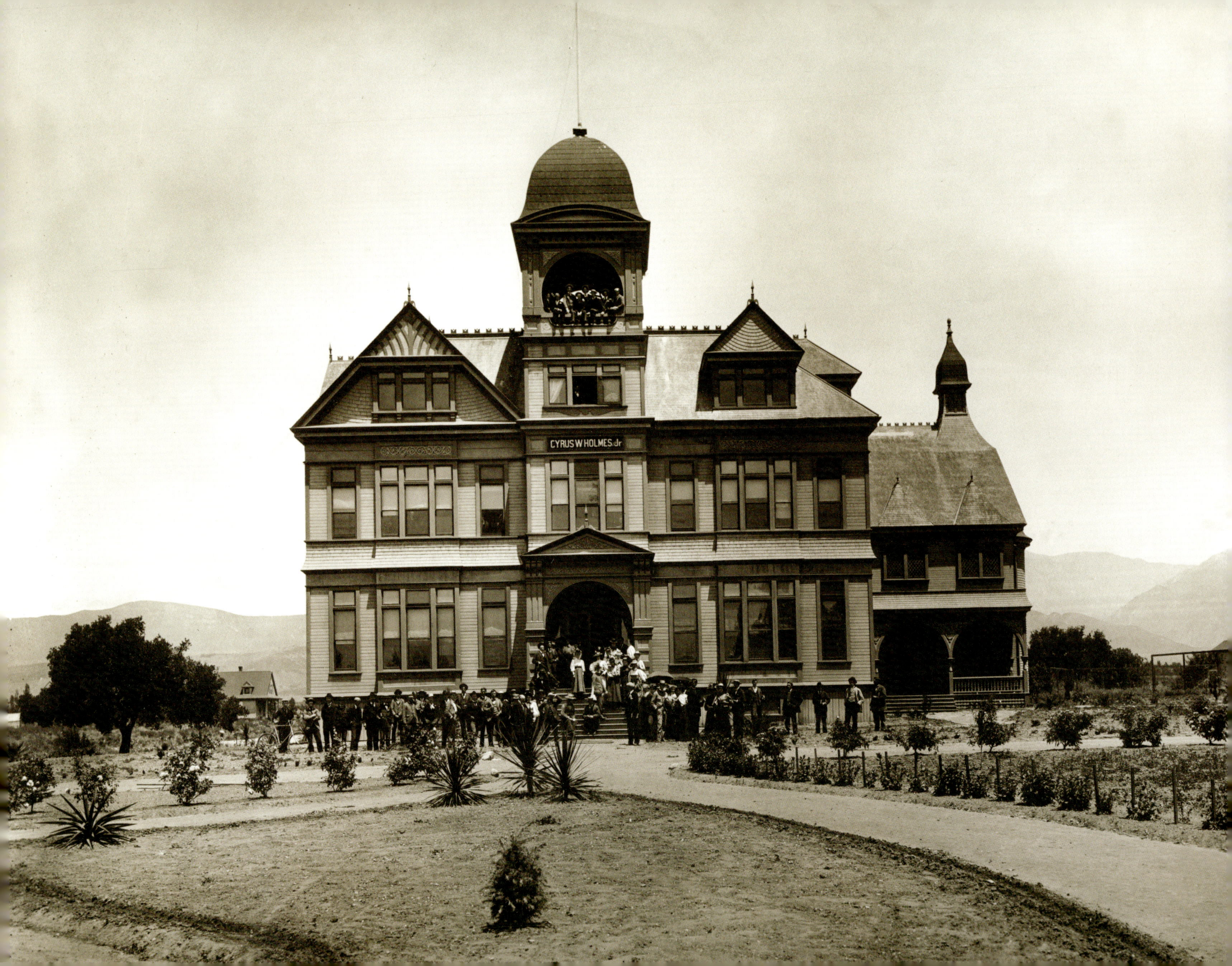
CYRUS W HOLMES Jr

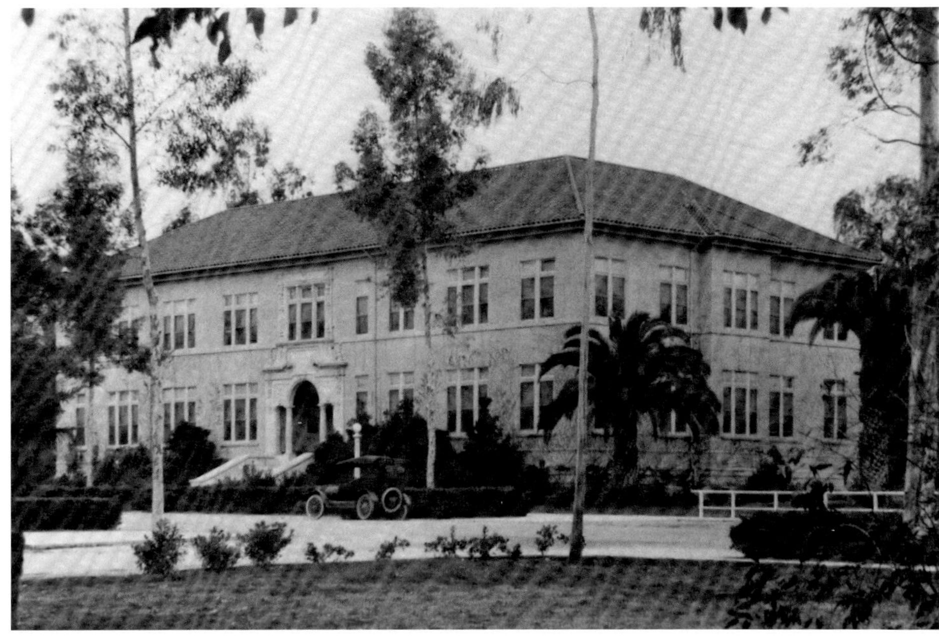

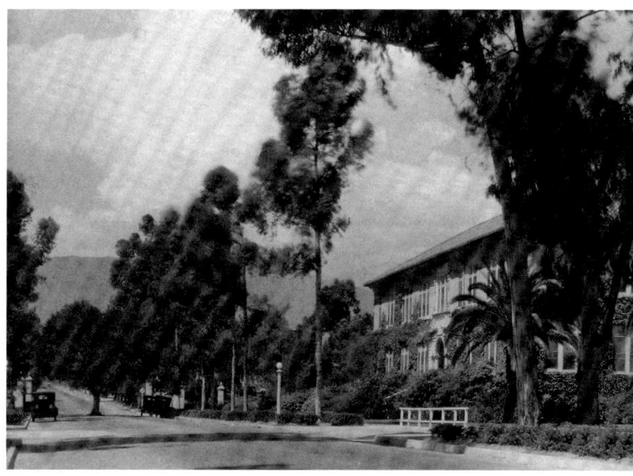

Joel McCrea '28, Robert Taylor '33, Richard Chamberlain '56, Kris Kristofferson '58." Perdita Horn Myers '54, who cites Holmes as her favorite campus building, remembers some of its dramatic glories: "*Ethan Frome*, and especially *Of Thee I Sing* (involving one tenth of the student body); the co-author of this Pulitzer Prize-winning show, Morrie Ryskind, attended a performance and came onstage to congratulate the principals during the curtain call." She also notes that "Holmes Hall was not in great shape even then (early 50s): one day during French class, a booted foot crashed through the second-story classroom ceiling directly over the teacher, M. Thomas. The foot promptly retreated into the attic, leaving a shaken professor. Good old Holmes Hall!"

It is likely that no one remembers the dilemmas presented by Holmes Hall with greater clarity than David Alexander who, as president, found it necessary to order its removal in 1990.

> *Holmes Hall went through several cycles of patching and alterations, mostly mandated by the Fire Marshal. Soon after I came, we were forced to prohibit any use of the auditorium balcony. "Rickety" is the word that comes to mind. The fixed seats in the auditorium were removed, and the Theatre Department, which remained in the building, used this modified auditorium, so dear to the memory of alumni and townspeople, for several productions… The historic nature of Holmes Hall conferred upon it an almost sacred status. Alumni, townspeople, students, and faculty were determined to defend it. One trustee required the College to have a series of studies that ultimately demonstrated that the building could be restored only at great cost and with limited utility as an academic building. Its wooden construction was a serious handicap, and the substandard height of the basement meant either a major excavation and lifting job or closing it off. Much passion was spent, but finally a demolition permit was granted with certain conditions, such as some commemoration of the building. In the meantime, the Byron Dick Seaver Theatre* (see Chapter v) *gave the drama and dance faculty and students a splendid, state-of-the-art facility.* ■

Cyrus W. Holmes, Jr. Hall

BUILT 1892–93
LOCATION Southeast corner College (then Warren) Avenue and Sixth Street
PRESIDENT IN OFFICE Cyrus Grandison Baldwin
PURPOSE "recitation" (classroom) building
ORIGINAL MATERIALS redwood frame
COST $22,400
DONORS Mrs. S.B. Holmes and Miss Esther R. Holmes
ENLARGED 1904
RECONSTRUCTED 1916 (under President Blaisdell)
RECONSTRUCTION ARCHITECT James P. Jamiesen
RECONSTRUCTION MATERIALS stucco, tile roof
REPLACED 1991, by Alexander Hall

Pearsons Hall of Science

BUILT 1898; dedicated January 1899
LOCATION 551 North College Avenue
PRESIDENT IN OFFICE Franklin La Du Ferguson
ORIGINAL PURPOSE Chemistry, Physics, Biology; President's Office; Library
ARCHITECT C.H. Brown
MATERIALS pressed brick
DONOR Dr. D.K. Pearsons
RENOVATED 1934 (C.T. and W.P. Stover); 1958; 2003–04 (Brian Bloom/Tovey Schulz)
CURRENT USE History, Philosophy, Religious Studies

Pearsons Hall of Science

Completed in 1898, during the brief administration of President Franklin La Du Ferguson (1898–1901), Pearsons Hall is the oldest of Pomona's buildings still in use on its original site (southwest corner of College Avenue at Sixth Street). Third of the College's early structures, it was originally dedicated primarily to science, with classrooms and laboratories for chemistry, physics and biology, and also housed the president's office and the College's first library. Pearsons was constructed of cream-colored pressed brick and featured an open, central hall finished in oak, gas lights, and steam heat. Its porch and steps served as a gathering place for rallies and photographs. The building's inset windows and round-arched entry with rusticated detail reflected the influence of renowned Boston architect H. H. Richardson, and its sober, cubic design, use of permanent materials, and modern facilities contrasted sharply with Sumner and Holmes halls. As Robert A.M. Stern, architect of the Smith Campus Center, has commented, when Pearsons was completed "Pomona began to take on the character it has had ever since—that of an imposing group of buildings that in varying ways addresses the issues of local climate and conditions and the idea of a college as a public institution with a deliberately civic rather than residential image."

The building was named for Chicago philanthropist Dr. D.K. Pearsons (1820–1912) whom President Ferguson had interested in Pomona. A physician and farmer who later turned to real estate and then railways, Pearsons, who had no children, gave generously to a large number of American colleges. His gift to Pomona of $20,000, in tandem with a $12,000 grant from the Congregational Educational Society, gave the trustees sufficient confidence to purchase the necessary land for the hall in 1898. Over his lifetime, Pearsons gave Pomona a total of $200,000, always at times of great need and with an interest in the potential of his philanthropy to stimulate further donations. President Blaisdell once remarked: "In my judgment, Dr. Pearsons's gifts have been nothing less than epoch-making in the history of American education."

Pearsons Hall served memorably as the site of an address in May 1903 by President Theodore Roosevelt (the only U.S. president ever to visit Claremont) whom Pomona President George Gates had invited, hoping to enhance the College's visibility and reputation. Arriving at the Claremont train station, Roosevelt was transported by carriage to campus where he spoke to a crowd of thousands from a podium constructed in front of Pearsons, later planting a California oak nearby to mark the occasion. The tree, alas, died soon thereafter, though College lore attached the Roosevelt name to succeeding oaks.

In 1934, in the wake of the Long Beach earthquake of 1933 that raised concerns about the strength of current structures, Pearsons was rebuilt with funds provided by founding Trustee George W. Marston and others. By this date, Pearsons was dedicated entirely to physics, with Mason and Crookshank halls now serving the other sciences. In 1958, with the move of physics to the newly completed Millikan Laboratory, Pearsons became a humanities center, housing the departments of History, Religion, Philosophy and Classics. The building's most recent renovation, in 2003–04, not only significantly upgraded the building's structure, interior spaces, and facilities, but also recovered original architectural details and features including the wooden windows and handsome staircase. ■

Gene Sasse

OPPOSITE *Pearsons Hall, after renovation of 2003–04*

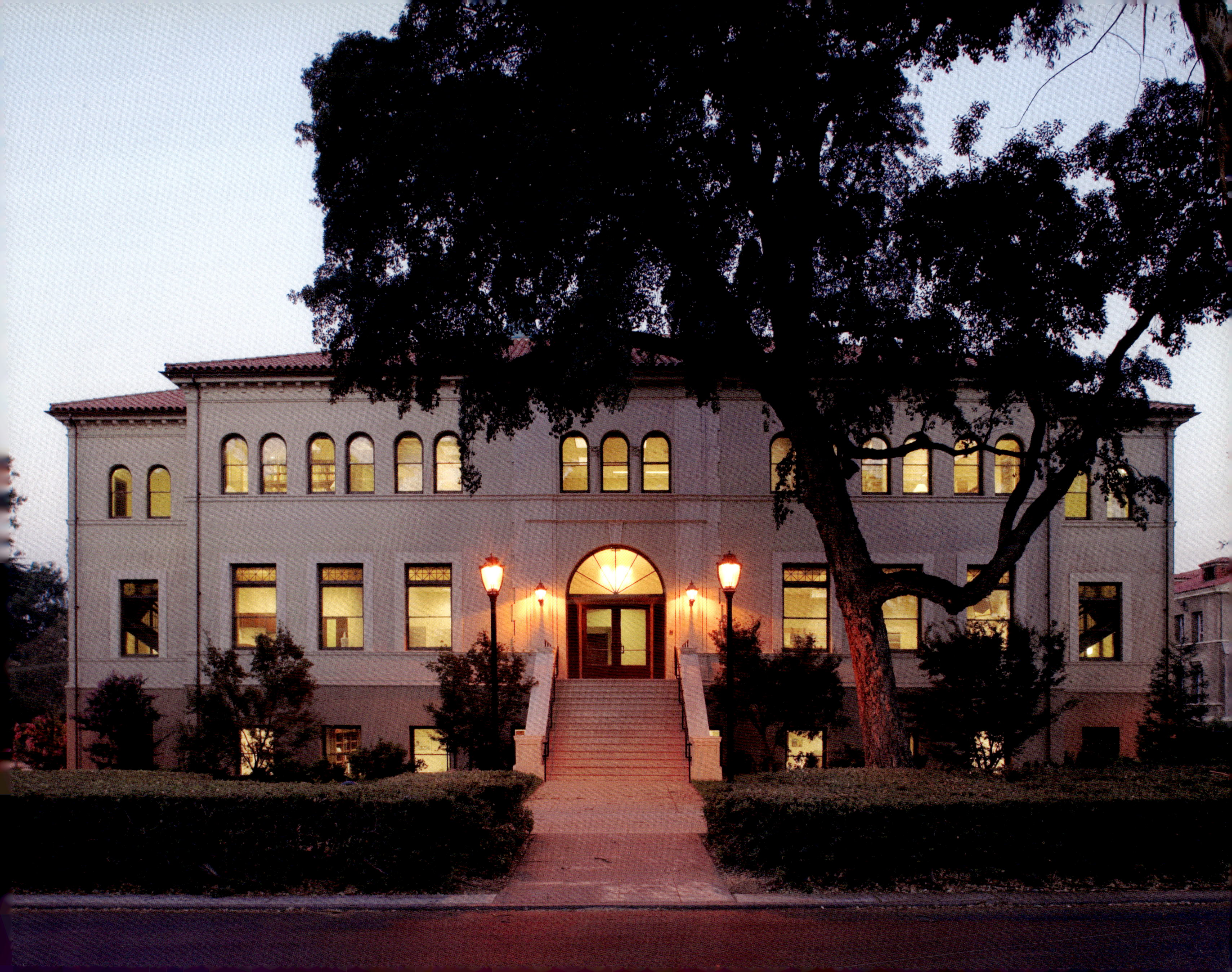

Renwick Gymnasium

BUILT 1899–1900
LOCATION East of Holmes Hall
PRESIDENT IN OFFICE Franklin La Du Ferguson
ARCHITECT Carroll Brown
MATERIALS wood frame; stucco façade
COST $5,500
DONOR(S) Mrs. Helen Goodwin Renwick, Claremont; additional funds raised by students
NAMED FOR William Renwick, late husband of donor
MOVED 1931
DESTROYED by fire 1952

Renwick Gymnasium

Most alumni who remember "Renwick Gymnasium" will associate the name with a different building and site than the original built in 1899–1900 during the tenure of President Ferguson. The confusion stems from the fact that the Renwick name fell out of use early in the building's history, and when a larger facility, originally built to house the Student Army Training Corps in 1918 (see Chapter III), was converted to use as a gymnasium in 1919 and dubbed the "Big Gym," the original became the "Little Gym." In 1930, in order to make room for the construction of Bridges Auditorium, it was moved to a site north of its larger partner. In 1950, when Memorial Gymnasium was completed east of Smiley (where Rains Center now stands), the two earlier wooden gyms were joined, re-christened William Renwick Gymnasium to preserve this important early College name, and dedicated to physical education for women. The 1899 structure was destroyed by fire in 1952.

The original Renwick Gymnasium contained "a bowling alley, chest weights, rings, bars, etc. for systematic exercise," and (outside) an improved track, baseball diamond and tennis courts. Its construction was funded by a $2,500 gift from Mrs. Helen Goodwin Renwick, Claremont; $1,600 raised by students, with the remainder contributed by the College. According to E. Wilson Lyon, Pomona's teams responded to the new building with a series of highly successful football and track seasons. Architect Robert A.M. Stern has described its design as "South African Dutch Baroque cum Mission Style," noting that in the context of Holmes and Pearsons halls, it suggested that the College had not yet established a consistent image.

At the time of Pomona's founding, colleges and universities were just beginning to acknowledge the importance of physical as well as intellectual development in higher education, and by the 1890s, intercollegiate activities were recognized as beneficial to institutions as well. Gyms, fields, and swimming pools soon came to be seen as essential, for women as well as for men. "No longer the pastime of idle hours," wrote Charles Sumner in 1914, "athletics have come to be regarded as a vital part of the college curriculum," echoing President Ferguson's remark at the dedication of Renwick that: "It is not too much to affirm that no other form of investment of five thousand dollars could have made a richer contribution to the wholesome life of the student body, or the most permanent welfare of the institution."[3]

Equally enthusiastic, Pomona's students managed and financed their own athletic association and, although membership was not required, it included nearly every student and member of the faculty by the 1892–93 academic year. The earliest intercollegiate sports were "field days" (track meets), at which Pomona excelled, competing primarily against USC and Occidental College. Football was first played in 1895, discontinued for a year because it was considered too dangerous, then reinstated in 1897. ■

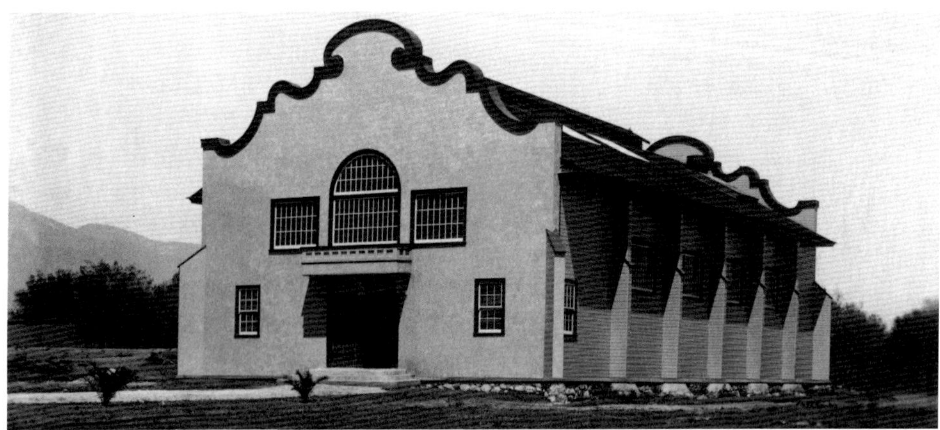

Claremont Inn

The Claremont Inn was initially a joint project of the College, which purchased the land, and the City of Claremont. Offering dining facilities and commons rooms, it served both communities. Pomona students not boarding in town were required to eat there, thus freeing space in Sumner Hall for additional student rooms. Although faculty presided at table, the more intimate atmosphere of Sumner Hall was difficult to recreate and, initially, students were resistant, arguing that they could cook more cheaply for themselves. By 1907, however, when the College took full ownership, services improved and the Inn increasingly became the center of the Claremont community, contributing to a close association between local residents and the College. In 1912 a wing containing guest rooms was added, and, until 1965 when these were closed due to safety hazards, the Inn was a convenient and popular hotel, describing itself in early brochures as "a friendly family inn" and "a quiet hotel of the New England type." Pomona students waited tables, and meals were reasonably priced; in 1940 one could dine on rice croquettes with chipped beef for 40 cents or splurge on rack of lamb (75 cents); a multi-course Christmas dinner cost $1.25.

A sense of the Inn in its early years is conveyed in the following from the 1916 *Metate*:

> *The Commons is the center of social life during the week and vies with the college library as a point of departure for 'queeners' [dating couples]. An orchestra furnishes music once a week and the room is filled at every meal with the happy bubbling chatter of divers [sic] young men and sundry coeds. 'Mixed tables' are a feature of the Commons. Owing to the fact that the men are outnumbered they are distributed gracefully around the room as long as they last.*

Dining for male students moved to Frary Hall when that refectory was completed in 1929, and in 1931, Harwood Dining Room began serving women. From that time until its closing in 1968, the Inn, managed from 1941 by Paul J. Scott, served as a center for faculty, community and the general public. After the closing of guest facilities in 1965, dining continued until 1968, when a feasibility study indicated that renovation would be impractical. Although sensitive to the community's fondness for the Inn, the trustees ultimately decided the building should be demolished. It was razed in July of that year after 62 years of service to the College and city. Plans to build a new inn were ultimately abandoned, and the site remained empty until the arrival of the Seaver House in 1979.

The Inn's architect, Arthur Benton, had previously designed the first section of the Mission Inn in Riverside (1902) and the house on College Avenue at Eighth Street now home to the president of Claremont McKenna College. The design of the Inn exemplified the popular Craftsman style, characterized by "rustic" timber construction, airy rooms, hand-crafted detail, and use of outdoor spaces. A legacy of the Arts and Crafts movement that flourished in England and America from the 1870s to around 1916, Craftsman architecture reflected the desire for a return to simplicity, in social and political life as well as aesthetics, and the creation of an affordable, "democratic" style that contrasted sharply with the ostentation and elaborate ornamentation and furnishings of Victorian homes. Patterns for Craftsman homes in various styles (Mission, Stone Cottage, Battened Board Cottage, etc.), published from 1909 by Gustav Stickley, increased the accessibility and popularity of the style, which can be seen in a number of Claremont residences today. ■

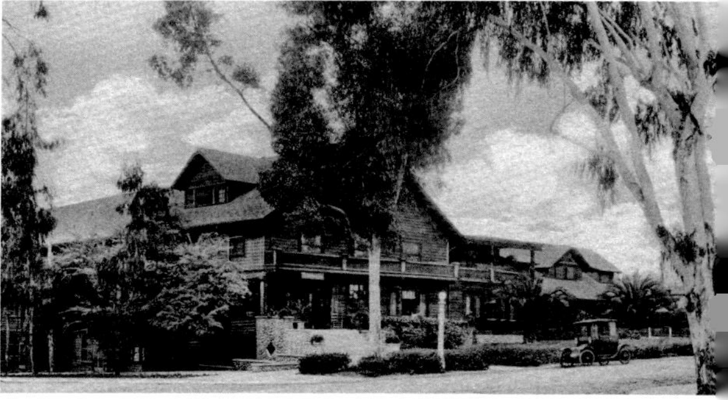

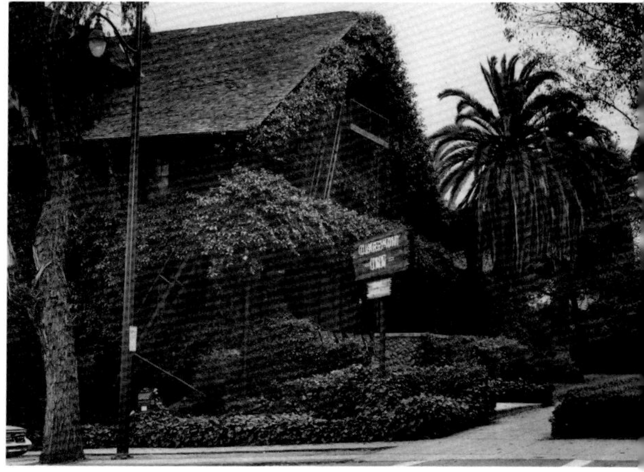

Claremont Inn

BUILT 1905
LOCATION Northwest corner North College and Bonita Avenues (current site of Seaver House)
PRESIDENT IN OFFICE George A. Gates
PURPOSE Dining and guest facilities for College and local community
ARCHITECT Arthur Benton
MATERIALS redwood frame
DEMOLISHED July 15, 1968

The President's House

BUILT 1900
LOCATION 345 North College Avenue at Fourth Street
PRESIDENT IN OFFICE Franklin La Du Ferguson
MATERIALS wood shingle (upper story), clapboard siding (lower)
COST $5,280
RENOVATIONS periodic

The President's House

Pomona's trustees first discussed the need for a new president's house in March 1899, and by April of 1900, three lots on College (then Warren) Avenue south of Fourth Street had been acquired and the house completed. The third major building of President Franklin La Du Ferguson's brief tenure, it has since been home to eight Pomona presidents and their families and has the distinction of being the oldest presidential residence still in use at any college or university in California.

The design of the President's House typifies the post-Victorian style known as American Foursquare. Box-like in shape, the Foursquare generally had two and a half stories; four rooms per floor; a hipped roof with dormers, wide entrance stairs; and wood siding. The style was popularized by pattern books and mail order "kits" that could be ordered from Sears, Roebuck & Company, and Foursquares could be found throughout the country from the 1890s to the 1930s. The house originally had four bedrooms and one bath on the second floor, and two bedrooms on the third. The entry is marked by a semicircular porch with Ionic columns and topped by a Georgian balcony.

Under President James Blaisdell (1910–28) a sleeping porch was added to the second floor along with a second bathroom. Early in the tenure of President Charles Edmunds (1928–41), the living room was enlarged and a large dining room was added on the north to accommodate weekly dinners given by Edmunds for as many as 45 students and faculty at a time. President and Mrs. E. Wilson Lyon, who occupied the house with their two children from 1941–1969, improved the gardens and added a new sun room off the living room. David and Catharine Alexander (1969–91) and Peter and Mary-Jane Stanley (1991–2003) added a powder room, opened the Edmunds Room to the re-landscaped backyard, and upgraded the house for wheelchair access. Finally, with the arrival of David and Claire Oxtoby in 2003, the house underwent major renovation that included a redesigned kitchen, enlarged patio, and French doors leading to the garden.

The President's House has always served as both private residence and symbolic "home" to the College community, a double life that has affected its residents as well as the many students, faculty, and staff who have been entertained there over the years. Carolyn B. Lyon, wife of sixth president E. Wilson Lyon, remembers dozens of dinners for seniors—at least one a week—in the "big room in the back, which had no interior design and no heat! The best use of that room was as a place to thaw the Thanksgiving turkey, but we used it anyway. Over the years, many enjoyed comradeship in that room."[4] The Lyons' daughter Elizabeth Lyon Webb, who lived in the President's House from the age of four until she left for college in 1954, recalls: "I always felt the house was very public. One of my friends once told me she didn't like coming over because she was afraid she'd have to be introduced to someone! To maintain privacy, my father made a ritual every night of putting down all the Venetian blinds. In the daytime they were up, and we were in the midst of the campus as the students passed by on their way to class."[5] Carolyn Lyon was determined to use the house as fully as possible and was responsible for developing the back yard (including planting its magnificent roses) so that it could be used for College functions. ■

OPPOSITE *President's House, built 1900*

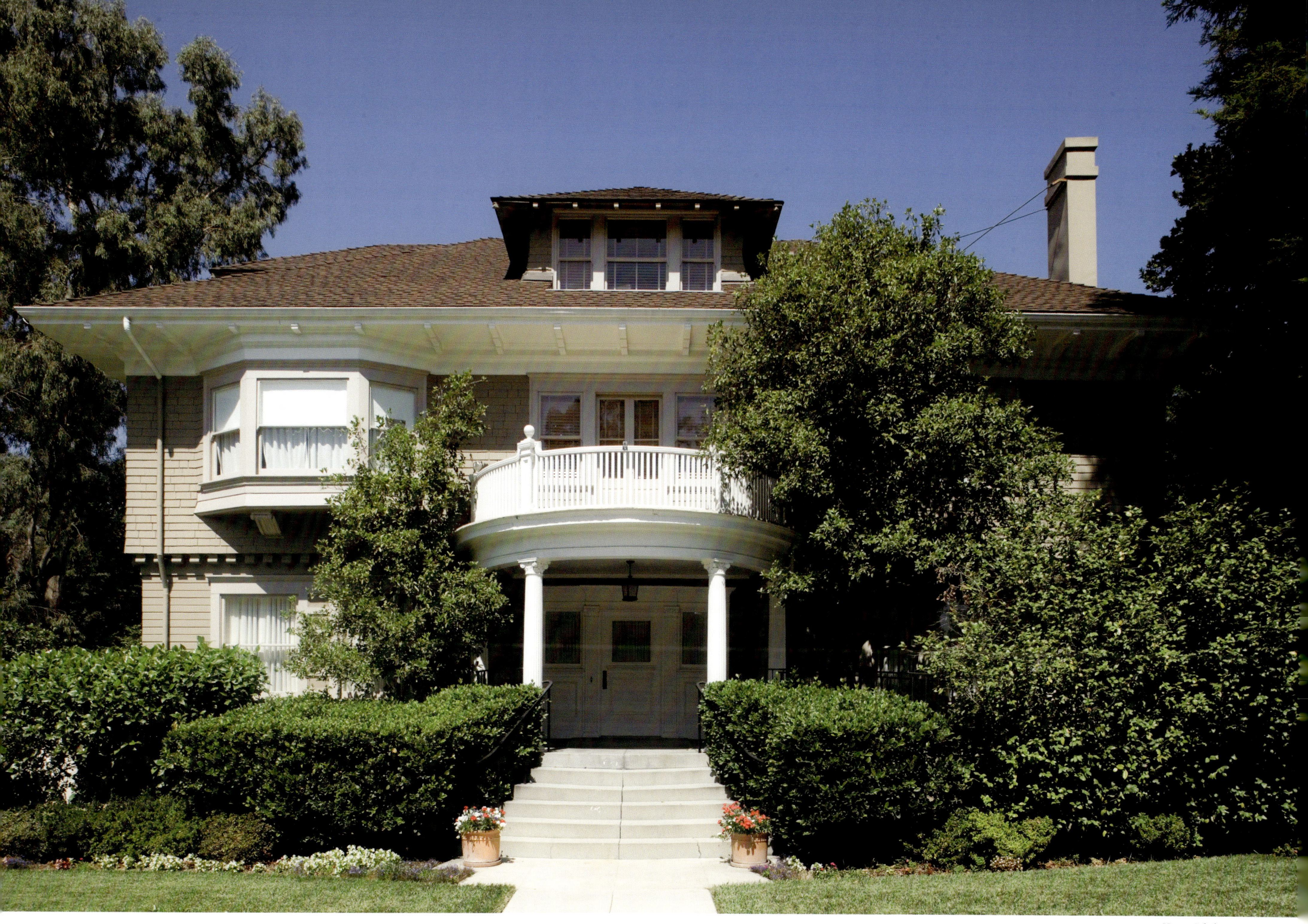

Henry Cabala

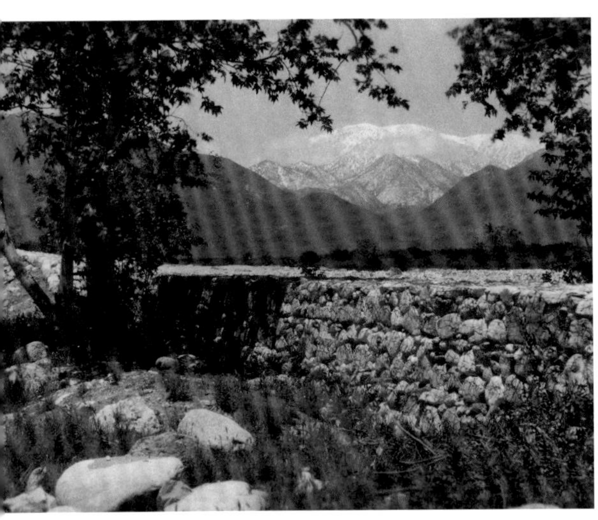

Blanchard Park (The Wash)

ACQUIRED 1905
LOCATION Southeastern edge of campus
PRESIDENT IN OFFICE George Augustus Gates
DESIGNER Samuel Parsons and Company, landscape architects, New York
COST $2,500 (to develop park)
DONOR Nathan W. Blanchard (land)

Blanchard Park (The Wash)

The acquisition of the 64-acre parcel of land to the east of the campus between First and Sixth streets was due largely to the efforts of founding Trustee George Marston who, in 1905, held what turned out to be an auspicious meeting with a landscape architect named Cooke, representing the New York firm of Samuel Parsons and Co.; Trustee Albert Smiley; and his brother, Daniel. All present were deeply interested in gardening and landscaping—Marston had a large garden at his home in San Diego, and the Smiley brothers were then developing property in Redlands and at Lake Mohonk, New York. Motivated by concern that the land might be purchased by investors and developed, Trustee Nathan W. Blanchard, a successful citrus rancher in Santa Paula, offered to support the creation of a park if the College would purchase the parcel. Marston and fellow Trustee Charles Sumner persuaded Blanchard instead to buy the land as a gift to the College, which, in turn, pledged $2,500 to develop a park named for him and to devote a minimum of $300 a year for maintenance.

The Wash, as it has always been known to students, consisted of an old stream bed and plateau filled with live oaks, sycamores, native shrubs and wildflowers. The area had been a favorite place for picnics and other outdoor activities since the College's earliest days in Claremont. A Wash ceremony was part of Commencement in 1897, and the 1901 *Metate* noted that: "The Wash has always been appreciated by the dreamers and lovers of trees and solitude."

At the time of its acquisition, the Wash was traversed by a mountain stream that later fell prey to irrigation needs, over 1,000 California live oaks, and an abundance of other native flora. Ralph D. Cornell '14, who later served the College as landscape architect, remembered the Wash in 1909 when he arrived as a freshman. "The oaks and sycamores lifted into the blue sky with majesty and beauty and a sense of strength...associated with them were the native elderberry, the mountain cherry, and the lovely toyon....The Whipple yuccas were generously dispersed around the oaks like tall white candles against the sky....The undercover of small plants added a springtime fillip of color and animation that provided all the charm of an open woodland, with flower carpets at the feet of majestic trees."

Cornell's rapturous reminiscences, written in a letter to Trustee Leonard A. Shelton '32 in 1966, were followed by an expression of concern about the current condition of the Wash and itemization of preservation efforts that he believed should be undertaken. In 1970, the generosity of trustees Morris Pendleton '22 and Herbert Rempel '23 permitted more regular care including judicious pruning, the installation of an irrigation system, and fire prevention measures.

The portion of the Wash maintained in its natural state has diminished over the years; indeed, the area has always been vulnerable to incursion. A baseball diamond and football field in the northwest section were authorized soon after the Wash was acquired; Brackett Observatory was built on the knoll in 1908, and the Greek Theatre designed by Myron Hunt (but never completed as he had envisioned) followed in 1914. Today, playing fields, tennis courts, and a track occupy large sections of the Wash, which is edged by Pendleton Pool and Seaver Theatre. The gradual loss of native habitat, lamented by many, has been counterbalanced by the gains offered by new facilities, and the Wash continues to play a central role in college life. An organic garden first established by students in the 1990s has recently enjoyed renewed attention, the now-restored Sontag Greek Theatre continues to be the site for weekly gatherings, and the park still offers the visual and spiritual respite that generations have enjoyed. ■

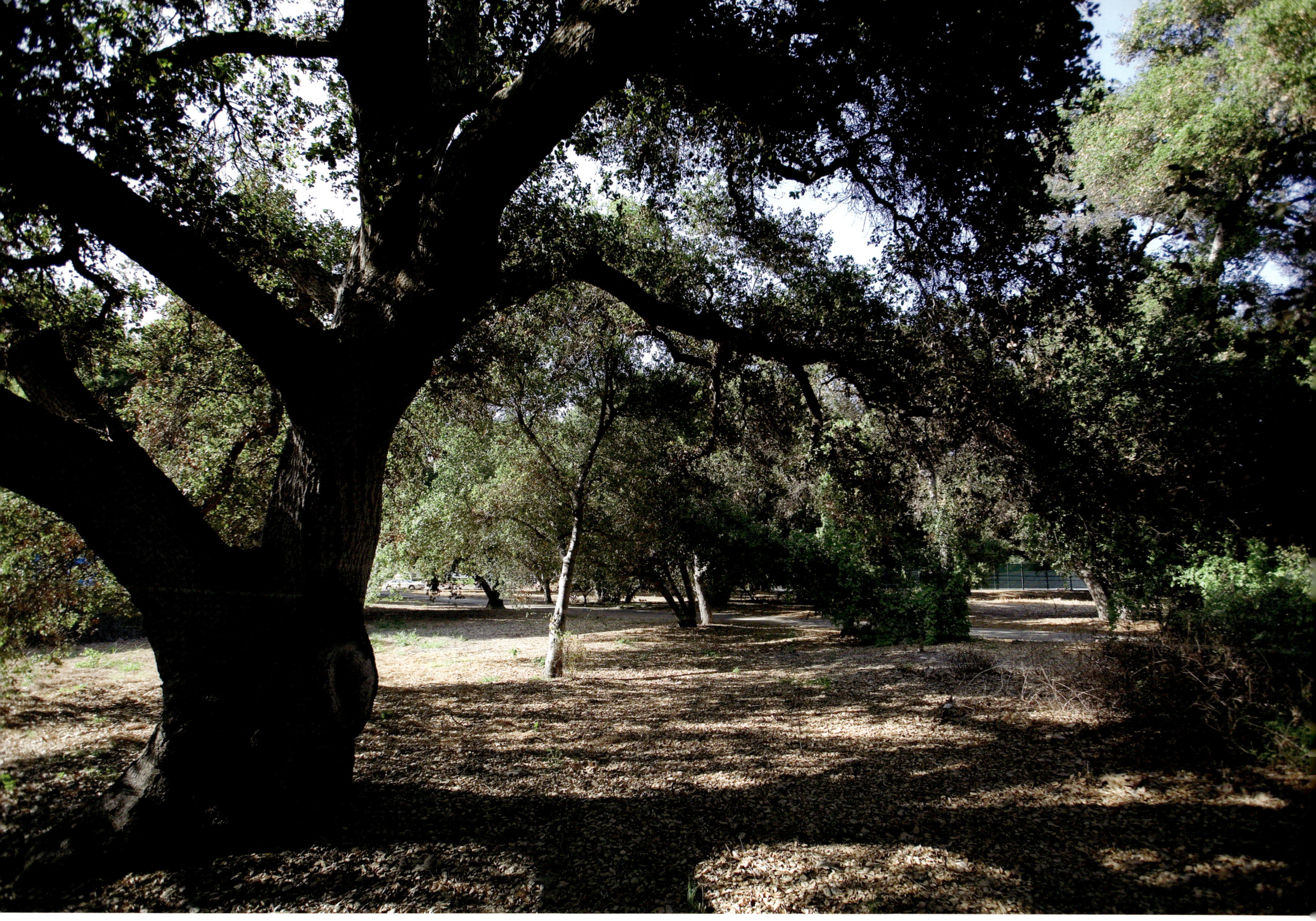

Henry Cabala

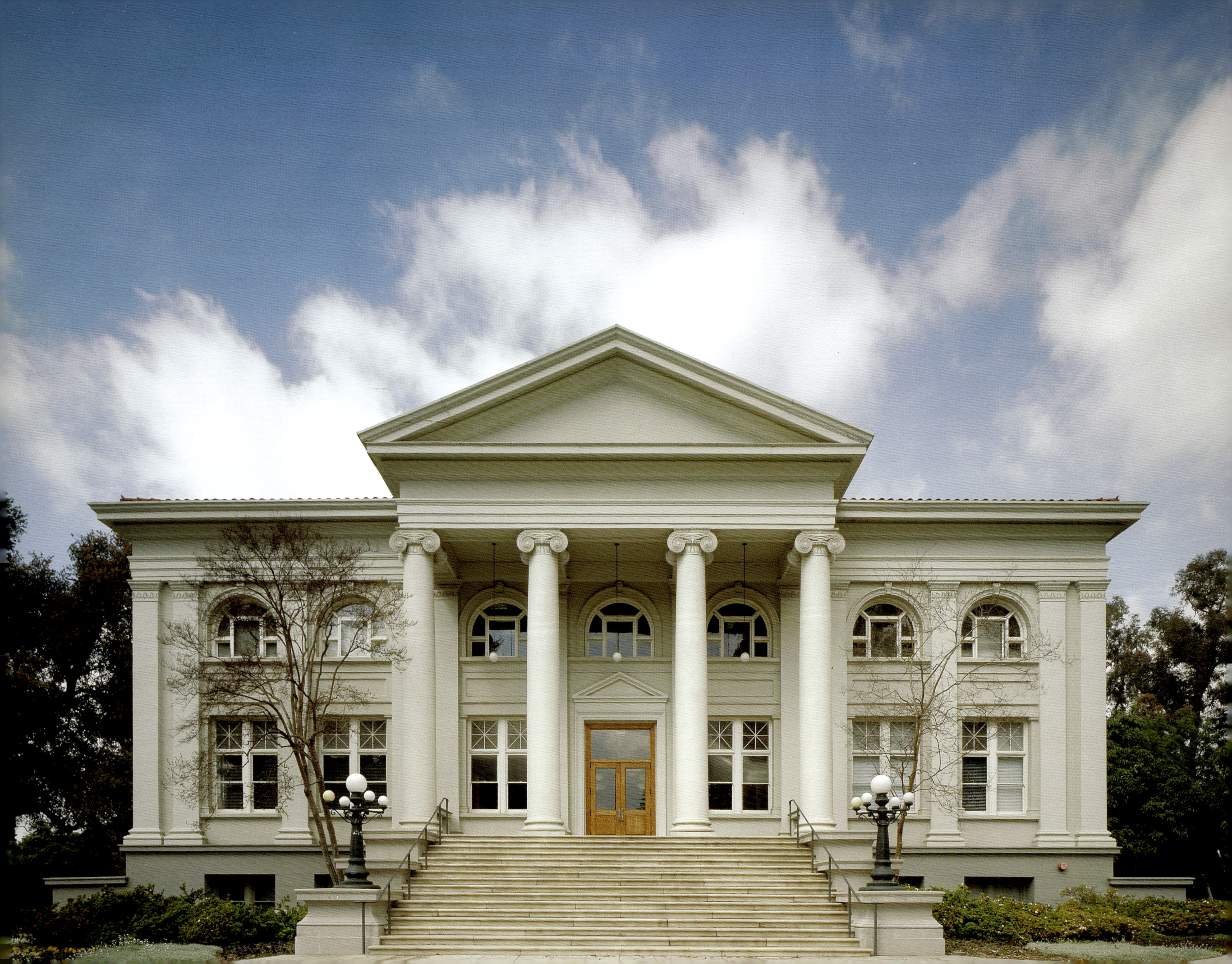

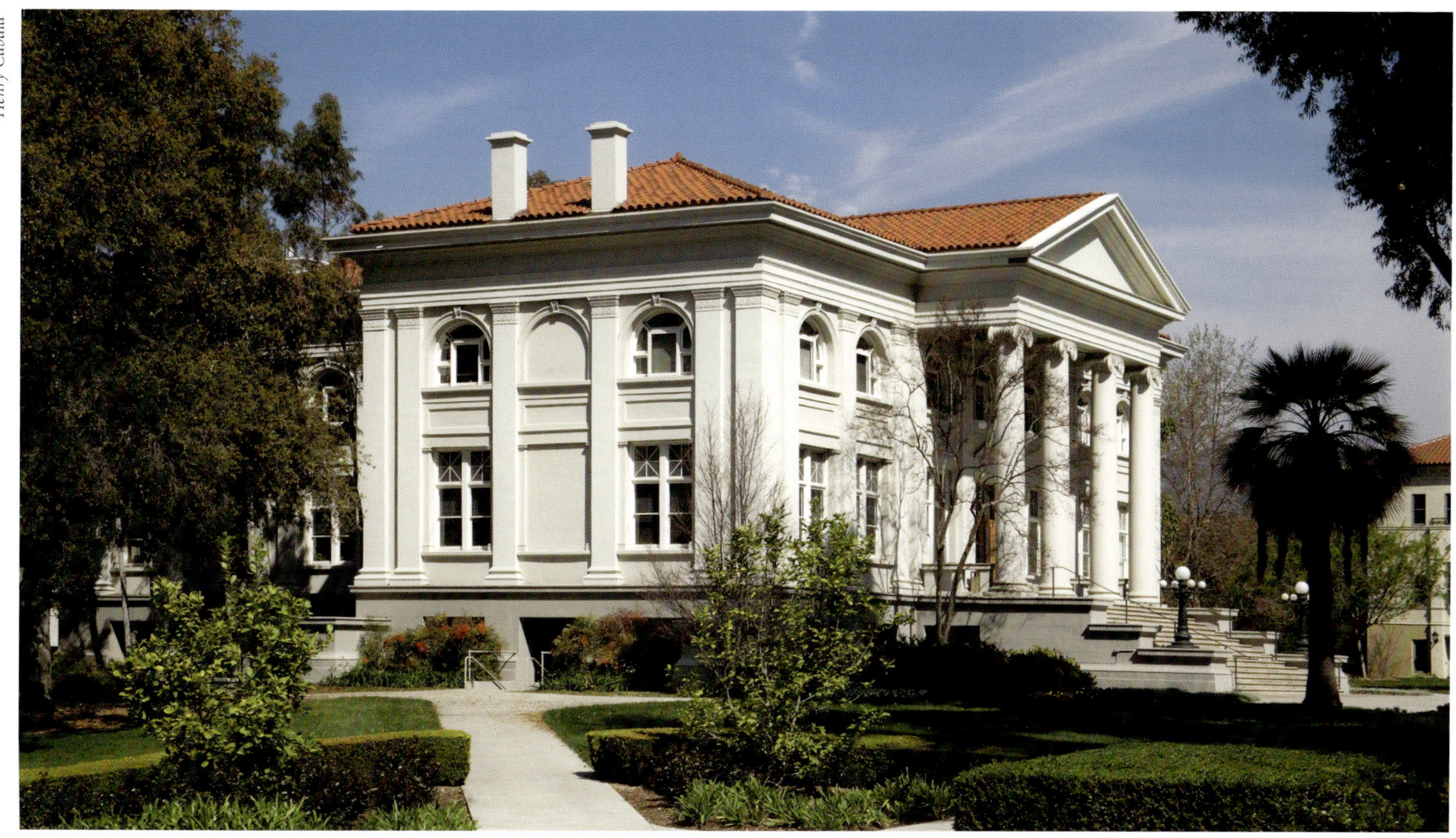

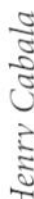

Henry Cabala

Andrew Carnegie Building

At the dedication of the Carnegie Library in 1908, President Gates declared: "There is not a college or university in the land that would not be ornamented by it," and, for many, Carnegie remains one of Pomona's "signature" buildings, anchoring the campus on College Avenue facing Marston Quadrangle. A favorite of photographers and filmmakers, it has served as the backdrop for annual faculty photographs, countless wedding and family portraits, and several Hollywood movies.

The College's first library had been housed in a single room in Pearsons Hall, but by 1906 its 8,000 volumes had taken over the entire south half of the first floor. The need for a separate library building was clearly a priority, and philanthropist Andrew Carnegie, who was, at that time, engaged in a massive program to develop libraries (which would number over 2,500 by 1918), was the logical source. Carnegie's pattern was to fund buildings but to require the recipient institution or community to provide site and maintenance. In April 1905, the foundation responded to the College's solicitation with a gift of $40,000, which the College agreed to match in new endowment. This was accomplished by 1906; the building was under way by January 1907 and completed the following year. Carnegie initially served the City of Claremont as well, a situation that lasted until 1914, when a drive was initiated to found a community library; Claremont's public library, on the corner of Harvard and Second Street, occupies land sold to the City by the College.

Andrew Carnegie Building

BUILT 1907-08 on land purchased 1902; cornerstone laid February, 1907; dedicated November 21, 1908, along with Smiley Hall and Brackett Observatory

LOCATION 425 North College Avenue between Fourth and Fifth Streets

PRESIDENT IN OFFICE George A. Gates

ORIGINAL PURPOSE Library (1908–52)

ARCHITECT E. P. Burnham, Los Angeles

MATERIALS reinforced concrete

COST $37,987

DONOR Andrew Carnegie

CURRENT USE Economics, Politics, Public Policy Analysis

RENOVATIONS 1952, 1969 (Criley and McDowell, Claremont); 1990 (McDowell); 1997–98 (Brian R. Bloom)

OPPOSITE AND ABOVE LEFT *Andrew Carnegie Building after renovations of 1997–98*

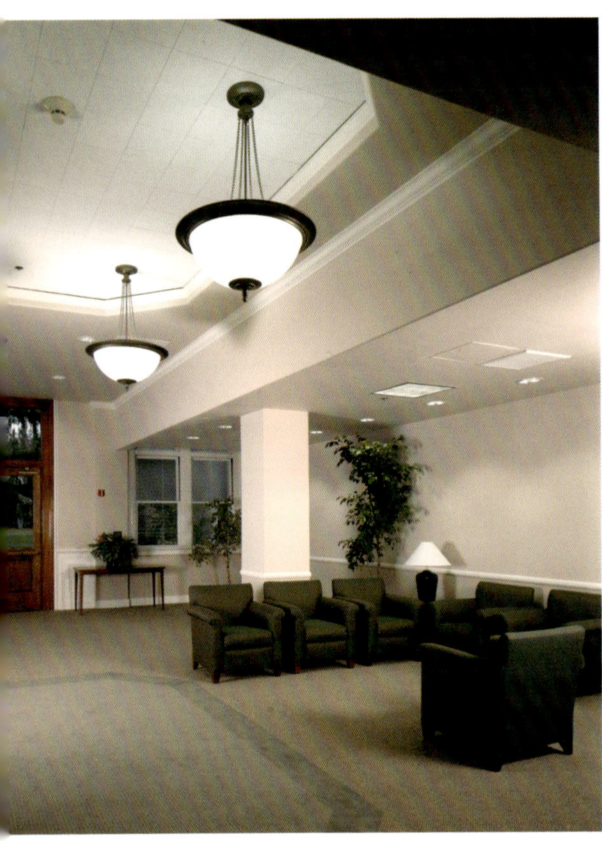

Gene Sasse

Carnegie was built of reinforced concrete, a relatively new material at the time. As work was beginning, a reinforced concrete hotel in Long Beach collapsed; construction was halted and engineer Edwin Squire investigated, leading to revised specifications including strengthened foundations and floors. Despite the bankruptcy of the contractor that cost the College an additional $8,860, the building was considered a great success.

Carnegie's design is prototypically neo-classical, the beautifully scaled, symmetrical block fronted by a raised entrance portico adorned by Ionic columns supporting a triangular pediment, its walls cadenced by paired Doric pilasters surrounding slightly recessed, rectangular and semi-circular windows that echo those of Pearsons Hall to its north. Carnegie libraries were often classical in design—indeed, we have come to associate such architecture with libraries, museums, and other buildings of civic significance—but this was not because the donor or his foundation so dictated. Andrew Carnegie's interest was in efficient operation, and his libraries were more importantly innovative in terms of function than style. The latter was overseen between 1903 and 1911 by James Bertram, Carnegie's personal secretary, who eventually published a pamphlet detailing his planning advice and schematic plans. Bertram's "Notes on the Erection of Library Buildings" did not, however, address architectural style. To the contrary, it warned against stylistic innovations at the expense of a functional interior design. The "family resemblance" of so many classical Carnegie library buildings was, thus, the result of individual decisions and not, as is often presumed, imposed by the donor. Architect Franklin P. Burnham was responsible for a number of other Classical Revival Carnegie buildings in California cities, including Whittier, Ontario, Santa Maria, Corona, Covina, Oxnard and Colton; only the latter two, both museums, survive today.

In 1914, Carnegie's collections numbered 18,000 volumes, with an average of 2,000 being added each year. Although not large, the library's holdings had the advantage of having been purchased by the College and selected by department heads, so that every book was up-to-date and usable. By 1923, there were 40,000 volumes, 30,000 pamphlets, and the library had become a depository for publications of the U.S. government and Carnegie Institution in Washington, D.C. While it was recognized as early as the 1920s that Carnegie was inadequate to serve as Pomona's library, it was not until 1945, during the tenure of President E. Wilson Lyon, that a central library for the associated colleges was proposed. The building that resulted was made possible by the bequest of William Honnold, a Trustee of Pomona and member of the founding board of The Claremont Colleges (established in 1925), who died in 1950. Construction of Honnold Library was begun in 1951, and the building was dedicated and occupied the following year (see photo on page 190). Of the 230,000 books and 146,600 documents moved to the new structure, more than half were from Pomona. The opening of Honnold left Carnegie free for the social sciences, and the departments of economics, government, education, sociology, and Oriental affairs all moved from offices in Sumner and Holmes halls.

In 1980, Carnegie was one of the first buildings nominated to the City of Claremont's Register of Historic and Architectural Sites, but the building also suffered from a series of renovations that were more functional than historically sensitive and included the removal of half of the grand stairway to create offices (1946), further subdivisions of space for classrooms (1953), and the addition of a masonry block to house restrooms, a staircase, and utilities (1968). Ceilings were lowered and many original details discarded. In 1997–98, a year-long campaign, led by architect Brian R. Bloom, both modernized the building and restored a number of original details, such as the iron and oak staircase and glass skylight, and recreated the volumes and finishes of original spaces as seen in historic photographs. The "new" Carnegie, now stripped of ivy and painted in subtly contrasting, neutral shades to emphasize its structure, is once again dazzling, allowing one to understand the enthusiasm of librarian Victor E. Mariott who wrote of his arrival in September 1912: "A shadow of a rock in a weary land was my first impression of the Pomona College Library…waves of heat were rolling across the hot sands, but there was the Library in the midst of its oasis of green, and inside its walls was a delicious coolness." ■

Henry Cabala

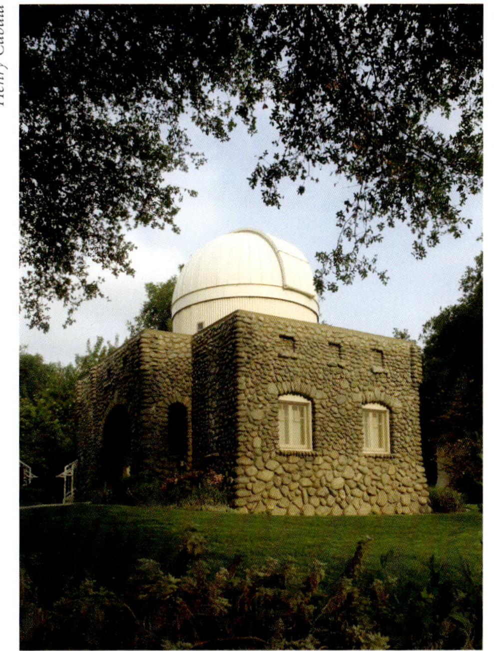

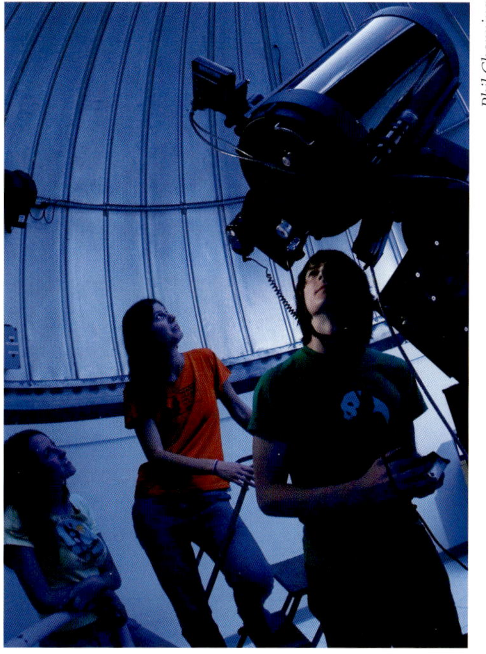

Phil Channing

Frank P. Brackett Observatory

Professor Frank Brackett, one of Pomona's original faculty members, was hired in 1888 to teach mathematics and Latin; he also taught astronomy beginning in 1892, when Thomas Barrows, an early friend of the College, donated a second-hand, six-inch telescope. The need to house it and enable astronomical observation on campus ultimately led to the construction of an observatory in 1908. Building funds were provided by Llewellyn Bixby, Class of 1901, a student of Brackett, and other friends supported the purchase of equipment. The observatory was dedicated in 1908 along with Smiley Hall and Carnegie Library.

Designed by Brackett, the observatory was constructed of local field stone and concrete, and surmounted by a manually controlled, revolving dome. Although increasingly sophisticated equipment was acquired periodically over the years, the building remained essentially unchanged until the 1970s. At that time, Pomona was maintaining a telescope at Table Mountain, a facility owned by the Jet Propulsion Laboratory near Wrightwood, California (elevation 7,500 feet) that offered the advantage of less smog and ambient light. By 1975, however, the inconveniences of depending entirely on an off-campus facility led astronomy professor Robert Chambers to make the case to upgrade Brackett, citing the need for an observatory on campus capable of supporting publishable research. In 1979, a $50,000 grant allowed the College to replace the dome that had been in place since 1949 with a new, electrically powered steel model; add an image processing system to the 22-inch telescope; and reinforce the building's structure.

In 2001, Brackett was completely renovated in a $300,000 project that included a new wing, doubling the size of the classroom and adding an office for an astronomy technician. The campaign also included the installation of one of the College's two robotic 14-inch computer-controlled telescopes, which joined a Coronado Instruments Helios solar telescope and a historic (1908) horizontal solar telescope still in working condition. Between 2001 and 2003, a grant known as the "Astronomical Computing Initiative" supported the upgrade of computers and multimedia equipment with the result that Pomona now enjoys a modern facility on campus that is used by students as well as by visiting school and community groups as part of the College's outreach effort. ■

Frank P. Brackett Observatory

BUILT 1908

LOCATION Western edge Blanchard Park (The Wash)

PRESIDENT IN OFFICE George A. Gates

PURPOSE Observatory

ARCHITECT Frank P. Brackett

MATERIALS field stone and concrete

COST $2,300 plus equipment

DONORS Llewellyn Bixby, Class of 1901, and others

NAMED FOR Professor Frank Parkhurst Brackett

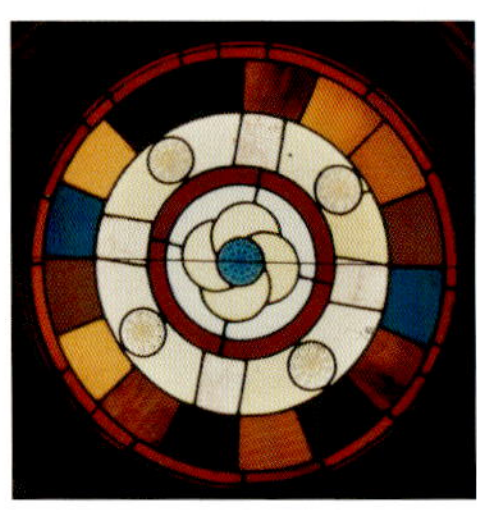

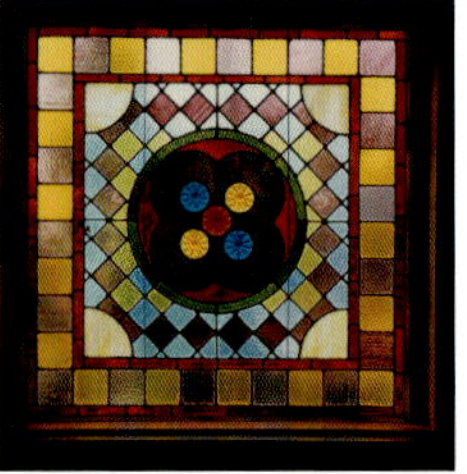

RIGHT *Sumner House, stained glass windows*

BELOW RIGHT *Baldwin House, Cook House, Renwick House*

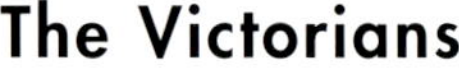

The Victorians

Pomona's first buildings were built near the end of the High Victorian period of American architecture that extended from the Civil War to the turn of the century. The original Sumner Hall and Holmes Hall exhibited the eclectic ornamentalism of the style, which can now be seen best in the domestic dwellings on College Avenue between First Street and Bonita Avenue, particularly the meticulously restored Sumner House. Although lavish in appearance, Victorian-styled buildings were made affordable by the new availability of pre-cut lumber, machined nails, pattern books, and ready-made decorative features (balustrades, cornices, etc.) that could be ordered and assembled on site according to the taste of the owner.

As Lawrence Cheek has written, "An upwardly mobile Victorian family could leaf through a pattern book and choose a floor plan dressed in any of half a dozen styles, from Tuscan and Persian to French Second Empire. Architects breezed from one style to another…They mixed and matched, often producing fantastic and outrageous hybrids.…But while it could be ridiculous, it was also symbolic and idealistic. In one sense, Victorian architecture represented the best of the American character: soaring imagination, individualism, boundless self-confidence.…After 1930, the fun came to an end. Ornamentation and imagery became architectural crimes, and Victorians seemed suddenly dated." ■

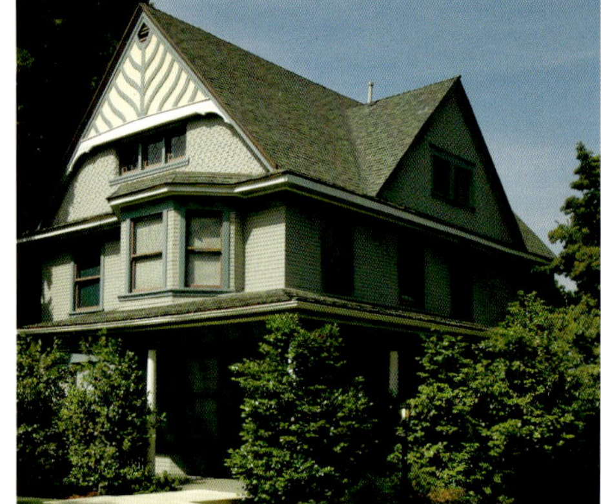

Mark Wood

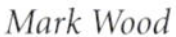

Baldwin House

BUILT 1890
LOCATION 137 North College Avenue
MATERIALS wood frame
Built by Pomona's first president Cyrus Grandison Baldwin and his wife Ella shortly after their arrival in Claremont. Baldwin House was later occupied by the Healy family and served as a boarding house and, later, a residence hall for Pomona students. Today, it houses faculty offices.

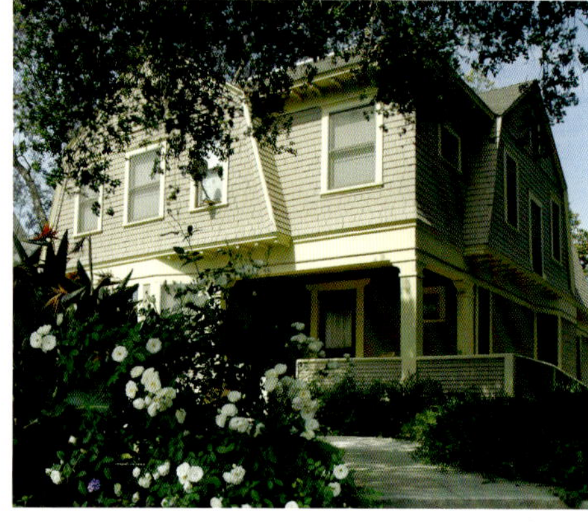

Mark Wood

Cook House

BUILT 1895
LOCATION 119 North College Avenue
MATERIALS wood frame
Cook House was built by Albert Cook, next door to the Baldwins. Although the house has been altered over the years, the stone wall is original. It is currently used to house new faculty.

Mark Wood

Renwick House

BUILT 1900
LOCATION 211 North College Avenue
MATERIALS wood frame
Built by Helen Renwick, a Claremont philanthropist who donated land for the public library, Rembrandt Hall, and Renwick Gymnasium, the house was later occupied by the McNamee family. Until 1989, it was used mainly as a college residence for students. Today it houses the Office of Annual Giving.

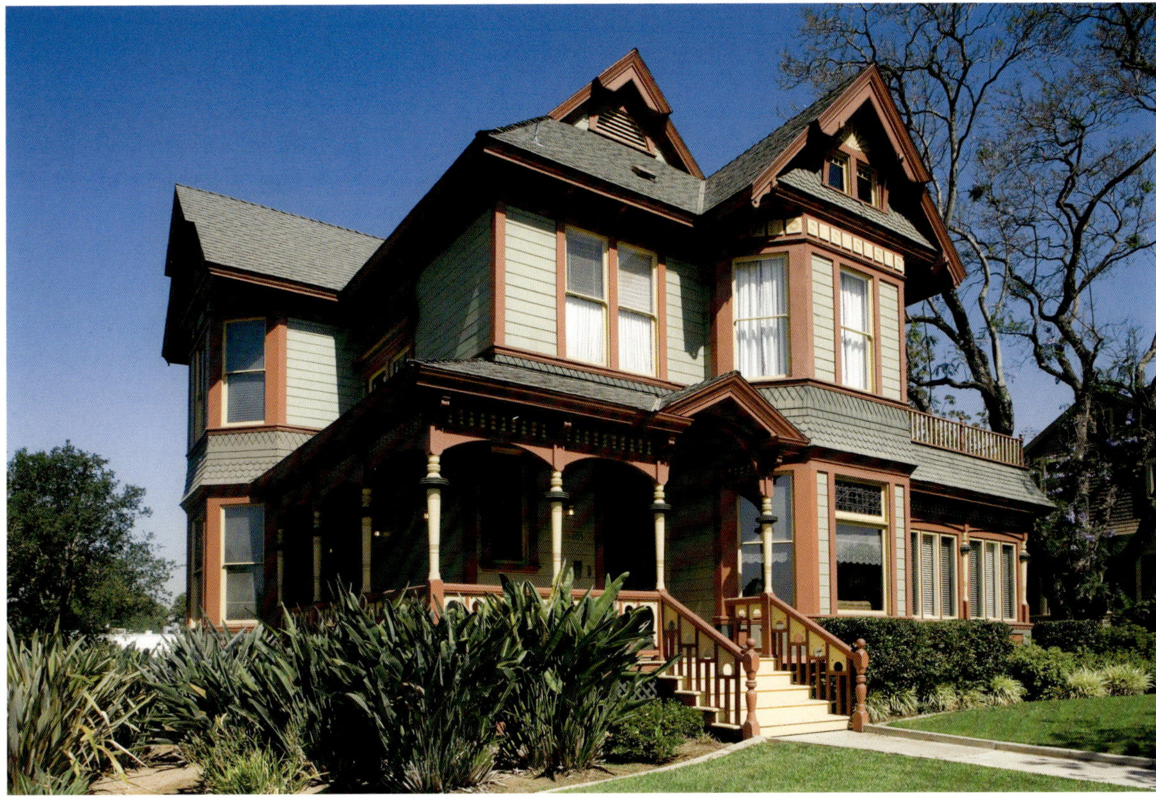

Henry Cabala

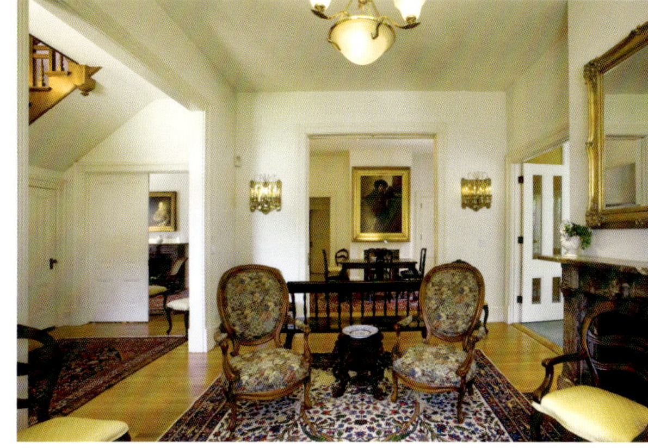

Sumner House

The home of pastor and Pomona College founder Charles Burt Sumner and his wife Mary Louisa Steadman Sumner (for whom Sumner Hall was named), Sumner House, originally named Twin Oaks, was built on 10 acres of land near the anticipated site of the College, and, in 1901, moved to its present site on timbers and rollers drawn by horses. The Sumner family lived in the house throughout the six-week move. The house was later home to the Sumner's son George C. K. Sumner, Class of 1894, who taught economics at Pomona and, in 1923, became College controller; and his grandson George Charles Sumner Benson. Over the years, Sumner House has been rented to faculty and, in the 1970s and '80s served as a dormitory for vegetarian students who prepared their own meals and dubbed it "veggie house." It was closed as a dormitory in 1989 and carefully restored in 1992. Since then, it has served as the College's guest house.

Sumner House epitomizes the exuberant "Queen Anne" Victorian architectural style that reflected equally the optimism and ostentation of what Mark Twain termed America's "golden age." Today, the house wears some of its original exterior colors—olive drab, forest green, muted yellow, brick red—though its interiors have been spared the wallpaper that once adorned every wall and ceiling. Highly ornamental, the house boasts a variety of gables and bays, wrap-around porches, and lavishly decorated woodworking. Sidings vary from scalloped and fish-scaled to diamond-shaped and both horizontal and vertical. ■

Sumner House

BUILT 1887
ORIGINAL LOCATION North Pomona; moved 1901
CURRENT LOCATION 105 North College Avenue at First Street
COST $7,000
MATERIALS wood frame construction
DONOR George S. Sumner, Class of 1894 and son of Charles B. Sumner
RENOVATED 1992

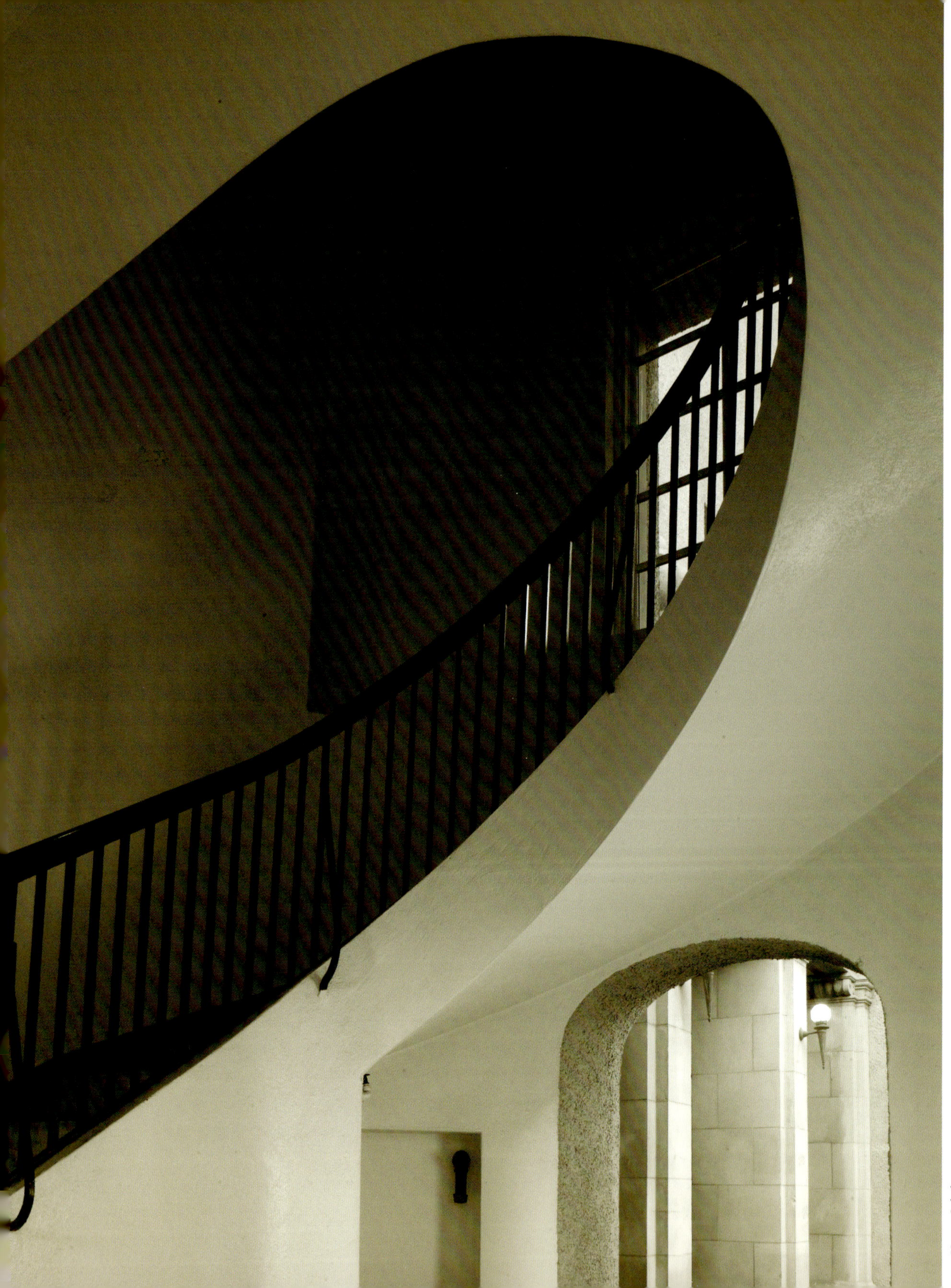

Henry Cabala

CHAPTER II

MYRON HUNT *at* POMONA COLLEGE 1908–15

Lebus Court

Myron Hunt and the "Academical Village," 1908–15

PRESIDENTS GEORGE GATES *and* JAMES BLAISDELL

Shortly before the turn of the last century, against the backdrop of the San Gabriel Mountains, the light of "California Eden" shone down upon two lonely structures—the picturesque Victorian Claremont Hotel (soon to be renamed Sumner Hall) and Holmes Hall, the first dedicated classroom building of newly founded Pomona College. A firm commitment to this "wilderness" site on the edge of an alluvial plain of rock, sagebrush and live oak, in a land previously occupied by Native American and Spanish-Mexican hacienda cultures, had brought the Congregationalist founders of this college "of the New England type" to what seemed a land of opportunity. A few short years later, the wilderness had been transformed by architect Myron Hunt into a pastoral expanse known as Marston Quadrangle, flanked by buildings he designed that, to this day, remain at the core of the College's campus.

How did this happen?

Conventional wisdom tells the story of disjunction between the area's Victorian beginnings—the result of Eastern and Midwestern Anglo-European railroad interests that encouraged migration to the "new frontier" of California—and the Mission Revival style of Myron Hunt's work at Pomona College. Hunt's campus plan of 1908 is an early example of regional identity and cultural appropriation, but the story is more subtle, part of a larger nation-building narrative. Out of the crucible of civil war and industrial revolution in the United States of the late 19th century, a new nation had been forged, melding pastoral, colonial-federalist agrarian ideals to urban, technological "progress."

At the very moment Frederick Jackson Turner dramatically announced "the end of the American frontier" at the annual convention of the American Historical Association in Chicago in July 1893, the World's Columbian Exposition—the White City—was rising, phoenix-like, from the ashes of the apocalyptic Chicago fire of 1871. Two architectural ideals shaped this modern city in the heartland, a blending of "picturesque" and "sublime" cultural ideals of Nature into the new frenetic urban landscape of commerce and politics. On the one hand, the skyscrapers of architect Louis Sullivan and the Chicago School transformed the horizontal Victorian city of brick and wood into a vertical complex of intricate spires and smooth, classicizing, "functional" structures made possible by steel frames and Otis elevators. A sublime vision, these "temples of commerce" rose over streets turned into canyons. At the same time, architect Daniel H. Burnham's central mall of the World's Columbian Exposition featured rational axial planning and monumental classical architecture adorned with colossal, allegorical sculptures.

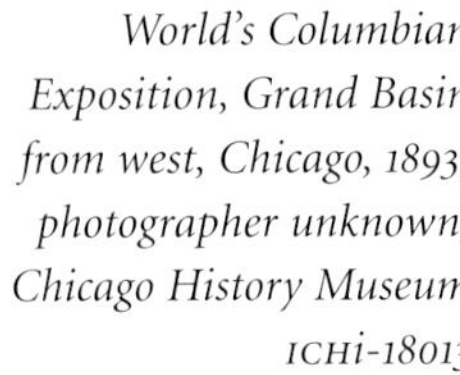

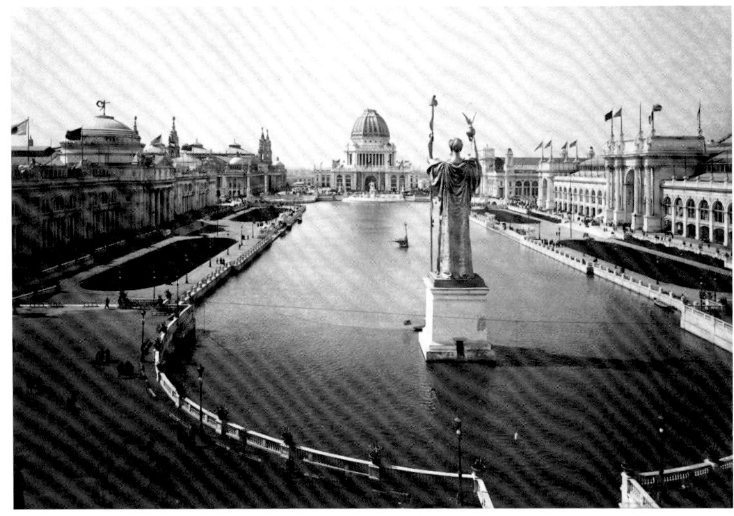

World's Columbian Exposition, Grand Basin with statue of the Republic in foreground, Chicago, 1893, photographer unknown, Chicago History Museum ICHi-02524

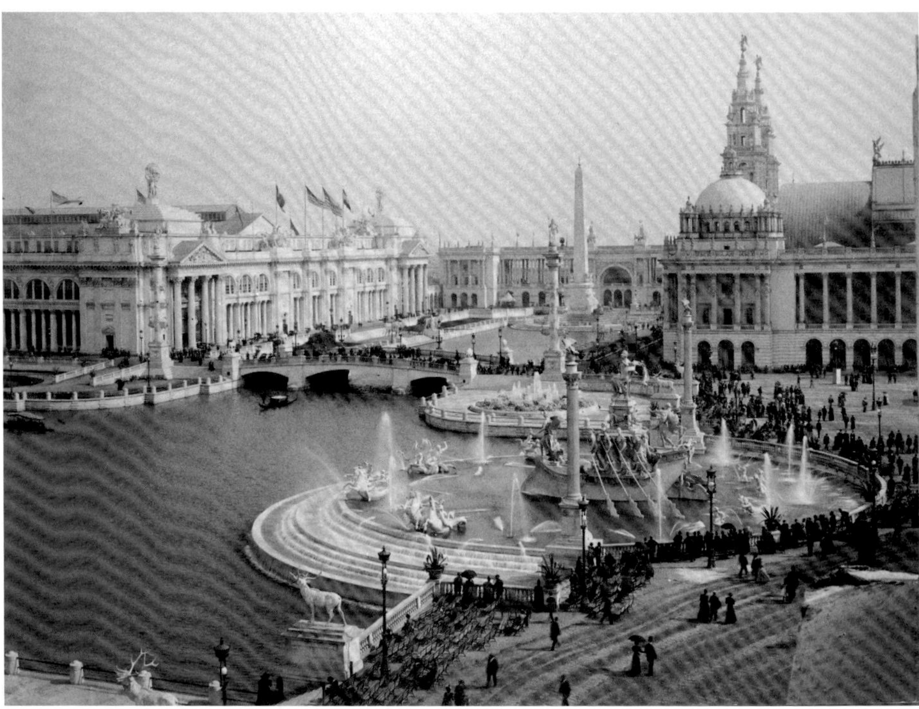

World's Columbian Exposition, Grand Basin from west, Chicago, 1893, photographer unknown, Chicago History Museum ICHi-18013

This was myth-making on a grand scale, a scenic "spectacle" in stucco and iron-frame. Through a blending of competition with and emulation of European imperial architectural styles, America had come of age, and the Colonial Revival and City Beautiful movements defined domestic and civic architecture from coast to coast in cities linked by a massive railroad system.

The Architect

Myron Hunt (1862–1952) played a vital role in the creation of an architectural identity that emerged through a transition from the revivalism of the 19th century to the modernism of the 20th. He was born in Sutherland, Massachusetts, a middle-class suburb of Boston, the son of a prominent nurseryman who influenced his approach to architecture as well as landscape. Hunt viewed nature in Romantic terms, as the source of virtue and health, a tradition exemplified in the work of such practitioners as Romanesque Revival architect Henry Hobson Richardson and landscape architect Frederick Law Olmsted. Hunt finished high school in Chicago and attended Northwestern University before pursuing an architecture degree at MIT from 1890 to 1893. Soon thereafter, he married Harriette H. Boardman, and the couple embarked on a Wanderjahr—a cultural pilgrimage to England, Scotland and Italy where, particularly in Florence, the young architect studied the Renaissance classical tradition. Returning to Chicago, Hunt took a position as draftsman in the local office of Richardson's Boston-based firm, Shepley, Rutan, and Coolidge, builders of his Chicago projects and also responsible for Stanford University's Spanish Romanesque Revival campus plan (1884–91); Stanford would later prove to exert formative influence on Hunt's understanding of the campus as a planned community as well as on his vision of the West. In Chicago, Hunt was also exposed to Louis Sullivan's functionalist Chicago School, to the Prairie Style of Frank Lloyd Wright, and, perhaps most importantly, to the American Colonial Revival and Beaux-Arts City Beautiful movements inaugurated in the visionary work of Daniel Burnham at the World's Columbian Exposition of 1893 and his ensuing radial city plan for Chicago of 1906–09.

Harriette Boardman Hunt suffered from tuberculosis, and in 1903, her illness brought the Hunts to Pasadena. Along with his partner Elmer Grey, Hunt established an architectural firm in downtown Los Angeles. The houses he designed, first in Evanston (1896), and then in Pasadena (1905) explored the domestic realm of Arts and Crafts "naturalism" in colonial, box-like forms with Shingle Style sheathing (like the bark of a tree), and trellised walkways leading to gardens. This was an "organic" American architecture that reflected the converging English and Japanese influences on such diverse practitioners as Richardson, Sullivan, the early Frank Lloyd Wright, Bernard Maybeck, Julia Morgan, and the Greene brothers. In his public commissions, however, Hunt pioneered the Spanish Mission Revival style, which he believed best suited the Mediterranean climate and local culture of Southern California and of which he became the leading and best known proponent. Significantly, through a series of campus commissions—Throop Polytechnic Institute (later known as Caltech, 1908-16), Pomona College (1908–15), and Occidental College (1911–44)—Hunt led the way in Spanish-inflected buildings and axial Beaux-Arts planning in Southern California that anticipated the City Beautiful civic centers of Pasadena, Los Angeles, and San Francisco of the late 1920s.

The Campus Plan

In 1908, Hunt was called upon by the trustees of Pomona College to design a comprehensive campus plan for the College. This appeared in a special supplement to the College's Bulletin of November 21, 1908, titled "Recommendations to the City of Claremont and to the Trustees of Pomona College, relating to the future development of the College Campus." Two photographs —an inviting one of the shady south entrance to Holmes Hall titled "Under the Peppers, Pomona Campus," and a stark ground plan of the central quadrangle of the "University of Virginia. Thomas Jefferson; McKim, Mead & White, Architects"—accompanied the opening paragraph:

> *Planning for the future growth of a college campus is an obvious necessity. Foresight in connection with such planning is as economically advantageous as it would be in the starting of a great factory plant. A few American colleges and universities have realized this fact soon enough to take advantage of it. The success of the general plan for the University of Virginia, the origin of which is to be credited to Thomas Jefferson, is an object lesson in point. On the other hand, the lack of any provision for adequate future growth on the part of the founders of Harvard and of Yale is an equally potent object lesson to the directors of college corporations whose institutions are still in their infancy.*

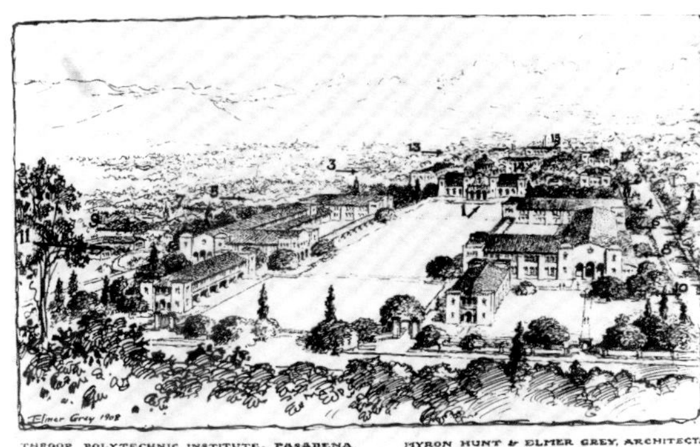

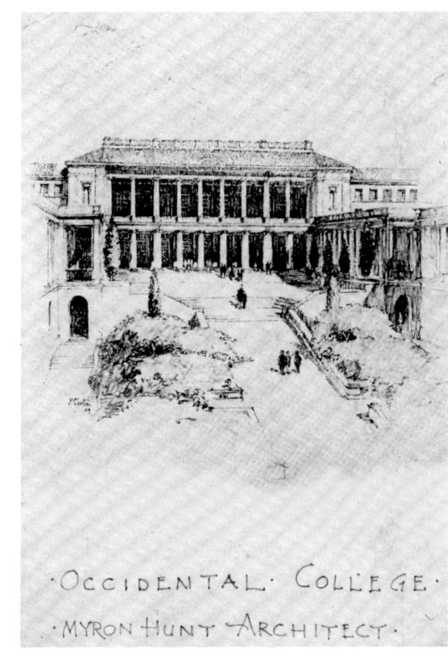

Myron Hunt and Elmer Grey, Proposal for a campus plan, Throop Institute of Technology (now Caltech), 1908, California Institute of Technology Archives

Myron Hunt, Proposal for an administration building, Occidental College, drawing, 1910, Hunt & Chambers Collection, Architecture and Design Collection, University Art Museum, University of California, Santa Barbara

Hunt's plan cited Thomas Jefferson's University of Virginia (1817–26), which had become an influential model for American campuses with the colonial revival of the late 19th century. Jefferson described his university as an "academical village" —a residential college focused on a central library (significantly, not a chapel) modeled, at two-thirds scale, on Rome's Pantheon to the pagan gods, an urban monument thus reincarnated in a garden setting. Importantly, the green space focusing the academic enterprise was not cloistered in the medieval pattern but open to nature in a manner reminiscent of colonial American communities designed around central commons. The individual pavilions flanking Jefferson's green, each specific to an academic discipline and linked with the others by colonnaded walkways, housed faculty families (a "familial" form for institutional learning) and classrooms. Students lived nearby along the green, and, behind each pavilion, benches for contemplation, reading and conversation formed a gentleman's "garden grove" enclosed by serpentine brick walls; on the margin were tiny rooms for servants, slaves, and horses.

In Hunt's plan for Pomona, the reference to the University of Virginia was less to Jefferson's vision of Enlightenment-influenced classical architecture in a "natural" field ("campus") than to its practical applications. The fact that UVA's pavilions were small, separate and affordable meant that they could be built over time as funding allowed, offering opportunities for the creation of memorials, a kind of expandable and sustainable memory theatre. In a pragmatic way, permanent masonry buildings were distinguished from removable, wood frame structures; thus, existing buildings (such as Pomona's Claremont Hotel/Sumner Hall) could be moved about and modified in style as the architectural identity of the campus took form. Hunt's recommendations for Pomona both reinforced and rationalized the original desire of the College's Congregationalist founders for a rural

University of Virginia from the south, engraving by B. Tanner, 1826, Special Collections, University of Virginia Library

University of Virginia, Rotunda and Lawn, aerial view, Records of the University Photographer, Special Collections, University of Virginia Library, RG-5/7/2.762

University of Virginia, Rotunda and Lawn, 1976, Records of the University Photographer, Special Collections, University of Virginia Library, RG-5/7/2.821

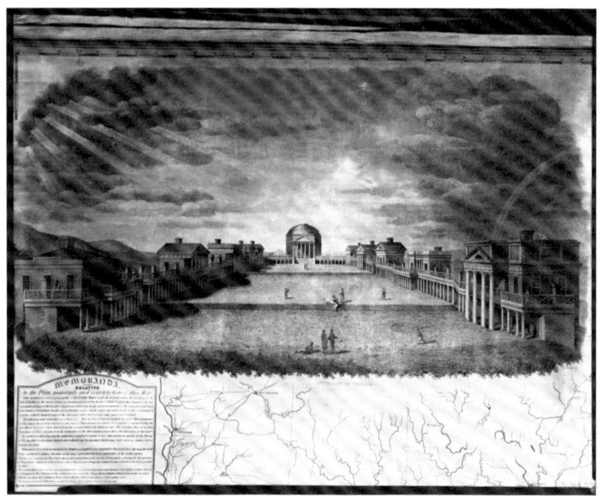

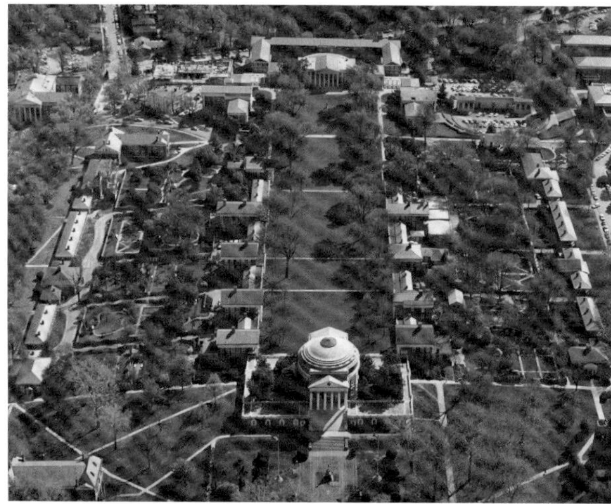

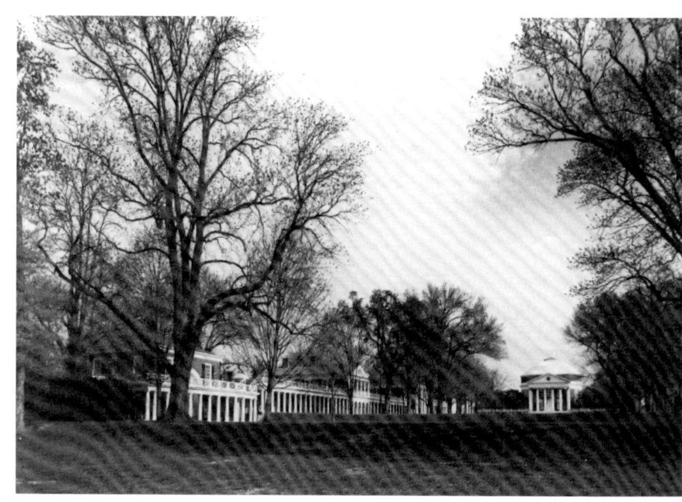

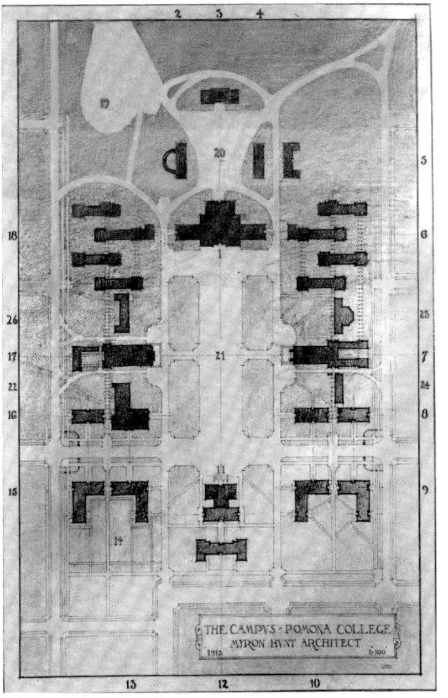

Myron Hunt and Elmer Grey, Proposed campus plan, Pomona College, 1908

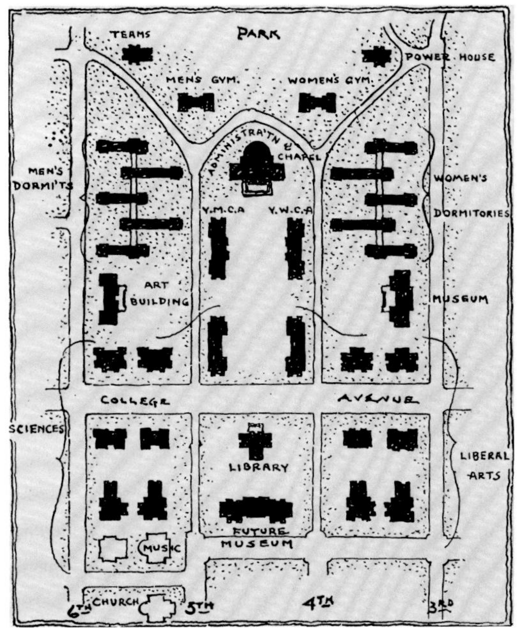

Myron Hunt and Elmer Grey, Proposed campus plan, Pomona College, 1908

educational institution by relating this aspiring West Coast college to the "classic" model of Jefferson's UVA, inspired by Greek and Roman tradition, a *locus amoenus* (amenable place) for contemplation on the edge of an urban center like the foundational "Academy" of Plato and Aristotle outside Athens.

Hunt's proposal for Pomona was well received. As at UVA, the new campus was to be focused on a central quadrangle. In due course, Trustee George Marston of San Diego provided the necessary funds to create the green that would ultimately bear his name; Marston Quadrangle took form between 1919 and 1923. The project required the relocation of the old Claremont Hotel (renamed Mary L. Sumner Hall in 1893), and this was accomplished in 1921; Sumner Hall was dismantled and reconstructed on the southeast side of the new quadrangle, an area as large as the one that served as the focus of Jefferson's UVA campus.

At the head of Pomona's "campus" (its true meaning—"field"—appropriate here) stood the raised Ionic "temple" of Carnegie Library (1908, see Chapter I) with its Corinthian pilasters and classical windows modeled after Andrea Palladio's mid-16th-century Renaissance villas of the Italian Veneto. Carnegie was in place when Hunt was hired, and if its scale appears small in relation to the expanse of Marston Quadrangle, this is because of its original position opposite the three-story Victorian Sumner Hall, an eclectic ensemble. Hunt's plan called for a central administration building at the east end of Marston Quadrangle facing Carnegie. The footprint of that projected structure, which was never built, indicates that the architect intended it to be of significant size; because elevation drawings were never completed, however, there is no way to be certain of the design he envisioned, although one can imagine something similar to Caltech's Throop Hall (1910) or Burnham's Administration Building at the Chicago World's Fair (1893), creating a classical unity. In fact, the eastern end of Marston Quadrangle was not defined until 1930–31 when Mabel Shaw Bridges Auditorium was constructed by the Claremont Consortium. (See Chapter III.)

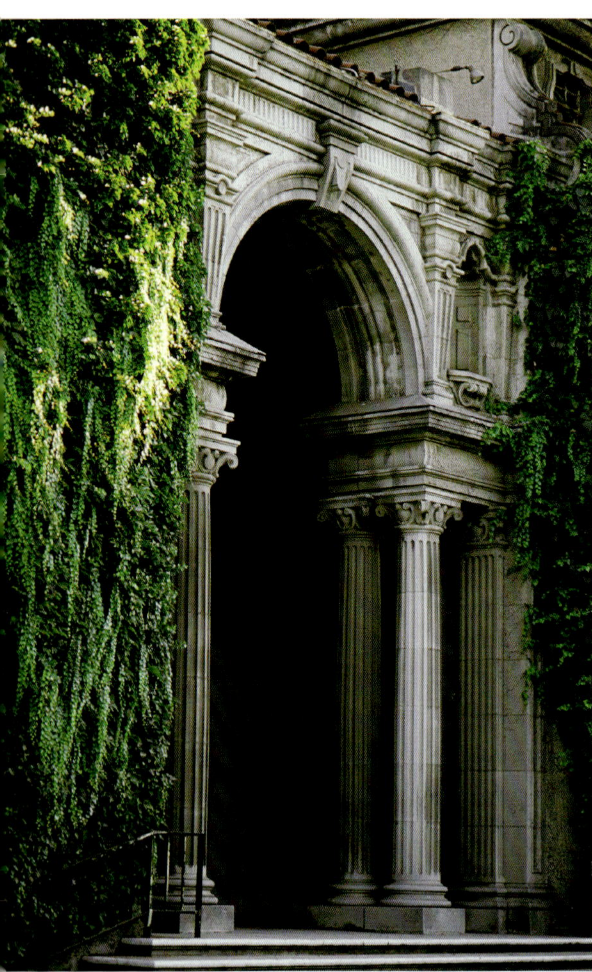

Bridges Hall of Music

Hunt's campus plan was gendered. His austere men's dormitory, Smiley Hall (1908), occupied Marston Quadrangle's northern side, which was projected also to be the site of science and social science buildings and a gymnasium. To the south were to be women's dormitories (Jamieson & Spearl's Harwood Court, 1921, realized this intent), arts buildings (Hunt's Rembrandt Hall, 1914; and Mabel Shaw Bridges Hall of Music and Lebus Court, 1915), and a separate gymnasium that was never built. In contrast to UVA, where Jefferson's pavilions and linking colonnades flanked and closed the central quadrangle, for Pomona Hunt projected staggered buildings in an open pattern that refers to but, at the same time, "ventilates" its source, with structures strung like beads on a necklace, linked by sight lines across the green. The arcades he favored relate to the trellises that extended his houses into gardens; whereas Jefferson used colonnades to provide cover between pavilions and to integrate his design, Hunt used their equivalent as a means of processing through the open space of his garden of learning. In further contradistinction to the Jeffersonian model, Hunt's notion was to position a mix of residence halls and administrative and classroom buildings around the quadrangle, with an academic science quad standing slightly apart in the northwest corner of the campus. By the 1920s, with the construction of Harwood Court south of Bonita Avenue and the Clark Campus north of Sixth Street, it was established that dormitories would occupy the periphery with Marston Quadrangle reserved for communal buildings.

Architect Robert A.M. Stern, who designed Pomona's Smith Campus Center (1999), has noted that Hunt's plan for Pomona College was not a departure from but, rather, part of the larger turn-of-the-century "taming" of the national architectural character seen in the transition from Victorian to Classical Revival styles. Already in an early photograph of the campus from c. 1893 (pages 28–9), one sees the contrast. Sumner Hall, built in 1887–88 as a hotel to attract investors, is an exuberant, picturesque, self-promoting salesman—a sort of Congregational cathedral for the westward-bound, Manifest Destiny-inspired migration of the American Enlightenment. In contrast, Holmes Hall to its north, built five years later, is relatively restrained, "classicized" and compact, although still many-gabled and topped by a Victorian bell tower rising like a straight-laced head above starched collar and tie. Directly across Warren (now College) Avenue from Holmes Hall, C. H. Brown's Pearsons Hall (1898, pages 37–8) presented a rational, compact, Renaissance revival block of classical symmetry, raised on a pedestal, with rounded windows and an arched entry. The three buildings reflected the dramatic stylistic shift that had occurred in a mere 12 years—from Victorian-Gothic Sumner Hall, to Victorian-Classical Holmes Hall, to Renaissance Pearsons Hall. Furthermore, when Holmes Hall was rebuilt in 1916, and Sumner Hall moved and reconstructed in 1921, both were stripped of their Victorian towers, overlapping gables, and elaborately ornamented porches, and transformed into a compact series of geometric, longitudinal buildings and open courtyards. Importantly, these were set at right angles to Marston Quadrangle rather than flanking it as was the case with UVA's disciplinary pavilions. At Pomona, an ensemble of structures was thus linked by major sight lines, through arches and gateways, reinterpreting the closed, Jeffersonian axial plan, and employing interior and exterior spaces in a manner characteristic of the architecture of California whose climate encouraged orientation to the out-of-doors and surrounding landscape.

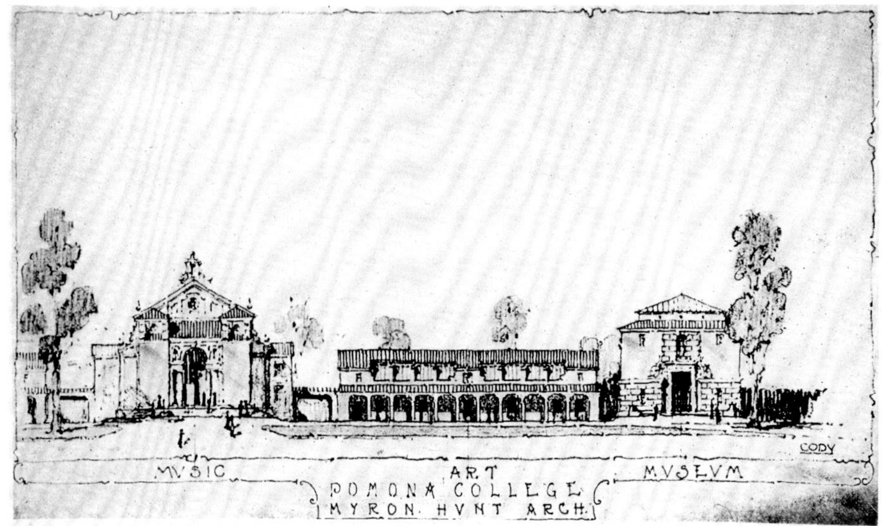

Myron Hunt, Elevation of Bridges Hall of Music, Rembrandt Hall, and Proposed Art Museum, Pomona College, drawing, c. 1913, Hunt and Chambers Collection, Architecture and Design Collection, University Art Museum, University of California, Santa Barbara

The result is a unique campus plan in union with a remade nature. Hunt extended the urban grid of Claremont to the new campus, which offered as well the "picturesque" Blanchard Park (The Wash), a "wild" ramble of serpentine paths and dense California oaks to the southeast that provided another type of "rural" experience; at its eastern edge Hunt designed a Greek Theatre (1914). The same year, he also created the College Gate, marking what was, at the time, the northernmost boundary of the campus.

Myron Hunt's campus plan for Pomona College was, ultimately, Southern in origin—a Mid-Atlantic (specifically, Virginian) pastoral vision of ordered, secular education for the landed aristocracy of a Jeffersonian Democracy, reinterpreted in terms of the Southern California mission tradition. Over the years, Jefferson's campus has been reinterpreted and redefined. A "plantation" for gentlemen eventually admitted women; slaves very gradually became students.

Today, the "academical village"—what architectural historian Paul Venable Turner calls "the distinctive American contribution to campus planning and higher education"—became (like the opening lines of the American "Declaration of Independence" of 1776) a vision as well as a challenge. In Southern California, a Congregationalist college of "the New England type" interwove a Virginian vision with local mission culture to create a unique West Coast model for campus architecture and planning. While Myron Hunt is justly renowned for the Beaux-Arts classicism of the Huntington home (now art gallery) and library set in its picturesque garden in San Marino (1910–20), and for his Mission Revival work seen in the Pasadena Public Library (1927) and Rose Bowl (1930), his collaboration with Elmer Grey and, after 1919, with landscape architect Ralph Cornell '14, at Pomona College was remarkable. From the axial grid of Marston Quadrangle to the picturesque California live oak ramble of Blanchard Park, an ideal model for liberal arts education was fashioned in Claremont, poised on the Pacific Rim and the future.[1] ■

George L. Gorse

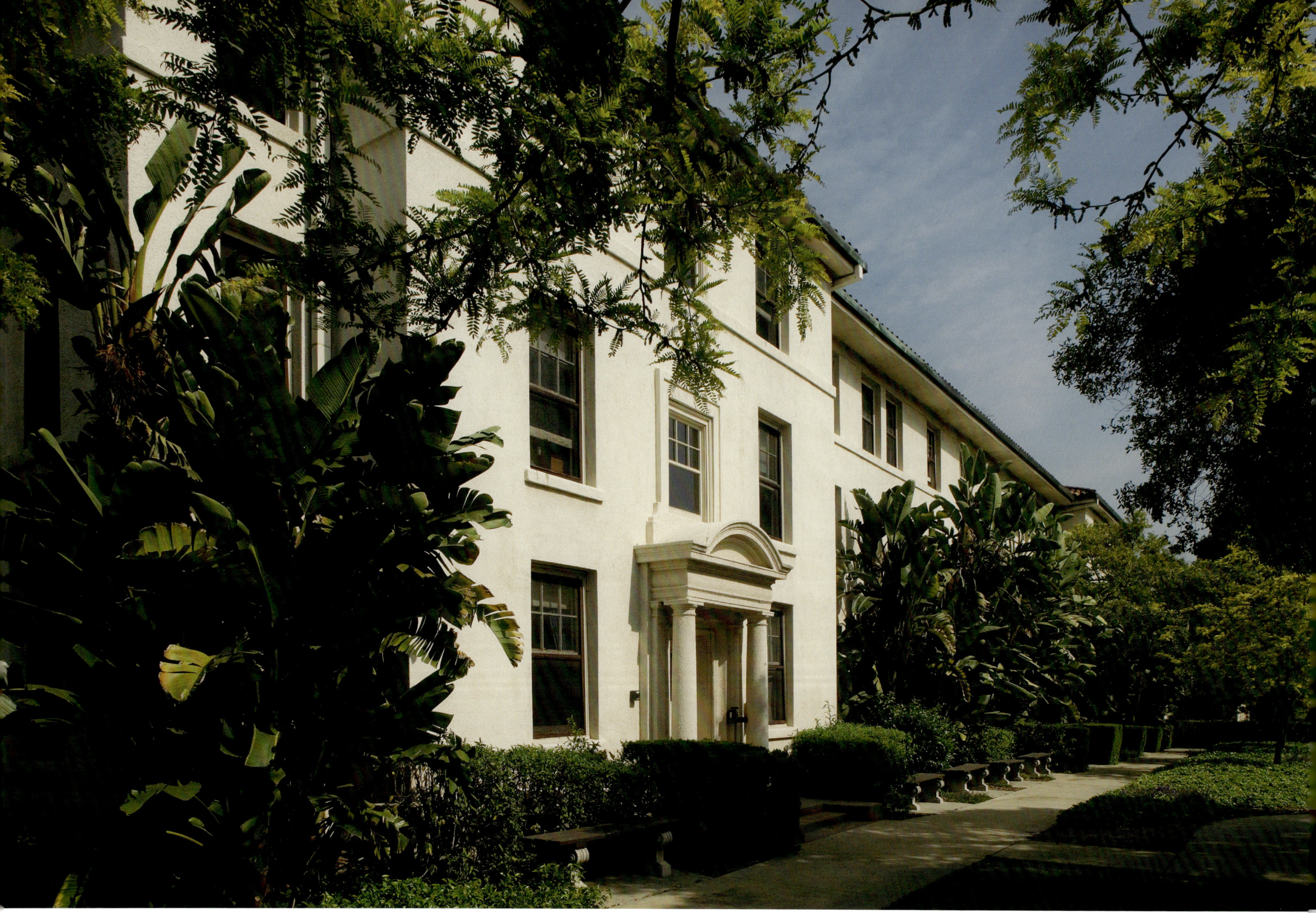

Henry Cabala

A.K. Smiley Hall

Smiley Hall was the first campus building designed to be a dormitory. Before it appeared (and with the exception of the College's first two years) most male students lived in private homes in Claremont, as was typical of the time; women students were then housed in Sumner Hall. Although the City of Claremont had grown from a population of 250 in 1900 to 1,114 in 1910, and had room to accommodate students, attitudes about dormitories were shifting, and many (including donor D.K. Pearsons) believed that living closely together could enhance students' educational experience (and not, as was formerly feared, lead to mayhem). It was Pearsons who suggested the building be named for Albert K. Smiley, a botanist, horticulturalist, and longtime trustee (1893–95, 1899–1908).

Built in an astonishing 100 days during the summer of 1908, Smiley Hall was the first of three campus buildings by architect Myron Hunt. It was sited east of Holmes Hall as prescribed in the campus plan he had presented to the trustees that same year, and its style—a simple, geometrically disciplined block with light-colored walls and a low, hipped, red-tile roof—offered, in Robert A.M. Stern's words, "a vernacular classicism…that deftly modified a Mediterranean-inspired architectural style for the Southern California landscape." Had a projected arcade (recorded in a 1908 drawing by Hunt's partner Elmer Grey) been built, Smiley would have resembled even more closely the architect's other campus buildings.

Three stories in elevation, Smiley was designed in three sections, each with its own entrance, and included a recreation room with a fireplace. It contained a few single rooms, but most were three-room suites, each occupied by two students; the building housed a total of 80 men at an annual lodging cost of $60. For several years, the Music department occupied the building's northern section, but enrollment increases soon resulted in its moving to other quarters.

Smiley is said to be the oldest American college dormitory in continuous use west of the Mississippi. Whether or not this is the case, more than a few of its residents over the years have reflected on its age, if not always in the most respectful terms. In 1924, a petition from 46 residents complained of insufficient heat; a member of the class of 1928 later recalled his neighbors' fondness for rolling a cannonball down the second floor hall at 2 a.m.; and stories about Smiley's plumbing, which (allegedly) required warning those taking showers before flushing the toilets lest the bathers be scalded, appeared regularly in *The Student Life*, such rueful reminiscences balanced by fond memories of the esprit de corps that developed among its residents.

Smiley was upgraded in 1968 and again in 1990 when it was discovered, just prior to the beginning of classes, that the building was not safe from earthquakes. As a result, 52 students were temporarily housed at Griswold's Inn where amenities such as maid service and a Jacuzzi tub helped compensate for the distance from campus. ■

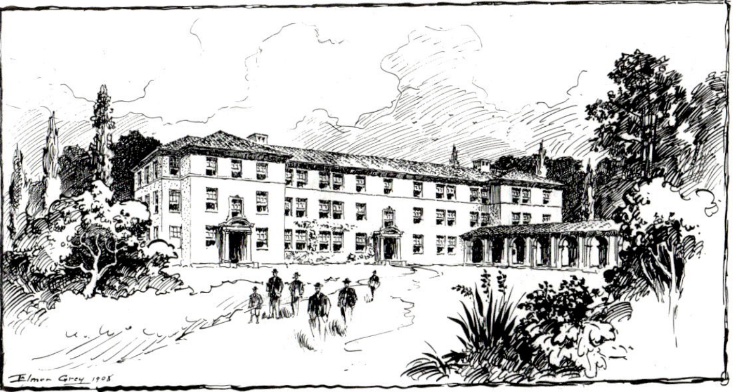

Elmer Grey, sketch for Smiley Hall, 1908

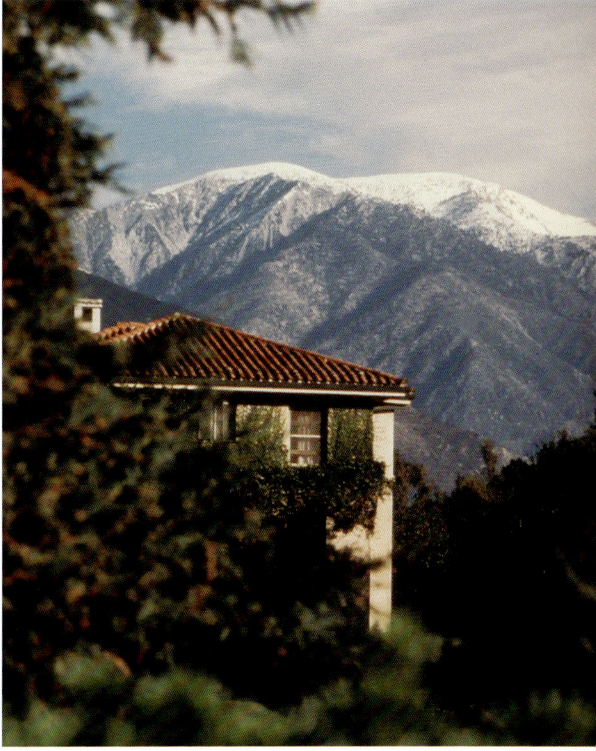

A.K. Smiley Hall

BUILT 1908 (summer, built in 100 days)
LOCATION 550 North College Way at Sixth Street
PRESIDENT IN OFFICE George A. Gates
PURPOSE Men's dormitory
ARCHITECTS Myron Hunt and Elmer Grey
MATERIALS reinforced concrete, double-shell construction, tile roof
COST $40,000
DONORS D.K. Pearsons, Nathan Blanchard, George Marston
NAMED FOR Trustee Albert K. Smiley (1828–1912)

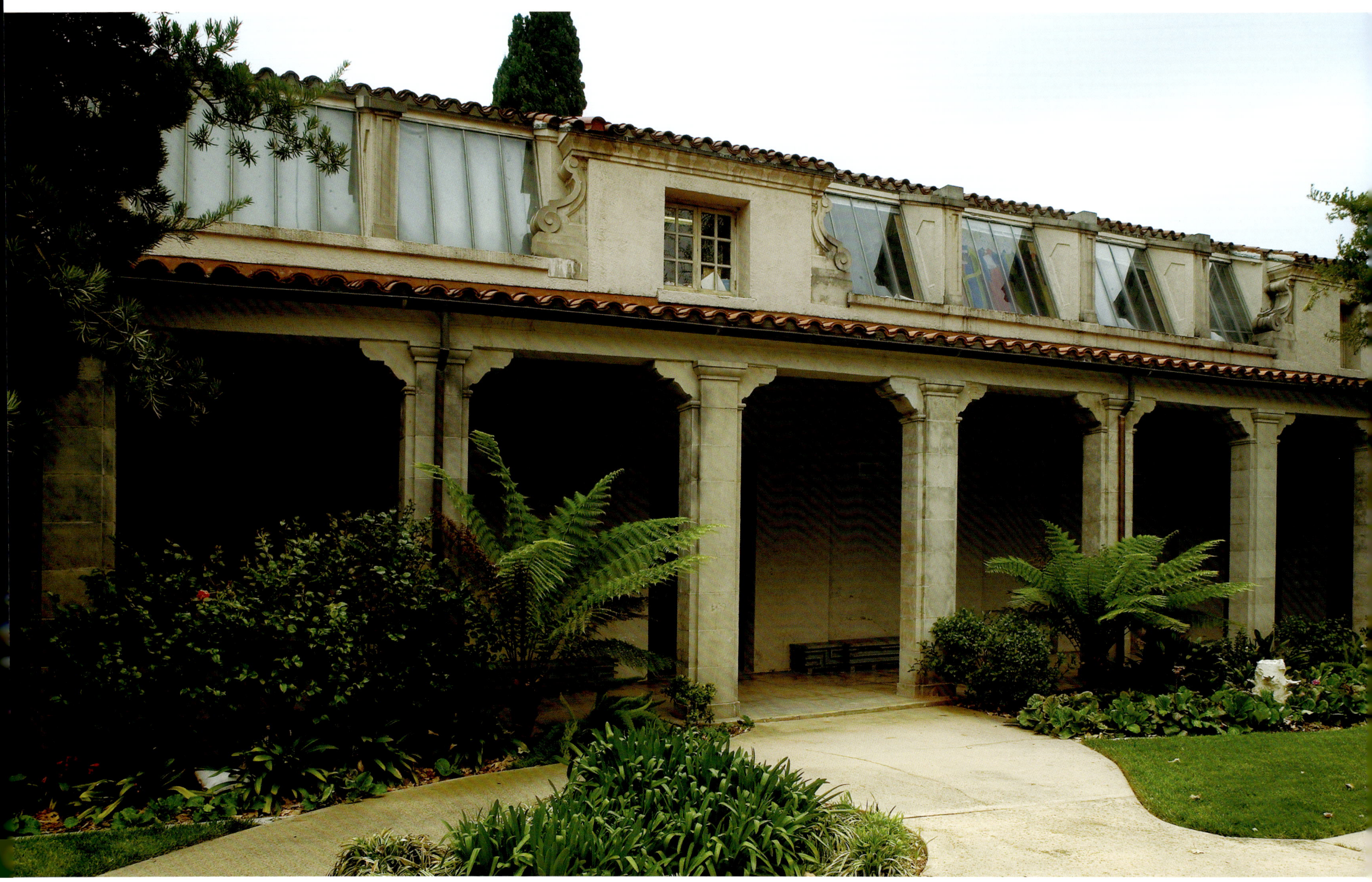

Henry Cabala

Rembrandt Hall

Rembrandt Hall was Myron Hunt's second building for Pomona and the first to be completed under President Blaisdell; it was also the first building devoted to art in the Pomona Valley. The need for space designated for art was recognized as early as 1908 by the Rembrandt Club, and a hall for this purpose was one of the goals of the College's Million Dollar Campaign undertaken shortly after President Blaisdell took office. The Rembrandt Club, which took the initiative and led the drive for the building, had been established in 1905 by Hannah Tempest Jenkins, who had been appointed that year as Associate Professor of Art and Design and Director of the School of Art and Design; Phebe Estelle Spalding, a professor of English literature who also taught art history and had created the College's first art gallery in her own office space in Holmes Hall; and Lucretia Brackett, wife of Professor Frank Parkhurst Brackett, who had taught mathematics and Latin since the College's founding. Mrs. Brackett had also played an important role in establishing the School of Art and Design at Pomona. The Rembrandt Club was dedicated to the "study of art and the fostering of the interest of the art department and gallery," a mission it fulfills to this day.

In 1914, the decision was made to turn both music and art into college departments rather than separate schools, and to situate their buildings close together. That year, Rembrandt Hall was built, with studio and gallery space for the new department; Hunt was commissioned at the same time to design the building for music (Mabel Shaw Bridges Hall of Music) that soon followed. The Rembrandt Club's involvement in the building that bore its name amounted to a partnership with the College. An agreement of 1917 states that "Rembrandt Hall is dedicated to the development and fostering of the aesthetic interests of the College and Community, more particularly on the side of Art." It goes on to list four primary constituencies—The Art Department, Rembrandt Club, "wider Community interests," and "wider College interests"—and to specify how the building was to be used. The Art Department was given use of the sky-lighted studio and office on the upper floor and was permitted to use the ground floor; the latter was, however, primarily the Club's domain, the site of its regular meetings, receptions, and exhibitions. The agreement also specified that the building was not to be used for student social activities, for large groups that might interfere with the work of the studios, or for classes other than art.

The location of Rembrandt Hall was dictated by Hunt's 1908 campus plan. The architect's original design also called for a museum at the western end, an idea realized only in 1958 with the building of Montgomery Gallery (see Chapter IV). In style, Rembrandt conformed to the model Hunt had established in Smiley Hall: stucco walls topped with a red tile roof, simple in form with Mediterranean details and arcades, which were a key feature of Hunt's plan for the campus. The north-facing portico of Rembrandt Hall resembles a stoa—the covered walkway common to ancient Greek and Roman architecture—but, in this case, with square piers supporting the roof rather than columns or arches. Until the construction of Thatcher Music Building in 1969, Rembrandt was open to Marston Quadrangle but recessed from its perimeter, creating, as George Gorse notes, the zigzag pattern—building facade alternating with open courtyard—that distinguished Hunt's plan. As in his other buildings, the architect here used reinforced concrete for the structure and cast stone for the building's decorative details.

In 1936, a western extension, also designed by Myron Hunt was added to Rembrandt Hall. This contained an exhibition gallery with "modern picture hanging fixtures," including walls covered in wire mesh and monk's cloth, and a new ventilating system. The use of the building has changed over the years as the art curriculum has grown and changed. The original gallery was used for faculty meetings under President Lyon and served for years as a lecture hall for art history and other classes. In 1995, prompted by the Northridge earthquake (1994) that raised concerns about the building's structural integrity, renovations were undertaken including the conversion of the lecture hall and a small adjacent seminar room for use by ceramics. In 2005, marking another curricular shift, the lecture hall became a computer lab for digital art and the former seminar room a student gallery. ■

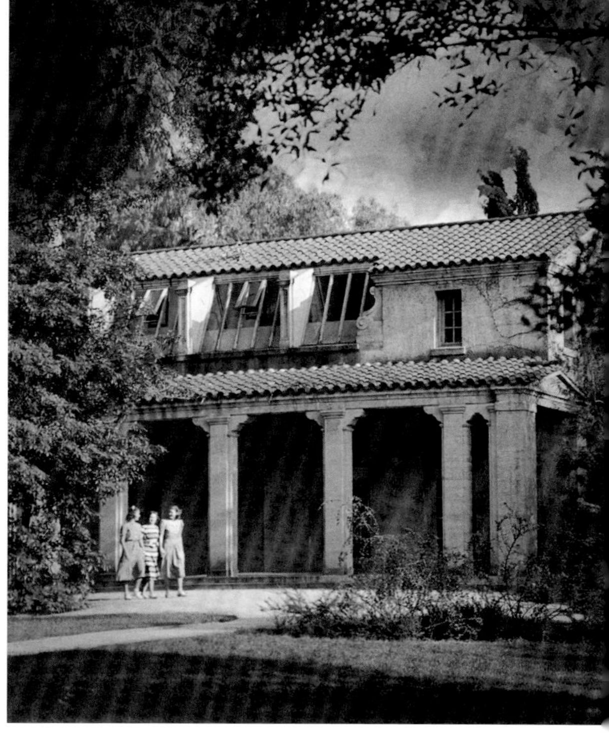

Rembrandt Hall

BUILT 1914; enlarged 1936–37 (see also Montgomery Gallery)
PRESIDENT IN OFFICE James A. Blaisdell
LOCATION 135 East Bonita Avenue
PURPOSE Art studios, gallery
ARCHITECT Myron Hunt
MATERIALS reinforced concrete, tile roof, cast stone details
DONORS/NAMED FOR Rembrandt Club

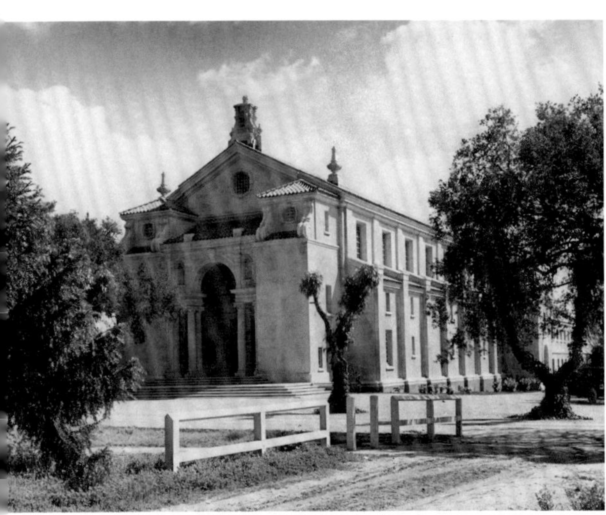

Bridges Hall, built 1915

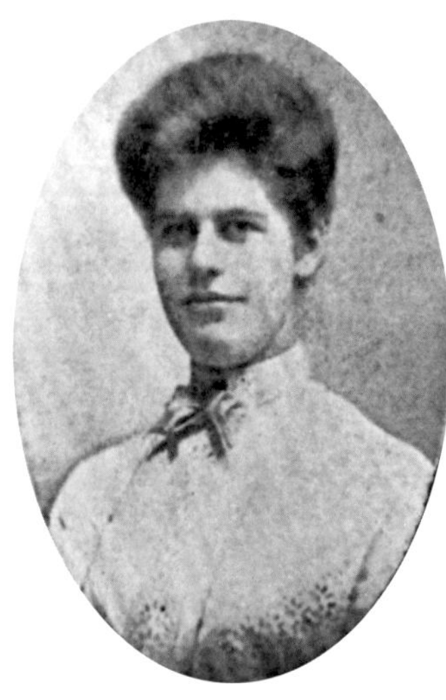

Mabel Shaw Bridges '08

Mabel Shaw Bridges Hall of Music

> *It may be said that no gift to the College has been transmuted into such high and golden value as the Mabel Shaw Bridges Hall of Music.*—FRANK P. BRACKETT

The Mabel Shaw Bridges Hall of Music is the architectural gem of the Pomona campus and, many believe, one of the finest buildings of Myron Hunt's career. Perfectly proportioned to its prominent site on Marston Quadrangle adjacent to the slightly recessed Rembrandt Hall, it conveys a sense of Hunt's larger plan for the campus. In a letter written in the early 1930s, the architect explained the basis of his design:

> *It was set by the desire of the college to have a room which could hold a thousand people but could be arranged to look as though there was a real audience if there were only three hundred and fifty. This was done by using the side benches of the parliament type and making the seats of the pit removable. When it came to the character of the detail, we worked back to Mexico, which means to Spain, which means to what the Spanish thought was the Renaissance.... The reason for this was because of our local Spanish traditions. Effort was made to spot the ornamental Spanish style, rather than spread it out, Italian style.*

Hunt gave his hall a festive entry porch that, according to his campus plan, was to have faced a chapel across Marston Quadrangle. Although a chapel was never constructed, the notion of an answering façade to the north was taken up many years later by architect Robert A.M. Stern whose Smith Campus Center, 1999 (see Chapter VII) has finally provided the visual dialogue between north and south sides of the quadrangle that Hunt envisioned. Writing about Bridges Hall of Music, Stern notes that it was "...certainly Hunt's greatest building on campus. More finely detailed and stylistically specific than his previous efforts, Little Bridges is a masterpiece that established a convincing sense of place." The concert hall itself is basilican in form, and one finds in the building references to French and Italian Renaissance ecclesiastical architecture as well as that of the Spanish missions. The auditorium was beautifully appointed—with dark paneling and a decorated ceiling—and expertly engineered acoustically.

Bridges Hall of Music is two-sided—its auditorium on the north, and, on the south, an elongated, U-shaped, courtyard (Lebus Court) surrounded by a graceful Ionic colonnade and rooms originally intended for music practice. Lebus Court, in turn, looks south to Harwood Court (1921), continuing the linear sequence of buildings, courtyards, and resulting sight lines that distinguished Myron Hunt's campus plan. At the center of Lebus Court, is a bronze fountain sculpture by Burt W. Johnson of a nude boy, in classic *contrapposto* stance and holding a flute, given to the College by the Class of 1915. Titled *The Spirit of Spanish Music*, the work reflects the "Arcadian" theme Hunt intended for Pomona's south campus.

Bridges Hall of Music was made possible by a gift of $100,000 by Mr. and Mrs. Appleton Shaw Bridges of San Diego in honor of their daughter, Mabel Shaw Bridges '08, who had died after a short illness in May 1907. Mabel Bridges had been active in music on campus as well as treasurer of the Rembrandt Club. At Commencement that year, a scholarship in her name was also established. The Bridges family

Henry Cabala

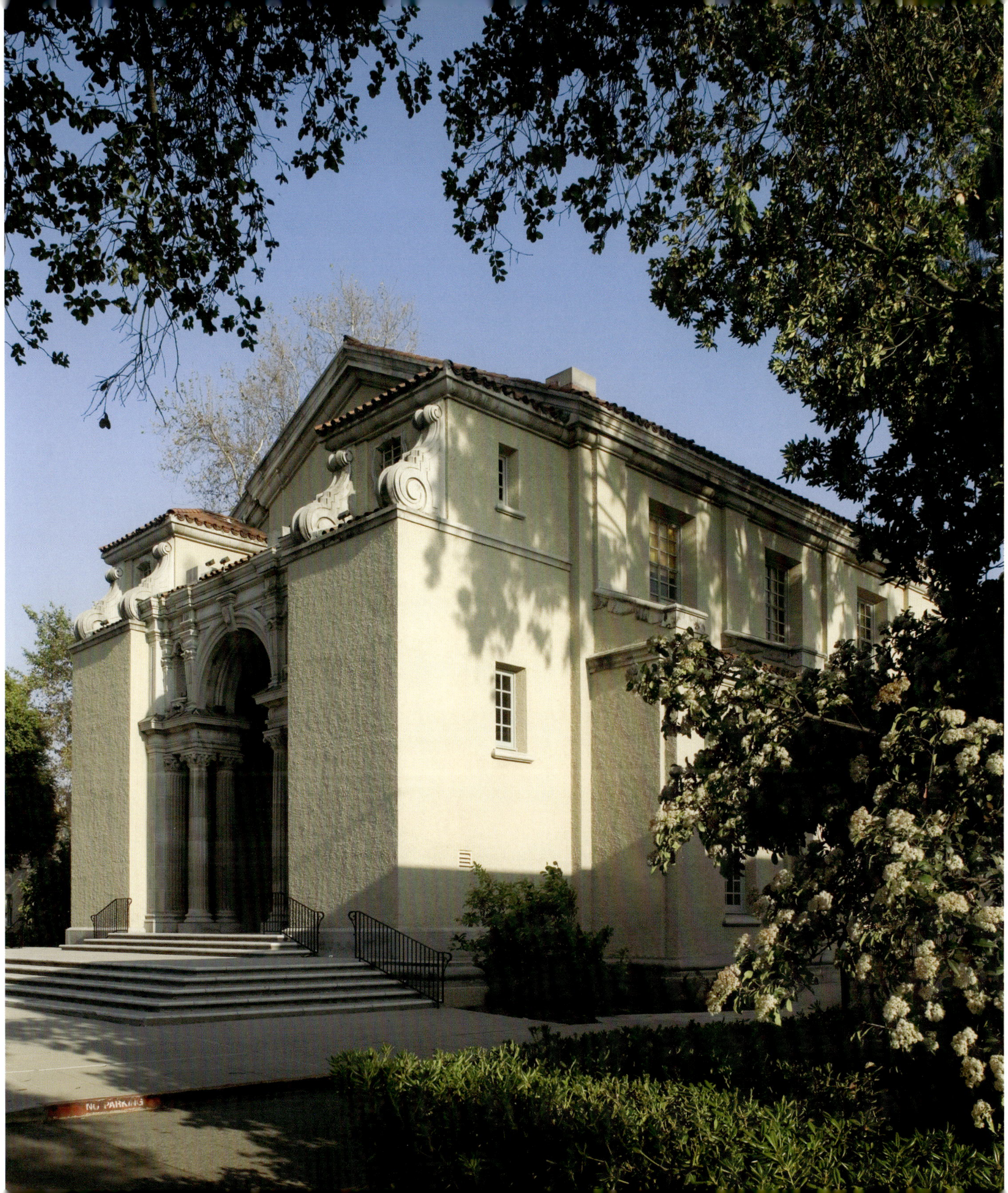

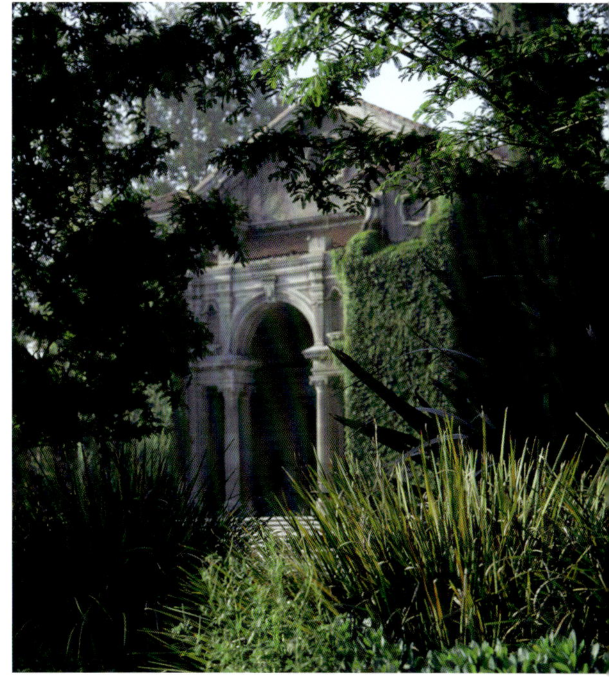

Mabel Shaw Bridges Hall of Music

BUILT 1915

PRESIDENT IN OFFICE James A. Blaisdell

LOCATION 150 East Fourth Street

PURPOSE Music auditorium; practice room, studios

ARCHITECT Myron Hunt

MATERIALS reinforced concrete, tile roof; cast stone details

COST $104,000

DONORS Mr. and Mrs. Appleton Shaw Bridges

NAMED FOR Mabel Shaw Bridges '08

RENOVATED 1971 (General Contractor, Noyes Roach Company of Los Angeles; Architects, Powell, Morgridge, Richards & Coghlan); 2000–01 (Claremont Environmental Design Group)

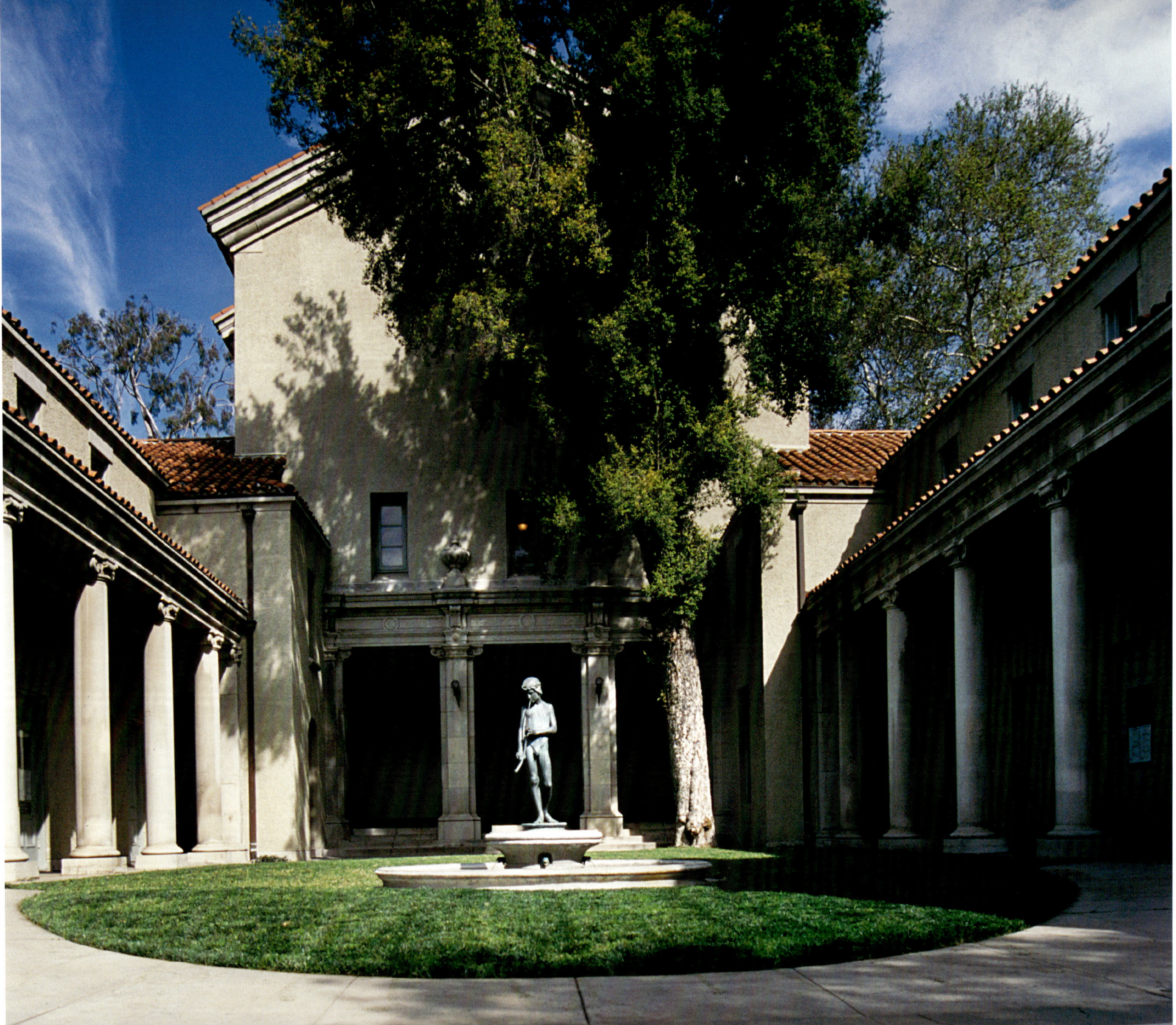

Ian Bradshaw

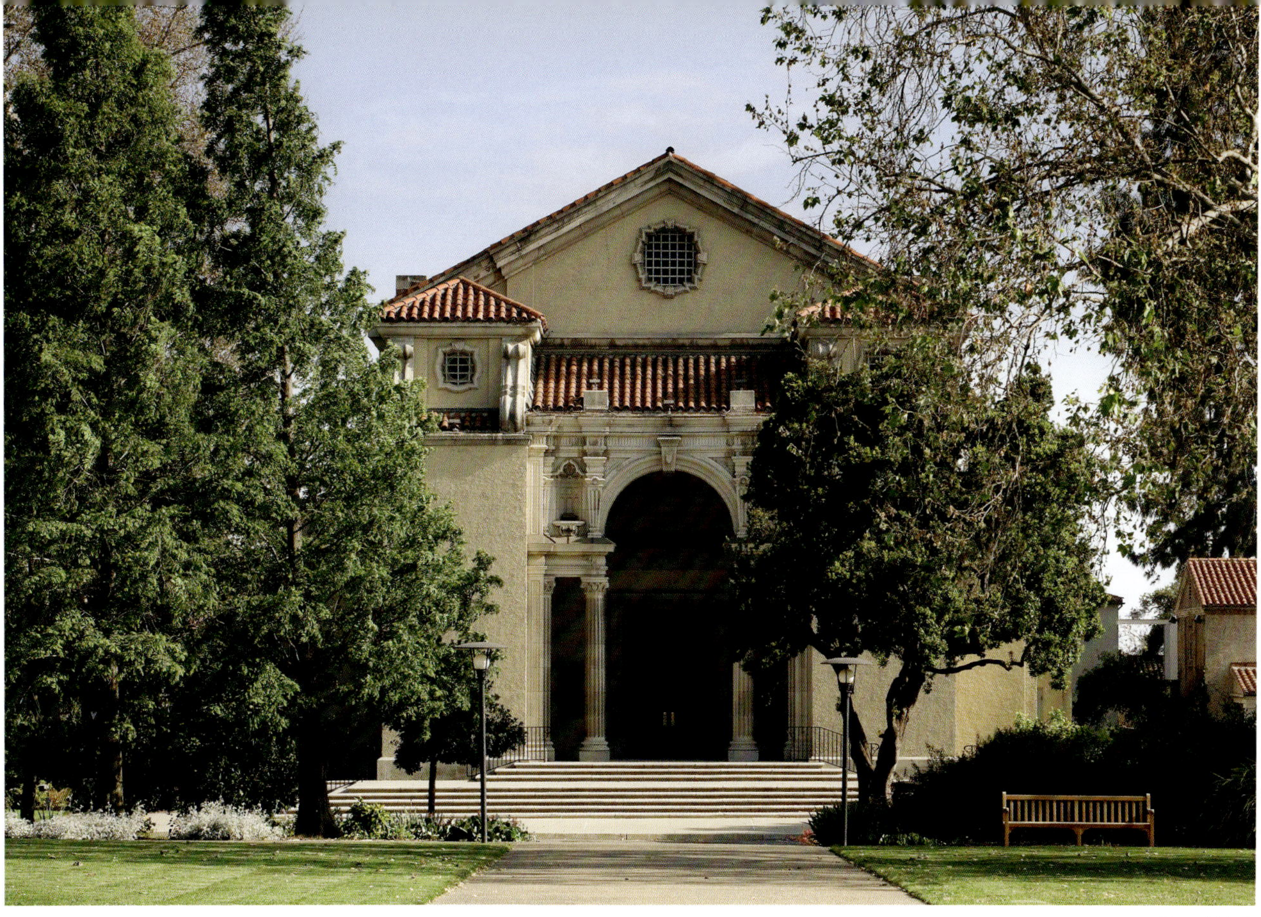

Henry Cabala

later supported the construction of Mabel Shaw Bridges Auditorium (1931, see Chapter III); thereafter, Hunt's building has been familiarly known as "Little Bridges," its larger neighbor as "Big Bridges."

In fall 2001, Bridges emerged from a 13-month, $5.2 million renovation—its first since 1971—that included a brilliantly restored ceiling and a new C.B. Fisk pipe organ. As Don Pattison has noted, less obvious, but no less important, were four large windows and two musician galleries recovered from an earlier seismic renovation, and new hardwood flooring, window glazing, lighting and audience seating. Outside the auditorium, changes included off-stage storage areas, an elaborate eight-inch honeycombed structure above the ceiling, an elevator, the addition of an accessible restroom and a new sprinkler system. "The most dramatic change, however, was in the ear of the listener. …'Little Bridges' had been in need of a more flexible acoustical environment, one that made it possible to tune the room—much as one tunes an instrument—for every kind of music, from chamber groups to ensembles to the impressive new organ. The challenge before the Department of Music was to transform what is considered architect Myron Hunt's 1915 masterpiece into a concert hall that ensured excellent acoustics for every performer."[1] The hall had excellent acoustics for solo or quartet but less so for the organ or a large orchestra; it also offered a better aural experience for the audience than for performers, a serious drawback. Addressing the problems required the collaboration of acoustical experts, engineers, architects and musicians, and involved such modifications as a new acoustical structure above the ceiling, glazing and adjustable banners for windows, reshaped walls, reinstalled balcony wainscoting, and newly designed chairs that allow sound waves to pass through and reflect off the floor. The net result is a superb musical environment housed within an architectural masterpiece. ■

OPPOSITE *Lebus Court, fountain sculpture by Burt Johnson,* The Spirit of Spanish Music, *gift of the Class of 1915*

Carlos Puma

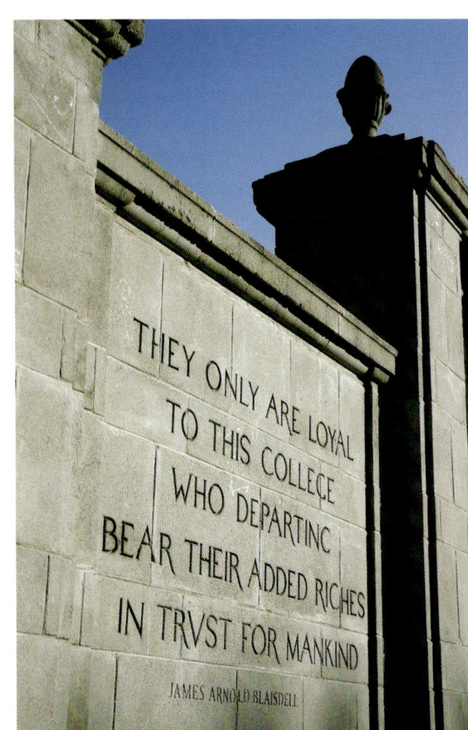

College Gate

BUILT 1914
PRESIDENT IN OFFICE James A. Blaisdell
LOCATION North College Avenue at Sixth Street
ARCHITECT Myron Hunt (with President Blaisdell)
MATERIALS concrete block, iron grille work
DONOR William S. Mason

College Gate

While Myron Hunt's Mabel Shaw Bridges Hall of Music was under construction, several campus beautification efforts were accomplished with support from William S. Mason, a Chicago businessman and friend of Pomona faculty member Judge Charles G. Neely. Foremost among these was an impressive gate flanking College Avenue at Sixth Street, which Hunt's campus plan had identified as the northern boundary of the campus. The gate was intended to provide a unifying point of entry to the College precinct, and at the ceremony celebrating the laying of the cornerstone on Founders' Day, October 14, 1914, President Blaisdell remarked: "This day marks the beginning of a new period of enrichment. We have struggled through the days of necessities; today, in a certain sense, we begin to glorify and beautify our life."[2]

The classic design of the gate, which consisted of matching concrete block panels and curving iron grilles, was the work of Hunt, but it was President Blaisdell who composed the flanking inscriptions:

Let only the eager, thoughtful and reverent enter here.
They only are loyal to this college who departing bear their added riches in trust for mankind.

Blaisdell was gratified by the positive reception to the gate and its message, noting "By nothing would I like more to be remembered." Many years later however, as E. Wilson Lyon writes, Blaisdell commented that, on reflection, the first of the inscriptions was perhaps "a trifle too prohibitive" for entering students and might have been better without the word "only"; but the second was "exactly as I still would wish it and I hope it may always express the final admonition of the college to its departing sons and daughters."

To carry Blaisdell's ringing statement of educational mission, which was inscribed in bold Roman script, Hunt designed a classically elegant gateway employing Doric and Ionic forms—pillars, architraves, pine cone pinnacles—and, in its placement and purpose, echoing the traditional ceremonial entryways to ancient Greek and Roman cities. The gate invites entry while also marking a physical and psychological boundary, and it is fitting that Pomona's incoming students traditionally process as a group through this portal as they begin their college career. Since Hunt's time the campus has expanded north of Sixth Street with the result that the Gate now marks the meeting place of north and south campuses rather than a point of entry; nonetheless, it continues to serve its symbolic purpose. ■

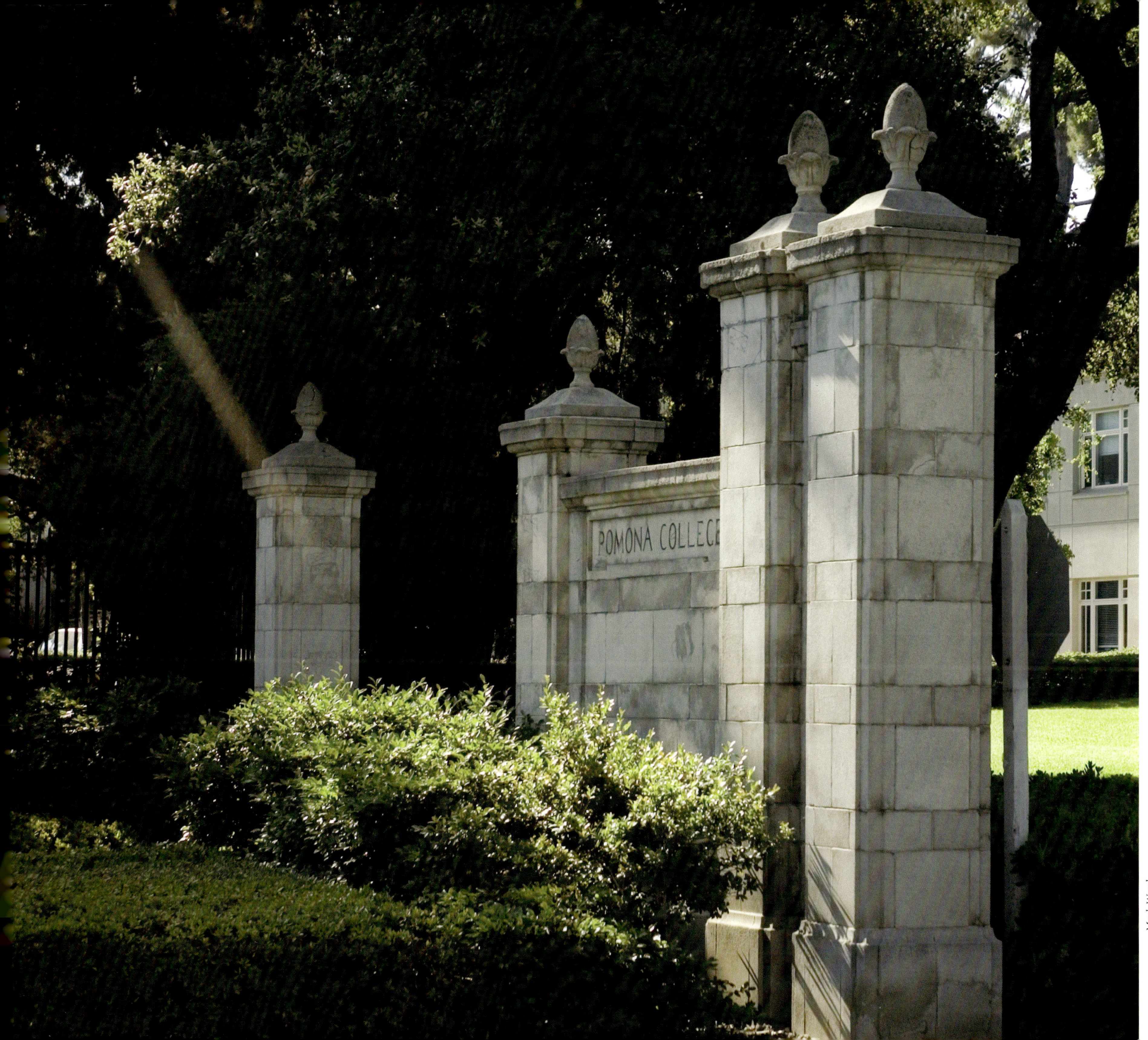

Mark Wood

Greek Theatre

BUILT 1914
PRESIDENT IN OFFICE James A. Blaisdell
LOCATION Western edge Blanchard Park (The Wash)
ARCHITECT Myron Hunt
RENOVATED 1996-97
NAMED FOR Frederick and Carol Sontag (1997)

OPPOSITE: *Myron Hunt, Greek Theatre, built 1914*

RIGHT: *Myron Hunt, original proposal for Greek Theatre, 1914, drawing reprinted in College publication*

FAR RIGHT: *Sontag Greek Theatre*

Greek Theatre (now Sontag Greek Theatre)

From the earliest days of the College, the western edge of the Wash had been the site of "fun-producing entertainment" traditionally offered by senior classes on the Tuesday afternoon of Commencement week, as well as for more formal performances and ceremonies. Over time, audiences became too large for the setting, and, in 1910, the senior class took the initiative in creating a permanent Greek theatre with a gift of $2,500. Invited to design the facility, Myron Hunt first visited the Greek Theatre at The University of California, Berkeley (1903). His proposal for Pomona included a stage, seating for 4,000, dressing rooms and stage facilities, all within a classical Greek structure. Although Hunt's design was never fully realized, the stage and amphitheater were completed, with several hundred concrete seats and wooden bleachers for 3,000 additional spectators.

The Greek Theatre provided a focal point for the College on the east and a gathering place for organized entertainments at the edge of the picturesque Wash. A civic space embedded in nature, it represented both an extension of the "college in a garden" concept and a reference to the classical groves of academe.

The Greek Theatre was handsomely renovated in 1996–97 and dedicated in 1997 to Professor of Philosophy Frederick Sontag and his wife Carol. ■

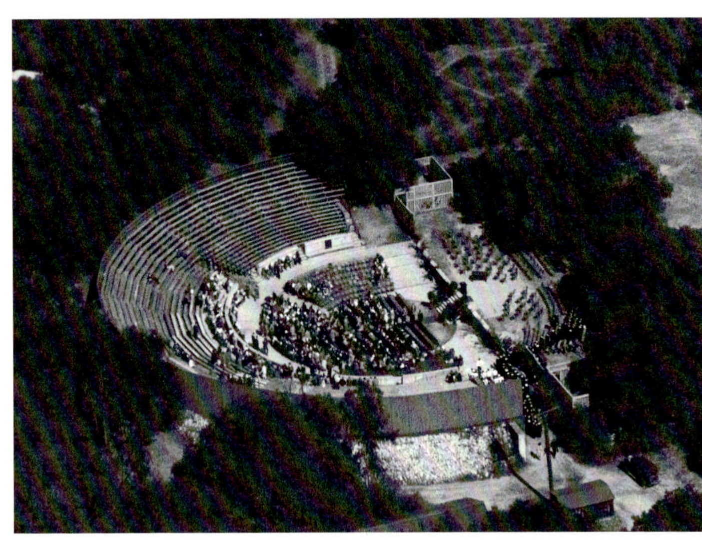

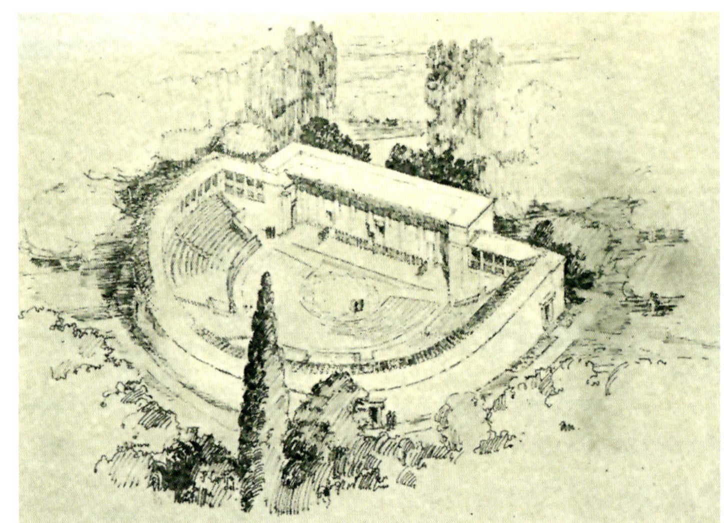

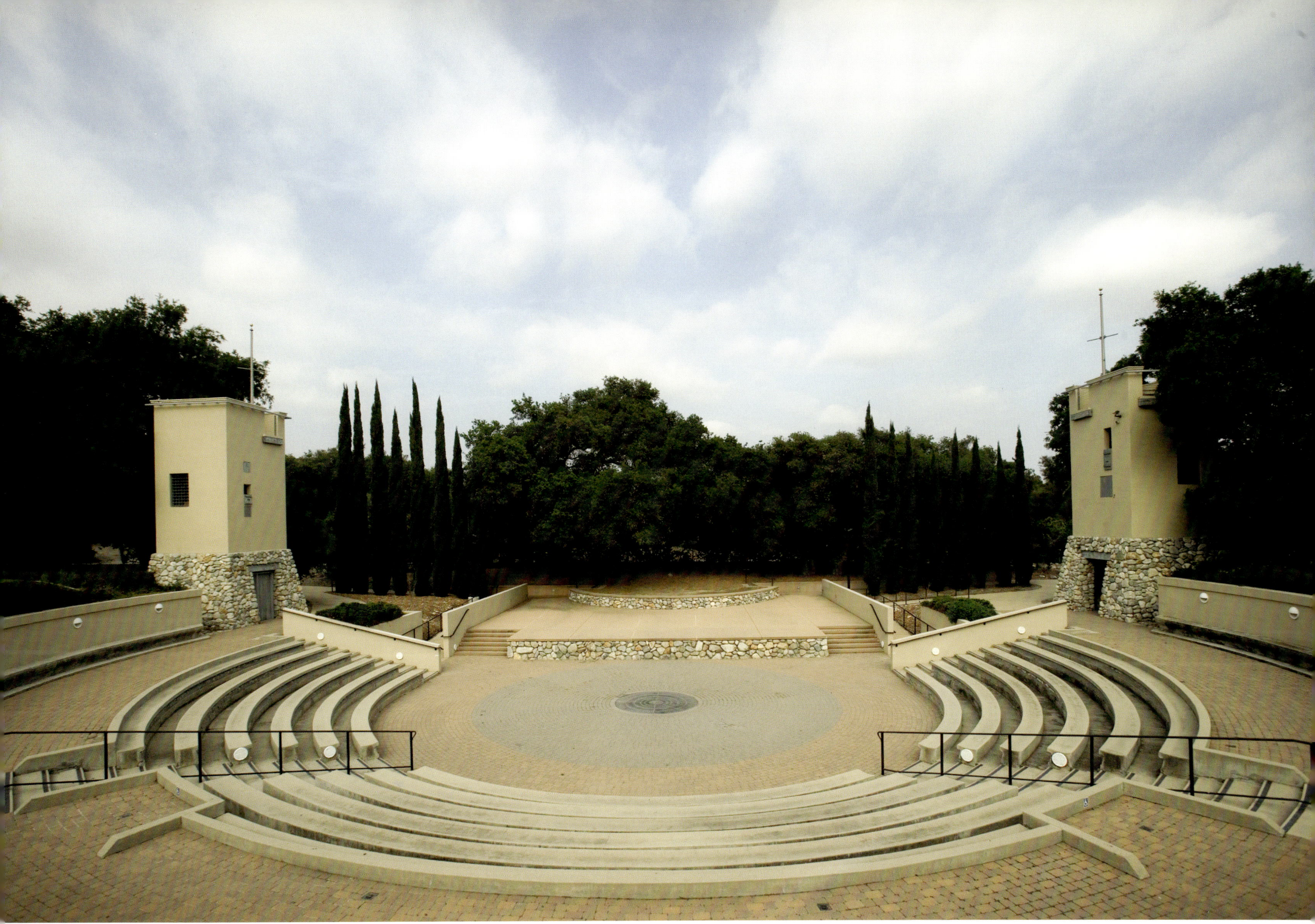

Henry Cabala

Henry Cabala

CHAPTER III CONSOLIDATION *and* GROWTH 1910–41

Bridges Auditorium

Consolidation and Growth, 1910–41

PRESIDENTS JAMES BLAISDELL *and* CHARLES EDMUNDS

The building of a college is like the building of a cathedral. Each is possible only by the faith, the idealism and the sacrifice of a multitude. There must be first a splendid and inclusive democracy sharing the courage and toil—life's richest experience of satisfying fellowship.[1]—JAMES BLAISDELL

THUS DID JAMES A. BLAISDELL, IN 1910, launch the first capital campaign of his 18-year presidency. Blaisdell's predecessor, George Gates, had resigned earlier that year, overwhelmed by the seemingly unending task of securing funds for the College, and the financial crisis Blaisdell inherited led in 1912 to his announcement of the "Million Dollar Campaign," which concluded successfully in 1919.[2] In that year, Blaisdell articulated his goals for the College in a report titled "The Making of an Adequate College." By "adequate," Blaisdell meant more than "sufficient"; he aspired to a "college of the highest character and standing," a goal that he readily admitted would be "endless."[3] By 1921, the College's resources had quadrupled, from $650,000 in 1910 to $2,885,000; in the same period, the endowment grew from $301,000 to $1,371,000, a truly remarkable record. Under Blaisdell, the College developed in other ways as well: the faculty increased from 40 to 70 in the first year of his administration alone[4]; art and music programs, which had held separate status as "schools," both entered the core curriculum as departments (with the understanding that their emphasis was not to be "professional") and were soon served by splendid new facilities (see Chapter 11); and the Preparatory Department, necessitated in the early years by the lack of adequate high school preparation for students, was terminated. The result was a single, cohesive instructional program.

Equally remarkable was the expansion of the College's land holdings that, in turn, enabled the growth of its physical plant under Blaisdell's leadership. The dual process of pushing back and protecting the relative wilderness that was Claremont in the 1880s, initiated by the acquisition of Blanchard Park (The Wash) in 1905, progressed significantly with the appointment of Ralph Cornell '14, landscape architect, whose first assignment, in 1919, was to begin the transformation of the College's central green space into what would be known as Marston Quadrangle. Through the exchange of lots, purchases, and gifts, the campus expanded in all directions, most notably though the generosity of Ellen Browning Scripps, whose name is associated primarily with Scripps College, which she founded in 1926, but who contributed importantly to Pomona as well. Miss Scripps, who lived in La Jolla, was an admirer of Blaisdell, with whom she shared a commitment to the education of women. Fittingly, Harwood

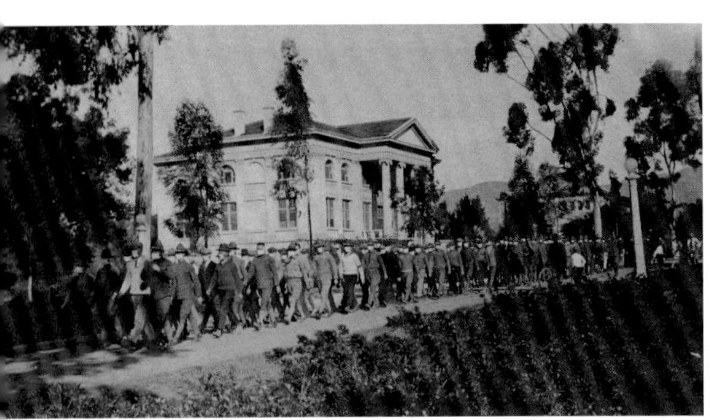

Soldiers marching, College Avenue, during World War I

Court, the first dedicated women's residence, was built on land donated by Scripps; she subsequently gave 253 acres in the area of Indian Hill (the mesa north of Foothill Boulevard near the current site of the Rancho Santa Ana Botanic Garden), and funds she provided enabled the College in 1924 to acquire some land between Sixth Street and the area bordered by College and Mills avenues.

Pomona's new quadrangle required the move and reconstruction of the College's first building—Sumner Hall (see Chapter 1), and Blaisdell's presidency also saw the transformation of the barracks built during WWI into (the second) Renwick Gymnasium ("Big Gym") along with the 1921 construction east of Smiley Hall of the Alumni Memorial Training Quarters for men's physical education. The same year, facilities for the sciences were radically improved with the addition of Mason and Crookshank halls, and the pressing need for a women's campus was addressed by the construction of Harwood Court and its Strong Hall wing.

Blaisdell had come to Pomona from Beloit, Wisconsin, where he was born and was, in 1909, teaching at Beloit College, his alma mater. After graduating from Hartford seminary in 1892, he was ordained a Congregational minister and served pastorates in Wisconsin and Michigan before returning to Beloit in 1909 to teach Biblical Literature and Ancient Oriental History. It was philanthropist D.K. Pearsons, who had supported Pomona richly in the past, who brought Blaisdell to the attention of the trustees. Although initially reluctant to leave Beloit, Blaisdell was won over by the opportunity Pomona offered to influence the development of a young institution in which he saw great promise.

Of Blaisdell's many accomplishments at Pomona, arguably the most significant—his role in founding the consortium known as The Claremont Colleges—was also, ironically, the one that ultimately led him to leave the presidency of the College. The increase in the College's endowment, physical plant, and land holdings during Blaisdell's first 15 years in office led to increasingly intense discussions about the future of the College, and, specifically whether (and in what ways) it should grow. To the apparent alternatives—remain a small, residential college or develop into a university—was added a third: combine the two in the manner of Oxford and Cambridge, where small, independent residential colleges flourished within a larger, umbrella organization. At Pomona's 1925 Commencement, invited speaker William Bennett Munro, Harvard professor of American government, posed the rhetorical question: "Can we develop in this country an institution which is large in its resources, broad and deep in its intellectual life, with an atmosphere that is stimulating to the highest type of creative scholarship, but which nevertheless preserves the wholesome community ideals of the small college, its rural environment, its religious spirit, its restfulness in the shadow of the hills?" The trustees, under Blaisdell's leadership, were already primed for such a bold experiment, and The Claremont Colleges consortium was incorporated on October 14, 1925, the 38th anniversary of Pomona's founding. Its purpose was to establish new colleges (a "central college," later Claremont University Center (CUC) and Scripps College, 1926, were the first of these) and to provide for the common concerns of present and future institutions. In 1927, Blaisdell, who had been

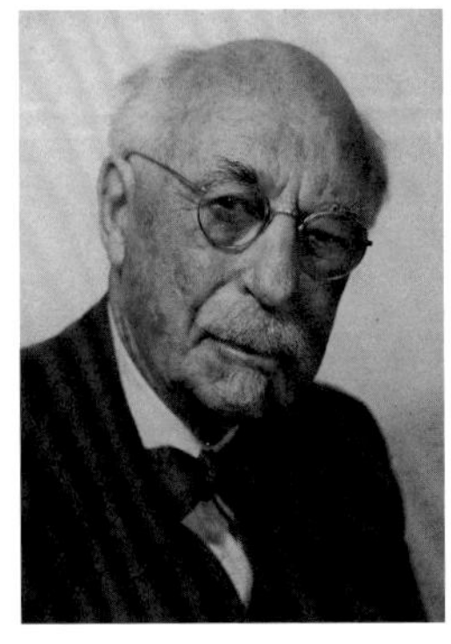

President James A. Blaisdell

appointed Head of the governing Board of Fellows, decided to commit himself fully to the new consortium, becoming its first president, and the search for his successor at Pomona College began.

President Charles K. Edmunds

With the inauguration of Charles K. Edmunds in 1928, attention shifted from Pomona's larger role in Claremont to its own campus and, specifically, its residential life. The period of his tenure witnessed the construction of several of the College's most visible and programmatically significant buildings, including the Eli P. Clark men's dormitories, Frary Hall with its magnificent fresco by José Clemente Orozco, Harwood Dining Hall, Mabel Shaw Bridges Auditorium (a project of the new Claremont Colleges), and the Student Union, later named in honor of President and Mrs. Charles Keyser Edmunds.

Charles Edmunds had graduated from The Johns Hopkins University and served as provost there from 1924 to 1926 when he became the New York-based director of Lingnan University (formerly Canton Christian College), Hong Kong, where he had previously been president. An engineer and physicist, Pomona's fifth president was the first who was not a Congregational clergyman. Upon taking office, Edmunds immediately made clear his desire to work closely with Pomona's students, whom he considered his primary responsibility; accordingly, his most pressing agenda was to complete Pomona's transformation to a fully residential college. At the time of his inauguration in 1928, only two dormitories existed—Smiley Hall for men and Harwood Court, which housed freshman women (older women students were still boarded in private homes and facilities near campus). Dining halls were also inadequate, and, except for women living in Harwood who dined at the Claremont Inn, students took their meals in homes and boarding clubs.

Early in his tenure, Edmunds commented: "Our most imperative needs have to do with those physical facilities which would make our life here together truly effective—dormitories, dining halls, and college-owned, properly located residences…To sleep in one building, go to another for meals, to yet another to entertain guests, and to another to read or to mingle with other members of the family is not a normal or an effective way of living. Properly arranged group life will create and maintain a high *esprit de corps*—a unity of feeling, sympathy and interest that will dominate every member of the group…A great many of the difficulties now constantly confronting us would be ameliorated, if not entirely removed, if we first put our students into healthy, congenial, attractive, well regulated homes."[6]

The 1920s was, until its final year, a decade of growth at the College, with increased enrollments and new buildings reflecting and, in turn, enhancing an expanding curriculum. The sciences gained significantly with the construction of dedicated buildings for Chemistry (Mason) and Zoology (Crookshank) that freed space in Pearsons Hall for the expansion of Physics and Mathematics. The period of economic prosperity and optimism during which Edmunds took the helm came to an abrupt end with the stock market crash of 1929 and the ensuing Depression. Although the Clark men's campus (1929–30) and Bridges

Henry Cabala

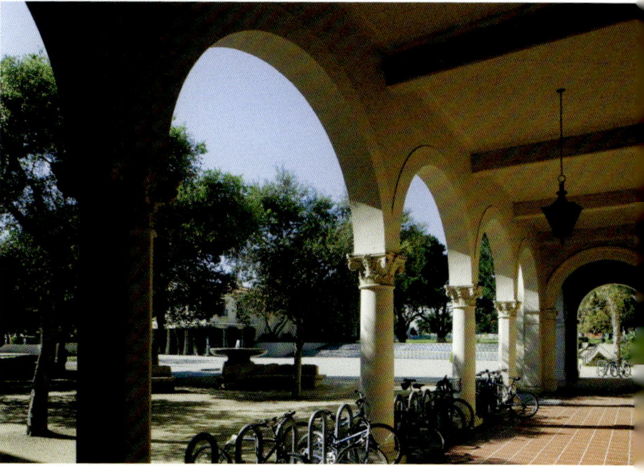

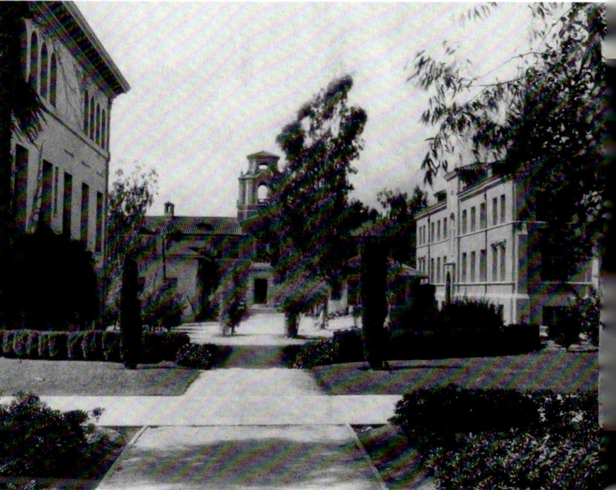

Eli P. Clark Dormitory

Mason Hall flanked by Pearsons and Crookshank Halls

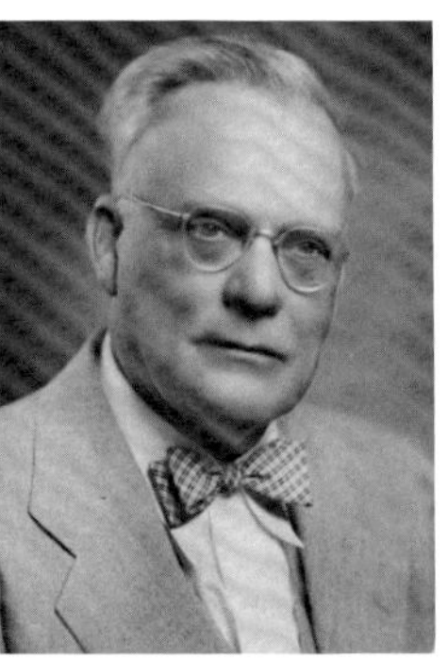

President Charles K. Edmunds

Auditorium (1931) were both completed during this time, there was no further campus construction until 1936. Consistent with the president's clearly stated priorities, the first buildings to be built after the economic situation had improved were a second women's dormitory (Blaisdell Hall) and a student union. As the country, and the College, recovered economically, however, the shadow of war in Europe was becoming increasingly oppressive, the fall of France to Hitler in 1940 leading to increased pressure on the United States to intervene. As President Edmunds, who would reach retirement age in September 1941, declined to extend his tenure, the search for his successor was thus undertaken at one of the most ominous moments in the country's history.

In terms of campus architectural history, the 1920s and 1930s witnessed divergence from the campus plan Myron Hunt had projected but, nonetheless, the continuation of his vision and of the style he established. Hunt was not retained as campus architect after 1915, moving on to Occidental College in Eagle Rock, where he supervised the development of that campus until 1944, and designing a number of important buildings in the Pasadena area. In 1916, Pomona hired architect James P. Jamieson whose first project was to transform Holmes Hall from a wood frame Victorian to a greatly simplified, classical stucco structure with a red tile roof, in keeping with the new campus vocabulary. This metamorphosis, like that of Sumner Hall, which went through a similar makeover when it was moved and reconstructed, also by Jamieson, in 1921, reinforced the stylistic direction of Pomona's campus architecture. In the words of architect Robert A.M. Stern, "Twenty-nine years after its founding, Pomona College had definitively left behind its pioneer, Victorian roots and emerged as an outstanding exemplar of a version of traditional Classicism that came to be widely identified as a Southern California style." The same year, Jamieson designed Harwood Court in a manner respectful of Hunt's vision, and in 1929, the Clark Hall men's campus and Frary Hall, by architect Sumner Spaulding, further extended this vocabulary in a way that both complemented and subtly distinguished itself from the College's earlier structures. The last building of President Edmunds's tenure, the Student Union, offered a spare version of the classicism established as Pomona's signature style. ■

OPPOSITE *Bixby Plaza and fountain*

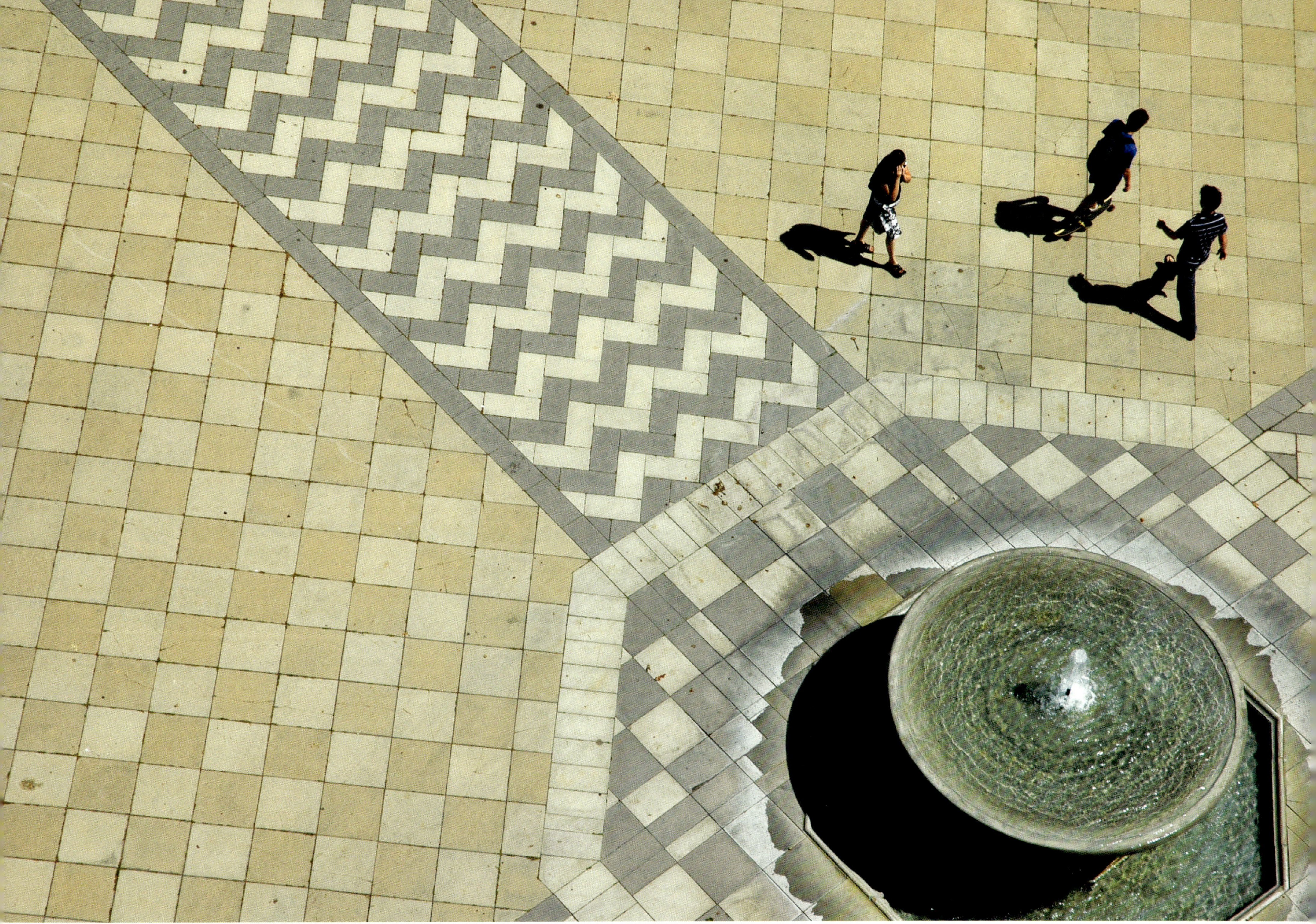

Carlos Puma

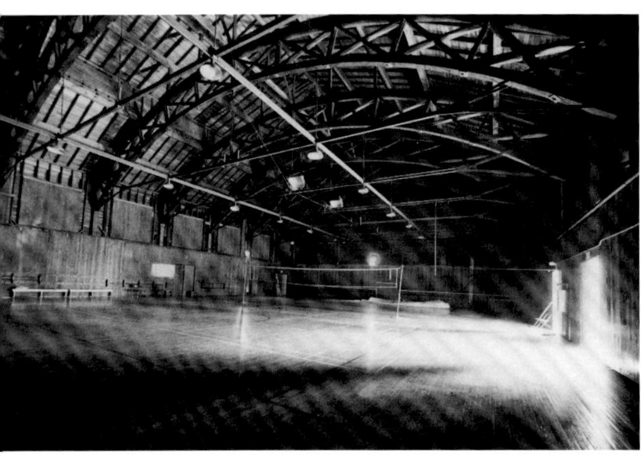

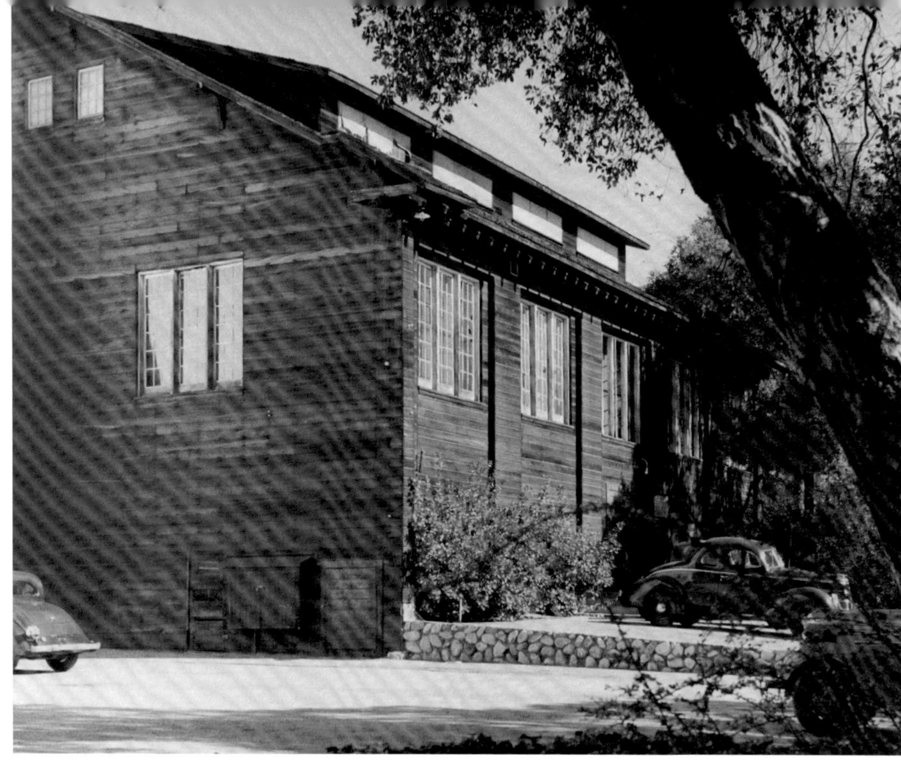

Renwick Gymnasium (Big Gym)

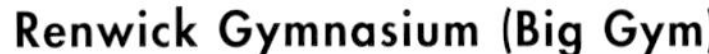

Renwick Gymnasium (Big Gym)

BUILT 1918
PRESIDENT IN OFFICE James A. Blaisdell
LOCATION east of current site of Bridges Auditorium
MATERIALS redwood frame
NAMED FOR William Renwick, late husband of Helen Goodwin Renwick, Claremont, who supported construction of first Renwick gymnasium
COST $16,000 (U.S. government, $10,000; donor $4,000 to prepare as future gymnasium; $2,000 from College)
DEMOLISHED 1982

The second gymnasium on the Pomona campus to bear the Renwick name (see Renwick Gymnasium 1899, Chapter 1), the 1918–19 building known to most as the "Big Gym," was originally constructed during World War I as barracks for the Student Army Training Corps. (The S.A.T.C. was part of a comprehensive government program initiated in May 1918 that used college and university facilities to train newly enlisted young men for military service; Pomona received two companies, housing them in the Claremont Inn, Smiley Hall, and the original Renwick Gymnasium.) From the outset, the College intended the building for eventual use as a gymnasium, and it served this purpose from 1919 until the construction in 1969 of the Pendleton Women's Physical Education Center. When Memorial Gym was dedicated in 1950, both Big and Little gyms were joined under the name Renwick and used primarily for women's physical education; men's facilities were in the Alumni Memorial Training Quarters, constructed east of Smiley in 1921, in memory of Pomona alumni killed in war.

The second Renwick had structural failings, including an incomplete inner east wall that served as a nesting place for pigeons, a honey storage area for bees, and a haven for woodpeckers and their acorns (the last leading to the popular moniker "Woodpecker Haven"). When the original Renwick Gym was destroyed by fire in 1952, students and staff lost their dressing rooms and offices, requiring temporary draperies to create private spaces for the then-required physical examinations of students, and dependence on Sumner Hall for restrooms. Elizabeth Cawthorne, who taught Physical Education from 1935 to 1973, later recalled life in Renwick:

> *"Our 'office' was a place of bedlam, with four desks for staff members and one for a student secretary; it was also the home of all equipment for basketball, badminton, volleyball. . . . I remember trying to interview a prospective staff member in . . . the gym where, amid woodpeckers, buzzing bees and birds flying around in the rafters, we tried to talk. Before we finished, in came a basketball class, so we moved outside. When the woman left, I thought, "If she's not willing to vie for the team of survival of the fittest, she'll decide this is not for her." But she was a survivor, and for many years we've had our fine dance teacher, Jan Hypes."*[1]

Cawthorne also remembered needing gloves to play badminton on winter mornings when the temperature could dip to 35 degrees inside, and an embarrassing episode when a prominent dance educator, on campus to give master classes, found herself drowned out by the sound of woodpeckers and their acorns dropping to the floor. Such dilemmas were once immortalized in a faculty show that featured faculty in woodpecker costumes singing the Woody Woodpecker song, and in the late 1960s, hoping to encourage donations for the beleaguered facility, tours were given during an Alumni Weekend and visitors treated to the dramatization of the building's hazards including heat exhaustion, bee stings, and frost bite.

Improbably, given its condition, Renwick also served a variety of community purposes including College dances and, on one occasion, a performance of the Los Angeles Philharmonic Orchestra. Claremont photographer Robert Frampton recalled actress Marion Davies filming *The Fair Coed* (1927) in Renwick, with townspeople as extras, followed by a dance hosted by William Randolph Hearst, "who sat on a dais with Miss Davies and watched the fun." In 1962, Renwick appeared in the Hollywood movie *The Absent-Minded Professor*, with Fred MacMurray, and in 1978, it served as a set for *Fast Break*, the story of a plucky basketball team at a failing college; to use the increasingly decrepit structure, the production company was required to resurface the floor and remove several thousand bees and their accumulated honey.

In 1980, safety concerns eventually led the Fire Department to refuse to issue a use permit. As reconstruction would have meant rebuilding in a new location (the site was needed for the physical education facility that was part of Pomona's master plan), Renwick was dismantled in 1982, during the tenure of President David Alexander. His recollections convey a poignant sense of the dilemmas faced by administrators responsible for dangerous but still beloved structures:

> *Renwick Gymnasium…was hopelessly inadequate and Memorial Gymnasium was bursting at the seams and suffering from any number of structural maladies. First, the Fire Marshal ordered us to clear the basement of Renwick, where the Theatre Department stored its props. Then we were confronted by an order declaring the building to be a fire hazard. The citizens of Claremont objected to our razing the building, and I was finally forced to write the City saying that the College was caught between the Fire Marshal and public opinion. If we were not given a demolition permit, the city would have to assume liability for the unusable structure. Reason prevailed, and we got the demolition permit. For my sins, one alumnus publicly called me a "thief in the night."*[2] ■

Harwood Hall for Botany

A new hall for science was part of the Million Dollar Campaign, but when that effort failed to provide the needed funds, A.P. Harwood stepped in to pay for a new botany building as a memorial to his son Alfred. The hall, constructed west of Pearsons, in the center of what is now the Academic Quad, was adjoined by a laboratory including both a greenhouse and a lath house. It remained home to Botany until 1942, when that department joined Zoology in Crookshank Hall. At that point, Harwood Hall for Botany became known simply as Harwood Hall, home to the Psychology Department. The building disappeared from the College Catalog and campus maps in 1966 and was quietly demolished in 1968. Reflecting, perhaps, its undistinguished character, there is little record of Harwood Hall in Pomona's archives, and though it was part of the campus for more than half a century, it can be glimpsed in only a handful of remaining photographs. ■

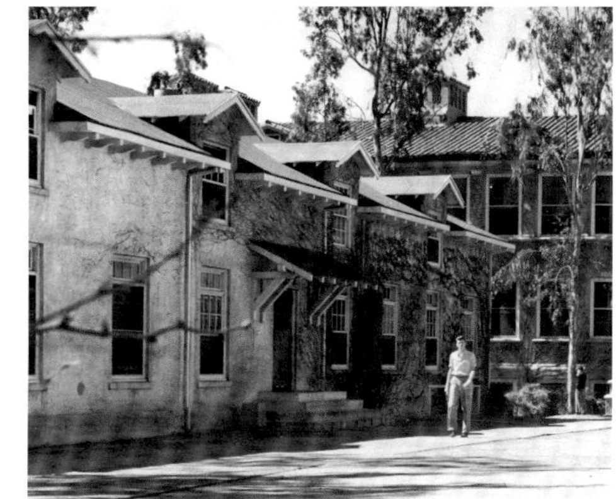

Harwood Hall for Botany

BUILT 1915 (summer)
PRESIDENT IN OFFICE James A. Blaisdell
LOCATION West of Pearsons (no longer extant)
DONOR A.P. Harwood
NAMED FOR Alfred Harwood (son of donor)
ORIGINAL USE Botany
LATER CHANGES/RENOVATIONS/DIFFERENT USES Used for Botany until department moved to Crookshank Hall in 1922, then converted to other uses until demolished
DEMOLISHED 1968

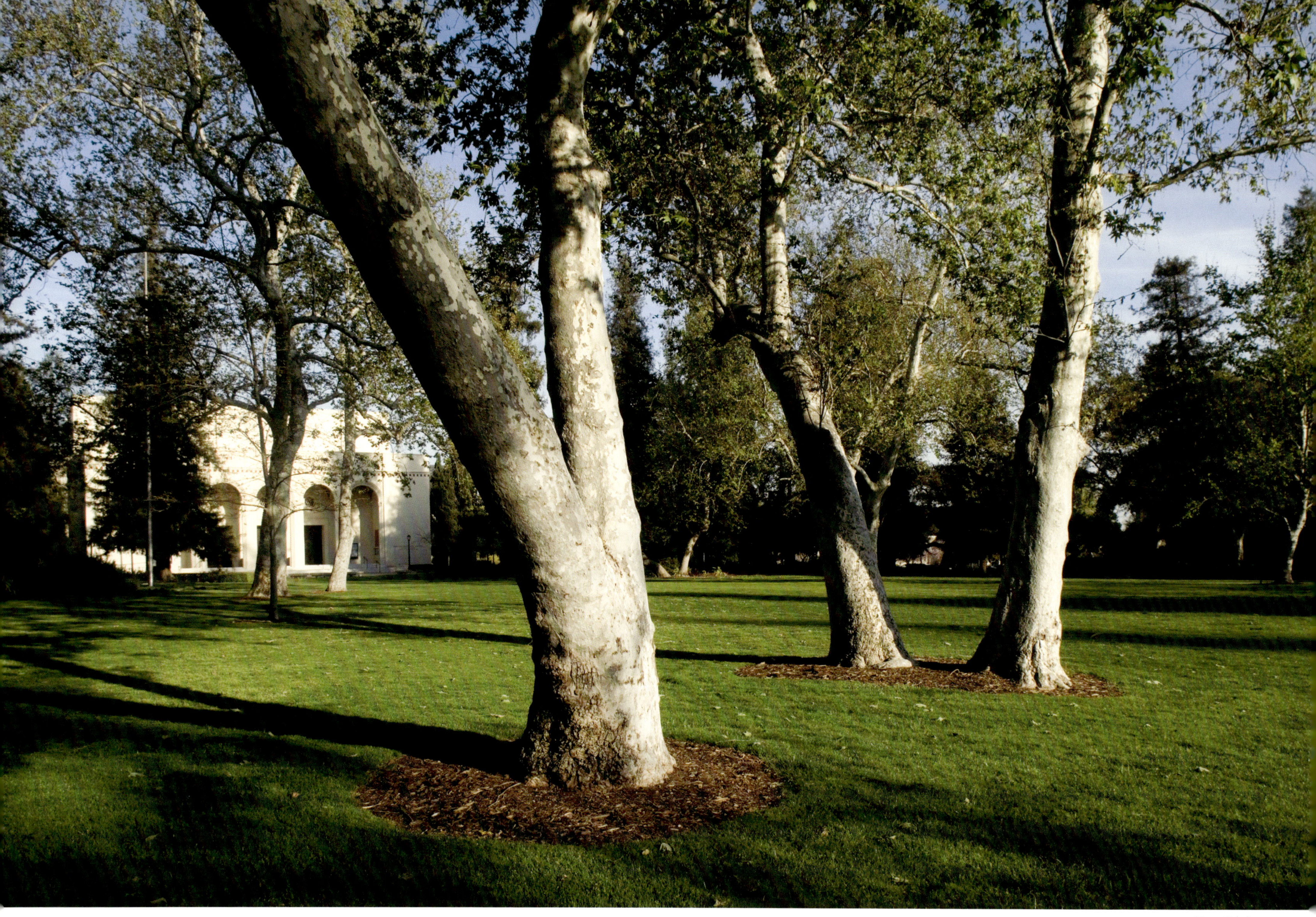

Henry Cabala

Marston Quadrangle

The primary organizing feature of Myron Hunt's 1908 campus plan was a central quadrangle reminiscent of Thomas Jefferson's much-admired design for the University of Virginia in Charlottesville (begun 1817). Like Jefferson's quad, Pomona's would be anchored by a library—Carnegie was newly completed—and flanked by buildings arranged on the north and south. With the quadrangle crossed by axes and vistas, Hunt created a serene garden environment to center the projected academic community (for further discussion see George Gorse's essay on Myron Hunt, Chapter II).

Founding Trustee and longtime Board Chair George W. Marston offered $100,000 to create and endow the central quadrangle. The work was undertaken in 1919, but the need to relocate Sumner Hall delayed the project, which was completed in 1921–22. This was not Marston's first contribution to the development of Pomona's grounds. During the presidency of George Gates, a landscape initiative led by Marston had resulted in the acquisition of Blanchard Park (The Wash) in 1905, and, shortly thereafter, he had funded the landscaping of Carnegie Library.

The landscape architect selected for the quadrangle project was Ralph Cornell '14, a graduate of the Harvard School of Landscape Architecture and the first professional landscape architect to establish a practice in Los Angeles. Marston Quad was Cornell's first work for the College (and the College his first client), and he would continue to oversee Pomona's landscaping for the next 53 years.[3] His design combined lawn, low shrubs around the perimeter, and trees, including an oval of sycamores that focus the longitudinal space. Cornell also designed Stover Walk and Memorial Court; his other work in the area included the median strip of Foothill Boulevard north of the Colleges, and the campus of UCLA. Early in the long (indeed, ongoing) development of the Quad, concrete curbs were laid out, and redwoods and evergreens were planted. The *Pomona College Quarterly* of January 1925 reported that that the boundaries of the Quad were now completed, leaving the main body for later planting and development, and that irrigation and lighting systems had been installed.

As Hunt envisioned, Marston Quadrangle has played a central role in campus life, offering a literal and figurative breathing space whether observed from a distance, traversed on one's way elsewhere, or indulged in for longer periods, as it is routinely by students who find its spacious and shady lawn a haven for reading, sunbathing, sleeping, and more active pursuits, like Frisbee. One sees art students sketching, Shakespeare classes performing, poetry classes reading. At Commencement, the Quad, which suddenly seems vast, overflows with the color of academic robes and celebratory flowers, and the joyful noise—laughs, shouts, camera clicks—of graduates and their families who queue to have pictures taken against the backdrop of the giant sycamore, at the eastern end, with its massive branch that sweeps the ground. In the words of Caroline Potter '04, "In a very real way, this enchanted garden is the heart of Pomona's campus. With its color, foliage and open space, Marston Quad may be precisely what Pomona's founders had in mind for their 'college in a garden.'"[4]

Marston Quadrangle, like all of the College's grounds, is a continuously evolving landscape. Walkways, irrigation systems, and lighting have all been upgraded periodically, and plantings have changed over time in response to changes in taste and, most recently, to environmental concerns such as water conservation. In this effort, drought tolerant and native plants are replacing other species, sprinklers are being replaced with less wasteful drip irrigation, mulch is used to reduce evaporation, and sensors indicate when an area needs to be watered. ■

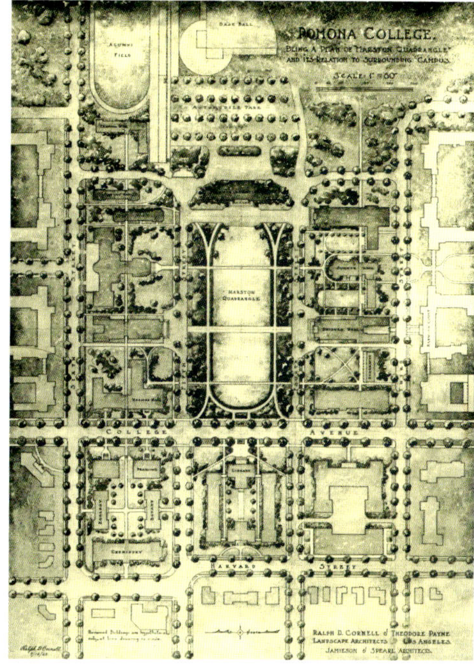

ABOVE *Study for Central Quadrangle, Ralph D. Cornell and Theodore Payne, Landscape Architects, James P. Jamieson and George Spearl, Architects, 1922, drawing*

OPPOSITE *Marston Quadrangle and Bridges Auditorium*

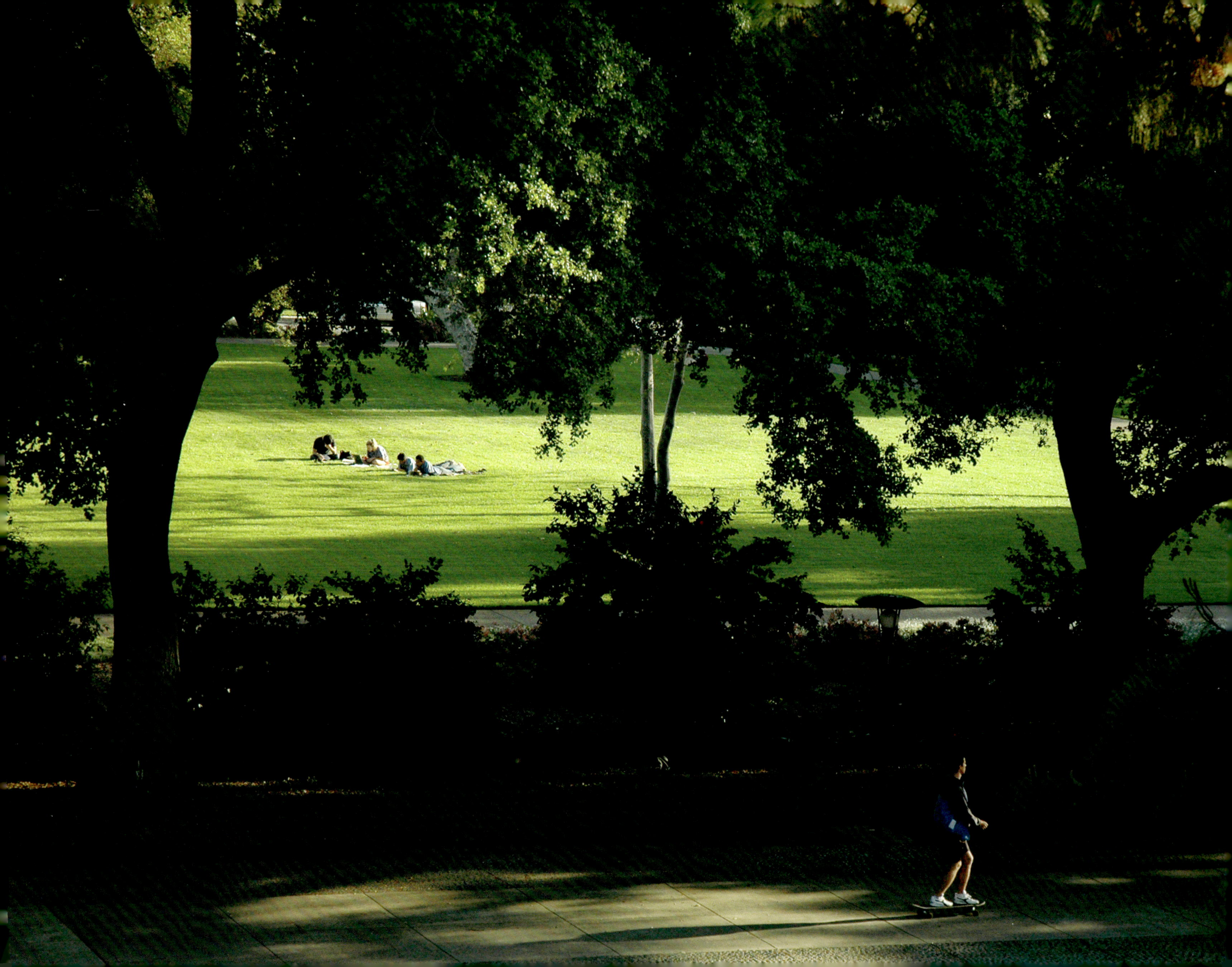

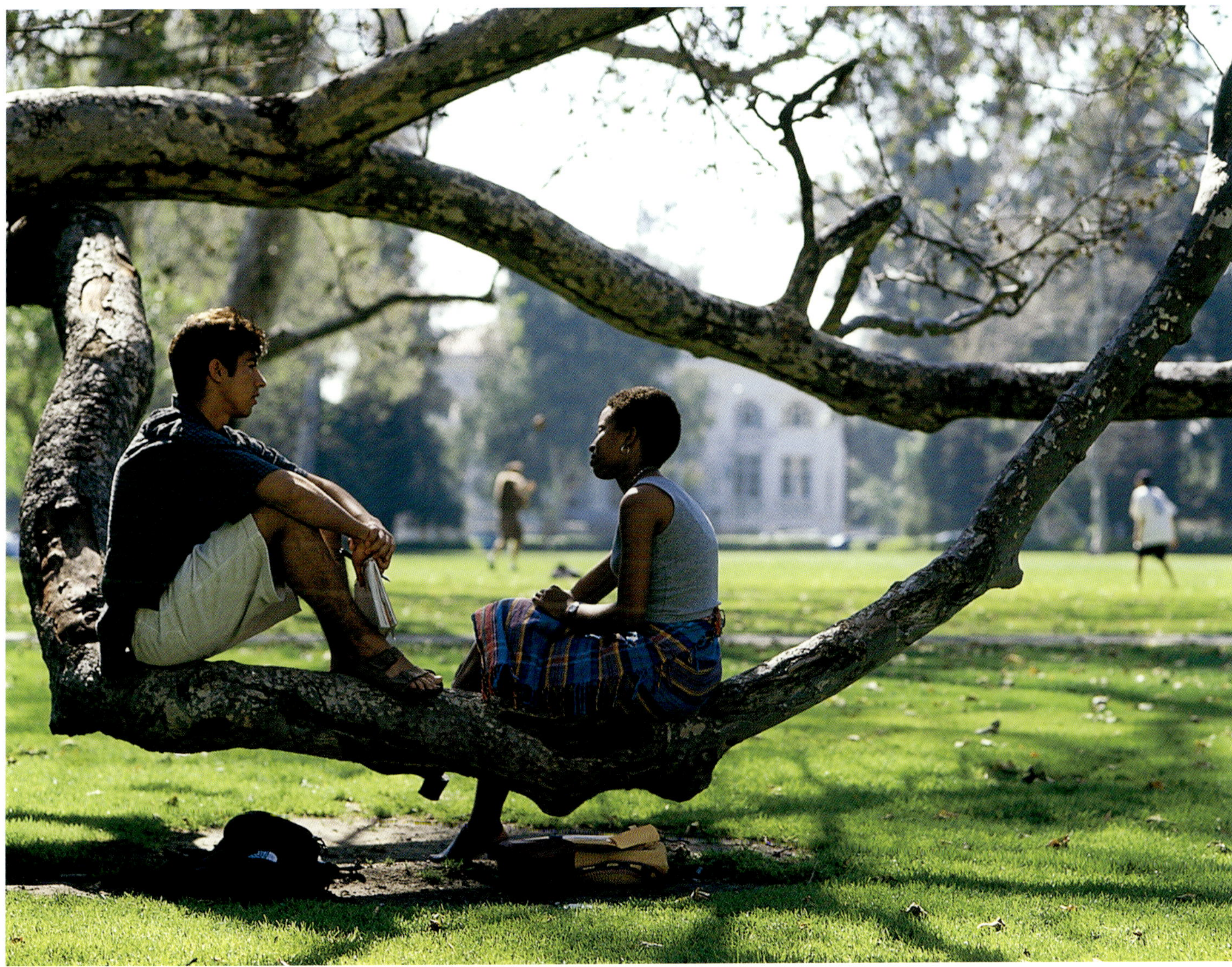

Phil Channing

Carlos Puma

OPPOSITE AND ABOVE *Marston Quadrangle, built 1919–23*

Marston Quadrangle

BUILT 1919–23
PRESIDENT IN OFFICE James A. Blaisdell
LOCATION bordered by College Avenue, College Way, Sixth Street, Fourth Street
ARCHITECT Myron Hunt (general plan); Ralph Cornell '14, landscape architect
COST $100,000 (original gift)
DONOR/NAMED FOR George W. Marston, trustee 1887–1946

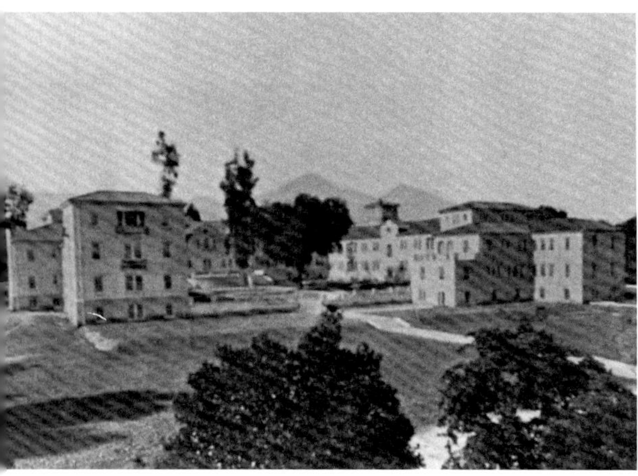

Harwood Court / Harwood Memorial Dining Hall / Olney Dining Hall

BUILT 1919–21; dedicated Feb 22, 1921
PRESIDENT IN OFFICE James A. Blaisdell
LOCATION 170 East Bonita Avenue (east of College Avenue)
PURPOSE/USE Women's dormitory
ARCHITECTS Jamieson and Spearl
MATERIALS stucco, tile roof
COST $200,000 (approx.)
DONORS Judge C.E. Harwood, trustee; Schuyler W. Strong (east wing)
NAMED FOR Memory of Catherine Henry Harwood; late wife of Schuyler Strong
LATER CHANGES 1950, dining room (east) renamed for honorary Trustee Mrs. Warren Olney, Jr.

Harwood Court / Harwood Memorial Dining Hall / Olney Dining Hall

Constructed between 1919 and 1921 to house 135 students, Harwood Court replaced Sumner as the primary residential hall for the College's women. Male students had been housed in Smiley Hall since 1908, and, by 1917, enrollment increases and growing concerns about the safety of wood-frame Sumner Hall led to the decision to construct a women's dormitory. Although construction was postponed because of the war, the site—between First and Third streets, east of College Avenue—along with additional land, was acquired by 1919. Construction costs were supported in part by a $50,000 donation by Trustee Judge C.E. Harwood, and in part by the College; income from room rents, then $125 per student, were expected to offset expenses over time. Still, however, funds were restricted, and construction of the easternmost of the three wings, expected to be delayed, was made possible in 1920 by a gift from businessman Schuyler W. Strong. The dormitory was named in memory of Judge Harwood's late wife Catherine Henry Harwood, and in gratitude for his service to the College; the east wing was named for Schuyler Strong. By September 1920, 100 rooms were ready for students, and the building was completed in February 1921. It immediately became the center of women's life on campus.

Architecturally, Harwood Court's three simple blocks, enlivened by ornamental detail, reflected the influence of Myron Hunt whose signature blend of classicism and Southern California regionalism could be seen in Bridges Hall of Music and its adjoining courtyard (Lebus Court) directly across Third Street. The large, landscaped courtyard that lay behind Harwood's Palladian entrance façade represented a new integration of interior and exterior spaces that took advantage of the local climate and distinguished Harwood from the majority of Pomona's earlier buildings, whose closed plans were derived from Eastern and Midwestern collegiate models. Harwood's elegant design also contrasted with the relative austerity of Myron Hunt's Smiley Hall (1908) and Sumner Spaulding's later Clark men's dormitories (1929), demonstrating an association of style with gender. As architect Robert A.M. Stern has noted, Harwood's handsome courtyard, with its fountain filled with goldfish and water lilies, also reflected an "appreciation of physical fitness and outdoor living that was one of Southern California's great contributions to American life."[5] The building's dedication in February 1921, held in the Greek Theatre, was part of a larger celebration of the 10th anniversary of James Blaisdell's presidency of the College.

Although Harwood Court was widely admired—the 1923 *Metate* judged it "probably the most artistic and beautifully appointed women's dormitory in the country"—and represented significant improvement in accommodations for women students, it was soon judged inadequate. By 1930, with the completion of the Eli P. Clark men's campus and Frary Dining Hall, all of Pomona's male students lived and took their meals on campus; by the same year, Scripps College boasted four completed residence halls with dining facilities and was, likewise, accommodating all of its students on campus. By contrast, Harwood was overcrowded—with 185 students in rooms planned for 135—and even by using nearby cottages, the College was still housing half its women students in privately-run boarding houses near campus. Dean of Women Jessie E. Gibson, who had been appointed in 1927, appealed to President Blaisdell: "The splendid and adequate new residence units for Pomona men and the attractive residences halls for women at Scripps provide a contrast with the conditions under which Pomona women live which is hard to meet."[6]

OPPOSITE *Harwood Court, entrance on Bonita Avenue*

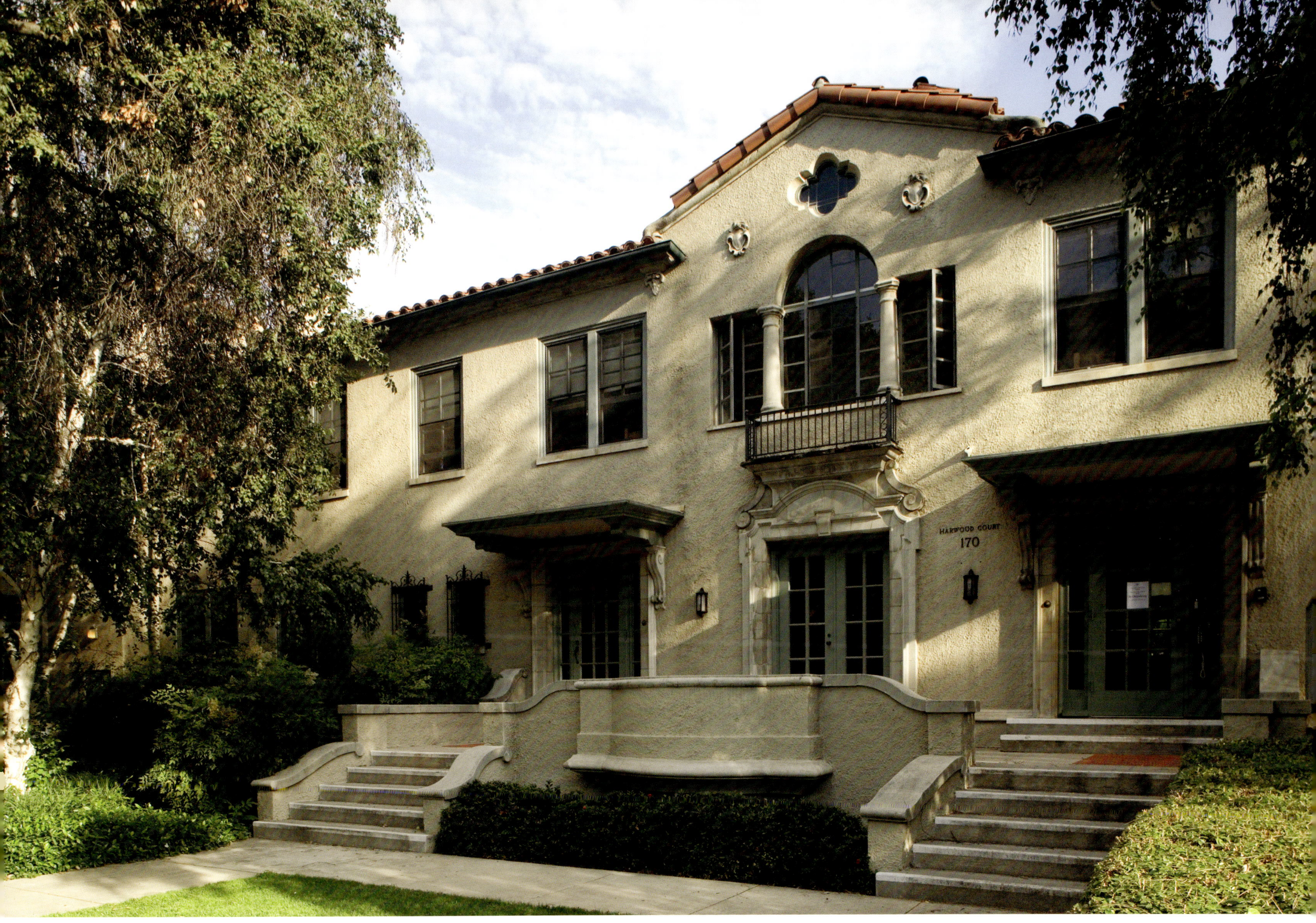

Henry Cabala

The first response to this dilemma was the addition of a kitchen and dining hall on the southern side of the building in 1930–31, a gift of the children of C.E. Harwood in memory of their sister Aurelia Squire Harwood, who had been the first woman president of the Sierra Club. Designed by Webber and Spaulding (architects of Clark/Frary), the hall featured high ceilings, bay windows, and pillared archways. Its completion marked the end of 25 years of student dining at the Claremont Inn. The kitchen was expanded and additional seats were added in 1935, when it became clear that its original size was no longer adequate. The opening of Frank Dining Hall in 1982 marked the end of the useful life of Harwood Dining Hall, and the building was demolished in 1987.

In 1974, Harwood Court underwent reconstruction to fulfill the city's fire and earthquake regulations, as well as to add 39 new beds. Other changes included a newly fire-resistant roof and renovated interiors. Construction was scheduled to be completed during the summer, but several workers' strikes in the building trades unions left the work unfinished at the time fall semester began. Students were housed at Griswold's Inn, in Claremont, until October, when the construction was finished. The building was further renovated in 1992 to provide wheelchair access and update the structure—an endeavor that was not without its drama. While attempting to remove vines from the building's exterior, workmen accidentally set the attic on fire. Twelve fire trucks were required to extinguish the flames as the disaster threatened to destroy the entire building.

In recent times, the residence hall has become famous for its Harwood Halloween celebration—an annual event rumored to be one of the nation's most rambunctious parties. Articles in *The Student Life* over the years have debated whether the bash should be the financial responsibility of Harwood residents. Although still known as "Harwood Halloween," it is no longer held in the residence hall's courtyard and student fees cover the expenses of the evening. ■

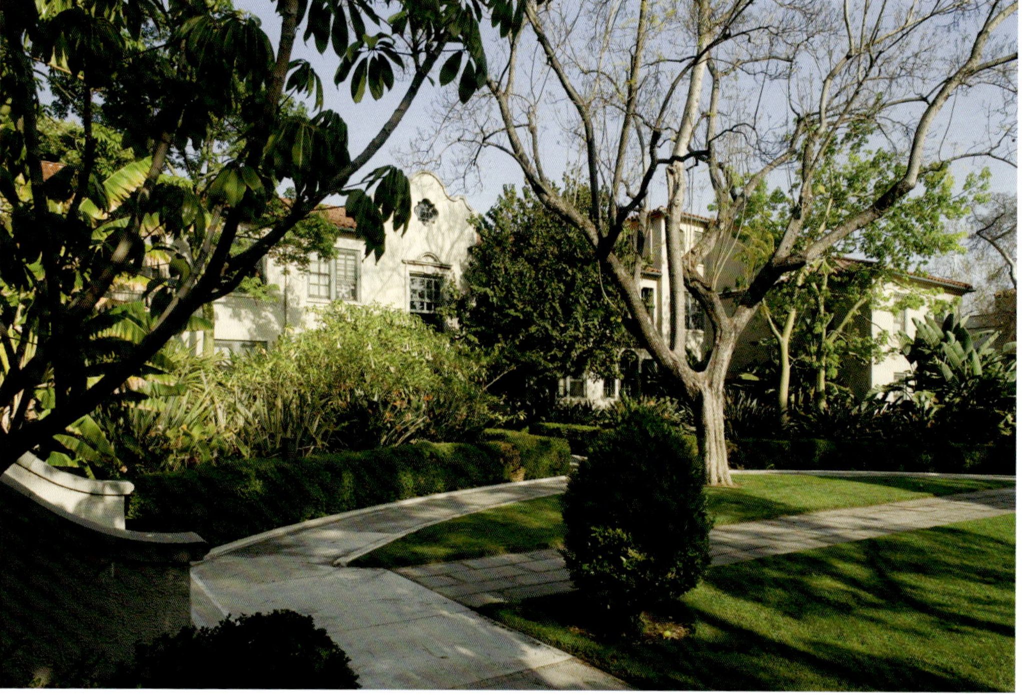

Henry Cabala

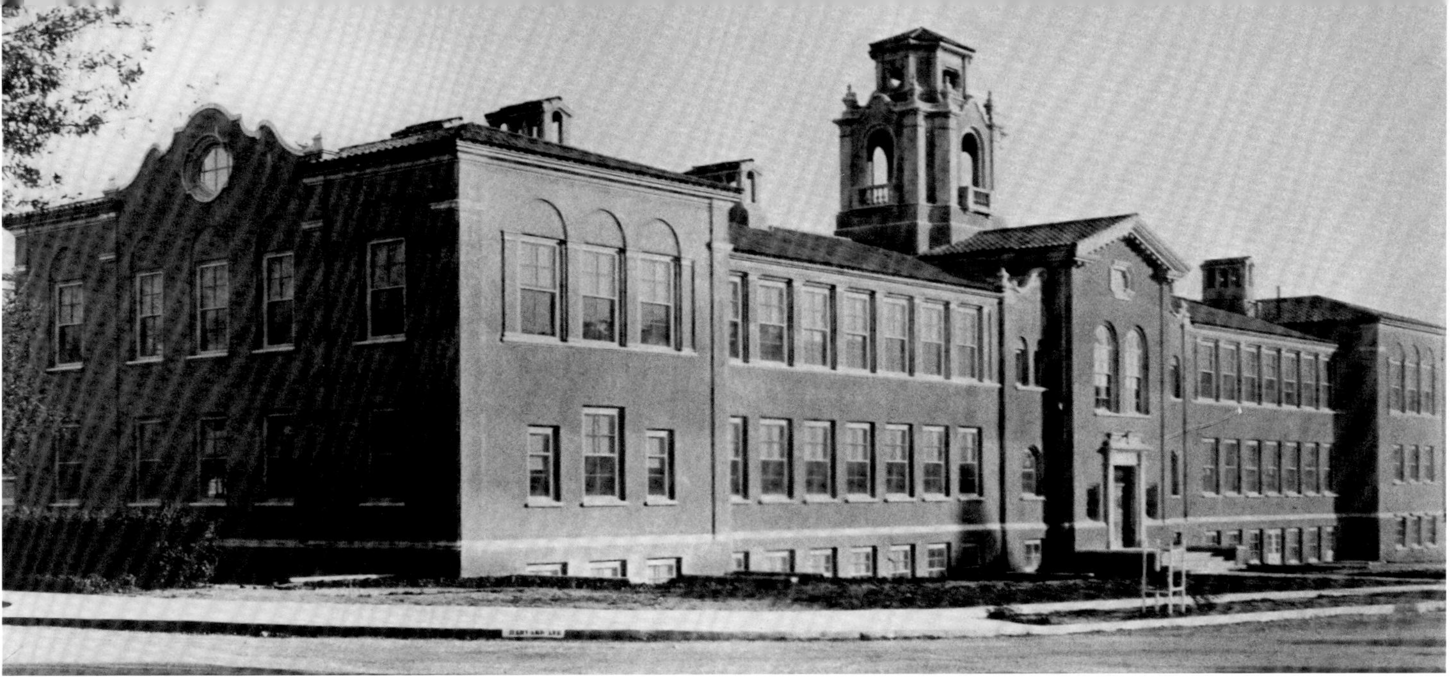

Mason Hall of Chemistry

In 1923, students and faculty at the College were excited to see the completion of construction of Mason Hall, a state-of-the-art chemistry facility. The impressive reinforced concrete structure stretched the entire length of the block from Fifth to Sixth streets on Harvard Avenue; then the westernmost of Pomona's buildings, it extended the boundaries of the campus. Wilson Lyon wrote that the building was considered "an ornament to the campus and to the city," not only for its design, which included an imposing tower, but also because its more than one acre of laboratory space and up-to-date science facilities were among the most coveted in the nation.

Planning for Mason Hall was initiated by a gift from Chicago businessman, philanthropist, and College Trustee William S. Mason; Mason, a friend of Judge Charles G. Neely who had taught Constitutional History and Law at Pomona since 1912, had, in 1915, covered the cost of landscaping the south side of Sixth Street between Harvard and Dartmouth avenues. According to Neely's remarks at the dedication of Mason Hall, Mr. Mason, who had requested that his name not be mentioned, had visited the College one day and asked President Blaisdell what was needed. When a women's dormitory, an athletic field, and a gymnasium were suggested, Mason seemed uninterested, but he was excited about the idea of a chemistry building, and thus the building was conceived.

Mason's first thought was to extend Pearsons Hall to create improved facilities for chemistry, but over the course of several years, it was decided that an entirely new building would be constructed. With the onset of war, the cost of the projected building nearly doubled. Mason cemented his position as a great friend of the College by donating $100,000 over and above the $200,000 he had already given. The design of the building followed the recommendations of Associate Professor Edward P. Bartlett, who had studied the newest chemistry facilities throughout the country. Bartlett was determined that Pomona would be "one of the strongholds of chemistry in the Southwest," and the completion of Mason Hall launched a new era of science at Pomona College. In Wilson Lyon's words: "The two stories and basement of Mason Hall of Chemistry, with its eighty rooms and an acre of laboratory space, must have seemed a paradise to the students and faculty who previously had known only the chemical laboratories in the basement of Pearsons Hall."[7]

Mason Hall of Chemistry

BUILT 1923 (dedicated March 24, 1923 along with Memorial Training Quarters, Crookshank Hall of Zoology and reconstructed Sumner Hall)
PRESIDENT IN OFFICE James A. Blaisdell
LOCATION 550 North Harvard Avenue between Fifth and Sixth Streets
PURPOSE Chemistry; also housed Geology
MATERIALS reinforced concrete, tile roof
COST $200,000 (building and equipment; ($50,000 endowment each for building and grounds)
DONOR/NAMED FOR William S. Mason
RENOVATED 2007 (WWCOT)
CURRENT USE Languages and History

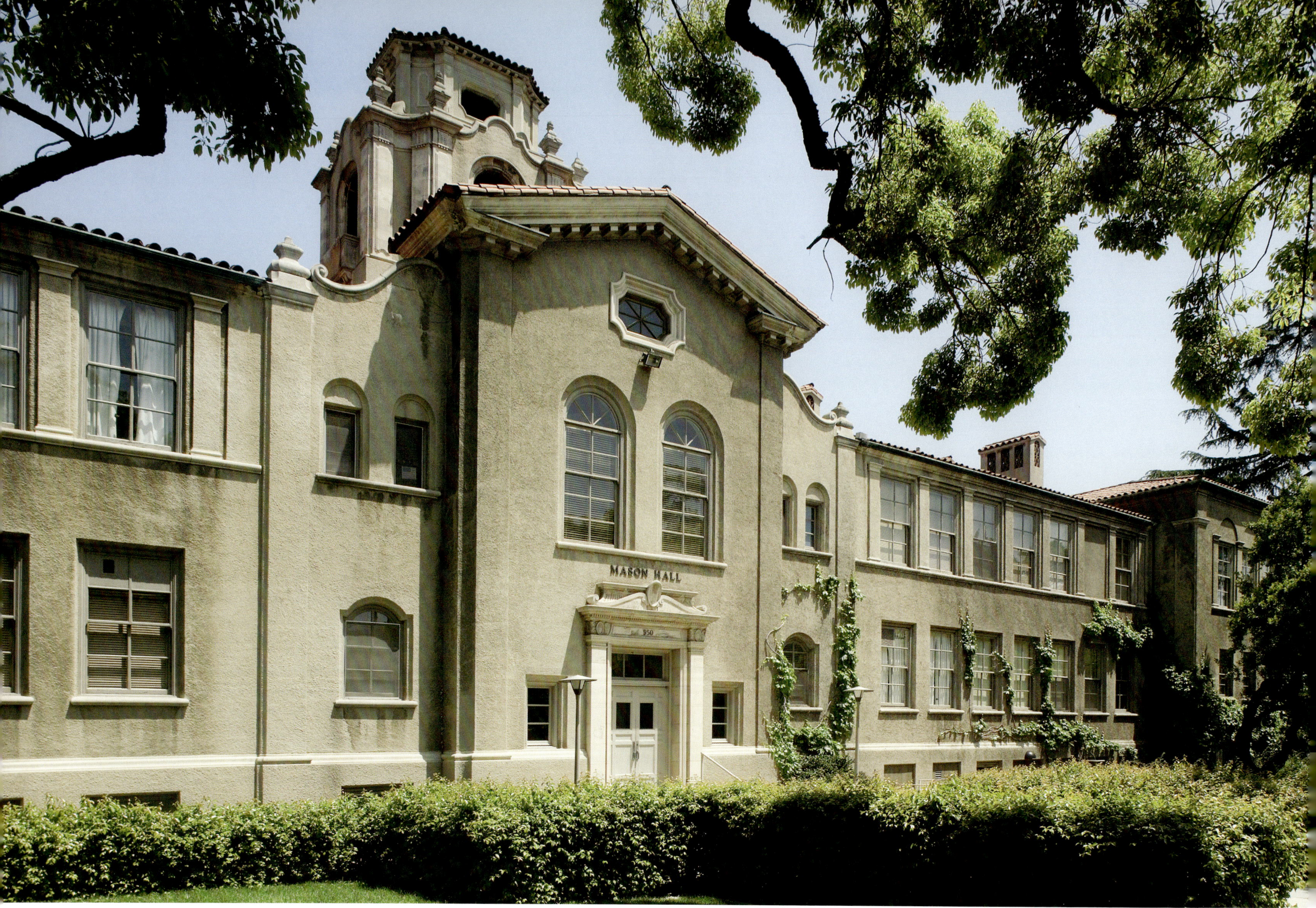

Henry Cabala

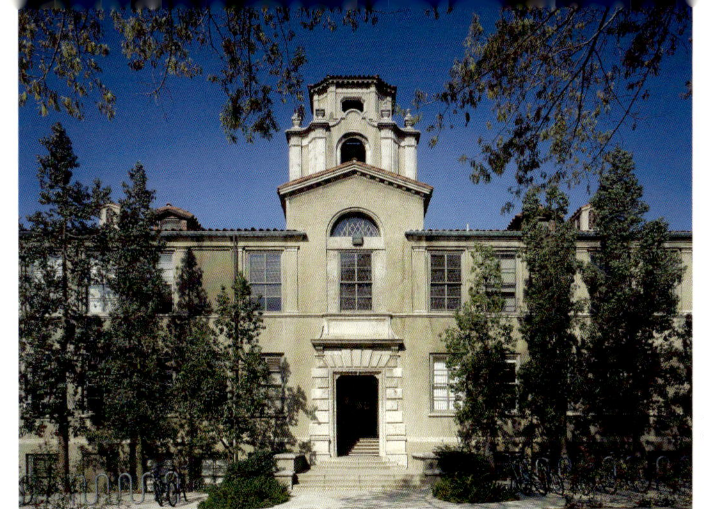

Henry Cabala

Mason Hall served as the College's chemistry facility until 1965, when the new Seaver Chemistry Laboratory opened. At that time, in a remodeling that cost approximately $500,000, Mason was converted into a home for Psychology, Modern European Languages (newly formed by the unification of former departments of German, Romance Languages, and Russian), and Chinese Language and Literature. The remodeled structure, completed in 1966, contained new and greatly improved psychology facilities, including laboratories for the department's animal, social and child research; a library space for displaying the College's Asian art collection; and language laboratories with 36 individual, soundproof booths overseen by a full-time director. The handsome and spacious classrooms and offices were a welcome contrast to the tiny quarters previously allotted to language faculty in Holmes Hall. According to Wilson Lyon, the "successful conversion of Mason Hall set a new standard for subsequent reconstruction of other historic Pomona buildings."[8] At the same time, the new Mason enhanced the quadrangle shared with Crookshank and Pearsons halls. In 2003, Mason's large and, by then, underutilized lecture hall (Room 101) was converted into two floors of faculty offices for the newly created department of Linguistics and Cognitive Science.

Reminiscence:

Coming from my home in the Arizona desert, Pomona College was a cool green oasis—grass, trees, ivy everywhere. I'd never seen so much green all in one place. The classically styled buildings, with their open stairways, echoing halls, and long rectangular windows, made me feel worthy of the education I was about to get. I was the first in my family to go to college, so every impression weighed on my future, and Pomona's physical impressions felt like the weight of a better destiny than I had ever imagined.

As a psychology major and Chinese language minor, I spent a lot of time in Mason Hall. In the lower southwest corner of Mason is a tiny room hidden from the main corridor of the building. You turn right and walk down a few steps, then left into this room large enough for about four people, with beautiful radiant light streaming through two tall windows. Apparently the room was once used as a staging area for talks given in a lecture hall nearby, but by the 1980s no one really staged their talks, so it was empty most of the time. A small blackboard was mounted on the wall. I was fortunate enough to be a teaching assistant for Dr. Bill Banks during my years at Pomona, and I held my "office hours" in this room. When I discovered that it was usually empty, I used it as my private reading nook as well and spent many an afternoon soaking up cognitive psychology beneath those generous windows.

Today, I'm a professor of psychology at a public liberal arts college in the Rocky Mountains of Colorado. Every now and then, while explaining something to a student during office hours, I think back to that magical room where I first tried writing with chalk and thinking out loud. What a privilege it was. —Janet L. Jones, '84 ■

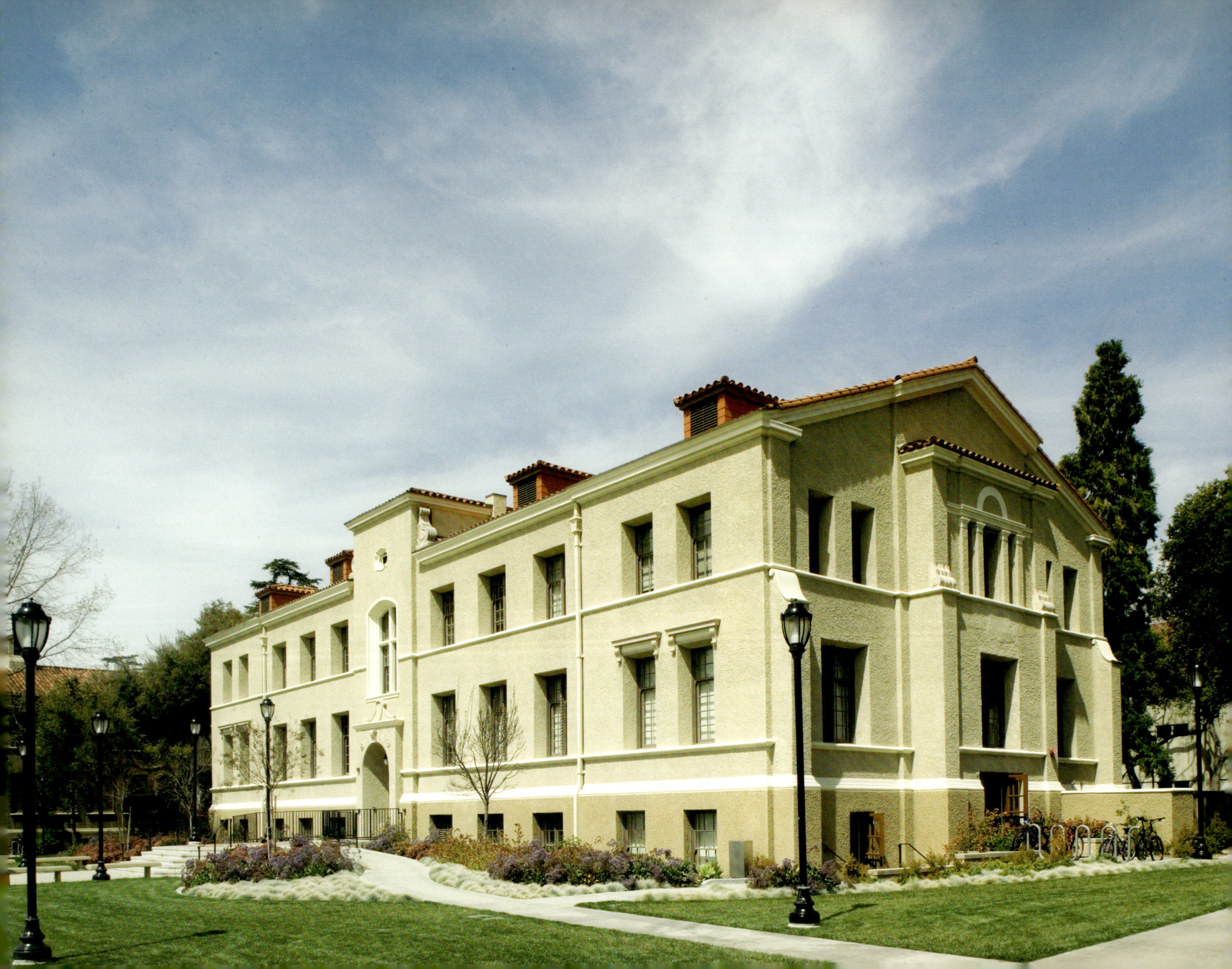

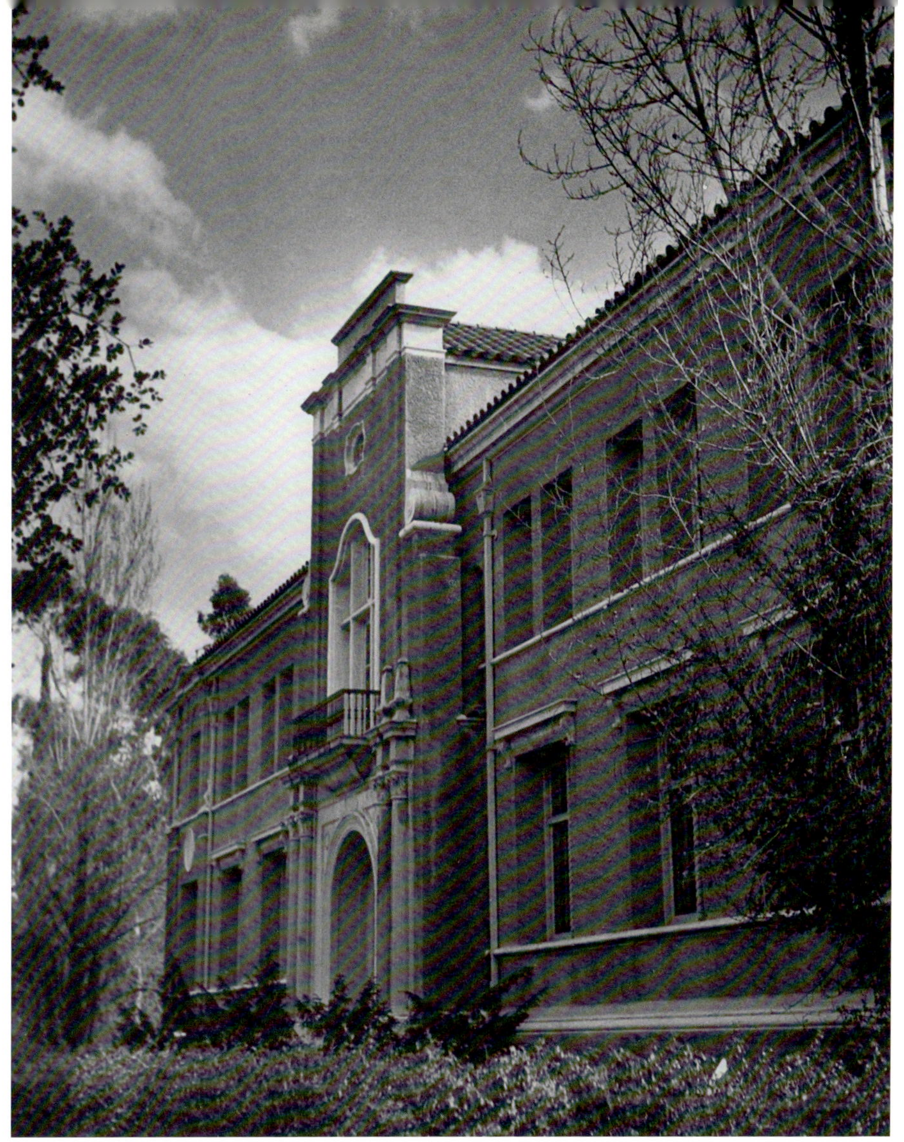

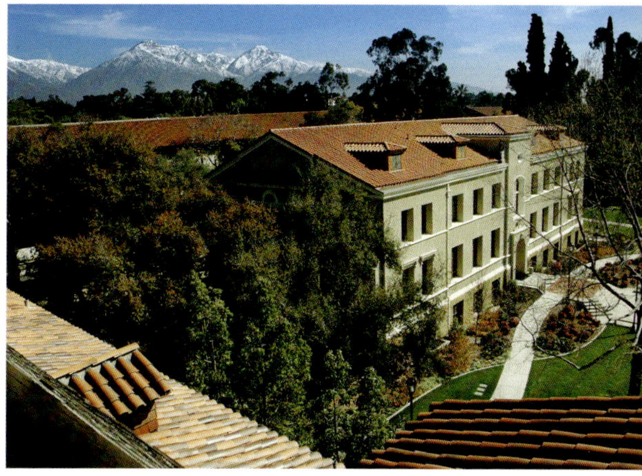

Mark Wood

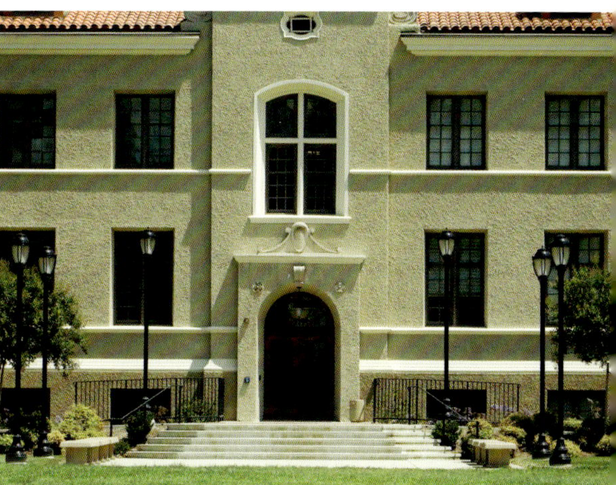

Mark Wood

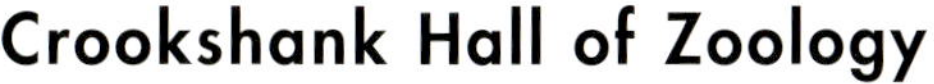

Crookshank Hall of Zoology

The north side of Pomona's science quadrangle took form more quickly than anticipated. In 1921, with plans already in the works for Mason Hall, another friend of the College, David Carnes Crookshank, offered to give a building for Zoology. Crookshank owned citrus acreage in La Verne and was a member of the board of directors of the California Fruit Growers Exchange. He was also a contractor—his work for the College had included the renovation of Holmes Hall and the construction of Harwood Court—who foresaw the benefits of combining construction projects. Although his donation of $100,000 to the College came in the form of common stock and bonds (from the Keystone Iron and Steel Works in Los Angeles), the trustees worked out financing that allowed the project to be undertaken at the same time as Mason Hall. Taking advantage of a dramatically rapid course of events, President Blaisdell, during morning chapel on April 25, 1921, announced that construction was set to begin immediately. As Charles Burt Sumner wrote: "The assembly was excused, marched to the ground, and at the President's word the steam shovel started the work."

Henry Cabala

ABOVE AND OPPOSITE *Crookshank Hall of Zoology, built 1922*

RIGHT *Crookshank Hall, Bonita Avenue entrance*

FAR RIGHT *Crookshank Hall, seminar room*

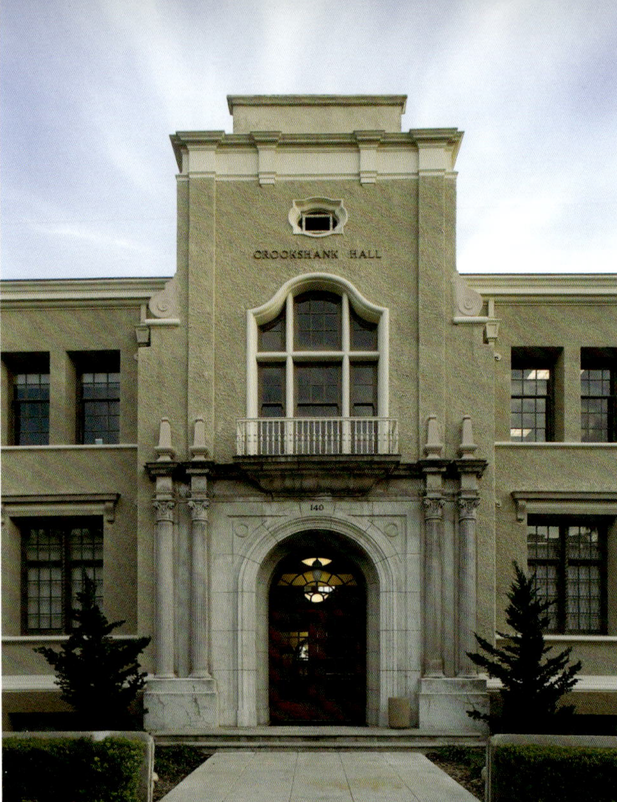

Henry Cabala

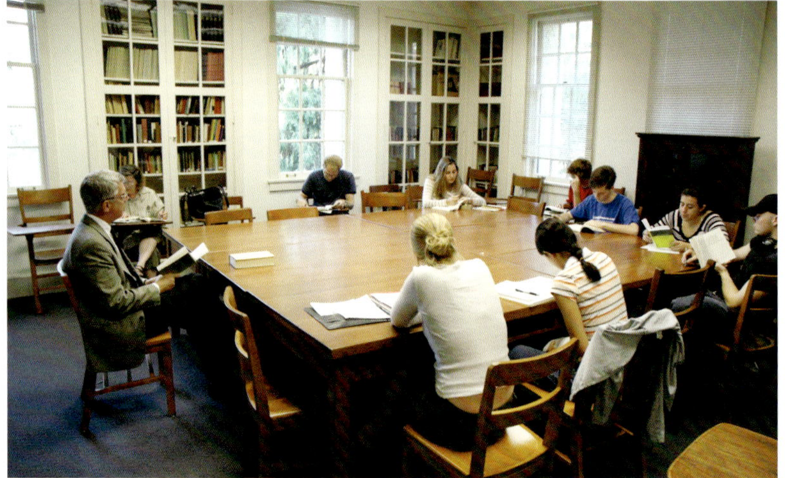

Carlos Puma

Crookshank Hall of Zoology

BUILT 1922; dedicated March 24, 1923 (along with Memorial Training Quarters, Mason Hall of Chemistry, and reconstructed Sumner Hall)
PRESIDENT IN OFFICE James A. Blaisdell
LOCATION 140 West Sixth Street (between Harvard and College Avenues)
PURPOSE Zoology/Botany
ARCHITECT Robert Orr; Jamieson and Spearl
MATERIALS reinforced concrete, tile roof
DONOR/NAMED FOR David Carnes Crookshank
RENOVATED Upgraded 1950s; remodeled 1977 (Criley and McDowell) for English, Classics; renovated 2003–04 (Brian Bloom)

Crookshank Hall's facilities—21,000 square feet of laboratories and classrooms designed with the participation of Zoology Professor William Atwood Hilton—could accommodate 200 students working simultaneously. The building was shared with Botany and housed that department's herbarium. Along with the equally new Mason Hall, and with improvements in Pearsons Hall for Physics and Mathematics, Pomona now boasted state-of-the-art facilities that would serve for years to come.

Crookshank was rededicated in 1977 when the building was remodeled for the Classics and English departments. The $364,000 renovation began in the fall of 1976, and included moving the Botany department across the street into the new Seaver Laboratory. Crookshank's interior was updated with new carpets, furniture, and modernized restrooms in addition to 10 classrooms and several faculty offices. A reading room and library named after Ena H. Thompson (1888–1980), a generous patron of the College, was also part of the renovated building.[9]

In 2003, Crookshank was again renovated as part of a $4.9 million project including the new Seaver Biology Building and an updating of Mason Hall. While the large-scale changes to the building included seismic upgrades, an elevator, and new utilities infrastructure, students and faculty responded particularly to the sensitively restored interior of the building. Spacious faculty offices (larger than any on campus) were equipped with floor-to-ceiling wooden bookshelves, complete with rolling ladders, and the Mulhauser Seminar Room quickly gained fame for its gargantuan, 12-foot diameter table.

Professor Martha Andresen, Chair of the English Department, was particularly entranced by the redesign of the interiors. "They built in more elegance and made it more functional, while keeping the integrity of the building and fostering the sense of relationship between students and faculty," she commented in an article in *Pomona College Magazine*. ■

Henry Cabala

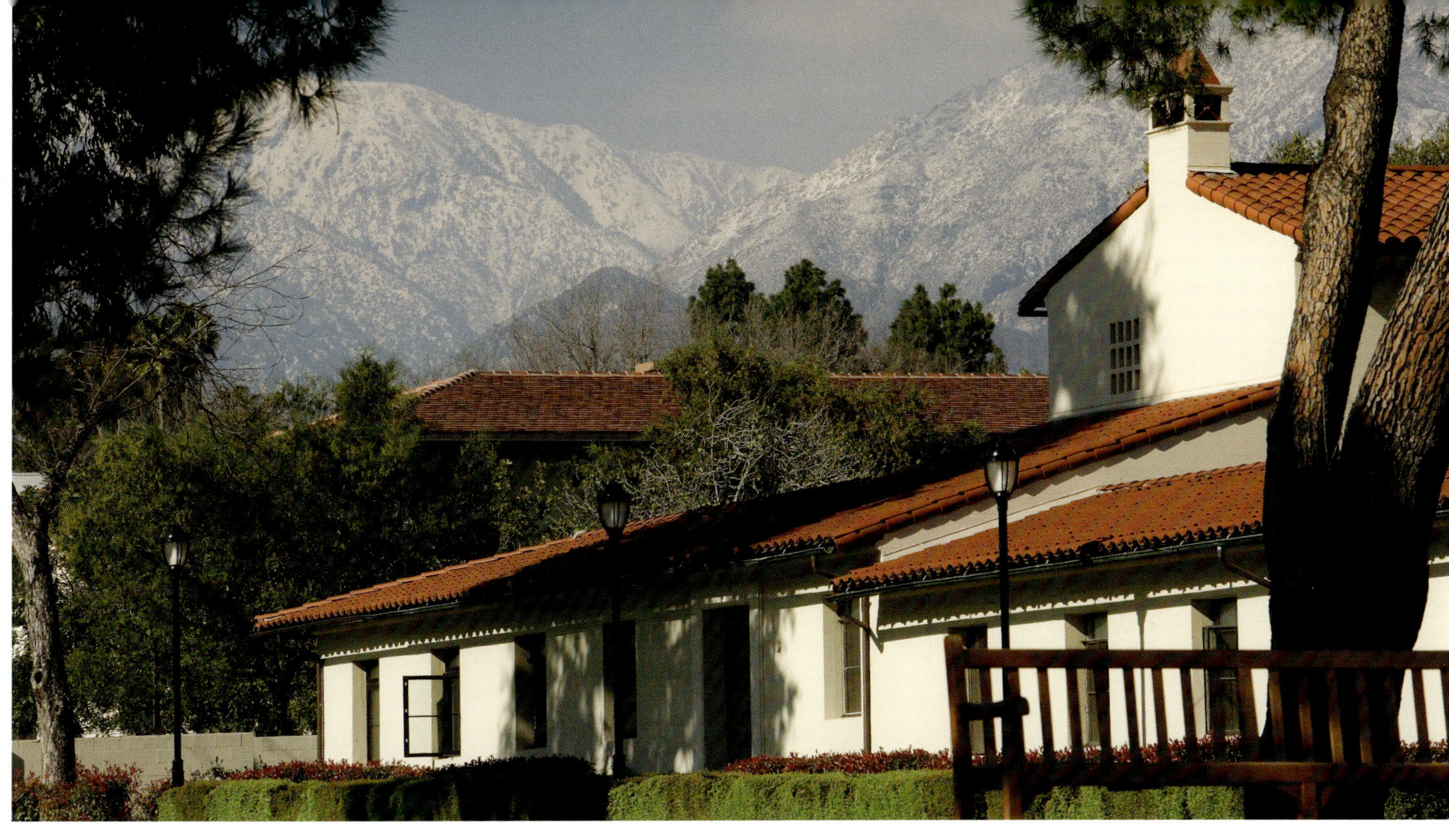

Clark I dormitory

Eli P. Clark Dormitories

At the time of his inauguration in 1928 as Pomona's fifth president, Charles K. Edmunds identified residential needs as primary. It was fortunate that funds for creating a men's campus were already in hand. In 1920, during the tenure of President James Blaisdell, Board Vice-President Eli P. Clark had donated to the College 150 acres of land at the mouth of Las Flores Canyon (now Malibu). Then valued at $10,000, the parcel was sold in 1926 for $600,000 to a land company owned by William Randolph Hearst. It was immediately suggested that the resulting "Clark Trust," which was designated for capital improvement, be used for dormitories. In November 1926, the trustees approved a contract with architect Sumner Spaulding, of Webber and Spaulding, Los Angeles, for a men's residence that, it was hoped, would be under way by 1927. In fact, construction was delayed by financing issues and indecision about the site and scale of the project, and did not begin until February 1929. The single unit of dormitories and refectory that had been approved were completed by fall 1929 and dedicated on October 12, and two more units were completed by September 1930; after that date, work on the men's campus was halted until 1953.

Eli P. Clark, for whom the men's campus was named, was an Iowa native and a civic, philanthropic and social leader in Los Angeles. With General M.H. Sherman, brother of his wife, he formed Los Angeles Consolidated Railway Company, the first successfully operated street railway system in California. In 1898, the city lines were purchased by Henry Huntington and became the Pacific Electric "Red Car" system. Clark served as a college trustee from 1909 until his death in 1931.

Architect Sumner Spaulding had studied in Europe from 1921 to 1926, and it was there that he met President Blaisdell during the latter's yearlong leave of absence in 1925–26. When hired by Pomona several years later, Spaulding had just completed the design for the Los

Eli P. Clark Dormitories

BUILT 1929–30
PRESIDENT IN OFFICE Charles K. Edmunds
LOCATION Between Dartmouth and Amherst Avenues, Sixth and Eighth Streets (Clark I, 328 East Eighth Street; Clark V, 225 East Sixth Street)
PURPOSE Men's dormitory and refectory
ARCHITECT Sumner Spaulding (Webber and Spaulding, Los Angeles)
MATERIALS reinforced concrete, tile roof
COST $305,000 (first dorm unit, Eli P. Clark Hall and refectory (Frary Hall); $450,000 for two additional dormitory units)
DONOR/NAMED FOR Eli P. Clark, Vice-President of the Board

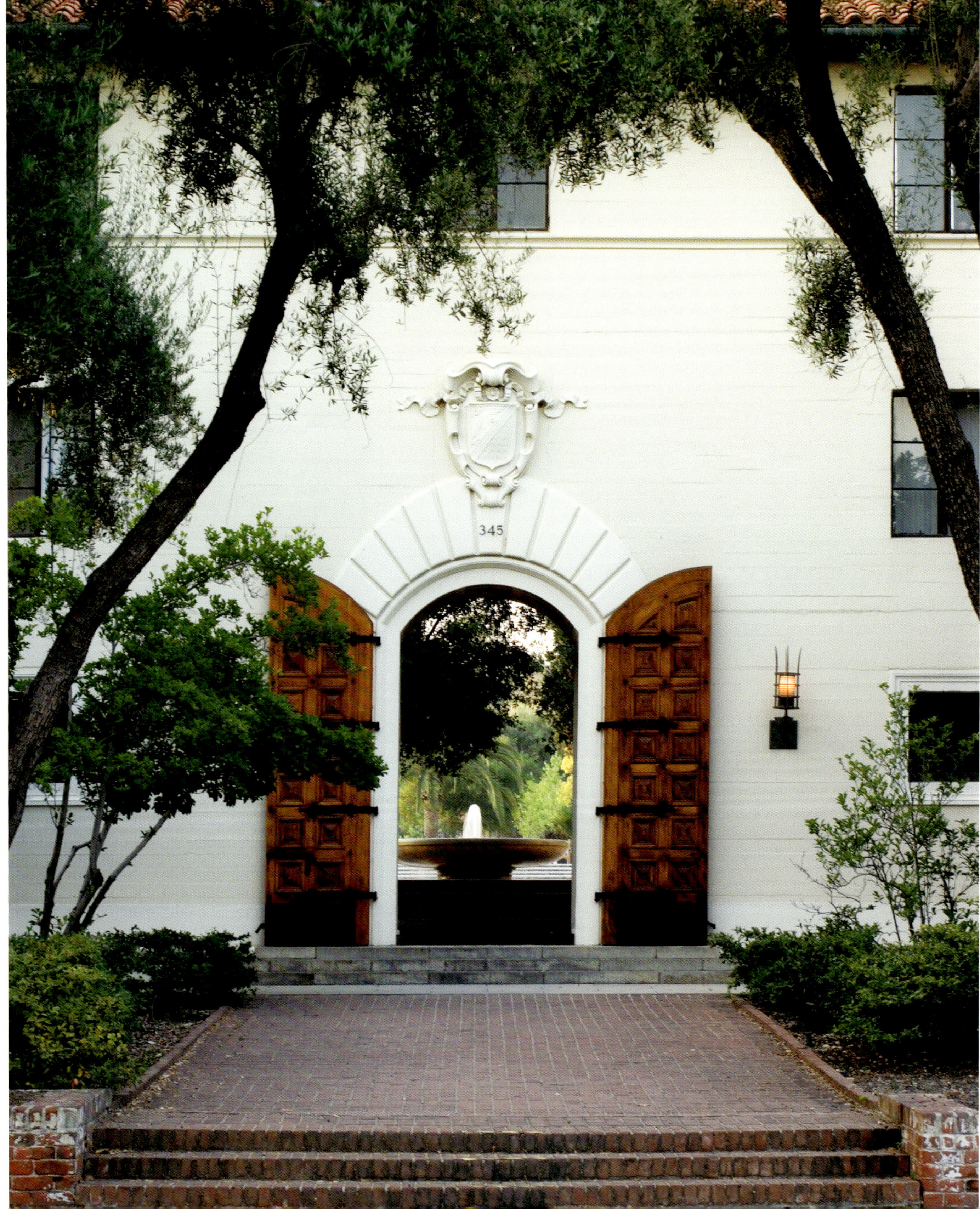

Sophomore Arch, Clark II

Henry Cabala

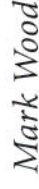

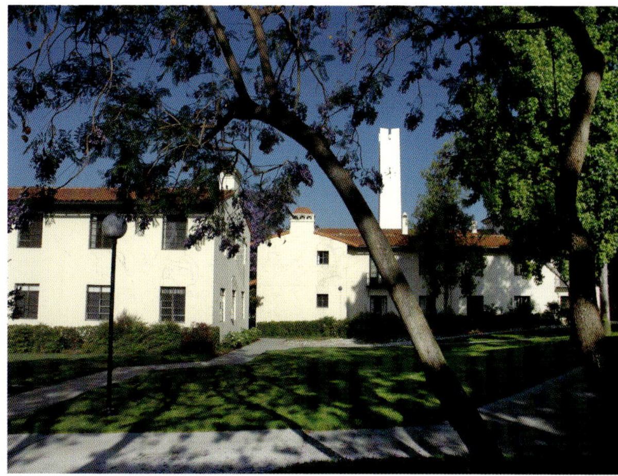

Angeles Civic Center. His design for Pomona's dormitories and refectory, which were constructed of light-colored reinforced concrete with red tile roofs, was consistent with existing campus buildings, particularly those of Myron Hunt. At the same time, the Romanesque arches, cloistered walks, intimate courtyards, spacious plaza with fountain, and such details as the carved wooden door leading into the dining hall, all reflected the architect's recent exposure to European architecture, particularly that of Spain where he had traveled in the Balearic Islands. According to architect Robert A.M. Stern, the Clark dormitories and Frary Hall, created "in the spirit of (Myron) Hunt's vision…marked a major evolution in the growing college as well as in its architecture."

Spaulding's original plan for the men's campus projected eight units: four residence halls, a lounge, an assembly room, and a tower. The first to be built, Eli P. Clark Hall (now called Clark 1), provided residences for 108 freshmen, a faculty adviser, and three instructors. Their design reflected features Blaisdell had admired at Oxford: student rooms, many with fireplaces, grouped around courtyards, most accessible directly from outside. As at Oxford, every Pomona student in Clark had his own room, whether a single or part of a suite. In 1930, two additional dormitories accommodating 175 upperclassmen were added to Clark Campus; along with Clark I and Smiley Hall, Pomona now had residences for 342 men. By 1930, then, men's living had been transformed, and almost all male students were now housed on campus and dining in Frary Hall. Pomona men, George Marston, noted, "lived like kings," a fact that accentuated the lesser quality of the now-overcrowded women's residence, Harwood Court.

In 1956, the Clark campus was extended to the west by an addition—Norton Hall—on Sixth Street at College Way (see Chapter IV, Norton Hall).

Reminiscence:

How many Pomona grads remember the time when women were encouraged to live in Clark? Indeed during the World War II years with the low enrollment of men and the departure of the ASTP program from campus, women (including myself and my freshman suite-mate) were so assigned and a great time we had for the next two years!

We were housed in the western section of Clark—suites of four single rooms and a bath built around several adjoining patios, as well as in the "dorm" section just to the east of the steps leading from Sixth Street up to the fountain area. Here, where my brother "Linc" Spaulding '36 had lived, the rooms of more traditional design opened off long cinder-block corridors with a single, multi-stall bath. (Some of the facilities intended specifically for men were discreetly covered with unpainted plywood.)

We ate at Frary, cafeteria-style, for all meals, and the food was surprisingly good considering wartime rationing. As I recall, however, "heels" were still expected for dinner wear.

Mice also managed to live in the dorm walls, and I remember midnight trappings in my wastebasket to catch "treats" for the Zoology Department snake." —Lois Spaulding Harmsen '47 ■

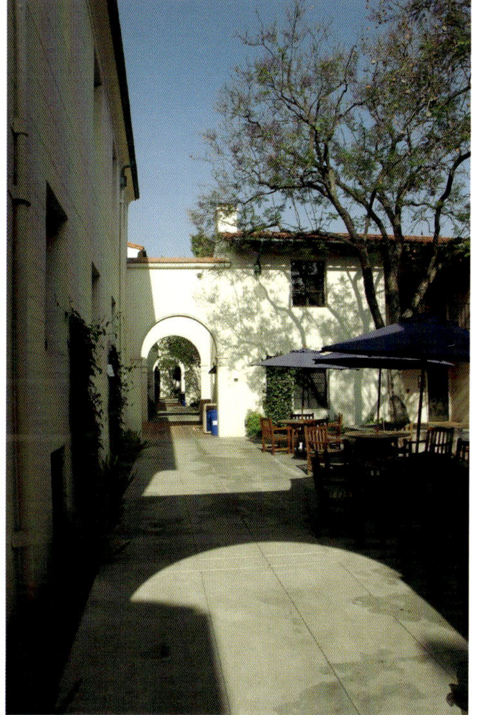

Mark Wood

Norton Hall

Clark V courtyard

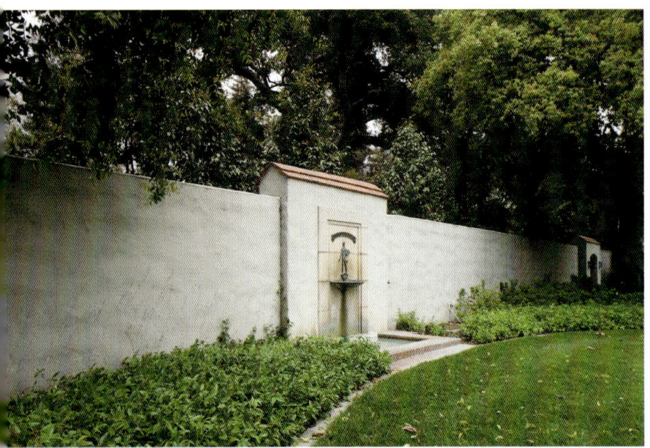

Henry Cabala

Memorial Court, wall fountain and sculpture by Burt Johnson, Theodore Edwin Norton Memorial Fountain, c. 1923, bronze, Gift of the Class of 1915

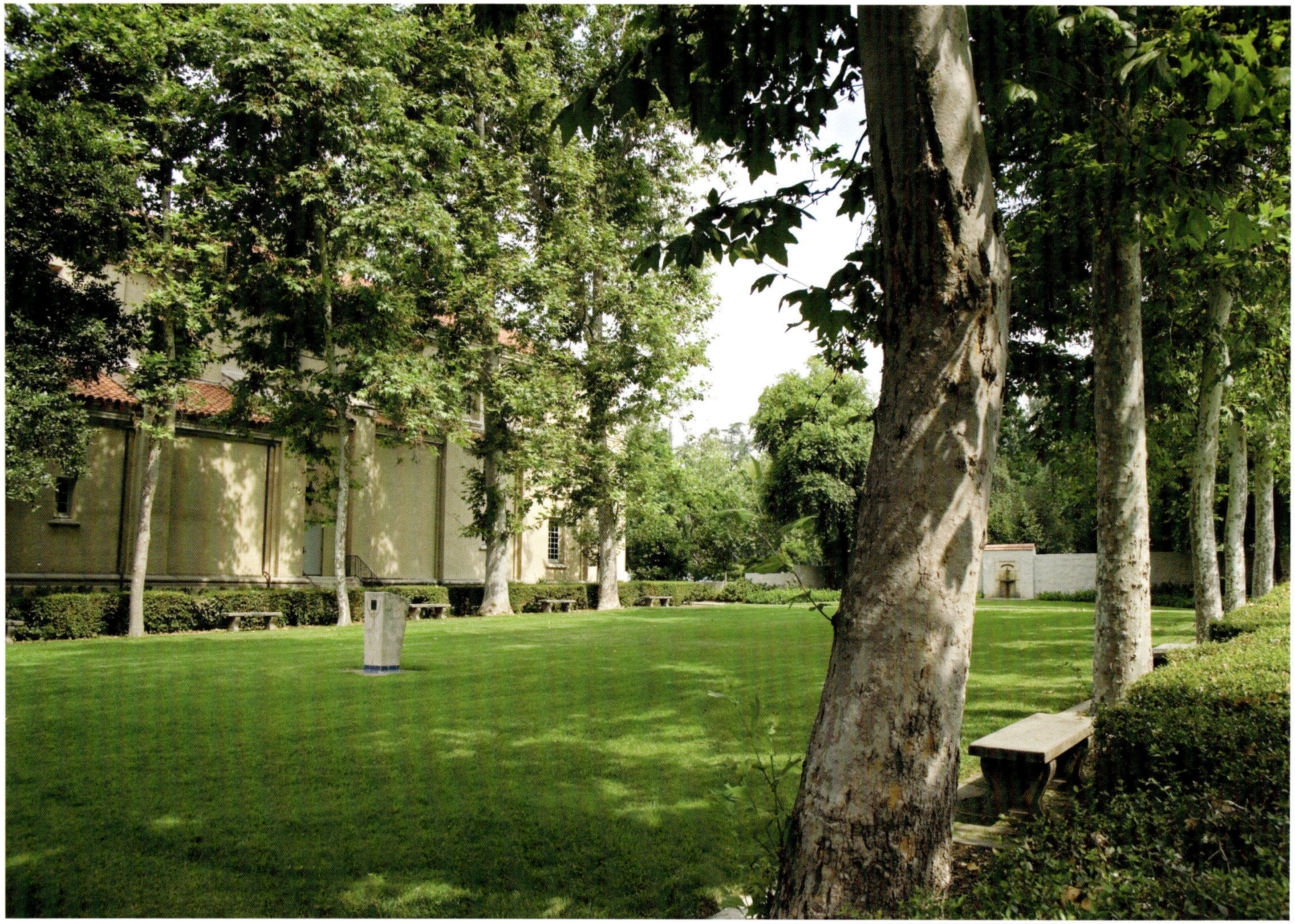

Henry Cabala

Memorial Court

BUILT 1929; dedicated May 28
PRESIDENT IN OFFICE Charles K. Edmunds
LOCATION Between Sumner Hall and Bridges Hall of Music
ARCHITECT Sumner Spaulding (gates and wall); Ralph Cornell '14 (landscaping)

Memorial Court

Created when the east end of Marston Quadrangle was being developed and Bridges Auditorium was under construction, Memorial Court provided a contemplative garden setting used since that time by the College for memorial ceremonies. The north wall of the courtyard is enhanced by a wall-mounted *Rainbow Fountain* by sculptor Burt Johnson '15, dedicated to the memory of Theodore E. Norton '24, by his parents Edwin C. Norton, dean of the College 1888–1926, and Frances Rice Norton. ■

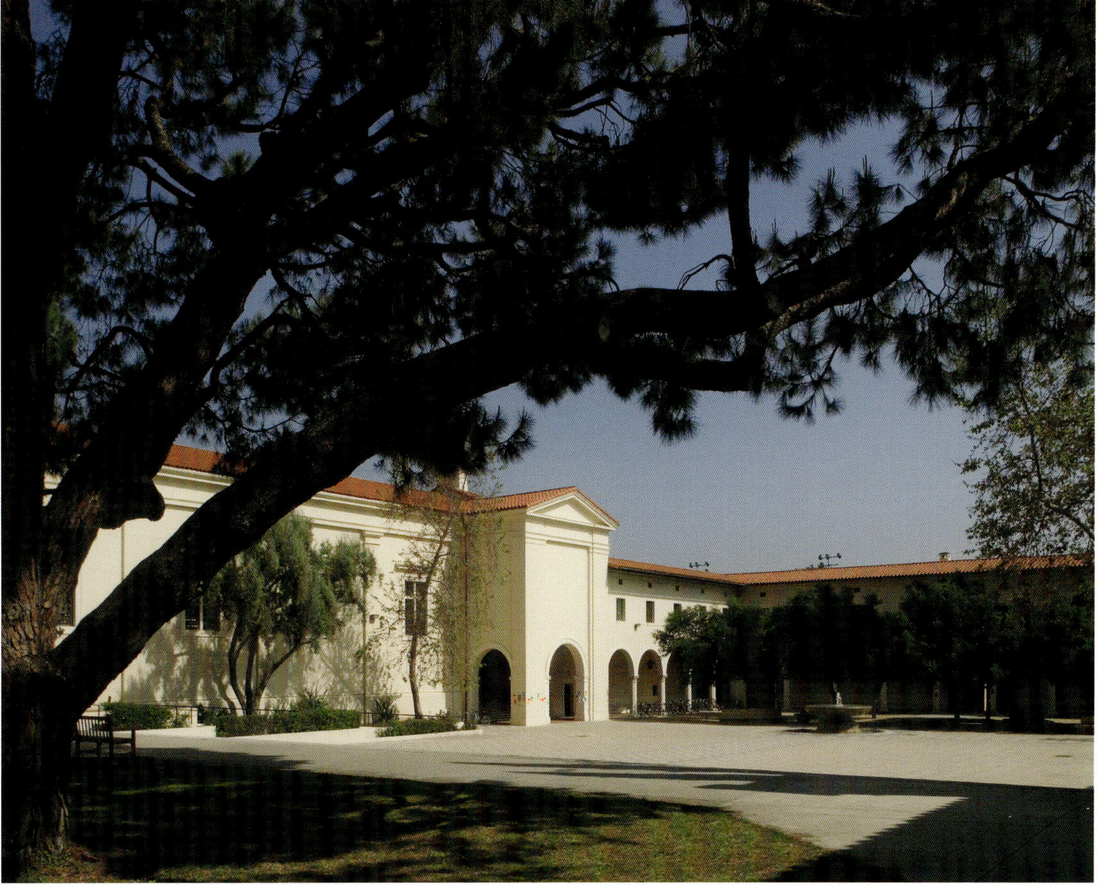

Henry Cabala

Phil Channing

LEFT *Frary Hall, built 1929, from northwest*

ABOVE *Frary Hall, interior, mural by José Clemente Orozco, 1930*

Frary Dining Hall

Frary Hall was a central feature of the Clark campus designed by architect Sumner Spaulding. A men's refectory was badly needed at the time; the Claremont Inn, which once served all students, had been given over to women living in Harwood, and men were dining in private homes or in boarding clubs. Built in 1929, at the same time as Eli P. Clark Dormitory (Clark I), Frary initially served all freshmen and some sophomores and upperclassmen. Other male students continued to eat off campus until fall 1930, when two additional Clark dormitories were completed; after that date, all men ate at Frary. Breakfast and lunch were cafeteria style, but dinners were served, and the men were required to wear coats and ties.

Funds for Frary Hall were provided by Trustee George W. Marston, who insisted on anonymity at the time and suggested the hall be named for Lucien Frary, a Congregational minister who had taken over as pastor of Pilgrim Congregational Church in Pomona when founding Trustee Charles Burt Sumner was persuaded to leave that post in 1887 to become the College's first administrator.

The Frary kitchen and servery were renovated in 2002–03. While the extensive work was under way, students were served in a "Garden House" structure temporarily added to the north side of Walker Hall. Constructed of steel, polycarbonate and glass, it resembled a large greenhouse, particularly after being filled with tropical plants.

Frary Dining Hall

BUILT 1929–30
PRESIDENT IN OFFICE Charles K. Edmunds
LOCATION 347 East Sixth Street
ARCHITECT Sumner Spaulding
MATERIALS reinforced concrete, tile roof
DONOR George W. Marston (anonymous)
NAMED FOR Lucien Frary, former pastor, Pilgrim Congregational Church, trustee 1892–1903

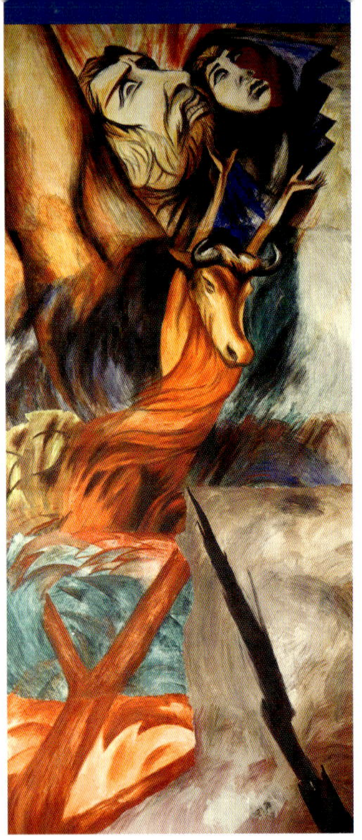

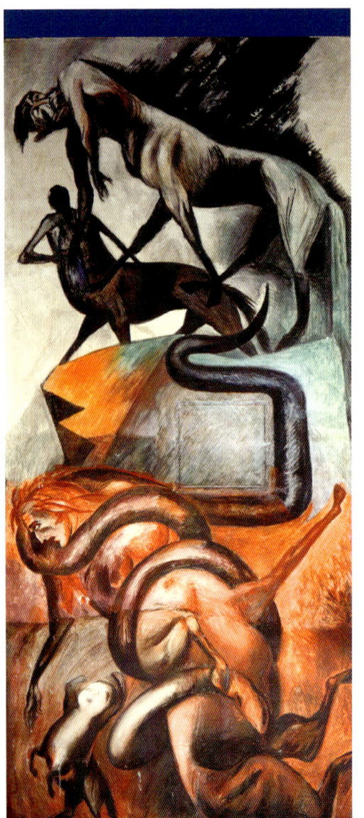

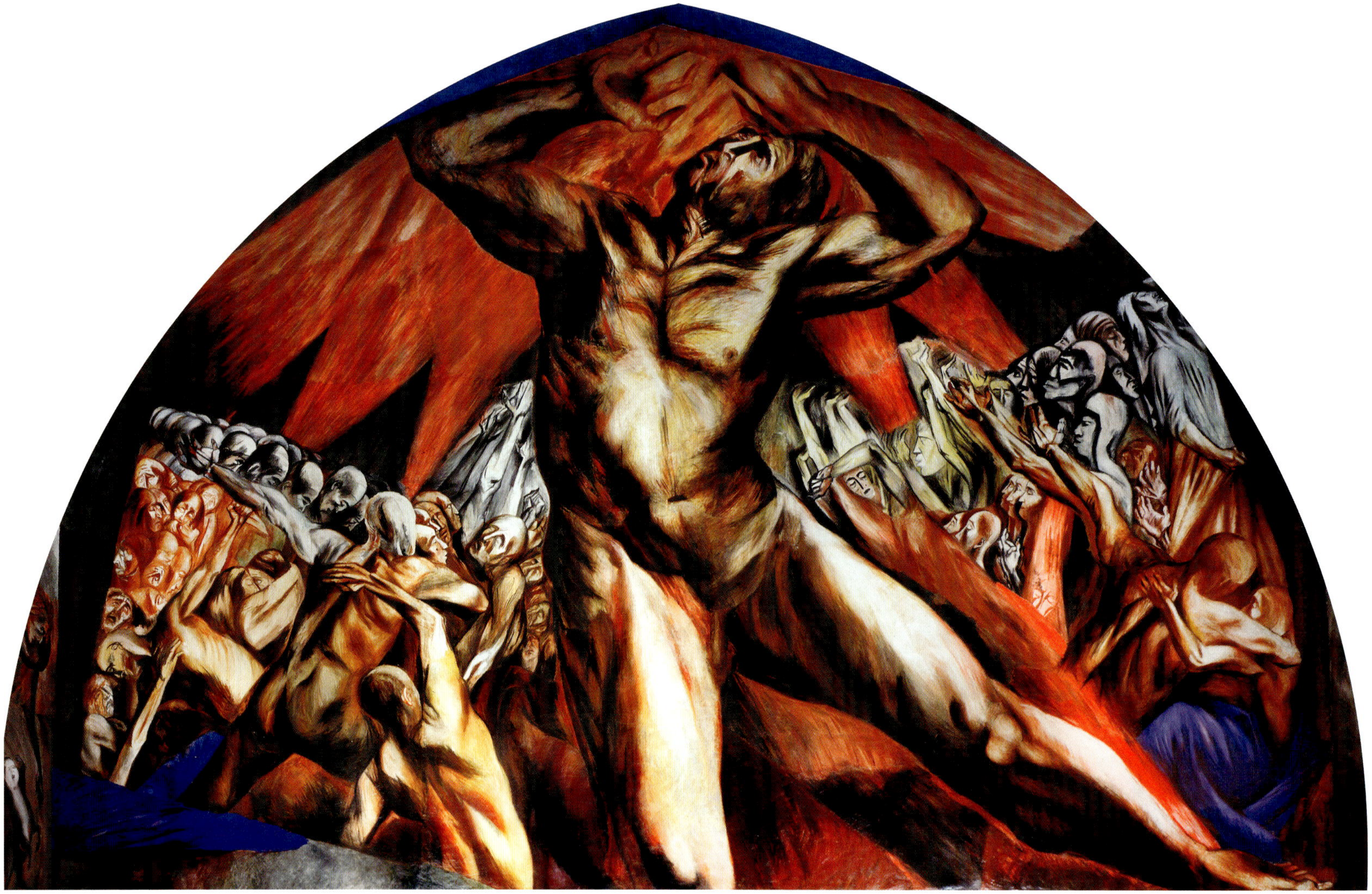

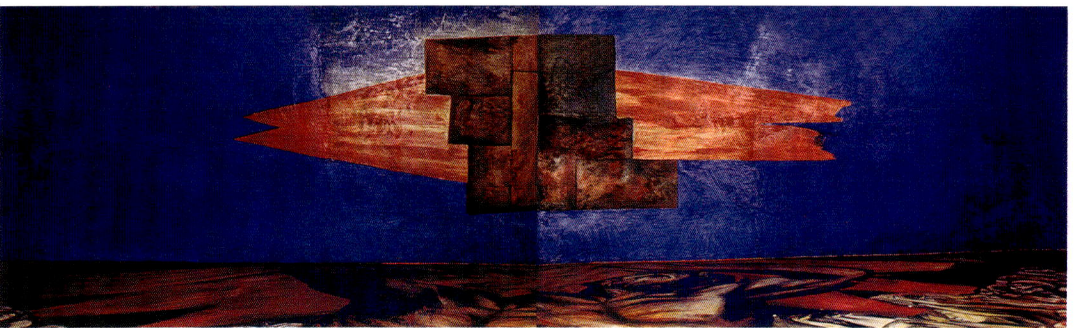

José Clemente Orozco, Prometheus, *1930, fresco, Frary Hall*

CLOCKWISE FROM LEFT

ceiling panel, abstract representation of Godhead; right (east) lateral panel, centaurs; left (west) lateral panel, Zeus, Hera and Io; central panel

The Murals

Frary Hall has the distinction of being the site of two of the College's most treasured works of art: José Clemente Orozco's *Prometheus* mural, which presides over the great north wall of the refectory, and *Genesis*, painted in 1960 by Rico Lebrun on the west wall of the building's entrance portico.

Orozco's fresco is significant in several respects. The first mural painted in the United States by the great Mexican muralist, who would later move on to ambitious commissions at the New School for Social Research in New York City and Dartmouth College, *Prometheus* marks the launching of the Mexican mural movement in this country. Orozco was invited to Pomona at the urging of José Pijoan, a popular professor of Hispanic civilization and art history. While on campus, the artist was housed in Clark Hall and took his meals in Frary Hall. He befriended students, who watched the mural take form and helped raise funds for the artist's fee.

An audacious choice at a time when American mural painting was typically bland and decorative, Orozco, whose style was influenced by sources as diverse as Michelangelo and the political murals of his native Mexico, gave Pomona a startlingly expressive interpretation of the Titan of Greek mythology. As scholar David Scott has written: "In at least one fundamental sense, the *Prometheus* was the first major 'modern' fresco in this country…It revealed a new concept of mural painting, a greatly heightened direct and personal expression. It challenged accepted conventions which decreed that wall decoration should be flat and graceful, pleasant, decorous, and impersonal. In *Prometheus*, Expressionism achieved a monumental scale."

As the fire Prometheus stole from the gods is generally understood to represent enlightenment, the myth offered a fitting metaphor for the task of the College. There may also have been a degree of personal identification in the choice of subject: Orozco, whose work was still largely unappreciated in 1930, saw himself as a heroic rebel whose efforts to enlighten, like those of Prometheus, were spurned and punished. The skill with which Orozco had scaled the composition to its architectural environment was particularly applauded. In a *Time* magazine interview in 1930, architect Spaulding was asked how he liked the mural; he responded: "I feel as though the building would fall down if the fresco were removed."

Scale was at least as difficult a challenge for Rico Lebrun whose *Genesis* was painted to be seen—and thus required to be legible—from viewpoints ranging from ground level to the small balcony in the opposing wall, further complicating the task of the muralist who must create at close range objects intended to be seen from a distance. And like Orozco, Lebrun used his wall as a means of expressing convictions he felt obliged as an artist to convey.

Rico Lebrun first visited Pomona College in November, 1956. Captivated by Orozco's fresco, he expressed interest in working on campus and, through the efforts of art history professor Peter Selz, was given a commission. Selz later persuaded Los Angeles art patrons Donald and Elizabeth Winston to sponsor the work as a gift to the College.

In *Genesis*, Lebrun was interested in portraying what he called "the evolution of form, of becoming." The story of Creation—the original "becoming" of Christian doctrine—was an ideal vehicle for expressing the artist's belief that reality is a complex interweaving of ideas, an inextricable blending of opposites, where good and evil coexist side by side. With its epic events and universal themes of tragedy and redemption, the story of Genesis provided the narrative framework for what was to be a highly personal aesthetic and political statement.

Lebrun and Orozco were both profoundly humanist painters, committed to the notion that art has a responsibility to deal with the human predicament and to do so in a public way. Pomona's two great murals epitomize the challenges as well as the rewards inherent in works of art in public places that are intended to be experienced as part of daily life rather than in the protective environment of a museum. ■

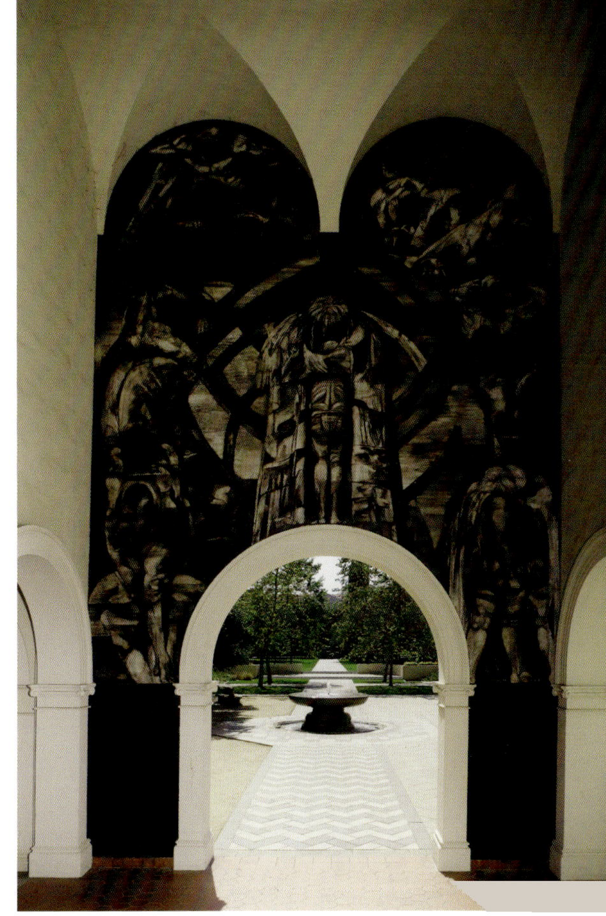

Henry Cabala

Rico Lebrun, Genesis, *1960, mural, Frary Hall*

Bridges Auditorium
(The Claremont Colleges)

BUILT 1931
PRESIDENT IN OFFICE Charles K. Edmunds (initiated by James A. Blaisdell)
LOCATION East side Marston Quadrangle
PURPOSE Music auditorium
ARCHITECT William Templeton Johnson
MATERIALS steel and reinforced concrete
COST $650,000
DONORS Mr. and Mrs. Appleton Shaw Bridges and family (H.H. Timken)
NAMED In memory of Mabel Shaw Bridges '08

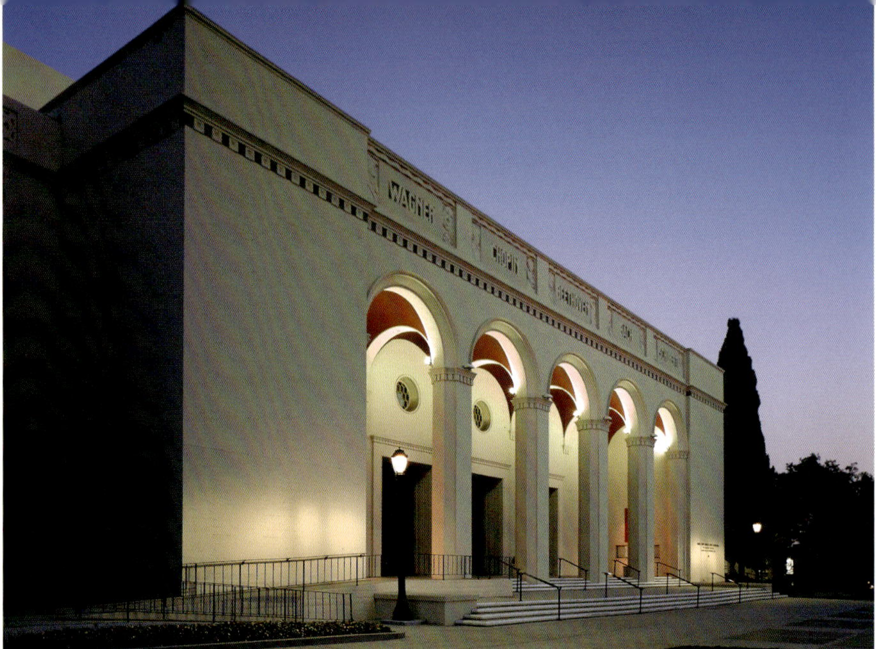

Henry Cabala

Bridges Auditorium
(The Claremont Colleges)

The story of Bridges Auditorium belongs to the tenure of two Pomona presidents: James Blaisdell, who had maintained a close relationship with donor Appleton Shaw Bridges, who funded Bridges Hall of Music in 1915, and Charles Edmunds, who followed Blaisdell as president in 1928. In 1925, Mr. Bridges expressed his continuing interest in music and mentioned the possibility of supporting the construction of a large auditorium. Bridges, joined by his brother-in-law H.H. Timken (brother of Amelia Timken Bridges), president of Timken Roller Bearing Corporation in Ohio, made the gift in May 1928, at the end of Blaisdell's presidency. Construction began in 1930, and the auditorium was completed and dedicated in the fall of 1931, during the presidency of Charles Edmunds.

The site selected was the eastern perimeter of Marston Quadrangle, occupied at the time by an unsightly heating plant, complete with tall smokestack. College buildings flanked the other three sides of the quad, and George Marston, who was also a friend of the Bridges family, donated funds to clear the site, a process that also involved moving the original Renwick gymnasium farther east and removing a swimming pool. According to Wilson Lyon, Marston believed that: "Since this would inevitably be a very massive building it should have an ample foreground, and with Bridges Hall of Music the companion building nearby, a location east of the large open quadrangle framed in a vista of trees and shrubs seemed ideal."

Although constructed on land owned by Pomona College, Bridges Auditorium was a joint undertaking of the relatively new entity known as The Claremont Colleges, which had held its first organizational meeting in December 1925. When completed, Bridges Auditorium was, in the words of Wilson Lyon, "a dramatic illustration of the value of joint facilities for the Associated Colleges"[10] and a focal point for the campuses.

Before drawing plans for the auditorium, architect William Templeton Johnson toured the major concert houses of Europe, and the resulting design, referred to at the time as a "free adaptation of northern Italian Renaissance architecture," was at once restrained and grandly monumental. The massive exterior of Bridges Auditorium—with its columns, vaulted arches, three massive wooden entrance doors facing west, and arched porticoes on the north and south—conveyed a sense of dignity and moment. Above the entrance portico, in the fashion of civic buildings of the time, were engraved the names of composers Richard Wagner, Frederick Chopin, Ludwig van Beethoven, Johann Sebastian Bach, and Franz Schubert. The 34 x 90-foot foyer had a terrazzo floor, Carrara marble columns, cast stone pilasters, and a hand-painted coffered ceiling. The auditorium boasted unobstructed views from all seats, an innovation made possible by the cantilevered 500-seat

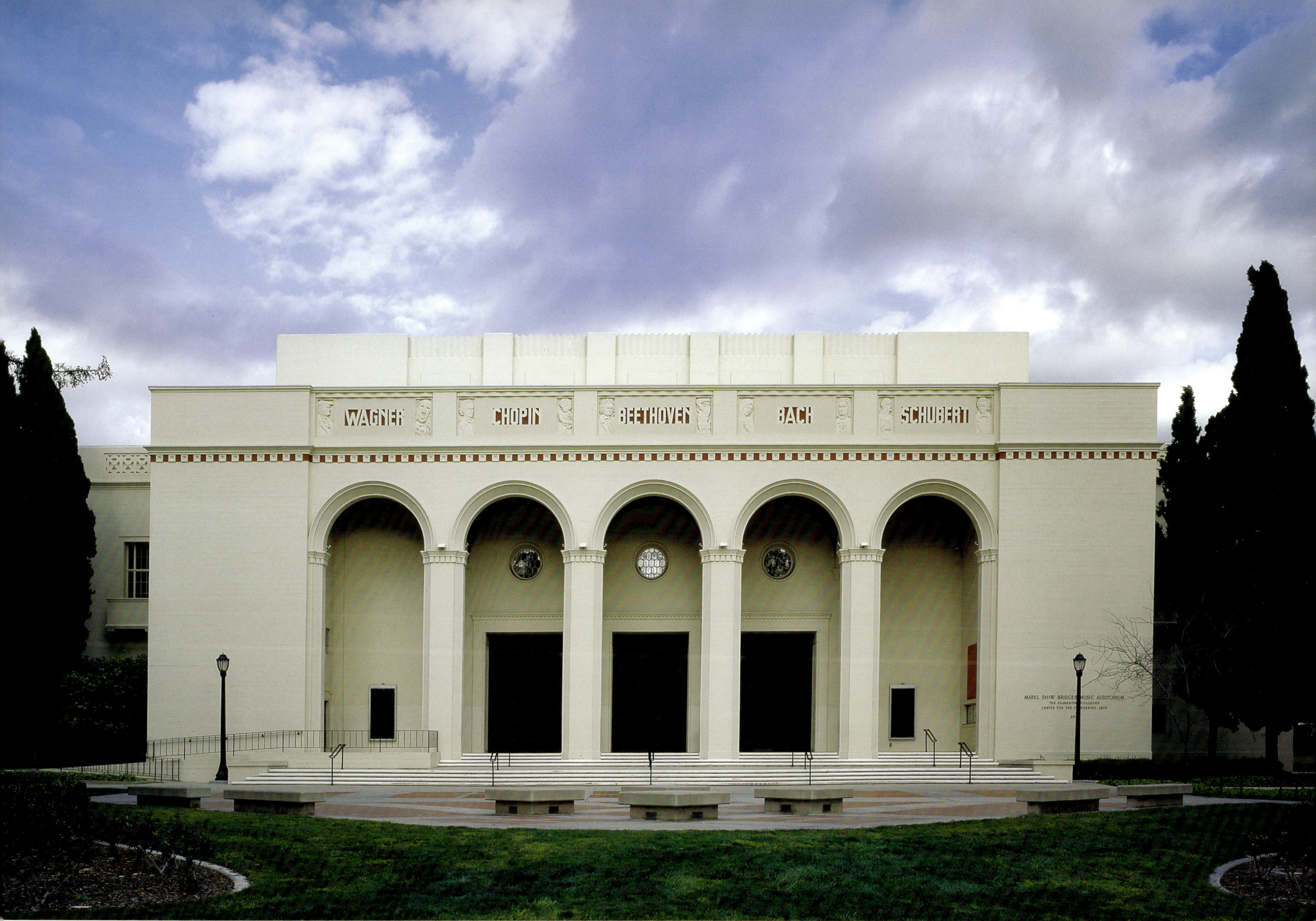

Henry Cabala

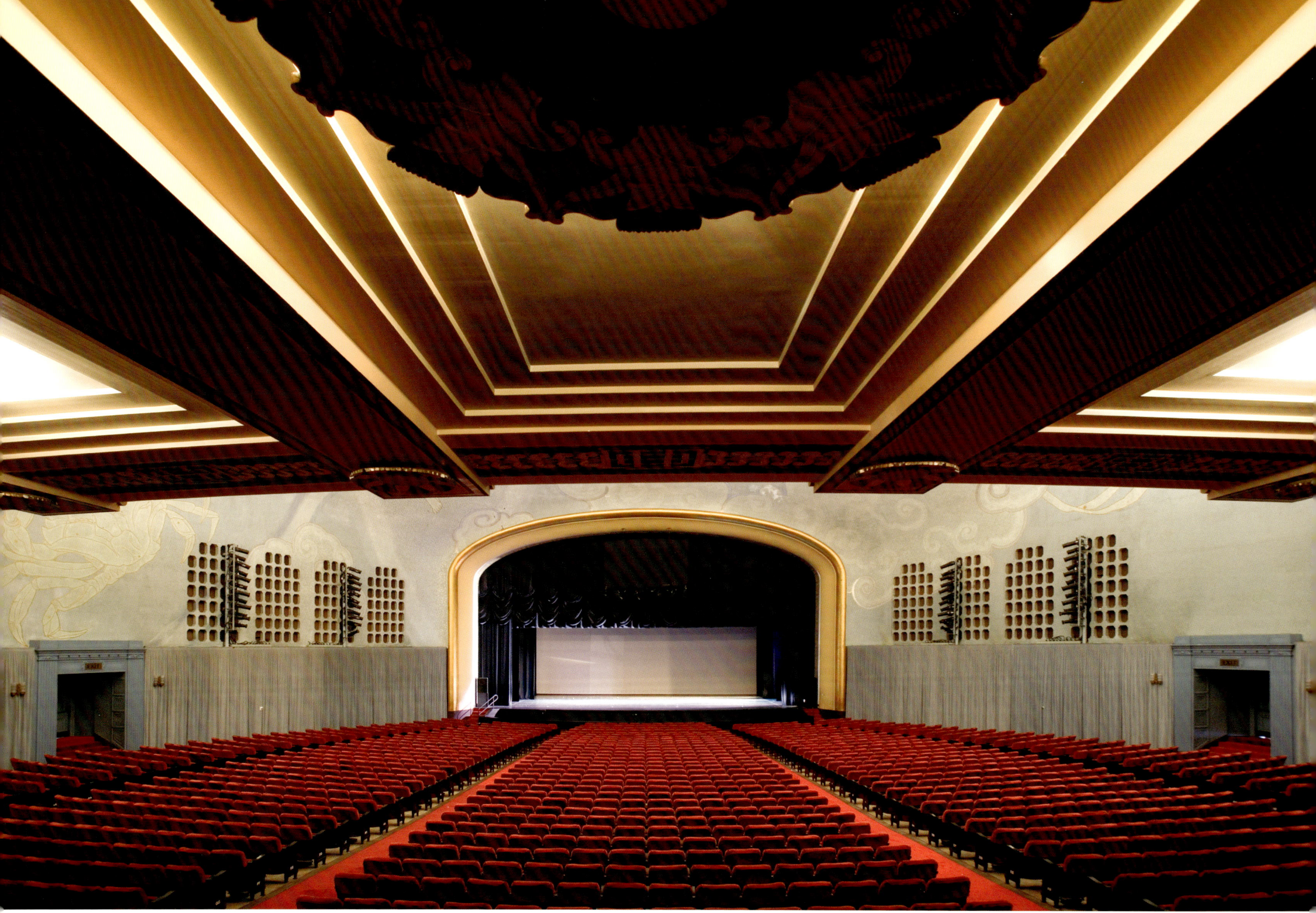

Henry Cabala

balcony that obviated the need for supporting pillars; a 6000-pipe organ; indirect lighting; and a downdraft ventilating system that could exchange the air in 10 minutes. The proscenium, 62 feet high by 36 feet wide, could accommodate a 100-piece orchestra. Perhaps most spectacular was the 22,000-square-foot ceiling, a parabola extending from the top of the proscenium arch to the rear wall, designed to offer ideal acoustics for vocal and instrumental music. On its concave surface a fresco by artist John Smeraldi, who had created the star-filled ceiling of New York City's Grand Central Station, depicted the signs of the zodiac in silver and gold against a blue field.

At the time it was built, Bridges Auditorium was the largest college or university auditorium on the West Coast. Although enrolled students numbered 1,300 in 1931, the Bridges family, with faith in the College's growth and the civic value of such a facility, provided seating for 2,500 (then the population of the City of Claremont). It proved superbly suited for concerts, drawing large audiences for major artists and ensembles, among them Sergei Rachmaninoff, Arthur Rubinstein, Andres Segovia, Kirsten Flagstad, Helen Traubel, Joan Sutherland, the Metropolitan Opera, and the Bolshoi Ballet; and was equally accommodating for convocations and speakers such as Eve Curie, Admiral Byrd, Amelia Earhart, Eleanor Roosevelt, and Will Durant. Over two million people attended programs between 1931 and 1975, when the building was temporarily closed.

Bridges Auditorium has a history rich with memories and anecdotes. According to his son Alan, architect William Templeton Johnson met the young Leopold Stokowski during his European sojourn, and the musician suggested he use Paris's Salle Pleyel as his model for the hall's acoustics. Several years later, as Bridges was nearing completion, Johnson invited his now-distinguished friend, who was then working in Hollywood several months each year (and would soon conduct the orchestra for Walt Disney's *Fantasia*), to review the hall's acoustics. Stokowski did so, concluding, "Mr. Johnson, she is fit for the fiddle."

Probably the best loved of Bridges Auditorium stories concerns rock musician Frank Zappa and his group The Mothers of Invention (1965–69). Around the time of a performance they gave in Bridges, it was noticed one morning that the northernmost façade frieze, depicting Wagner, had been replaced by one that read "Zappa." To the left of the letters was an outline of the rock artist's face; on the right, a marijuana leaf. The cleverly fashioned wooden facsimile had been adroitly slipped into place without damage to the building (or Wagner). Those responsible were never identified.

Bridges Auditorium was closed for renovation in 1975. Although, in 1930, the Fellows of The Claremont Colleges had authorized additional funds to assure the structural integrity of the building, safety codes had become more stringent in the wake of the Long Beach earthquake of 1933, and by the 1970s, the auditorium was deemed substandard; it was also facing a large deficit. The price tag for upgrading was substantial, $1.5 million along with a performance support component of $118,000, but the goal was met and Bridges reopened in 1977.

In 1991, a pedestrian mall was created in front of the building, closing College Way between Fourth and Sixth streets to automobile traffic and installing decorative paving and seating. The mall had been designed as a unifying element in the College's Campus Landscape Master Plan that had been approved in 1983; once again the Timken Foundation provided funding.

Today, Bridges Auditorium is used by The Claremont Colleges, collectively and individually, for ceremonial occasions, public lectures, and live performances. It is also used by outside organizations throughout the year. Since 1954 it has been home to the Fiske Museum, a collection of over 1,200 European and American musical instruments including many historically significant examples. ■

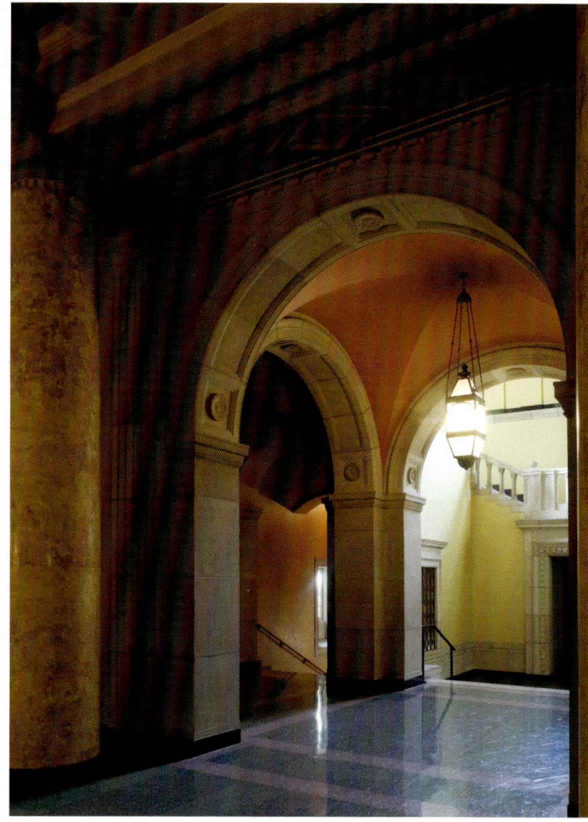

Henry Cabala

ABOVE *Bridges Auditorium, foyer*

OPPOSITE *Bridge Auditorium, interior*

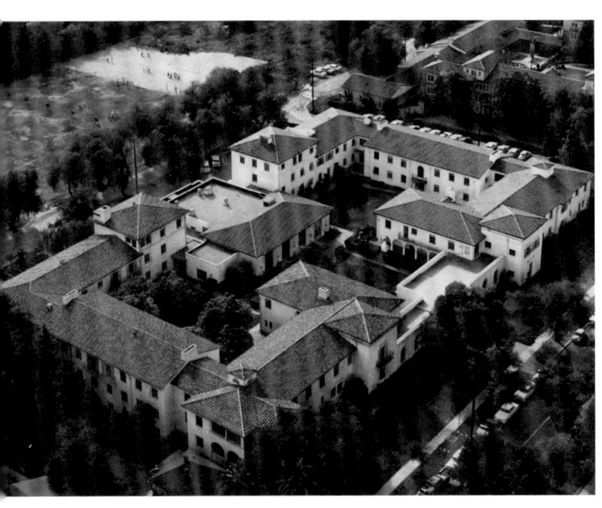

Florence Carrier Blaisdell Hall; Della Mulock Mudd Hall (Mudd-Blaisdell Hall)

BUILT 1936 (Blaisdell); 1947 (Mudd)
PRESIDENTS IN OFFICE Charles K. Edmunds; E. Wilson Lyon
LOCATION 230 East Bonita Avenue
PURPOSE Women's dormitory
ARCHITECT Allison and Allison, Los Angeles
MATERIALS reinforced concrete
COST $210,000 (half gifts, half loan from endowment)
DONOR George White Marston ($50,000 matching grant)
NAMED FOR Mrs. James Blaisdell; Mrs. Della Mulock Mudd

Florence Carrier Blaisdell Hall; Della Mulock Mudd Hall (Mudd-Blaisdell Hall)

Blaisdell Hall was the first building to be undertaken as the College, and the country, began to recover from the effects of the 1929 stock market crash and ensuing Depression. Given the priority President Edmunds placed on residential life, it is not surprising that the first capital project in five years was a dormitory. The plans first drafted by architects Allison and Allison were for two residence units, housing 164 women and including a dining hall, situated in a quadrangle. Concerned about costs (projected to be $230,000 for each unit), the trustees opted to begin with a single unit funded by gifts and a loan from the College's endowment. Despite this reduction-by-half, the completed building was nonetheless considered a great success, in the words of E. Wilson Lyon, "hailed as a 'milestone in the social history' of Pomona."[12]

Named for Florence Carrier Blaisdell, wife of former president James Blaisdell, the horseshoe-shaped concrete structure housed 85 women within its Georgian-styled rooms. The interior decor and furnishings were described as striving for "an atmosphere of femininity" and blended mahogany furniture with carefully matched pink, blue, and white upholstery. A large recreation hall on the first floor became famous for its informal dances and social gatherings.

It was not until after WWII that the second half of Blaisdell residence hall—Della Mulock Mudd Hall—could be constructed, and, by this time, a new president had taken office. The return of veterans to campus beginning in 1945 exacerbated an ongoing campus housing crisis. Between 1945–46 and 1947–48, enrollment increased from 659 to 1,110. Veterans accounted for 488 of these, but the number of women students had also grown to the extent that they were being housed in one unit of Clark Hall and in the northern section of Smiley, formerly "a masculine citadel." In response, Lyon pushed the completion of Blaisdell Hall's second residential unit to the forefront of his agenda. Trustee Seeley G. Mudd agreed that his family would pay for the building, which was designed by the same architects who designed Blaisdell Hall. Construction began in 1945, a year before the government restricted the use of building materials exclusively for housing; two-thirds of the rooms were ready by September 1946, the remainder by Thanksgiving. The parlors and a connecting corridor to Blaisdell Hall were completed in early 1947, and the building was dedicated in April, named for Della Mulock Mudd. Three members of the Mudd family had served the College as trustees: Mrs. Mudd's husband Colonel Seeley W. Mudd (1914–26), and their two sons Harvey S. Mudd (1926–30) and Dr. Seeley G. Mudd (1930–52)

Today Mudd-Blaisdell is the largest dormitory on campus, housing 283 students. In 2001, a $5 million renovation added air conditioning and updated the interior. Despite the relatively small size of its rooms, Mudd-Blaisdell's wide hallways and comfortable climate have made it popular among the freshmen Sponsor Groups it currently houses. ■

LEFT *Florence Carrier Blaisdell Hall, built 1936; Della Mulock Mudd Hall, built 1947, aerial view*

OPPOSITE *Blaisdell Hall*

OVERLEAF *Mudd-Blaisdell Hall*

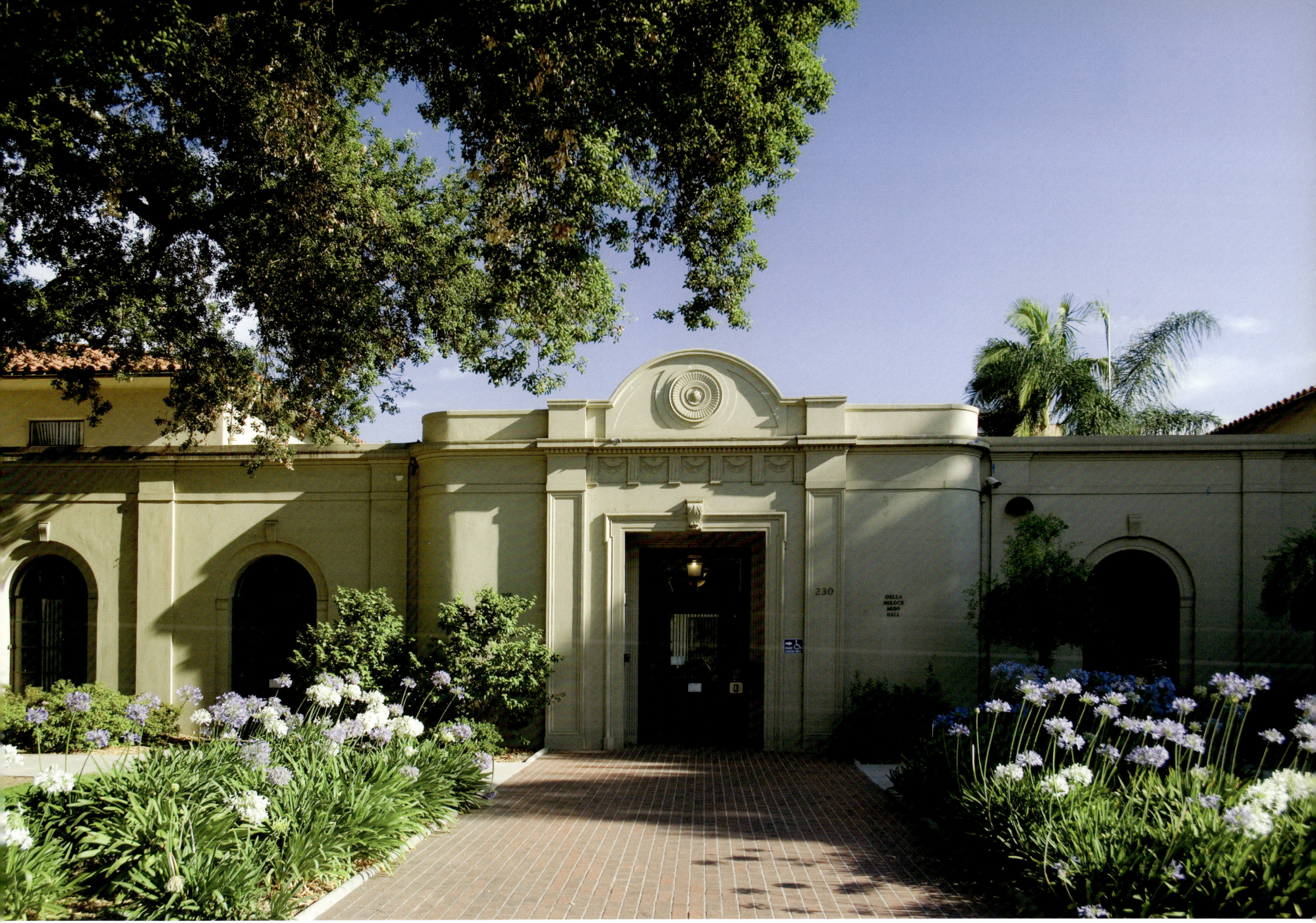

Henry Cabala

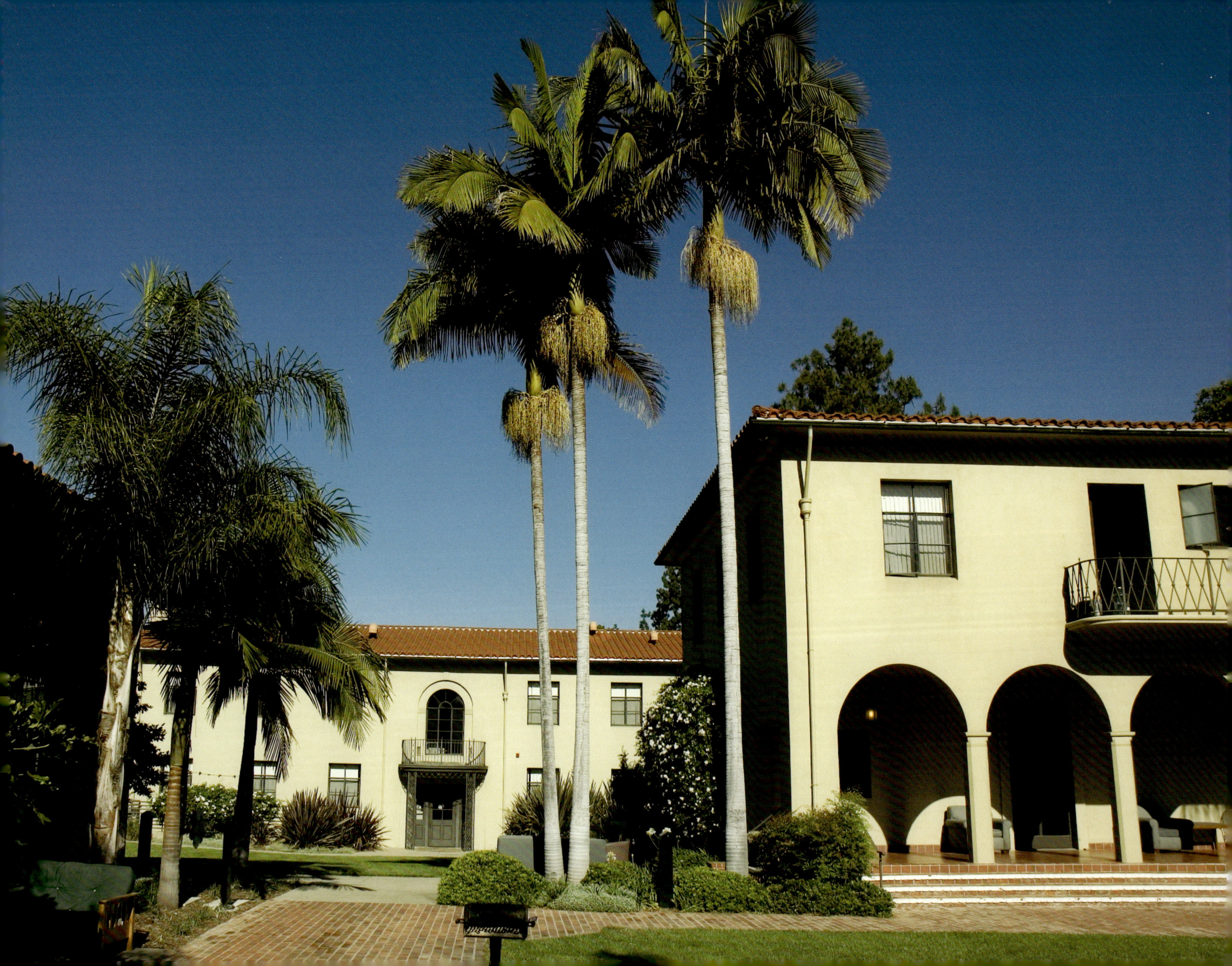

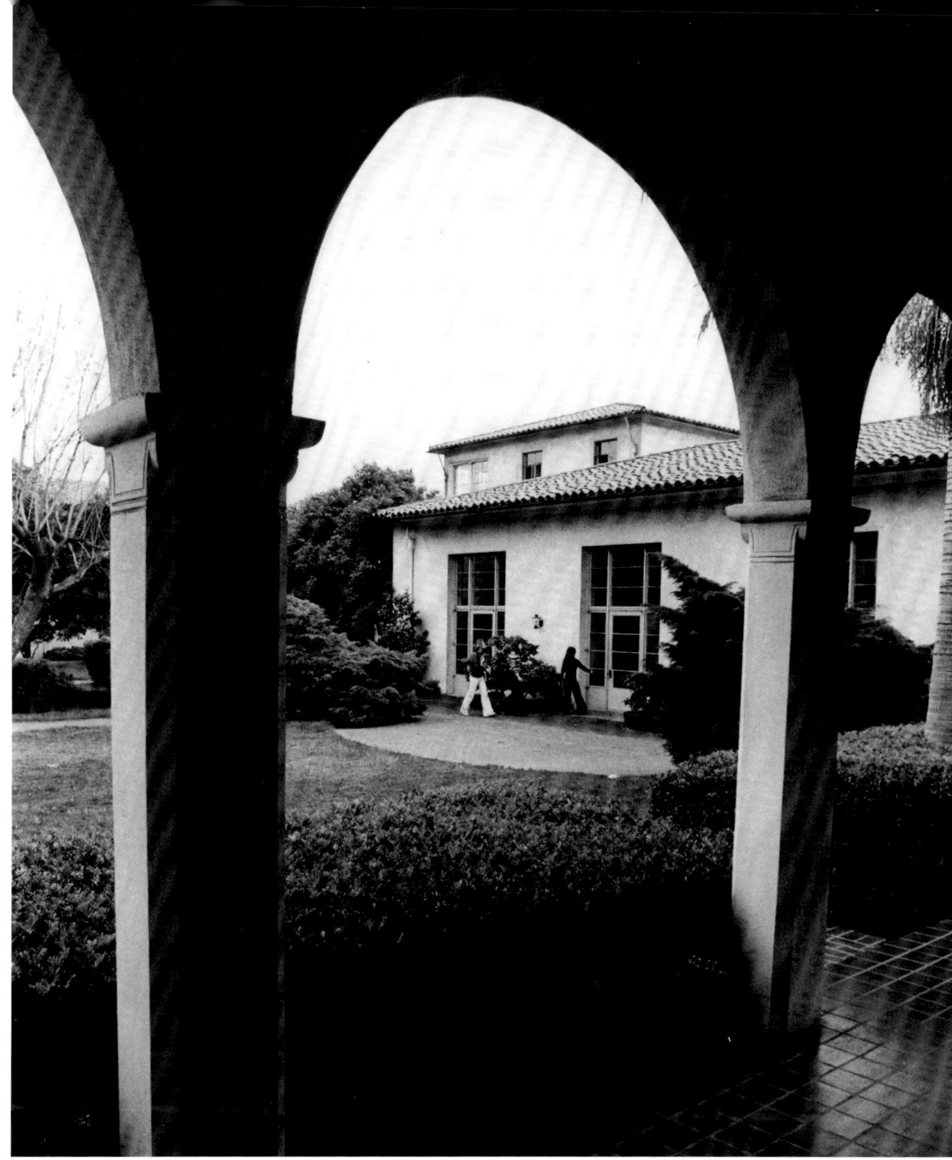

Mark Wood

Gibson Dining Hall

As Mudd Hall was under construction in 1946, the Women's Campus Club agreed to help raise funds for a new dining hall south of the combined residence halls it would serve. The Club, formed in 1940 under President Edmunds, included mothers of students, alumnae and friends led by Mrs. Victor Montgomery and Mrs. Edmunds; its principal goal was to develop the women's campus. Through solicitations and benefit events, it raised nearly $97,000, the remaining funds needed were borrowed from the College's endowment. Ground was broken in March 1949, and the hall was ready for use by September of that year. The hall contained round tables seating a total of 262 in two rooms decorated with watercolors by Milford Zornes '34.

After the construction of Frank Hall in 1982, Gibson Dining Hall was converted to other uses, including a computer lab and, in the old private dining room, the Pomona Student Art Gallery (PoSA); in 2005, Gibson was converted to dormitory rooms, and the gallery moved to Rembrandt Hall. ■

Gibson Dining Hall

BUILT 1949
PRESIDENT IN OFFICE E. Wilson Lyon
ARCHITECT Allison and Rible
MATERIALS reinforced concrete
COST $97,000
DONORS Women's Campus Club
NAMED FOR Dean Jessie E. Gibson, 1927–49

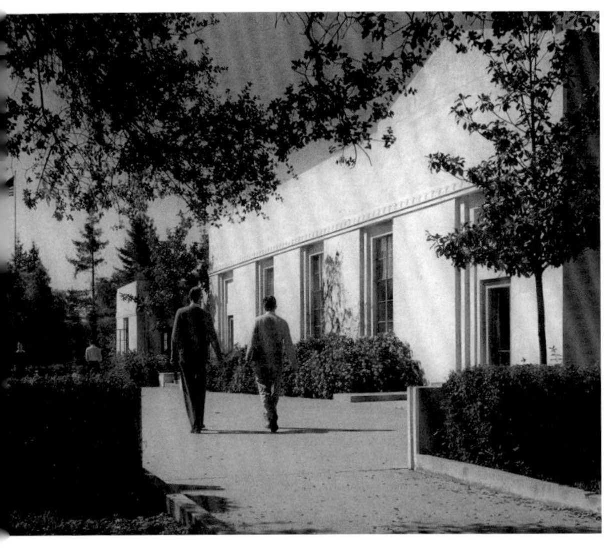

Edmunds Union

As is the case on many campuses, Pomona's student union has always occupied a special place in the hearts, as well as the daily lives, of the student body. Although students' need for a congenial place to gather is perennial, their diversity has always been reflected in the widely varied, and occasionally conflicting, preferences for such a structure. Furthermore, these change over time; while one generation prefers large spaces for community gatherings, the next might well favor smaller, more intimate areas. Not surprisingly, the functionality of the student union building has been (and continues to be) questioned with regularity, and change is more or less constant.

A student union was first proposed in 1929 and, had it not been for the Depression, might well have been in place the next year; the need had long been acknowledged, the trustees had already approved a site between Holmes and Smiley halls, and students had requested that their annual activity fee be increased from $3.50 to $5.00 with the understanding that the additional $1.50 would be reserved for a student union. By the time the plan was taken up again, in 1936, the need was exacerbated by the fragmentation of campus life resulting from the increased use of automobiles. A pamphlet detailing the need for a union was circulated, and in 1937, sufficient funds had been raised that architectural drawings were requested from architects Marston and Maybury of Pasadena.

Even with the additional support of parents and trustees, however, fundraising efforts fell short of the projected $128,000 cost (of the $64,000 raised to date, nearly half came from the Associated Students), and it was decided to proceed with the construction of the main building and west wing, postponing the east wing for a later date. The $94,000 scaled-back plan was funded by gifts and a loan from the endowment to be repaid through continued assessment of students.

In the fall of 1937, the doors opened to a structure that bustled with student activity, from the offices of the Associated Students and *The Student Life*, to the cooperative store and numerous gathering places for socializing and snacking. A grand, two-story ballroom was used for formal and informal dances, relieving the need, reinforced by an increasing number of automobile accidents, to depend on off-campus hotels. Carolyn Lyon recalls that parties at Edmunds Union were "good fun, designed to bring the community together, to provide a sense of being a part of the whole college. People got all dressed up—long evening dresses and the men wore tuxedoes if they had them—very gala. Ray Noval and his band provided the music for years. The musicians were very melodic, which appealed to our generation. The faculty, trustees who lived nearby, and some townspeople—members of the school board, the City Council, the mayor—were invited. Everybody loved it, but no one as much as I. I loved to dance and I loved Ray's music. It kept lines of communication open at all levels."[12]

The building went unnamed until 1948, when the Board voted to christen it the Charles Keyser and Katharine Poorbaugh Edmunds Union, in honor of the former president and his wife (tragically, Edmunds died barely two weeks later). For most, however, the union would always be "the Coop."

The postponed east wing was finally undertaken in 1950 during the administration of President E. Wilson Lyon. Architect Wallace Neff designed the new wing to relate harmoniously to Memorial Gymnasium, then under construction. Ever-creative in finding ways to fund projects, Lyon developed a plan financed by surplus funds from the Associated Students, anticipated store profits, and continuance of the $1.50 student surcharge. The new wing faced College Way and offered a large, canopied porch and glass façade. A full basement, which could

Mark Wood

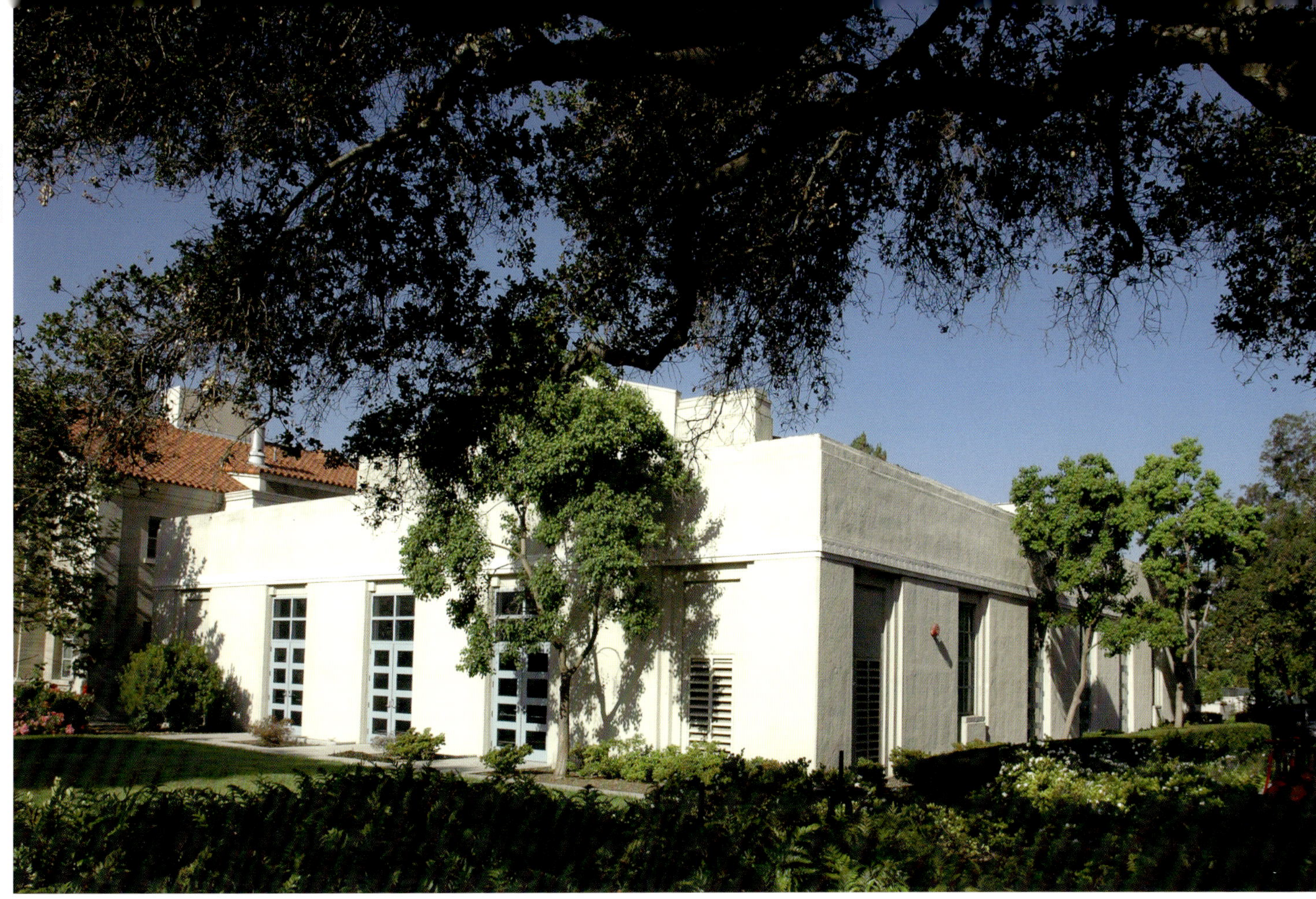

accommodate 250, was used for class parties and various recreational purposes. In 1962, a coffee house known as The Smudge Pot was opened. The intimate space, with wood paneling, booth seating and partitioned rooms for privacy, quickly became popular. Students gathered in the basement to listen to live music and enjoy conversation with friends, often filling the pages of *The Student Life* with debates over the cost of admission to hear their friends perform at the coffee house's nightly concerts.

By 1969, after 32 years, the Union was due for an upgrade. Students formed a committee to assess the needs of the building, and then pushed for renovation, requesting improved recreational facilities, a more flexible space for social events, a more efficiently designed bookstore, and an outdoor eating area that faced Stover Walk. The student body was responsible for $166,000 of the $407,500 needed for the project, which fundamentally restructured the building according to their specifications. The renovations, by architect Bernard Zimmerman, radically altered the building in a manner consistent with current architectural style but unrelated to campus context, a situation that, in the view of Robert A.M. Stern who designed the building that was to replace Edmunds Union, "reflected a condition which prevailed at many colleges across the country when trustees and architects ignored the past and built buildings that were belligerently self-referential." Nonetheless, in this form, Edmunds Union served the College for another 30 years before being replaced by the Smith Campus Center (see Chapter VII). ■

Edmunds Union

BUILT 1937; east wing 1951

PRESIDENTS IN OFFICE Charles K. Edmunds and E. Wilson Lyon

LOCATION 170 East Sixth Street (between Holmes and Smiley halls)

ARCHITECT Marston and Maybury, Pasadena

PURPOSE student union, offices of student organizations, Coop Store, ballroom

MATERIALS reinforced concrete

COST $94,000

DONORS Bequest of $10,000 from the estate of Florence Riley; increased student activity fees

NAMED FOR President Charles K. Edmunds and Katharine Poorbaugh Edmunds, in 1948

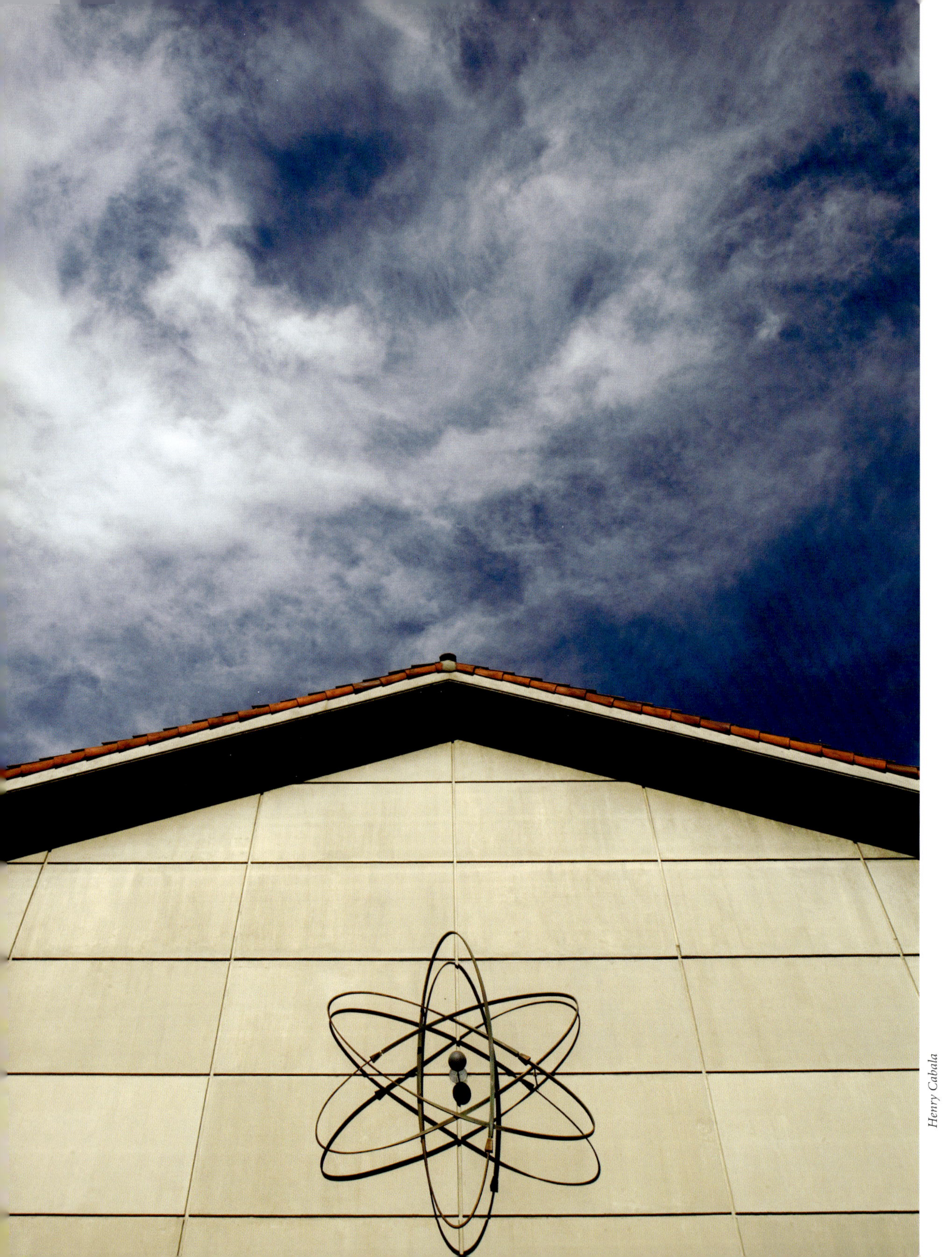
Henry Cabala

CHAPTER IV *The* LYON YEARS 1941–69

Millikan Laboratory

The Lyon Years, 1941–69

PRESIDENT E. WILSON LYON

THE 28-YEAR PRESIDENCY OF ELIJAH WILSON LYON WAS the longest in the history of the College. For that reason but more importantly because of Lyon's vision, dedication, and energy, the nearly three decades of his presidency were exceptionally significant for Pomona. Indeed, Lyon's administration was responsible for critical developments in every aspect of the College's life, including the growth of the campus that is the primary focus of this volume. That Pomona's story is recorded is also due to Lyon, who devoted the first eight years of his retirement to writing the College's history, a remarkable achievement without which the institution would have a far less rich sense of its own past. Lyon's chronicle of the years of his own presidency set a standard for objective scholarship.

When he was named the sixth president of Pomona College on April 25, 1941, E. Wilson Lyon was professor of history at Colgate University in Hamilton, New York. Born in Heidelberg, Mississippi, in 1904, Lyon studied Latin, Greek, French, English literature and history at the University of Mississippi where he earned a B.A. with special distinction in 1925. Upon graduation, he entered St. John's College, Oxford, as a Rhodes Scholar, completing a B.A. in the Honour School of Modern History in 1927 and, in 1928, a B.Litt. in Modern History. Returning to the States, he earned a Ph.D. in Modern European History from the University of Chicago (1932). After a year teaching at Louisiana Polytechnic, he was hired by Colgate University in 1929 as assistant professor of history; over the course of his 13 years there, he rose to the rank of professor and chair of the department and played a key role in the reorganization of the university's curriculum; during summers, he taught at Syracuse University, the University of Rochester, and the University of Missouri. As a scholar, Lyon's primary interest was modern European history, with particular focus on the history of France and its relationship to the United States. Lyon's academic and administrative experience at a small, liberal arts school (Colgate had fewer than 1,000 students at the time) and at Oxford, which had served as a model for The Claremont Colleges consortium and where the college system offered close student-faculty interaction, seemed perfectly suited to Pomona. The same was true of his wife Carolyn Bartel Lyon, who had attended Earlham College, graduated with a B.A. in French from Wellesley, and then earned an M.A. in history from the University of Chicago (1930). It was there that she met and, in 1933, married Wilson Lyon. The couple arrived in Claremont in September 1941 with their two small children, Elizabeth and John, then five and two years old.

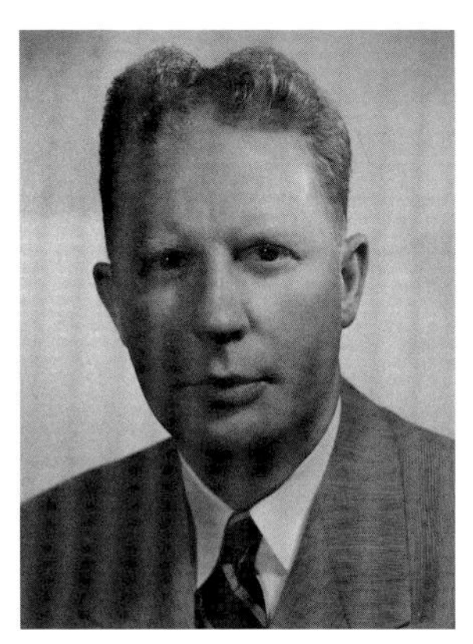

President E. Wilson Lyon

The addresses that celebrated Lyon's inauguration in October 1941 were dominated by concern about the war then raging in Europe, the threats to democracy it represented and the consequent need for colleges and universities to rededicate themselves to the intellectual and spiritual ideals that underlie liberal education. In his inaugural comments, Lyon himself noted that the world was in one of the "most far-reaching revolutions in modern history, a period resembling in many ways the religious upheavals of the 16th and 17th centuries in Europe," and stressed the College's responsibility to train its students to appraise political and economic institutions and to examine the place of the United States in the world. Within months, the country was at war, and that "place" had become even more critical.

Lyon found the College functioning efficiently in the fall of 1941, with 75 faculty, 850 students, and a permanent endowment that stood at $3.5 million, but any hopes of a smooth beginning to his administration were abruptly dashed by the bombing of Pearl Harbor on December 7. The following day, America declared war against Germany, Italy, and Japan, a momentous decision cast in terms of the preservation of freedom and democracy. On campus, the war led to a drop in enrollments, the temporary loss of male faculty and administrators, an optional accelerated program for men involving year-round classes and the arrival of military units whose barracks would ultimately serve the College's physical education program. In the absence of men on campus, women maintained many of the campus traditions and activities, gaining invaluable experience in the process.

REMINISCENCE:

Over the years, I have come to believe that the extra-curricular opportunities open, of necessity, to women on campus during wartime could prove of almost as much value as some class work.... Obviously, traditional social life was limited at Pomona in the mid-forties with so few men on campus, but that, of necessity, opened many opportunities never traditionally available to women. Major student body offices were prime examples, as were opportunities in stage production, a program which remained very active (if Virginia Allen, fondly known as "Teach," could find plays with only one or two male parts). My roommate, for example, would never have climbed to adjust the lights on the balconies of Holmes Hall, nor would I have been Business Manager for Drama Productions, for heaven's sake! What did women know about promoting a new plan for season ticket sales, fitting poster campaigns into budgets, etc.? Such experiences have stood many of us in good stead over the years. —Lois Spaulding Harmsen '47

By summer 1944, allied advances appeared to promise victory. In June, the passage of President Roosevelt's Servicemen's Readjustment Act (soon known as the G.I. Bill of Rights), which assured those who had served in the military a fully-paid education, initiated a new era in American colleges and universities. As veterans returned, enrollments nationwide rose markedly. A 1947 presidential commission described this growth as "phenomenal," with more than 2,000,000 students in American colleges; by 1951, that number had doubled. The trend continued as children of the postwar "baby boom" entered college in the 1960s, and in 1962 it was reported that nearly all of the country's approximately 2,000 institutions of higher learning had plans for expansion and that 200 new campuses were planned or under way.

At Pomona, whose student numbers grew from 659 to 1,110 between 1945 and 1947, housing again became an issue ultimately leading to the construction of five new dormitories—Della Mulock Mudd Hall (1945–47), Helen R. Walker Hall (1953), Norton Hall (1956), Anna May Wig Hall (1959), and Oldenborg Center (1966). At the same time, the curriculum was revised, with electives restricted and a renewed emphasis on a core curriculum that would provide, in Lyon's words, "the common fund of knowledge essential for a free society." Increasing competition with the USSR reinforced the centrality of the sciences—the biological, physical and social sciences were the first three of the seven "pillars of wisdom," those core areas of study required in the student's first two years—and at Pomona, as across the country, science facilities were built.

Pomona's new science buildings—Millikan Laboratory for Physics, Astronomy and Mathematics, and Seaver Laboratory for Biology and Geology (1958–59), soon followed by Seaver Laboratory for Chemistry (1964–65)—reflected this national trend as well as an important local decision. The concern to upgrade science instruction was shared by the other Claremont Colleges, and the possibility of sharing facilities that would be built on Pomona property north of Sixth Street was discussed at length. Ultimately, the College decided to retain control over its science curriculum, a decision with lasting consequences. As Don Pattison, the College's broadly knowledgeable historian, has noted, the new science facilities, which have been renovated and expanded over time and to which splendid additions are currently under way, put Pomona on the map, enabling it, perhaps for the first time, to claim facilities that rivaled or surpassed those of any liberal arts college in the country. The science quadrant (including space reserved for Seeley Mudd Library, which would soon follow) was certainly one of President Lyon's most significant legacies.

The postwar period also witnessed a rededication to the fine arts, on campuses and elsewhere. The threat to Europe's museums and cultural heritage during the war, including the Nazis' wholesale destruction of works of art deemed "degenerate" and the confiscation of others for Hitler's planned "museum of the fatherland," had the effect of reinforcing the significance of national patrimony and ushered in a period of growth for museums, whose value as humanizing educational institutions was recognized with renewed clarity. American museums, many of whose directors participated in the massive repatriation of works after the war, rededicated themselves to public education, a movement seen equally in higher education. Pomona had offered instruction in the arts from the time of its founding, and Lyon's postwar curricular reform included "literature, art or music" as one of the seven required areas of concentration in the student's first two years. Visual and performing arts curricula flourished, at Pomona as elsewhere, and the construction of Montgomery Gallery and Thatcher Music Building reflected this renewed emphasis.

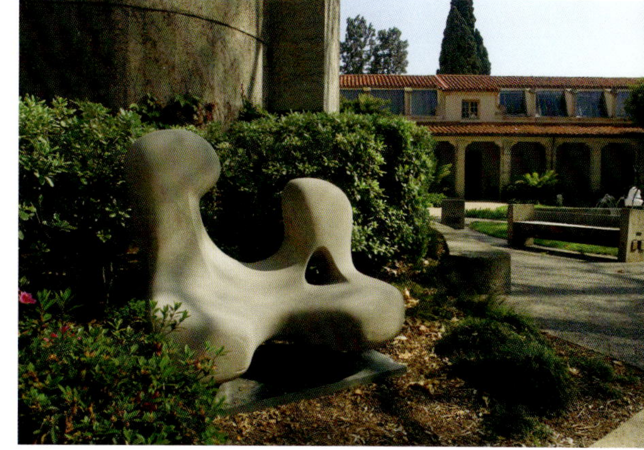

Charles Lawler, Untitled, c. 1950, bench/sculpture, gift of the Rembrandt Club, Lyon Garden

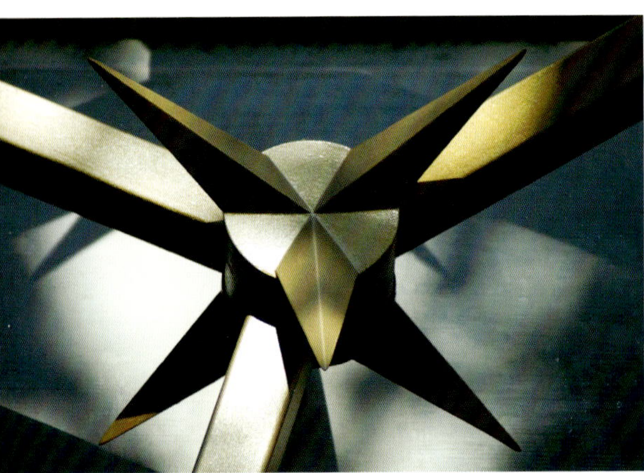

Mark Wood

Seaver Laboratory for Chemistry

The war in Europe had affected the intellectual life of the United States even before the country entered the conflict. The flight to America of artists and intellectuals, particularly from Hitler's Germany, significantly affected the visual arts here, with architecture the most visible manifestation of the new modernism. German architects Walter Gropius, Mies van der Rohe, and Marcel Breuer all arrived in America in 1938; Gropius became chairman of the department of architecture at Harvard, and Mies took over as head of the Armour Institute (later the Illinois Institute of Technology) in Chicago, where other former members of the Bauhaus established a small "New Bauhaus" in exile. Almost immediately, the sleek, functionalist "International Style" exemplified by the work of these architects occasioned debate about campus architecture. "To the modernists, all traditional collegiate forms were bankrupt, and the erection of any 'modern' building was a victory. To the traditionalists, the goal was just as simply to keep the American school free of the alien International Style."[1] Arguments about the most appropriate style for collegiate architecture continued during the war, with Mies van der Rohe's 1938–40 design for the campus of the Illinois Institute of Technology seen as a triumph for modernism. In ensuing years, the clean, spare lines of the new architecture took hold, in part because it appeared (misleadingly) easy to imitate and inexpensive to build relative to more decorative historicizing styles. At the same time, a premium on originality and individuality supported the notion of the building as a unique work of art, responsible only to itself and free of the obligation to blend in with its environment. Although most colleges continued to prefer unity over stylistic diversity, by the 1950s and 1960s, architectural variety was deemed not only acceptable but, in fact, desirable.[2] On Pomona's campus, this trend can be seen clearly in the three science laboratories, Oldenborg Center, Montgomery Gallery, and Thatcher Music Building—all composed of simple, block-like forms derived from their intended function and designed with only minimal deference to architectural context.

Wilson Lyon's presidency, extending from the Second World War to the Vietnam conflict, witnessed extraordinary changes in virtually every area of American life and higher education. The final decade of his tenure was a particularly tumultuous period, encompassing the birth of the Civil Rights Movement; the assassinations of John F. Kennedy, Martin Luther King, and Robert Kennedy; and the country's increasing involvement in Vietnam. At Pomona as elsewhere, students demonstrated an unprecedented level of activism and protest directed at both institutional and national issues. That the College not only weathered the crisis-ridden period but emerged stronger, its campus significantly enhanced, was a tribute to Lyon's leadership. His widow, Carolyn, recalled that the first thing to confront them when they arrived was the U.S. entry into the war, commenting, "One of his outstanding characteristics was his calm disposition in the face of really important and difficult times. He never scared easily. The College was always honorable in all its dealings. Pomona was built on the most solid integrity imaginable." ■

Memorial Gymnasium

In 1945, the trustees approved enlarging the College's facilities for physical education as a memorial to Pomona men and women who had died during two world wars (five men in World War I, 77 men and two women in World War II). The site and architect were selected by 1948, and ground was broken in 1950. Architect Wallace Neff integrated the old Memorial Training quarters (see Renwick Gymnasium, Chapter III) and added a dressing and shower room for women. The combined buildings offered a covered entrance on Sixth Street and a new gateway to Alumni Field. Neff had performed a similar transformation of an old building at Loyola University. The new facility, with a total 27,233 square feet of floor space, included everything required for Physical Education at the time.

The new gymnasium was the first priority of the Alumni Association's campaigns between 1946 and 1950, and the necessary funds were raised primarily from alumni, parents, trustees, and other friends of the College. Although there were several large gifts, most were small; the fund-raising effort included more alumni than had ever contributed to a single project.

In 1989, parts of Memorial Gymnasium were incorporated into the new Rains Center (see Chapter V). ■

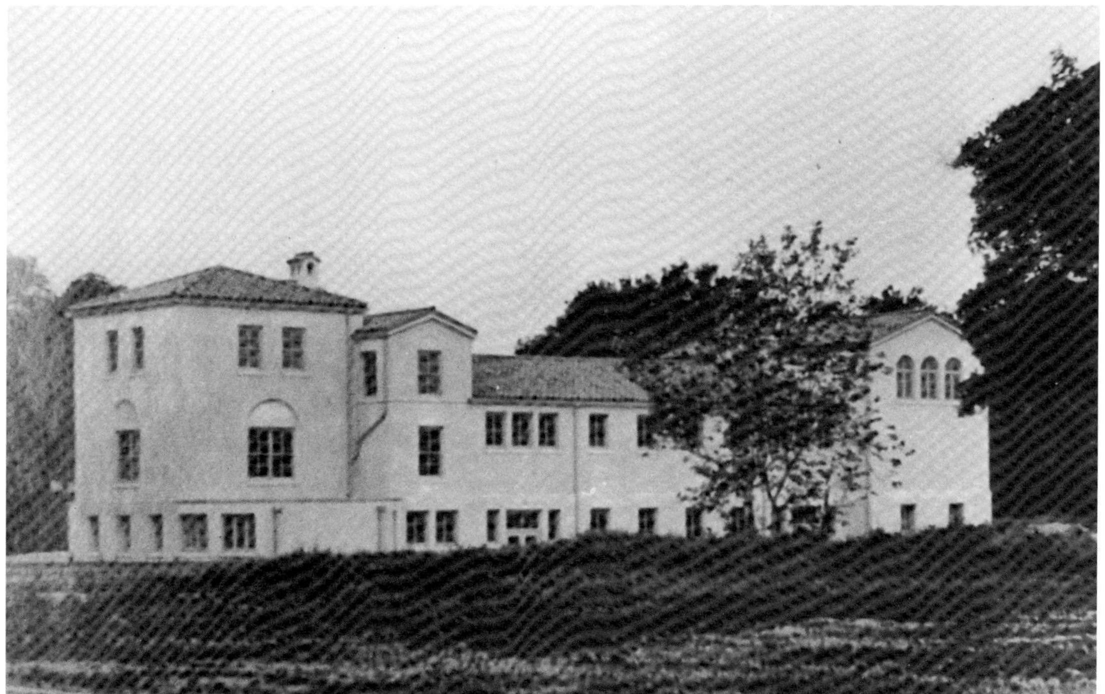

Memorial Gymnasium, built 1950

Memorial Gymnasium from playing field

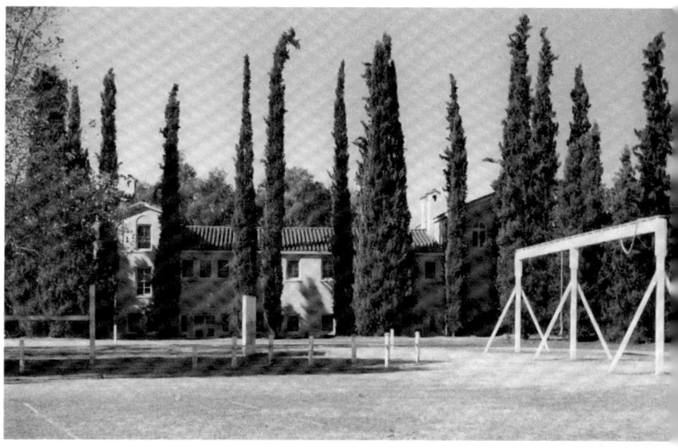

Memorial Gymnasium

BUILT 1950; dedicated November 11 (Armistice Day)

PRESIDENT IN OFFICE E. Wilson Lyon

LOCATION East of Smiley Hall (incorporating existing Memorial Training Quarters)

PURPOSE/USE men's gymnasium (some facilities for women)

ARCHITECT Wallace Neff, Los Angeles

MATERIALS reinforced concrete

COST approx $350,000 including equipment, landscaping

DONORS alumni, parents, trustees, friends of the College

NAMED FOR Pomona men and women lost in combat or war-related service

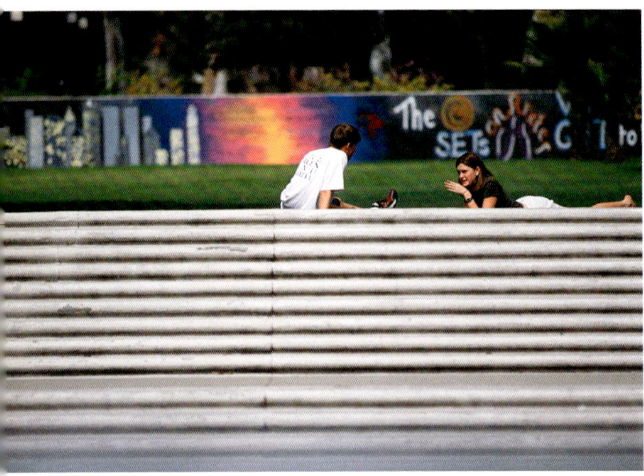

Phil Channing

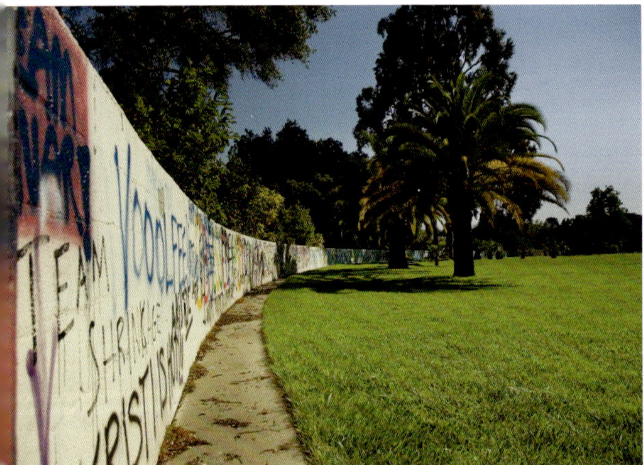

Mark Wood

"Walker Beach"

Walker Wall

Helen R. Walker Hall

The dedication of Walker Hall in 1954 was a momentous occasion, marking the completion of the men's campus (a 25-year building project) and resolving a housing crisis. In the early 1950s, with the number of male students approaching 600, the College could accommodate only 430 in Smiley and Clark halls. A new residence was clearly needed.

Plans for the men's dormitory and central lounge that would later become Walker Hall had been drawn in the late 1920s by architect Sumner Spaulding as part of his design for the Clark campus, but working drawings for the building were not commissioned until 1951. Construction of the new, 35,000-square-foot building began in 1952 and was completed in the fall of 1953. The timing was fortunate; although temporary units had been erected for returning veterans, the Claremont City Council, in September 1953, ordered that substandard emergency housing be removed—just in time for Walker Hall to open its doors.

The influence of Spaulding's travels in Spain's Balearic Islands in 1925, seen in the Mediterranean features of his and partner John Rex's design for the Clark dormitories and Frary Hall, was equally apparent in Walker, which reflected the earlier campus in its use of Romanesque arches and red tile roofs. The 35,000-square-foot structure housed 108 men in three wings, each of which included a sitting room, kitchenette, and patio. The design was praised for the manner in which it facilitated communal life. Walker transformed the appearance of the men's campus, ultimately forming a quadrangle with Norton Hall to the south. Friends of Frank H. Harwood converted the land north of Walker into a recreational field and garden now known as "Walker Beach."

Walker's lounge, with its glass wall facing Mt. Baldy, housed a game room, student offices and conference areas, a mail room, and a library. Directly below the lounge was an area known as "The Fishbowl," which contained a music-listening library and an organ, which supplemented concerts and outdoor programs in the Bosbyshell Fountain Plaza just outside its doors. The windows that lined the southeast corner of the lounge could be recessed into the walls, creating an open-air atmosphere.

Walker Hall was made possible largely through the estate of Helen R. Walker of Glendale, who left the bulk of her estate to Pomona College. Although she had no direct connection with the College and had never even visited the campus, Walker, according to her attorneys, "selected Pomona because it is a small college away from the distractions of a large city, and because of its reputation of developing not only the intellectual powers of its students but also their moral and social responsibilities." The Walker estate brought in over $700,000, at the time, the largest single gift ever made to the College.

The five-foot wall that curves along the northern edge of Walker Beach was built in 1956 as a flood break and remained untouched until the spring of 1975 when students painted "Free Angela" on its inner surface, referring to the imprisonment of activist Angela Davis. Significantly, College administrators decided not to remove the slogan, and since then, generations of Pomona students have turned Walker Wall into a public forum, expressing everything from whimsical musings to profoundly serious political statements. Perhaps most moving was the response to the attacks of September 11, 2001. On that evening, the wall was painted a uniform black; on the second day, the New York skyline appeared, with the Twin Towers restored and the words "You Are in Our Hearts." ■

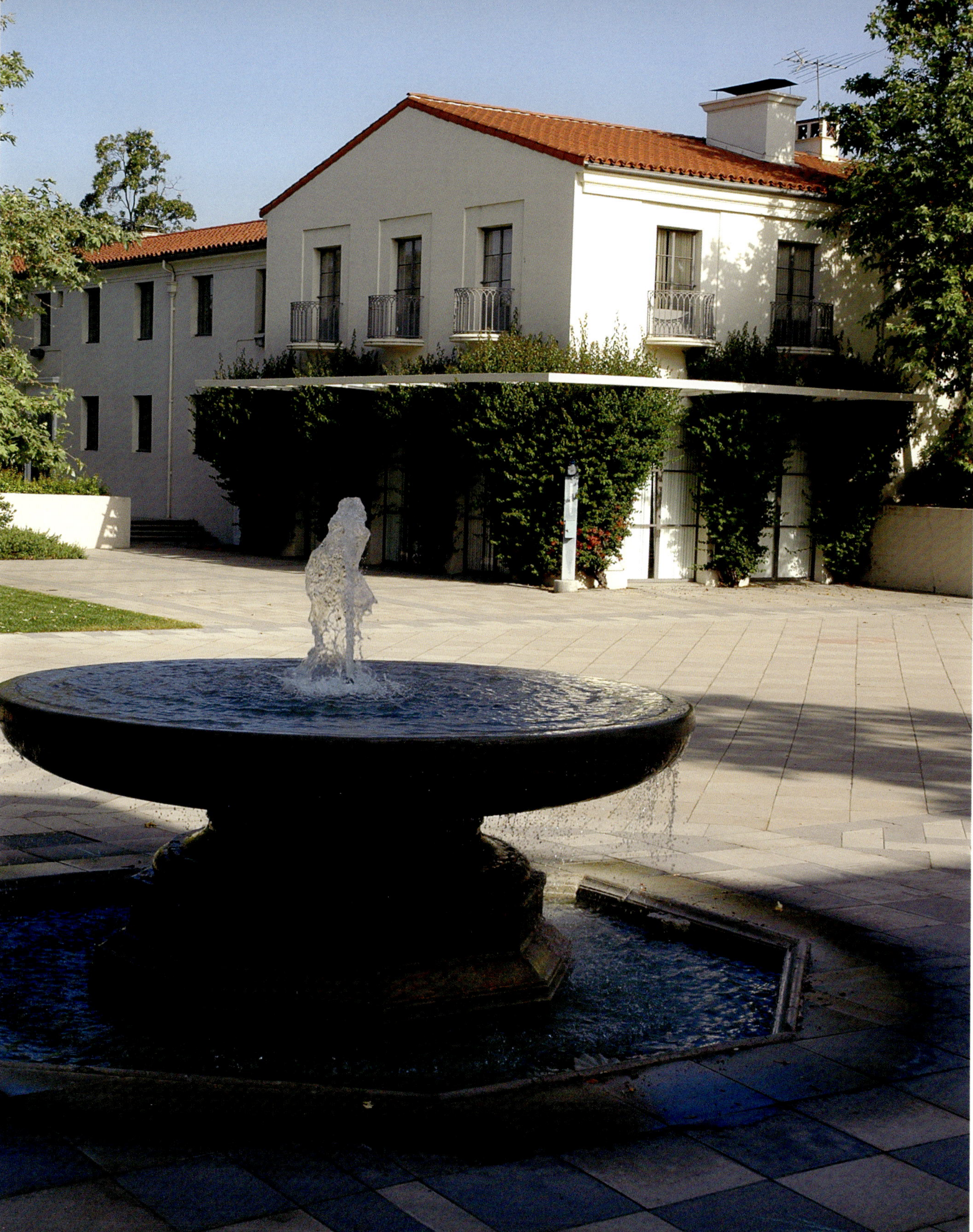

Mark Wood

Helen R. Walker Hall

BUILT 1953; dedicated 1954
PRESIDENT IN OFFICE E. Wilson Lyon
LOCATION 700 North College Way
PURPOSE/USE men's residence hall
ARCHITECT Sumner Spaulding and John Rex
MATERIALS reinforced concrete, tile roof
DONOR/NAMED FOR Mrs. Helen R. Walker, Glendale

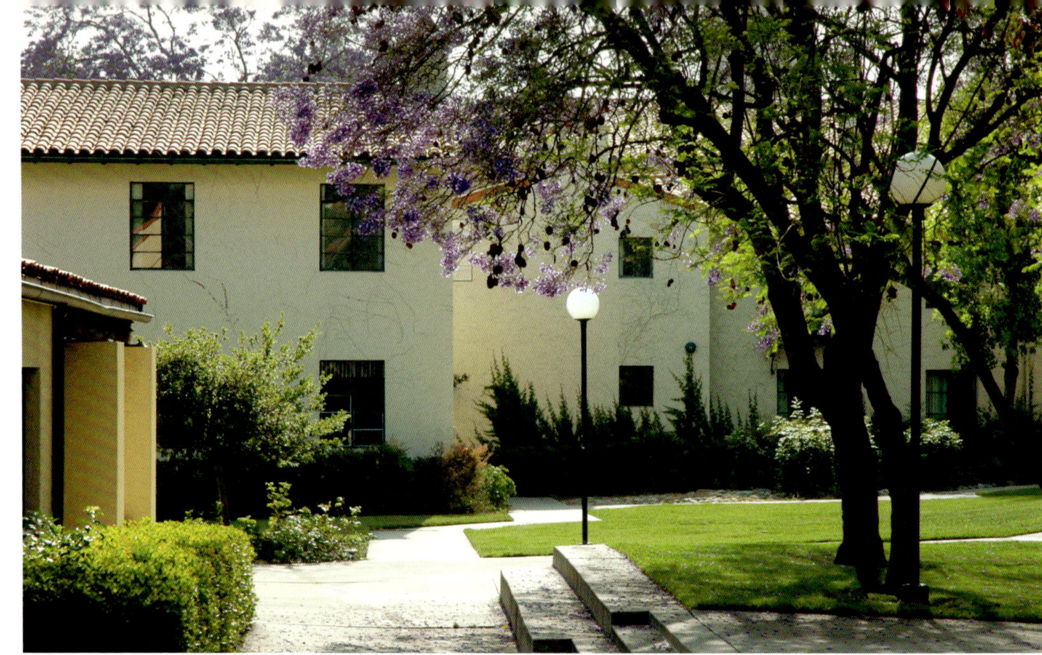

Mark Wood

Norton Hall

BUILT 1956
PRESIDENT IN OFFICE E. Wilson Lyon
LOCATION 355 East Sixth Street
ARCHITECT/BUILDER William J. Moran Co.
COST $114,000 (approx.)
MATERIALS reinforced concrete, tile roof
NAMED FOR Edwin Clarence Norton, dean of Pomona College

Norton Hall

In 1956, several years after the completion of Walker Hall, rooms for men were still needed, so 36 singles were added as an extension of Clark Hall along Sixth Street. Built in the same style as the rest of the Clark campus, the new unit, along with its inner courtyard, was named for Edwin Clarence Norton, appointed in 1888 as the first member of the original Pomona College faculty and later professor of Greek and dean of the faculty. ■

Smith Memorial Tower

BUILT 1961
PRESIDENT IN OFFICE E. Wilson Lyon
LOCATION North campus courtyard of the north campus (named Bixby Plaza in 1994)
ARCHITECT John Rex (Honnold and Rex, Los Angeles)
COST $150,000 (approx.)
MATERIALS reinforced concrete, glazed pre-cast concrete grilles
DONORS/NAMED FOR Mr. and Mrs. Edwin S. Smith, San Diego

Smith Memorial Tower

Architect Sumner Spaulding's original plan for Pomona's north campus in the 1920s included a tower, but more utilitarian concerns took precedence and the structure was not built.[2] In 1959, Mr. and Mrs. Edwin S. Smith of San Diego provided funds for a memorial tower that was subsequently designed by Spaulding's former partner, John Rex of the firm of Rex and Honnold, and completed in 1961. Installed in the 125-foot tower is a 2,350-pound replica of the Liberty Bell in Independence Hall, Philadelphia.

REMINISCENCE:
I have many favorite memories of my tenure at Pomona in the 1970s. The quad with the Frary fountain was the scene of East LA cumbia, a group of us, with Alejandro Gonzales (now president of Cal State Sacramento and a Pomona trustee), dancing with joy around the water. I swam in the fountain at the height of the hippie antics, and watched the indomitable Andy scale the clock tower, and of course, searched for the ambiguous Mufti stickers plastered along the courtyard walkways. —CAROLYN PEREZ-RODRIGUEZ '73 ■

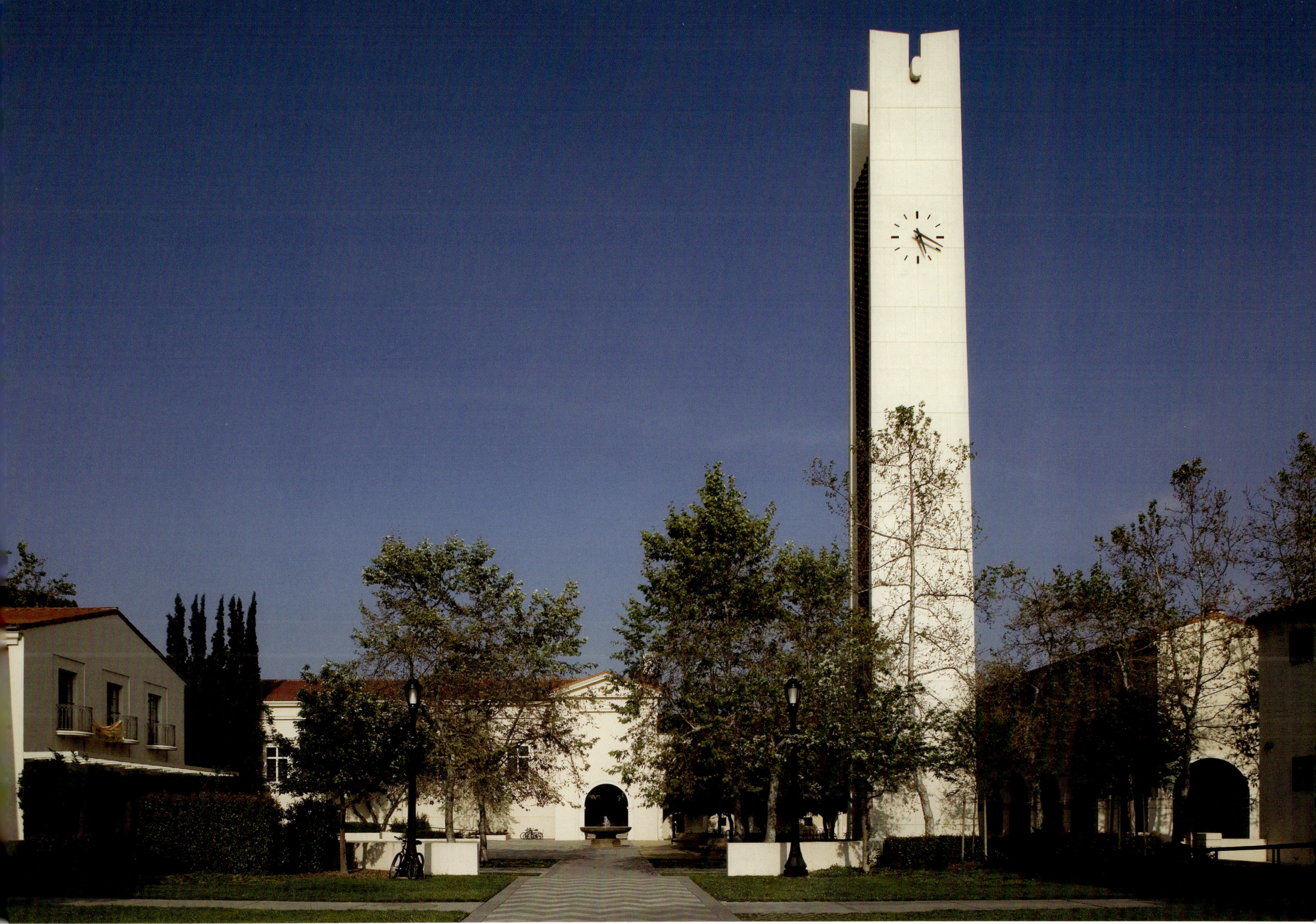

Henry Cabala

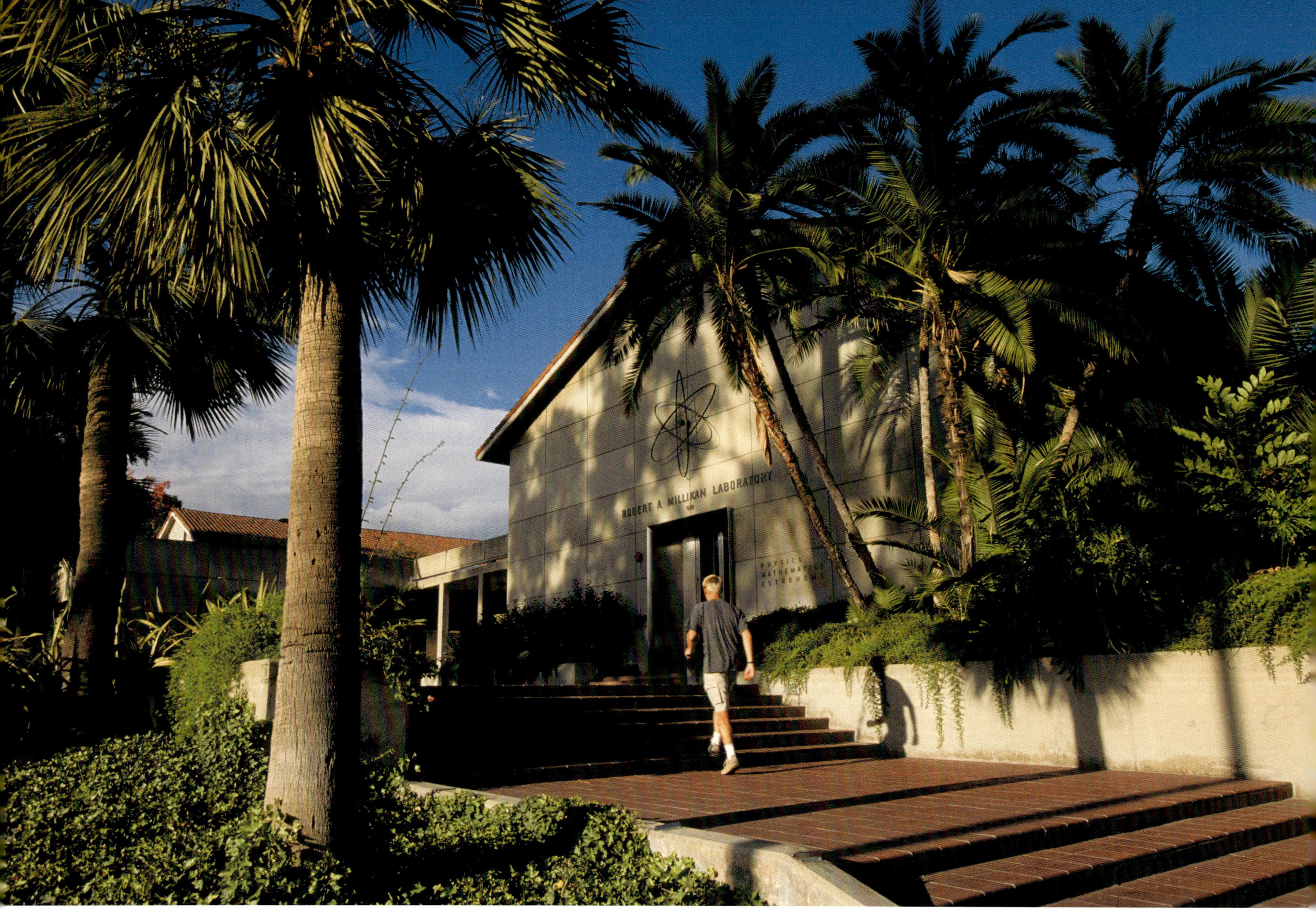

Phil Channing

Seaver Science Center

These new structures will provide the most modern facilities for instruction at the undergraduate level in the nation. They are designed particularly to meet Pomona's science instruction program which stresses the importance of individual student research. —E. Wilson Lyon on Seaver and Millikan laboratories

The development of Pomona's science complex, which now occupies the two blocks from Harvard Avenue to College Way between Sixth and Seventh streets, extends from 1958 to the present day; the most recent facilities—the Lincoln and Edmunds buildings—were dedicated in March 2007.

Science had held a prominent place in Pomona's curriculum from the time of its founding. Two of the original six faculty were science teachers, and by the early 20th century, Pomona was among the leaders in the percentage of alumni who went on to graduate study in the sciences; in 1959, the College ranked fifth among liberal arts colleges in the number of alumni members of the National Academy of Sciences.

The first two buildings in the Seaver complex—Millikan Laboratory for Physics, Mathematics, and Astronomy, and Seaver Laboratory for Biology and Geology—were dedicated together on December 6, 1958. The speaker on that occasion, Dr. Detlev W. Bronk, president of the National Academy of Sciences and of the Rockefeller Institute, referred to the two as "temples dedicated to the truth we seek." At the time, these facilities were believed to be unsurpassed for undergraduate scientific instruction. Facing each other across College Avenue, the matching structures were the gift of Frank R. Seaver '05 (trustee 1947–64). Seaver, who had already provided funds for chemistry equipment and, in 1950, had paid for an astronomy laboratory at Brackett Observatory, was the ideal patron—intensely involved, determined to have the best facilities irrespective of cost, and even willing to underwrite annual operating expenses as well as construction.

Plans for the building were first discussed by Dr. Charles A. Fowler, Jr., professor of physics and chair of the department, at a trustee-faculty retreat in 1956. The original idea was to site a new structure on Fifth Street between College and Harvard avenues, but ultimately the larger lot north of Sixth Street was selected. At Seaver's request, the new building was named for Robert Andrews Millikan (1868–1953), professor of physics at the University of Chicago, first president of Caltech, and Nobel prize-winner (1923); a close friend of Seaver, Millikan had made Southern California a world-renowned center of science education. The 43,927-square-foot facility included laboratories for nuclear, electronic and atomic and molecular physics; the College's first computer lab; the Spitz Planetarium, featuring a stellar projector that simulated the sky as seen by the naked eye; separate libraries for the three disciplines; an extensively equipped machine shop; a 150-seat demonstration auditorium; and an engineering drawing laboratory. Millikan doubled the space available for physics, mathematics, and astronomy, freeing Pearsons Hall, which was remodeled for the departments of History, Religion, Philosophy, and Classics.

Fowler noted at the time that Millikan intended to provide the research atmosphere students would find in industrial and graduate school laboratories after leaving Pomona. "While some colleges and universities provide this realistic atmosphere of research at the senior level, Pomona is one of the few that offer this type of instruction at the lower undergraduate levels, even in the freshman year."

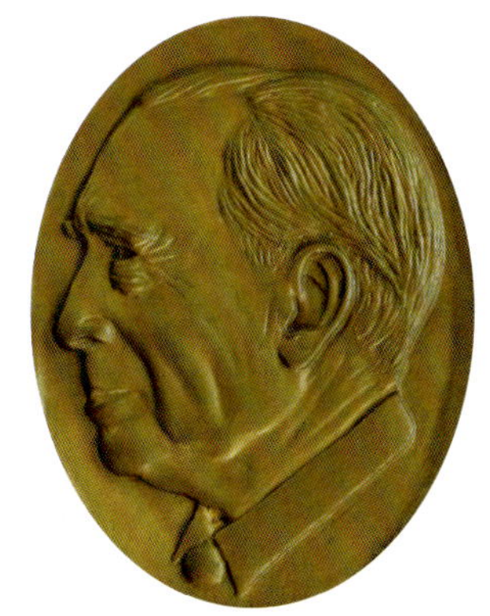

Frank Seaver

Robert A. Millikan Laboratory for Physics, Mathematics, and Astronomy

BUILT 1958

PRESIDENT IN OFFICE E. Wilson Lyon

LOCATION 610 North College Avenue (northeast corner College Avenue and Sixth Street)

PURPOSE Physics, Mathematics, Astronomy

ARCHITECT Herbert J. Powell (Smith, Powell and Morgridge), Los Angeles

MATERIALS reinforced concrete, tile roof (matching Seaver Laboratory)

COST $3,250,000 (with Seaver Laboratory and equipment)

DONOR Frank R. Seaver '05, Trustee 1947–64

NAMED FOR Robert Andrews Millikan (1868–1953), friend of Seaver, professor of physics, University of Chicago, first president and chairman of executive council of Caltech, Nobel Prize winner (1923)

Seaver Laboratory for Biology and Geology (Seaver South)

BUILT 1958
PRESIDENT IN OFFICE E. Wilson Lyon
LOCATION 609 North College Avenue (Northwest corner College Avenue and Sixth Street)
PURPOSE Biology/Geology
ARCHITECT Herbert J. Powell (Smith, Powell and Morgridge), Los Angeles
MATERIALS reinforced concrete, tile roof
COST with Millikan and equipment, $3,250,000
DONOR/NAMED FOR Frank R. Seaver '05, Trustee 1947–64
EXPANSION of the Department of Biology, February 26, 2005, dedication of new Richard C. Seaver Biology Building (see Chapter VII)

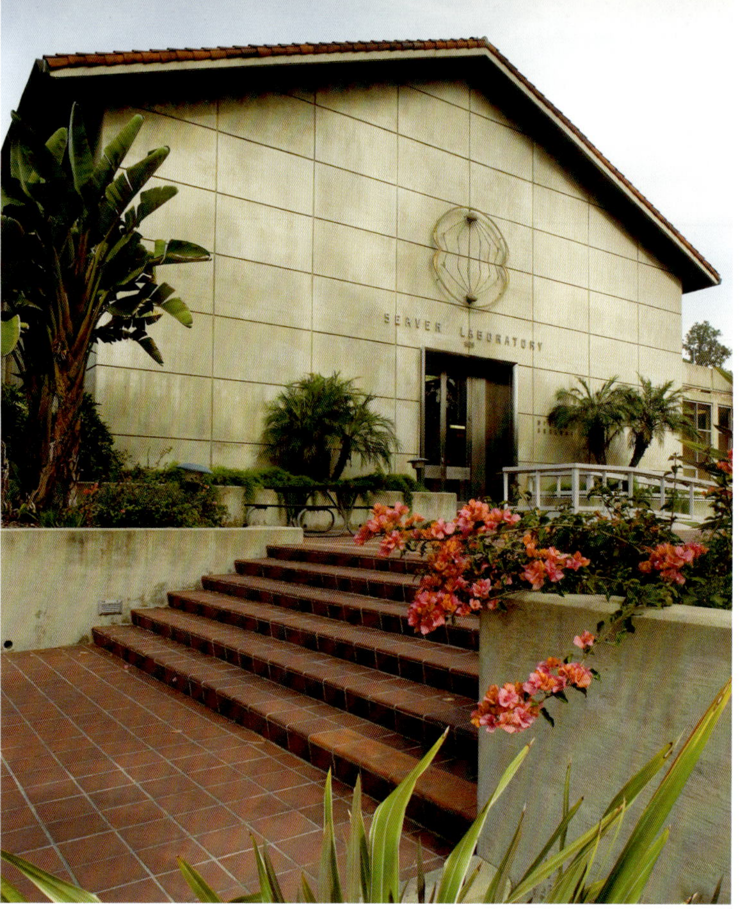

Henry Cabala

The Seaver Laboratory for Biology and Geology, now known as Seaver South, was constructed at the same time as Millikan Laboratory just across College Avenue. Encompassing 50,529 square feet, its facilities for biology included electron, phase and Baker interference microscopes; a radioactive-isotope laboratory patterned after Oak Ridge; experimental aquaria using seawater for marine-life study; and a controlled-temperature animal house. For geology, it featured a microscope room with Zeiss and Leitz instruments with four-axis universal stages for three-dimensional measuring purposes; an X-ray spectrograph for chemical analysis of rocks; a gravity meter for measuring earth tides; ultrasonic separator for breaking up rock material; an experimental lab where clay was used to simulate the earth's crust; and a rock-slicing room with diamond saws. The building also included libraries for both zoology and geology.

The construction of Seaver Laboratory freed space in Mason and Crookshank for chemistry, psychology, and botany. Although the trustees initially believed that Mason Hall would continue to suffice for chemistry, the completion of Millikan and Seaver laboratories soon led to a different conclusion. In September 1962, Frank Seaver met with President Lyon and Chemistry Professor R. Nelson Smith '38 in Mason Hall. He brought with him a check for $1,000,000 for a new science building. The gift was announced in November, and working drawings were complete by summer 1963. When bids came in higher than anticipated, Seaver characteristically insisted the building be constructed as designed; at the trustee meeting that September, he presented another check, for $1,600,000. Ground was broken on September 26, 1963 (the opening day of classes), construction extended through fall semester 1964, and the department moved in during Christmas break, offering classes there beginning in January 1965. Ultimately, Seaver donated nearly $3.4 million to the project, a figure that included

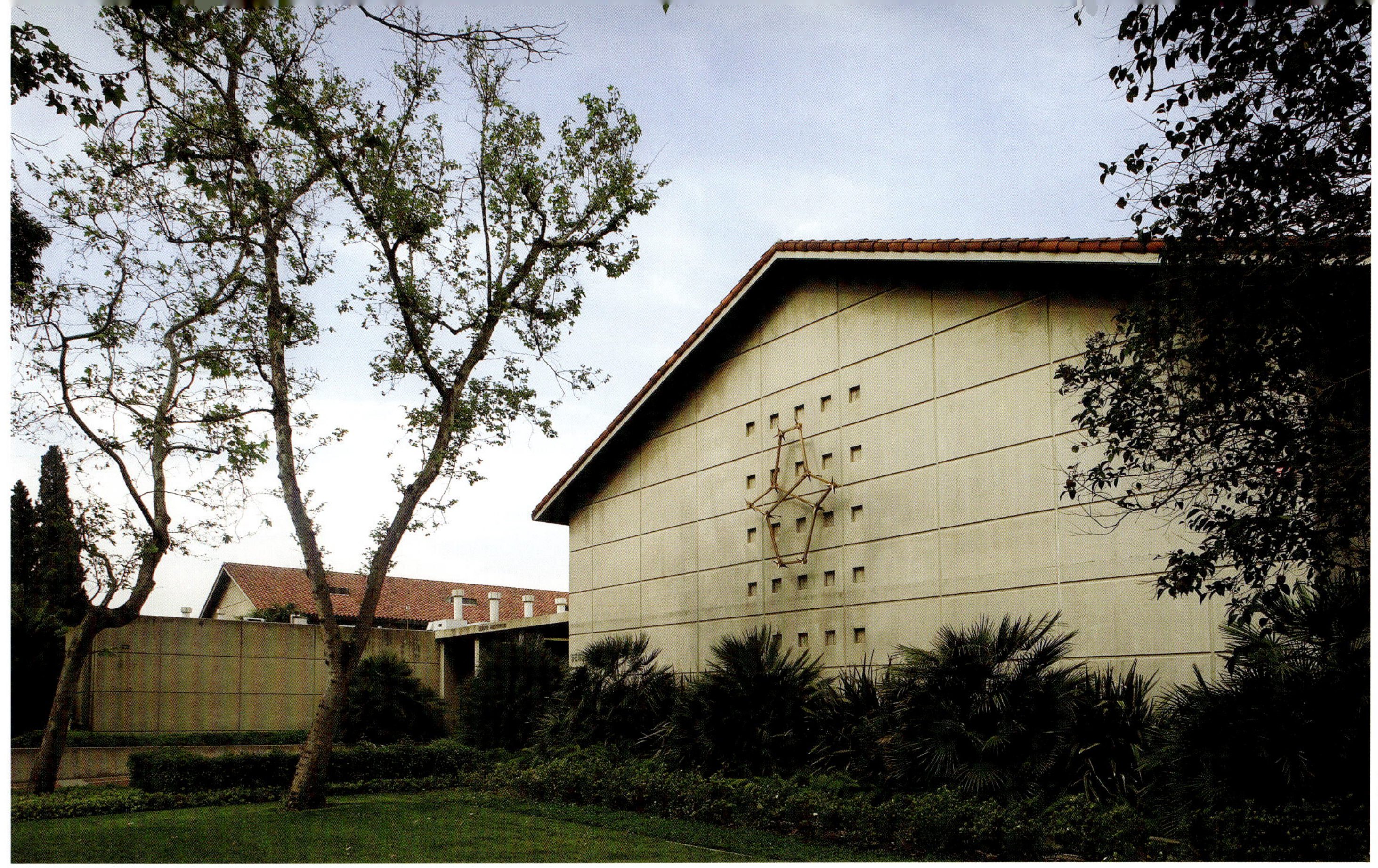
Henry Cabala

$650,000 for equipment. When he died in October 1964, he left the College interest in a trust fund to cover future needs; thereafter, Mrs. Seaver, who was named to the Board in 1965, continued the family's extraordinary history of support.

Pomona's new chemistry building, Seaver North, was the largest (60,319 square feet) and most complex of the three donated by Frank Seaver. It was an unusually well-equipped facility for an undergraduate college, featuring a lecture room with closed circuit and commercial TV and both slide and movie projectors; two freshman laboratories; a well-stocked chemistry library that Wilson Lyon declared one of the finest on the West Coast,[3] and an IBM System/360 computer (that cost $268,000 and was one of the first to be purchased by any American college or university in the nation). The research and teaching labs all had stainless steel distillation hoods and safety glass partitions. The building's specifications evolved through the close cooperation of members of the faculty, particularly Professor R. Nelson Smith, chair of the department, who devoted three academic years to the project.

The three buildings in the original Seaver Science complex were designed by a single architect, Herbert J. Powell of Smith, Powell and Morgridge, Los Angeles. Consistent in elevation and design details, all were constructed of reinforced concrete, similarly scored into blocks. While their red tile roofs linked them with their older neighbors Holmes and Pearsons halls, the spare, bunker-like architecture reflects a Cold War mentality that one finds in science buildings of the same period on other campuses. Together, they formed a cohesive complex that would later expand to include the Seeley Mudd Science Library, 1983 (see Chapter v); the Edward and Edith Andrew Science Building, 1999; Richard C. Seaver Biology Building, 2005; and the Lincoln and Edmunds buildings, 2007 (see Chapter vi). ■

Seaver Laboratory for Chemistry (Seaver North)

BUILT 1964
PRESIDENT IN OFFICE E. Wilson Lyon
LOCATION 645 North College Avenue (southwest corner College Avenue and Seventh Street)
PURPOSE Chemistry
ARCHITECT Herbert J. Powell (Smith, Powell and Morgridge), Los Angeles
MATERIALS reinforced concrete, tile roof
COST $3,379,334
DONOR Frank R. Seaver '05, Trustee 1947–64

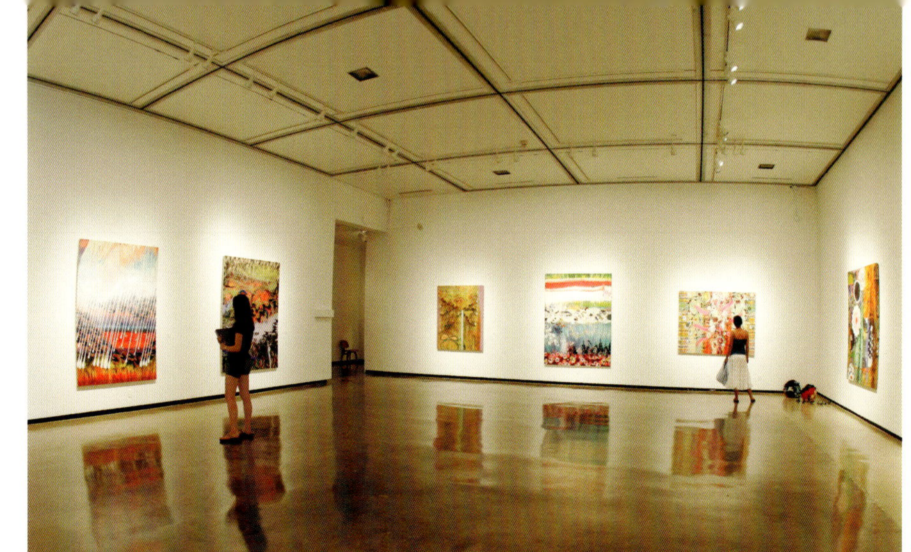
Phil Channing

Montgomery Art Center
(See Also Rembrandt Hall, Chapter I)

BUILT 1958
PRESIDENT IN OFFICE E. Wilson Lyon
LOCATION 330 North College Avenue (northeast corner College and Bonita Avenues)
PURPOSE art gallery, studios
ARCHITECT Herbert J. Powell (Smith, Powell and Morgridge), Los Angeles
MATERIALS reinforced concrete
DONOR Victor Montgomery
NAMED FOR Gladys K. Montgomery

ABOVE *North gallery, added 1977, after renovation of 2006*

RIGHT *Public entrance after renovation of 2006*

Montgomery Art Center/ Pomona College Museum of Art

(See Also Rembrandt Hall, Chapter I)

The growth of interest in art was one of most prominent post-war developments at the College, and the expansion of the fine arts curriculum, under the supervision of a series of distinguished faculty members, inevitably led to a demand for enhanced facilities. In the late 1950s, President Lyon encouraged art historian Professor Peter Selz, then chair of the department, and his colleague, Professor Seymour Slive, to present their needs to the Academic Affairs Committee of the Board, chaired by Gladys K. Montgomery; ultimately, her husband Victor would donate a new fine arts building named in her honor. Designed by Herbert Powell, who was working at the time on the Seaver science buildings, the reinforced concrete structure included a gallery, lecture room that also served as a gallery, space for permanent collections exhibitions and seminars, and a slide room. Completed in the summer of 1958, it doubled the space available to the art department, adding 8,000 square feet adjoining Rembrandt Hall on the south and west and freeing space there that was subsequently transformed into studios and classrooms.

The dedication of the new art center was celebrated with an exhibition titled "The Stieglitz Circle" that included paintings by Charles Demuth, Arthur Dove, Marsden Hartley, John Marin, Georgia O'Keefe, and Max Weber; art historian Seymour Slive, who had, by then, left Pomona for Harvard, gave the opening lecture. Also on view was the College's permanent collection, exhibited together in one place for the first time in its 71-year history.

As had been the case with Rembrandt Hall (see Chapter 1), the Rembrandt Club played an important role in securing the new art center, asserting the need for improved facilities and raising initial funds. Gladys K. Montgomery, for whom it was named, had been a trustee since 1948. She was also the first president (1940) of the Women's Campus Club of Pomona College, a large organization of mothers and friends of students, and a civic and cultural leader in Los Angeles.

Mrs. Montgomery's support of the arts at Pomona continued. In 1968, she funded renovations that nearly doubled the size of the art center, adding a second story on the eastern half of the building, a new room on the north, and a new entrance from College Avenue. And in 1977, under the directorship of David Steadman, a large exhibition space that featured ceiling-hung movable panels was added on the north, along with other important renovations, including the addition of climate control and conversion of an existing gallery into a print study room. This project, too, was funded by Montgomery, who had, by this time, also donated generously toward the Thatcher Music Building in memory of her husband. The enhanced gallery reopened with a major exhibition of drawings from Southern California collections.

From 1977 to 1993, Montgomery Gallery participated with Lang Gallery, Scripps College in a joint program known as The Galleries of The Claremont Colleges, and in 2001, Montgomery Gallery became the Pomona College Museum of Art, reflecting its role as an institution that houses a substantial permanent collection as well as serving as a gallery for the display of temporary exhibitions. ■

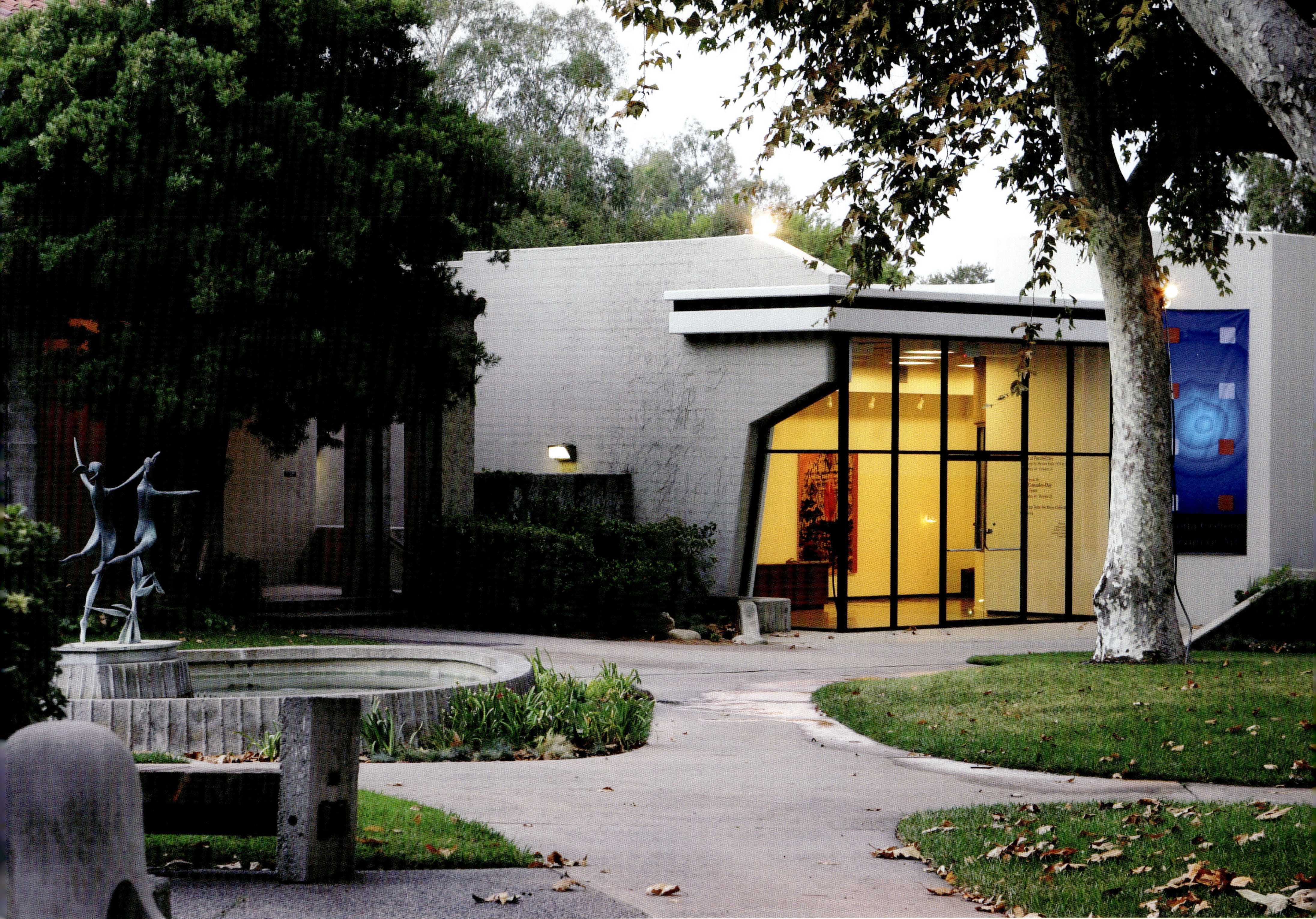

Phil Channing

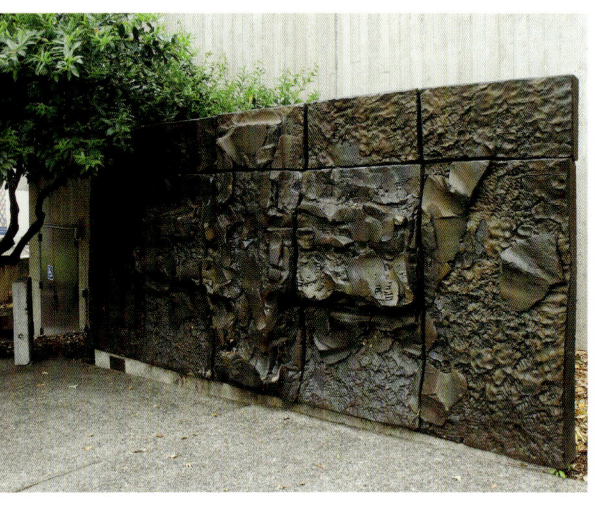

Henry Cabala

Carolyn Bartel Lyon Garden

BUILT dedicated 1970
PRESIDENT IN OFFICE David Alexander
LOCATION College Avenue between Bonita Avenue and Fourth Street; courtyard formed by Rembrandt Hall/Montgomery Gallery, Thatcher Music Building, Bridges Gallery, Thatcher Music Building, Bridges Hall of Music
NAMED FOR Carolyn Bartel (Mrs. E. Wilson) Lyon, wife of Pomona's sixth president

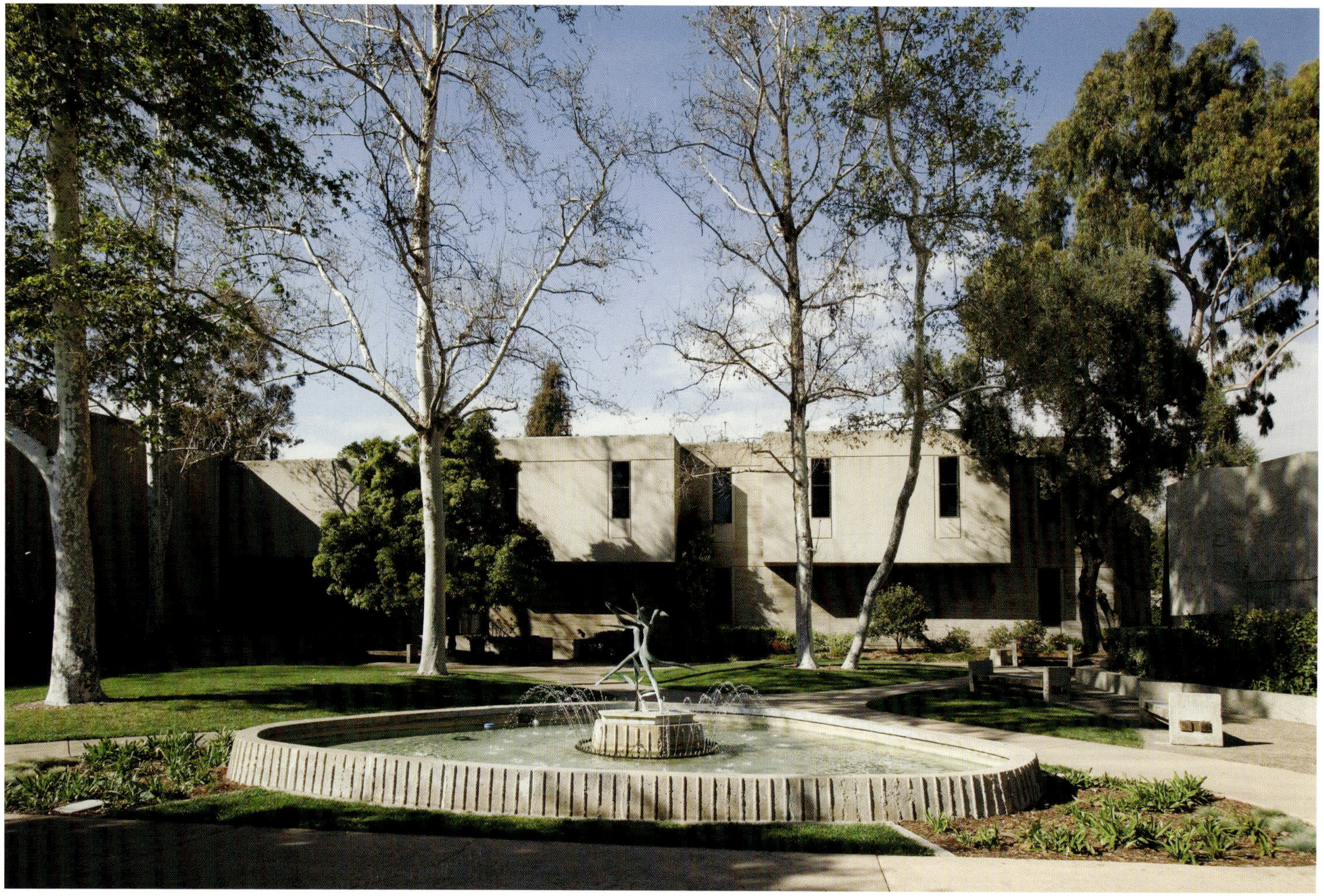

Henry Cabala

ABOVE LEFT *John Mason,* Cross Form, *1964, glazed ceramic sculpture, gift of the artist, Lyon Garden*

ABOVE *Lyon Garden and Thatcher Music Building; fountain sculpture by Robert I. Russin,* Joie de Vie, *1973, gift of Mrs. Victor Montgomery*

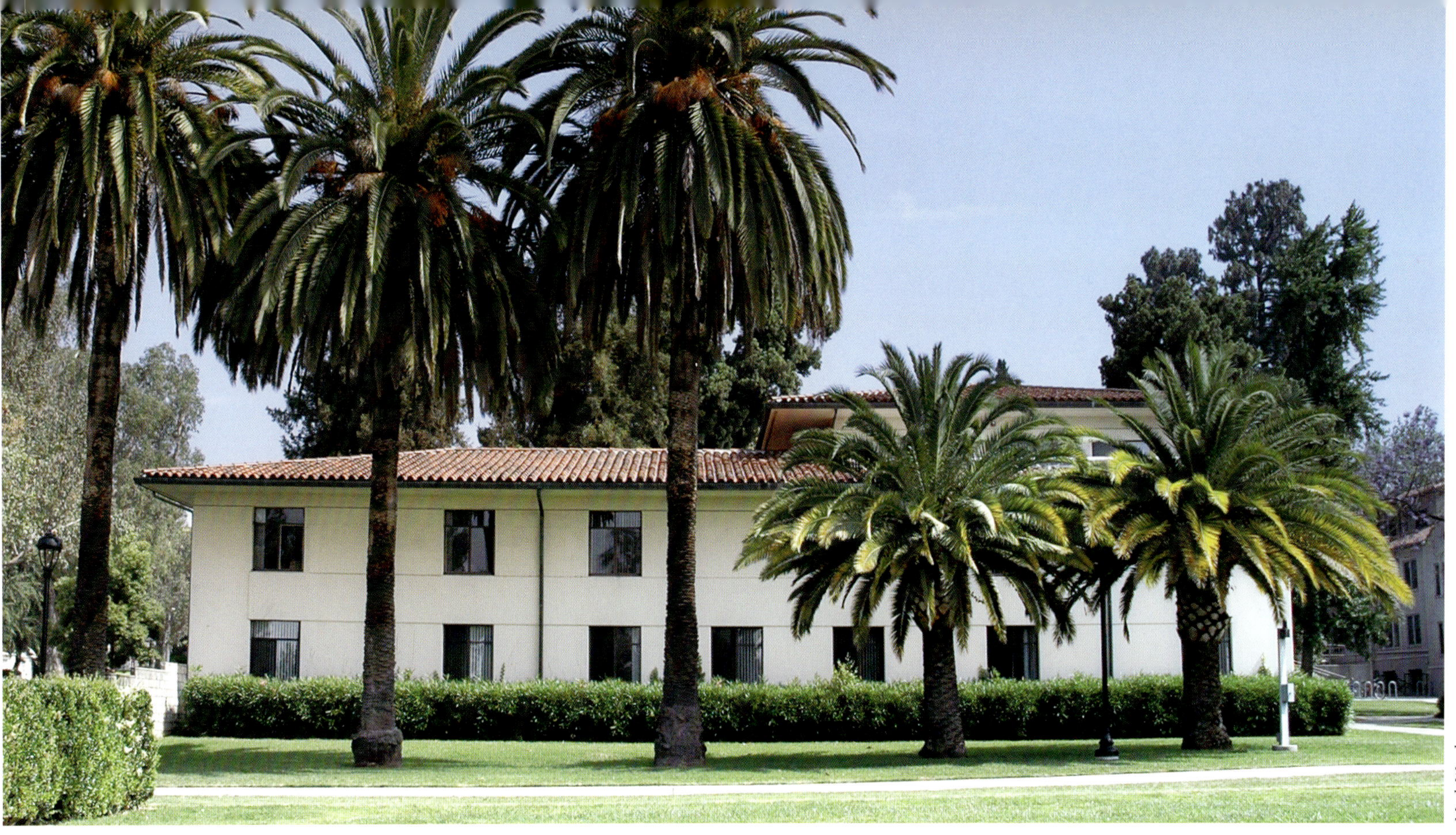

Mark Wood

Anna May Wig Hall

By the late 1950s, another women's residence hall was needed. With enrollment now at 1,000, the existing facilities for women— Harwood Court (1921), Blaisdell Hall (1936), Mudd Hall (1947); and three smaller residences, each accommodating a dozen students who spoke German, French, and Spanish—no longer sufficed; the College was still housing women in private homes and the Claremont Inn.

The Women's Campus Club, for which a new women's dormitory had been a goal for years, gave $24,000 that was used primarily for furnishings. The building itself was supported by Board Chair Rudolph J. Wig (trustee 1929–67), his daughter Mary, and her husband Stanley Johnson. It was named for Wig's late wife Anna May (Bartlett) Wig who had died in September 1956. A pianist who had studied at Oberlin and taught music in Chicago, she had been active in the Pasadena Presbyterian Church.

Consisting of a two-story structure facing Bonita Avenue and running south along College Avenue, and a three-story L-shaped wing on Second Street, the new residence housed 97 students. It featured a lounge, which extended east toward Harwood Court and boasted a massive fireplace with a raised hearth and stainless steel hood. Designed by Herbert Powell, architect of the Seaver Science Center and Montgomery Art Center, it was also built of reinforced concrete with a tile roof and formed a quadrangle with Harwood Court that gave access to the dining hall where Wig residents took their meals. Construction required the removal of several small houses and transformed the entrance to the College at Third Street. ■

Anna May Wig Hall

BUILT 1959
PRESIDENT IN OFFICE E. Wilson Lyon
LOCATION North College Avenue between Second Street and Bonita Avenue
PURPOSE women's dormitory
ARCHITECT Herbert J. Powell (Smith, Powell and Morgridge, Los Angeles
MATERIALS reinforced concrete, tile roof
COST $543,000
DONORS Rudolph J. Wig, trustee 1929–67, Mary (Wig) and Stanley Johnson, and the Campus Women's Club
NAMED FOR Anna May (Bartlett) Wig

Stover Walk

Stover Walk, which connects College Avenue and College Way along the northern edge of Marston Quadrangle, is one of the College's primary east-west axes. At Commencement, its role becomes ceremonial as well, serving as the gathering point for the annual procession of trustees, faculty, and graduating seniors to the site of the ceremony in Bridges Auditorium. The beautification project of which it was a part also included 10,000 ivy plants, a dozen new trees, including an olive and six Canary Island pines; automatic sprinklers, new lights, and benches.

The north side of the walk was enhanced by a bronze relief figure of Pegasus, created and donated by sculptor Albert Stewart, professor of fine arts at Scripps College, and installed on a terrazzo wall originally located between Edmunds Union and Holmes Hall. Stewart noted that he chose Pegasus, the winged horse, as a classic symbol of aspiration. When the Smith Campus Center was built in 1999, replacing Edmunds Union, Stover Walk underwent modifications designed in part to open north-south vistas across Marston Quadrangle. Pegasus now rises on a low wall on the south side of the walk near College Avenue.

Clarence T. Stover '21, whose family had moved to this area from Kansas, was a builder. Beginning in 1929, he and his brother William oversaw one of the largest and most successful construction firms ever to be established in the Pomona Valley. The C.T. and W.P. Stover Company was responsible for Clark, Frary and Mudd halls at the College as well as for many houses in Claremont, the Progress-Bulletin building in Pomona, and the Los Angeles County Fairgrounds complex including the Fine Arts Building and grandstand. A prominent civic leader, Stover was a trustee from 1952 until his death in 1955. ■

Stover Walk

CONSTRUCTED 1957–58; dedicated Alumni Day 1958
PRESIDENT IN OFFICE E. Wilson Lyon
LOCATION Extending from College Avenue to College Way east of Harrison Street
DONORS family and friends of Clarence T. Stover
NAMED FOR Clarence T. Stover '21, trustee 1952–55 (d. 1955), chair of Buildings and Grounds Committee; prominent civic leader

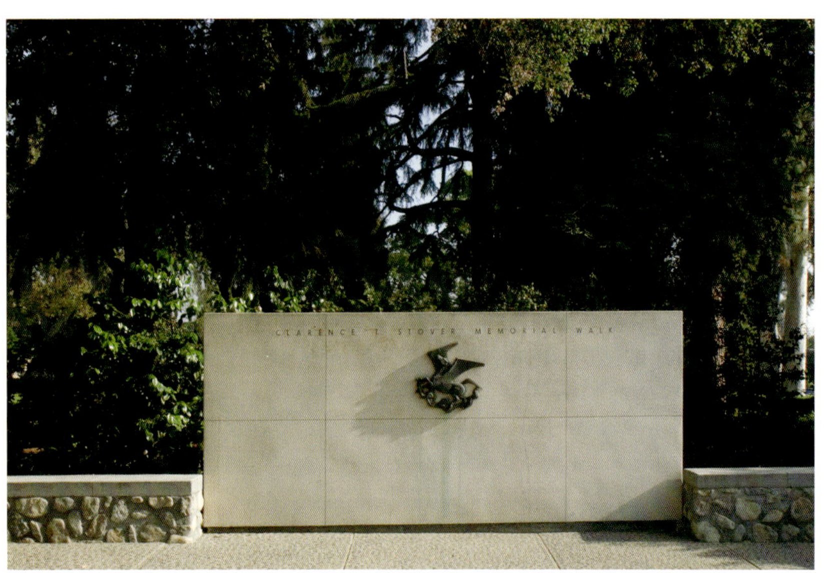

Henry Cabala

Albert Stewart, Pegasus, *1958, Bronze relief, Stover Walk, Pomona College commission in honor of Clarence T. Stover*

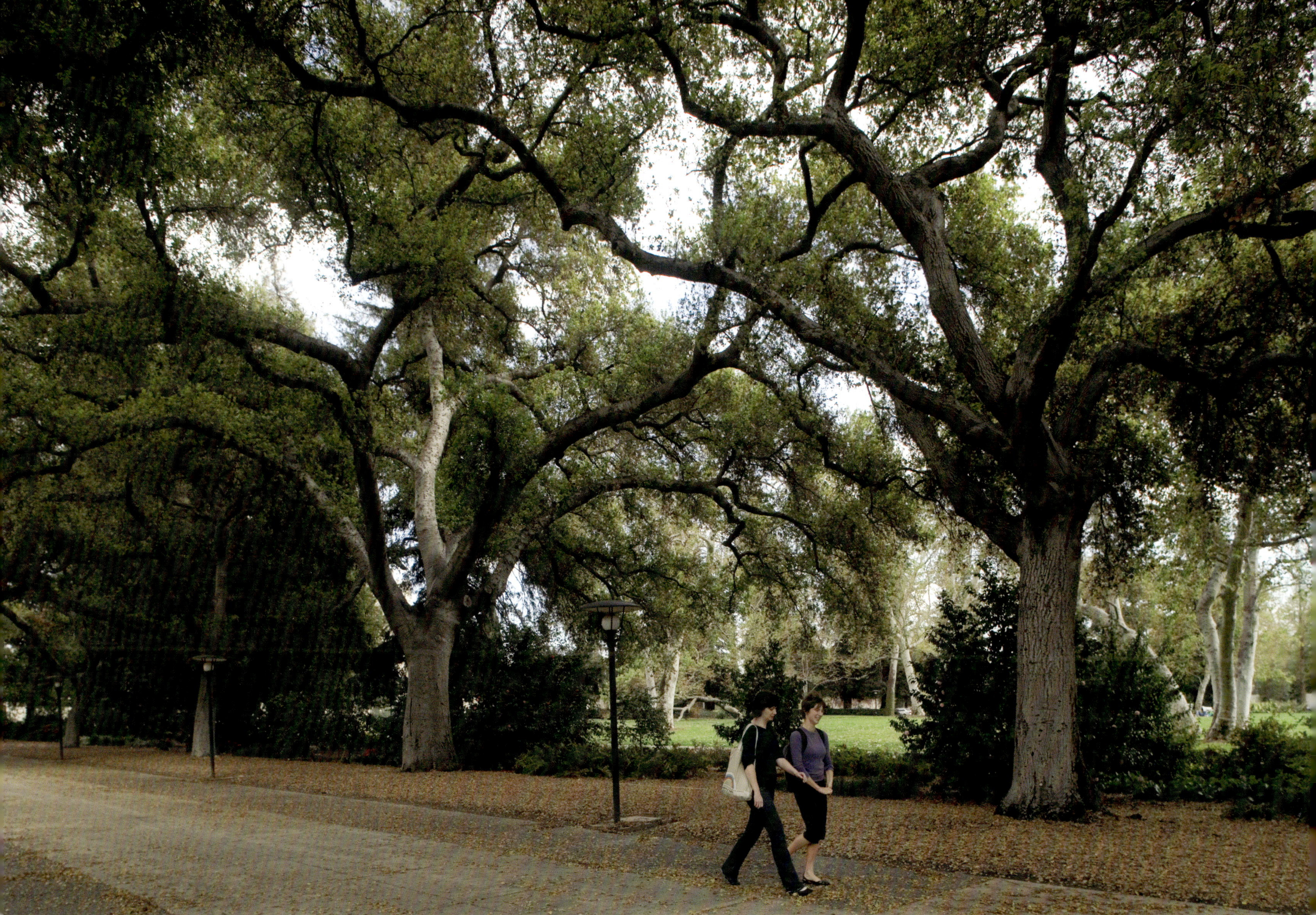

Henry Cabala

Oldenborg Center

When Oldenborg Center was built in 1966, it was believed to be the first facility of its kind to combine a language center, international house, and coeducational residence in a single building. Although other institutions, Columbia and Berkeley among them, had international centers for foreign students, and many others had modest language houses, no other American college or university offered a dormitory designed for the practice and use of foreign languages.

Pomona's Center was named for Dietrich C. Oldenborg, a retired businessman who had died in 1965. Born in Denmark and raised in New York, he had been a world traveler whose goal as a philanthropist was to "strengthen communication and understanding among nations and thereby contribute to world peace." Although a Yale alumnus, Oldenborg was attracted to Pomona by The Claremont Colleges consortium. Experience abroad heightened his interest in Pomona's need for new foreign language and international relations facilities, and his gift of $1.1 million was, at the time, the third largest in the history of the College.

Oldenborg Center was designed to facilitate the development of language fluency and better understanding of foreign cultures and international relations, offering opportunities second only to an actual sojourn abroad. At the time of its dedication in October 1966, it housed 144 students, grouped according to the languages they were studying, in separate wings for men and women; the dining area was also divided into language sections. The original five languages accommodated—French, German, Spanish, Chinese and Russian—had, by 2006, expanded to 26: American Sign, Arabic, Armenian, Bulgarian, Chinese, Farsi, French, German, Greek, Hebrew, Hindi/Urdu, Hungarian, Italian, Japanese, Korean, Nepali, Portuguese, Russian, Slovak, Spanish, Swahili, Swedish, Taiwanese, Thai, Turkish and Vietnamese.

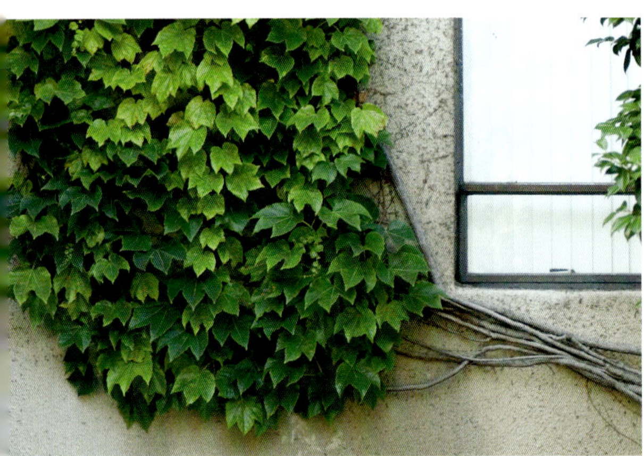

Mark Wood

Oldenborg Center

BUILT 1966
PRESIDENT IN OFFICE E. Wilson Lyon
LOCATION 350 North College Way at Bonita Avenue
PURPOSE residence and center for study of foreign languages and international relations
ARCHITECT John Rex (Honnold and Rex, Los Angeles)
MATERIALS reinforced concrete
COST $2,300,000
DONOR Dietrich C. Oldenborg

As Spanish Professor Howard Young commented at the time in *The Student Life*,[4] attitudes toward the teaching of language arose from the exigencies of war as well as the research of linguists and anthropologists. At the outset of World War II, when individuals familiar with foreign languages were suddenly in demand, it was discovered that although many could read, write and analyze, few could speak other tongues; verbal fluency, it seemed, was an afterthought. This realization led during the Cold War period to significant changes in college curricula. In the wake of Sputnik and through the National Defense Act, language became an urgent area of concentration. Furthermore, it quickly became apparent that continual practice was necessary for fluency. The Oldenborg concept, which insisted that meaningful study of language and international relations must involve personal, day-to-day living experience as well as a strong and varied program of course work, was unique in American education at the time.

The new facility included a dining hall seating 250 that could be subdivided into four sections; a multipurpose room; an international kitchen where students could prepare meals typical of their countries of origin; an international relations library (Virginia Glass Memorial Library for International Relations); four language lounges; apartments for language residents; electronic devices for language study; a short wave radio for foreign broadcasts; and a public address system allowing programs in five languages to be heard in student rooms.

When completed, Oldenborg (70,000 square feet) was the second-largest campus building (after Clark Hall), but the subdivision of the structure into definable units helped maintain a sense of human scale. Architect John Rex noted that the design deliberately avoided reference to any particular architectural style or culture but was, instead, "a bold and strong expression of a load-bearing wall." This form-follows-function approach was typical of Bauhaus-influenced postwar architecture and reflective of a Cold War mentality. The minimal use of glass, for example, was intended to enhance a "feeling of security and intimacy—a relaxed and comfortable environment to stimulate study and thought"—and to create an environment conducive to the broad and frequent exchange of ideas among various cultures. In fact, Oldenborg had a reputation for being the quietest environment on campus. Its eight-inch concrete walls also made it one of the safest buildings in Southern California.

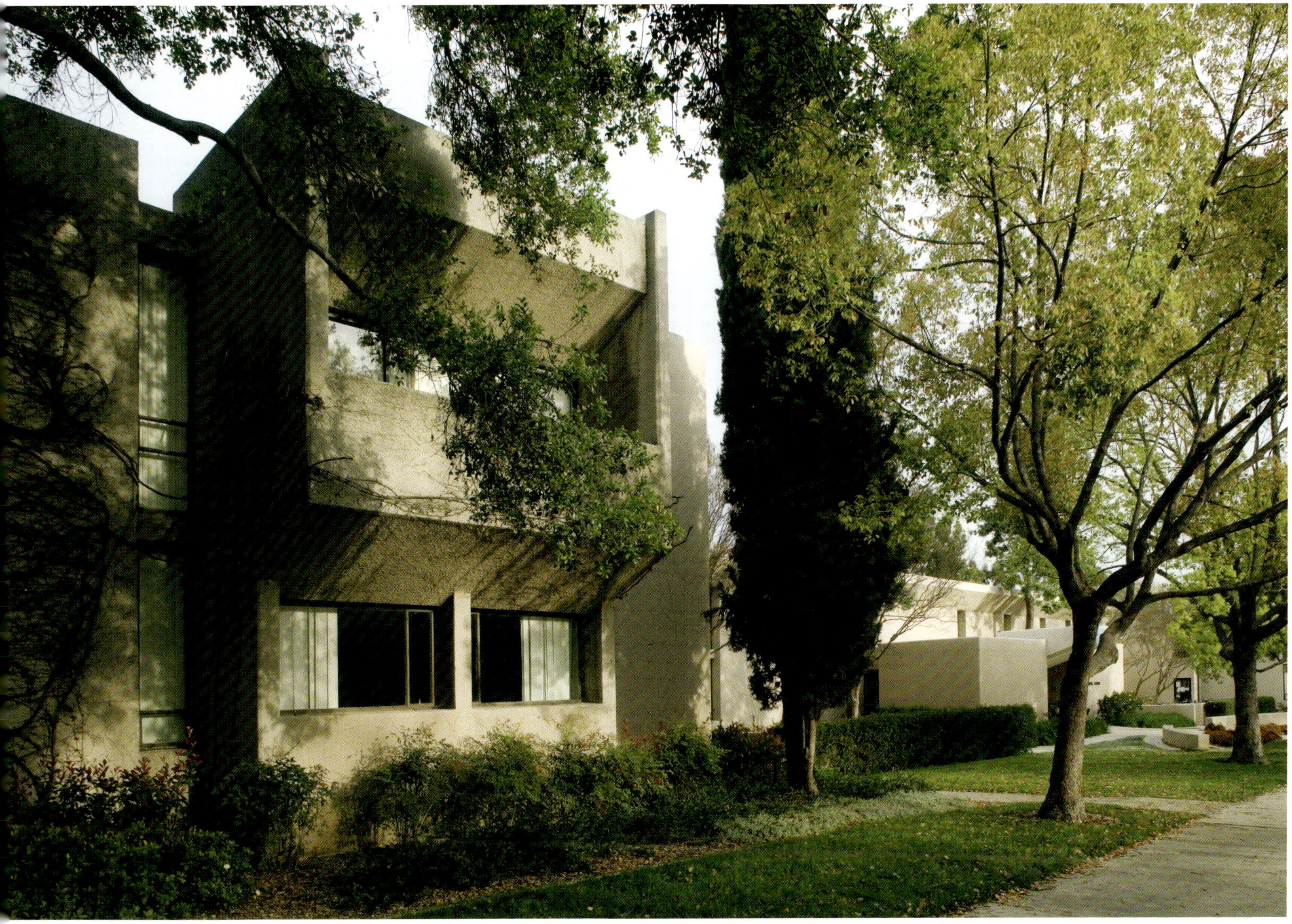

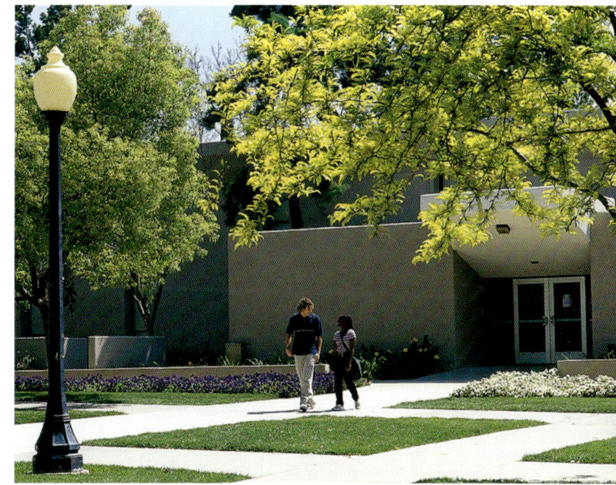

Phil Channing

Henry Cabala

Reminiscence:

My experiences in Oldenborg dorm were the highlight of my time at Pomona…with students from all over the globe living together. I have such fond memories of lunches there (I took French, Chinese and Indonesian.) It was a wonderful time. I started my education at Pomona after a year in France. I was so homesick that first year. Oldenborg was the closest thing to returning to Paris I could have found in the States. I hope they have continued that "United Nations on campus" feel at Oldenborg. What a great experience that was.—LAURA H. LUNDAHL '88 ■

Thatcher Music Building

BUILT 1969-70; dedicated March 7, 1970
PRESIDENTS IN OFFICE E. Wilson Lyon and David Alexander
LOCATION 340 North College Avenue (southeast corner College Avenue and Fourth Street)
ARCHITECT Allison, Rible, Robinson, and Ziegler
MATERIALS reinforced concrete
COST $1,882,665
DONORS Madge Rice Thatcher and the late Harry S. Thatcher; additional gifts from friends; federal grant

Thatcher Music Building

Architecturally Bridges (Hall of Music) and Thatcher are as different in timbre as coloratura and bass-baritone.
Little Bridges, fluted, curlicued and ornamented, remains the graceful lady of the South campus....
Thatcher is as beautiful, but like the music of today it looks to a different aesthetic canon.
Designed from the inside-out, its heavy concrete forms gain their integrity from the functions they serve.[5]

Music has always played a central role on Pomona's campus—both as a curricular offering and as one of the College's most treasured contributions to the larger community—and this is reflected in the prominent placement on Marston Quadrangle of the buildings dedicated to it: Bridges Hall of Music (1915, see Chapter II), Bridges Auditorium (1931, see Chapter III), and Thatcher Music Building. Given the needs of the Music Department at the time Thatcher was built, it is remarkable that it had managed to offer so full a program in the limited (if beautifully designed) spaces available to it.

Sharing the south side of the Quad with Myron Hunt's Bridges Hall of Music, Thatcher forms a courtyard (Carolyn Bartel Lyon Garden) with Hunt's second campus building Rembrandt Hall (1914, see Chapter II) and with Montgomery Art Center (1958) to its south. In sharp contrast to its historic neighbors but like other Pomona buildings constructed in the late 1950s and 60s (science laboratories, Oldenborg Center), Thatcher reflected the prevailing functionalist aesthetic of the time as well as a national trend toward conceiving new campus buildings as individual objects that contrasted with, rather than conformed to, their architectural contexts.

Designed for the teaching and playing of music, Thatcher's layout, engineering, and construction were carefully calibrated for the control of sound, a goal that required novel solutions to age-old dilemmas. Among remarkable structural aspects of the building was the configuration of practice rooms and studios that allowed as many as 30 individuals and/or groups to play simultaneously in different spaces. Potential sound and vibration problems were avoided by building rooms within rooms, with ceilings and walls suspended on springs from the outer concrete shell, and floors floated on cork cushions; each room was, thus, a self-contained entity with no direct structural contact with any other. Furthermore, to prevent the formation of troublesome "standing waves," none of the building's ceilings, floors, and wall surfaces was designed to be strictly parallel; the result was visually unusual, but aurally, Thatcher's rooms had the properties of much larger halls, aiding musicians in better judging the quality of their playing. Thatcher also had the distinction of being the first "Edison All-Electric" building on the Pomona campus and in Claremont.

The 35,000-square-foot building featured two back-to-back rehearsal halls and, in a perpendicular wing, department offices, classrooms, faculty studios, and large spaces that double as practice rooms for small ensemble playing and studios for visiting musicians. It also houses, in its basement, the broadcasting studios for KSPC-FM. Funding for the music building came from several sources including a federal grant ($462,043 under the Higher Education Facilities Act of 1966), and gifts from Madge Rice Thatcher and her late husband Harry S. Thatcher. The Thatchers, prominent Ventura County citrus ranchers from Oxnard, gave their ranch near Oxnard to Pomona as a life estate in 1949. Mr. Thatcher, who was also a pioneer in the California sugar beet industry and director and founder of Seaboard Lemon Association,

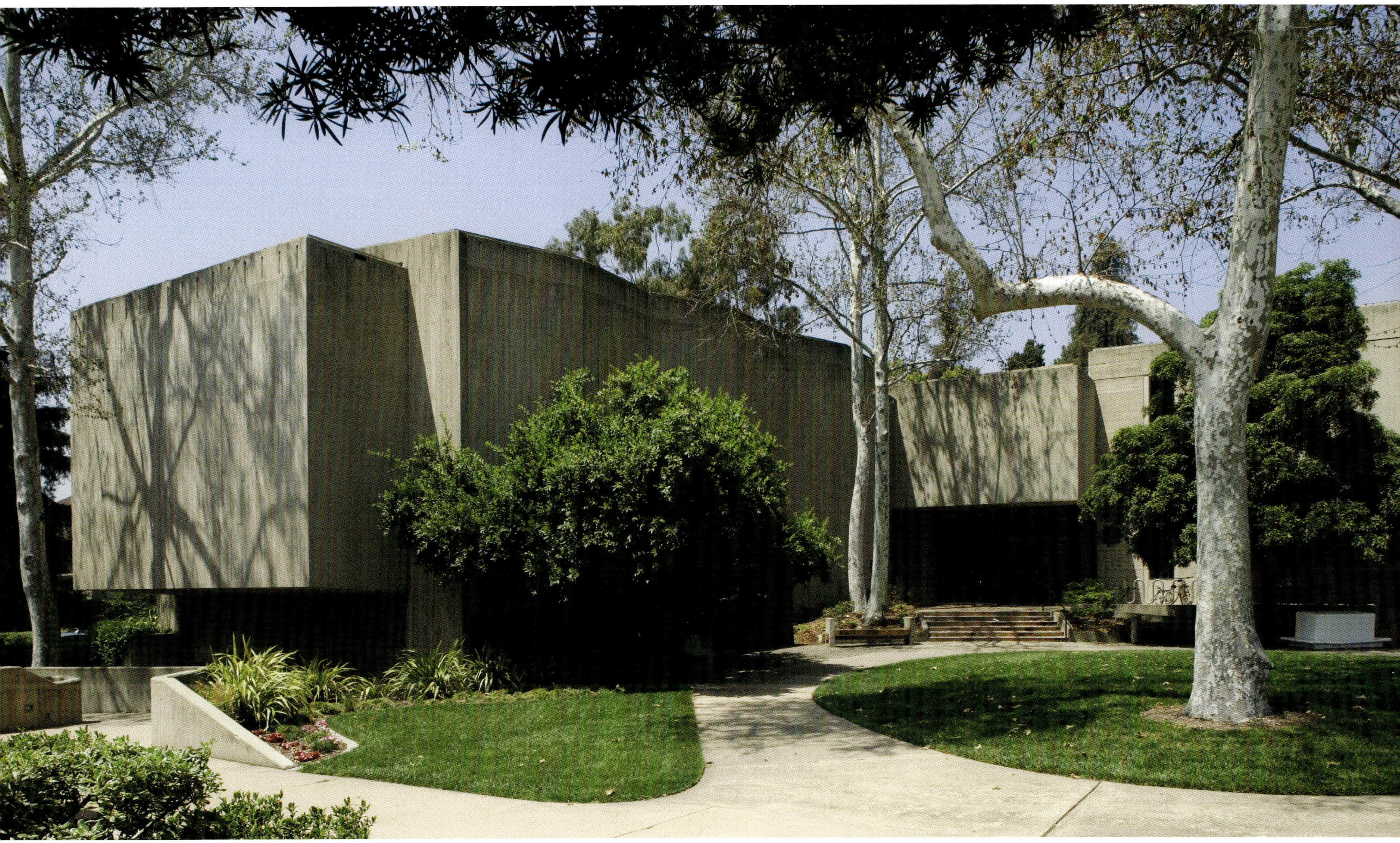

Henry Cabala

died in 1951. The College operated the ranch until 1969 when it was sold. The proceeds ($1,755,775) were used to construct the building ($500,000) and to endow two academic chairs.

The names attached to Thatcher Music Building's many amenities indicate the extraordinary patronage attracted by the needs of music on campus. The 250-seat Ralph H. Lyman Memorial Hall was designed for musical performances, choral rehearsals, and lectures. Ralph "Prof" Lyman was professor of music and director of Pomona's glee clubs and choir from 1917 to 1948; the hall was made possible by gifts from the Lyman family and alumni "in remembrance of the warm, witty 'Prof' who perhaps more than anyone nurtured the tradition of song at Pomona College." Lyman Hall houses the Smith Memorial Organ given in 1972 as a memorial to Grace Hobson Smith and Rodney H. Smith by the Fred W. Smith family; Mrs. Smith was a founding member of the Women's Campus Club and the mother of three Pomona graduates. The work of Rudolf von Beckerath, a renowned organ builder from Hamburg, Germany, the $75,000 instrument was designed to be suitable as a general teaching organ and also to supplement the larger organ in Bridges Hall of Music in the area of early music. Whereas the original Bridges organ was electric (the movement of air into the pipes controlled by electric switches and keyboards), the Smith "Bach" organ used electricity to blow bellows and control the choice of stops, but linkages between the keys and pipes were mechanical, thus suiting it to pre-19th-century music. Thatcher's Bryant Hall for Orchestra and Band was dedicated to the memory of Mrs. DeWitt Clinton Bryant, whose husband had left a bequest to the College; the Victor Montgomery Music Library on the second floor was donated by trustee and patron Gladys K. Montgomery in memory of her husband who had been president of the Hollywood Bowl Association; and the foyer was dedicated to the memory of Katharine Poorbaugh Edmunds, wife of Charles K. Edmunds, Pomona's fifth president (1928–41). ■

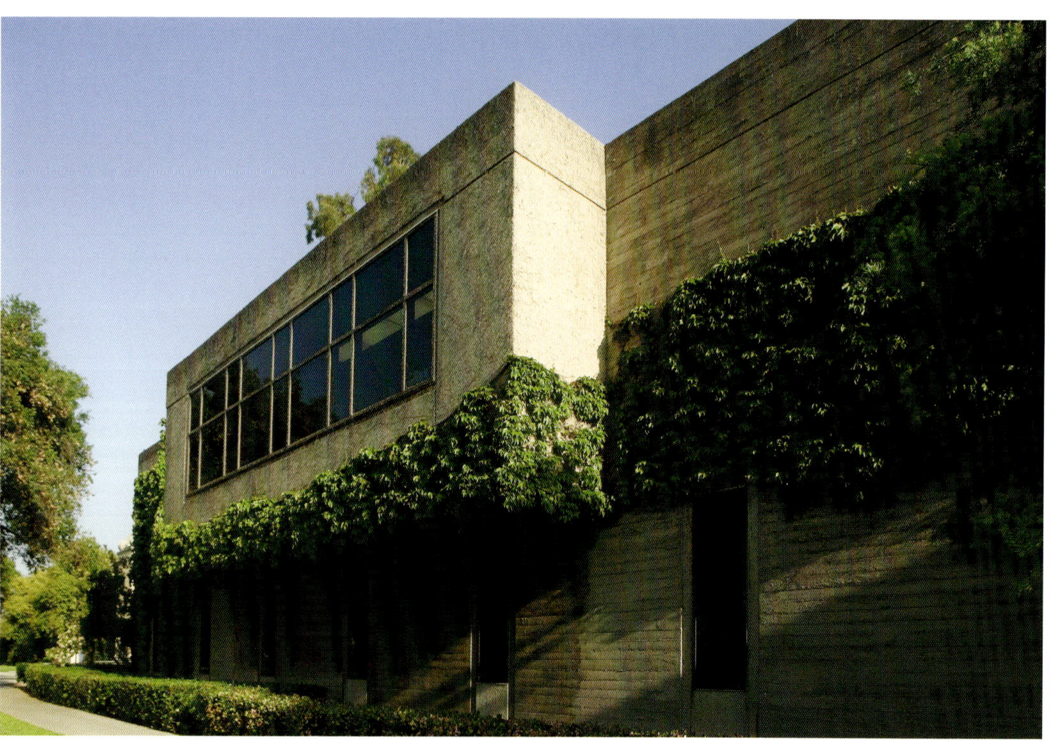

Henry Cabala

Thatcher Music Building

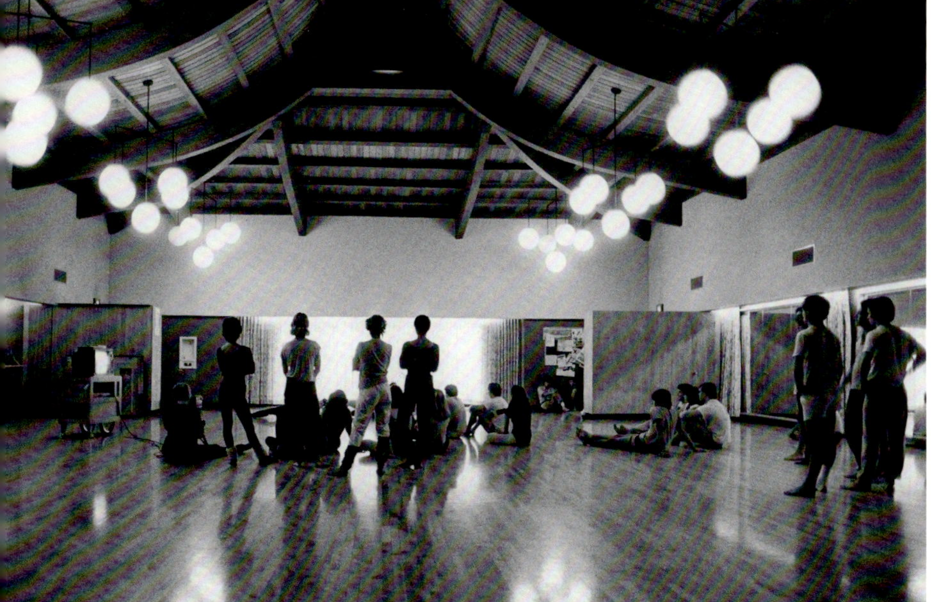

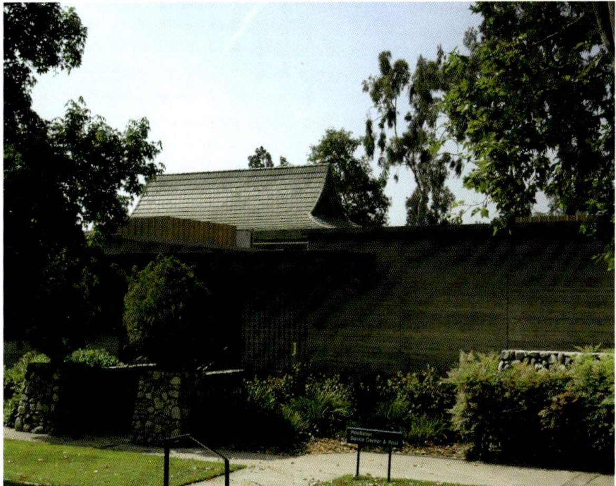

Mark Wood

Gladys Shepard Pendleton Women's Physical Education Center

BUILT 1969; dedicated April 18, 1970
LOCATION 210 East Second Street
PRESIDENTS IN OFFICE E. Wilson Lyon and David Alexander
PURPOSE Dance studio
ARCHITECT Herbert J. Powell, Powell Morgridge, Richards and Coghlan
MATERIALS concrete and wood
COST $565,000
DONORS Mr. and Mrs. Morris B. Pendleton both '22; additional gifts from alumni; federal grant
NAMED FOR Gladys Shepard Pendleton '22

Gladys Shepard Pendleton Women's Physical Education Center
Gladys Shepard Pendleton Pool

Like Thatcher Music Building, Pendleton Center was funded in part by a federal grant under the Higher Education Facilities Act that required the College to raise two-thirds of the estimated cost of the building (approximately $500,000). This was accomplished with a large gift from Mr. and Mrs. Morris B. Pendleton and a number of smaller donations by alumni.

The original Renwick gymnasium (1900, see Chapter 1) had been lost to a fire on December 20, 1952. It, and its later incarnation, originally built as barracks during World War I, had served for years as the women's physical education facility. The student body had more than doubled during these years, and this fact, added to the decrepit state of the second Renwick, only intensified the need for new facilities. At the Pendleton dedicatory ceremony in April 1970, Elizabeth Cawthorne, chair of the women's physical education department, "praised the new Center as a dream come true and happily consigned rickety Renwick Gym with its woodpeckers and antique plumbing to the rosy realm of memory."

The center was built adjacent to the Gladys Shepard Pendleton Pool, which had been constructed four years earlier, its dedication celebrated with a water polo demonstration and a synchronized swimming "aquacade" overseen by Professor Anne Bages. Pendleton Center contained 12,000 square feet of space, including administrative offices, a variety of teaching spaces, dressing rooms, and a multi-purpose room for conferences of the Women's Recreation Association and for visitors from other colleges. Of particular note was the 3,800-square-foot dance studio. Marking the southern edge of campus, its Japanese-inspired, wing-like roof echoed the grace and rhythms of the human movement it contained.

Other athletic facilities added to the campus during this period included Athearn Field, given by associates of the late Fred G. Athearn, Class of 1900, and built in 1958, including athletic fields used for soccer, touch football, softball and other sports; and several new facilities given by Carlton M. Rogers '37 and constructed in Blanchard Park in the mid-1960s, including five tennis courts named for Mr. Rogers's mother, built on the women's field, and a new all-purpose practice field named for Earl J. Merritt '25 on the east side of Blanchard Park. ■

Gladys Shepard Pendleton Pool

BUILT 1965; dedicated May 14, 1965
PRESIDENT IN OFFICE E. Wilson Lyon
LOCATION East Second Street
COST $60,000
DONOR Morris B. Pendleton '22, trustee 1947–73 and president of Pendleton Tool Industries, Inc.
NAMED FOR Gladys Shepard Pendleton '22

ABOVE LEFT *Dance Studio*
ABOVE RIGHT *Gladys Shepard Pendleton Women's Physical Education Center, built 1969*

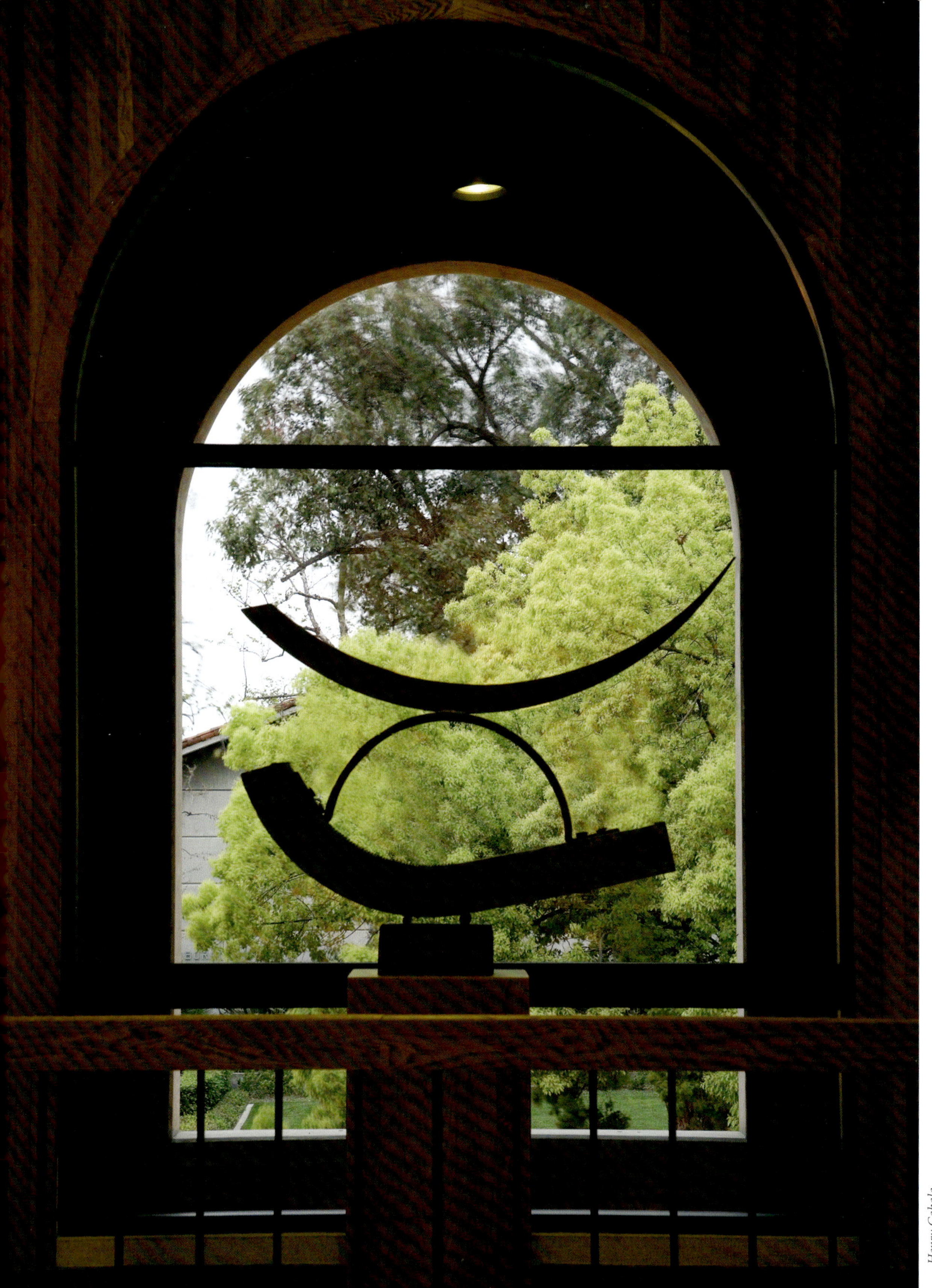

Henry Cabala

CHAPTER V *From* REGIONAL *to* NATIONAL 1969–91

Mudd Science Library

From Regional to National, 1969–91

PRESIDENT DAVID ALEXANDER

President Lyon, who would reach the age of 65 in summer 1969, had indicated as early as 1966 that he would not seek to extend his tenure beyond this date. A committee, formed to begin the search for his successor, announced on January 13, 1969, that Dr. John David Alexander, the 36-year-old president of Southwestern at Memphis (now Rhodes College), had been selected as the College's next president.

Born in Springfield, Tennessee, and raised in Kentucky, David Alexander had graduated from Southwestern at Memphis in 1953 with honors in Greek and election to Phi Beta Kappa. In 1954, following a year at Louisville Presbyterian Seminary, he entered Christ Church, Oxford University as a Rhodes Scholar, earning the D.Phil. in church history, Greek, and Hebrew in 1957. Ordained a Presbyterian minister, Alexander was named associate professor of Old Testament at the San Francisco Theological Seminary, from which he was called, in 1964, to the presidency of his alma mater. Southwestern at Memphis, modeled on Oxford, was seen to be particularly appropriate preparation for Pomona College. Alexander was inaugurated as Pomona's seventh president on October 18, 1969, his thirty-seventh birthday and the eighty-second anniversary of the College.

The new president came to Claremont with his wife and family. Catharine (Coleman) Alexander, born in Whitehaven, Tennessee, had graduated from Southwestern, Phi Beta Kappa, in 1955. The Alexanders were married in the summer of 1956 before embarking for Oxford. They arrived in Claremont in 1969 with their three children: Catharine (Kitty) aged 10, John 9, and Julia, nearly two. Like many of the presidential wives who preceded her, Catharine Alexander played an active role in the life of the College, highly regarded as an indefatigably gracious hostess and an astute and dedicated presidential partner.

David Alexander became president of the College at a tumultuous time in the history of the country and its institutions of higher learning. His inaugural address, titled "A Perspective on Renewal," dealt forthrightly with the threats to American society posed by the Vietnam conflict, which, unlike the war in Europe that had engendered a unified national response, was dangerously divisive. "Our task now is to winnow from the welter of changing values those transcendent values for which this college exists, so that while trying to move with society Pomona College will help move society through education." Always an eloquent speaker, Alexander addressed as well the College's capacity for self-renewal, amply demonstrated in the past and likely to be even more necessary in the years to come.

OPPOSITE *Norm Hines '61,* Lunar Libration, *1983, granite and steel sculpture, gift of the Chapman Family in memory of C. Stanley Chapman '10, Mudd Science Library*

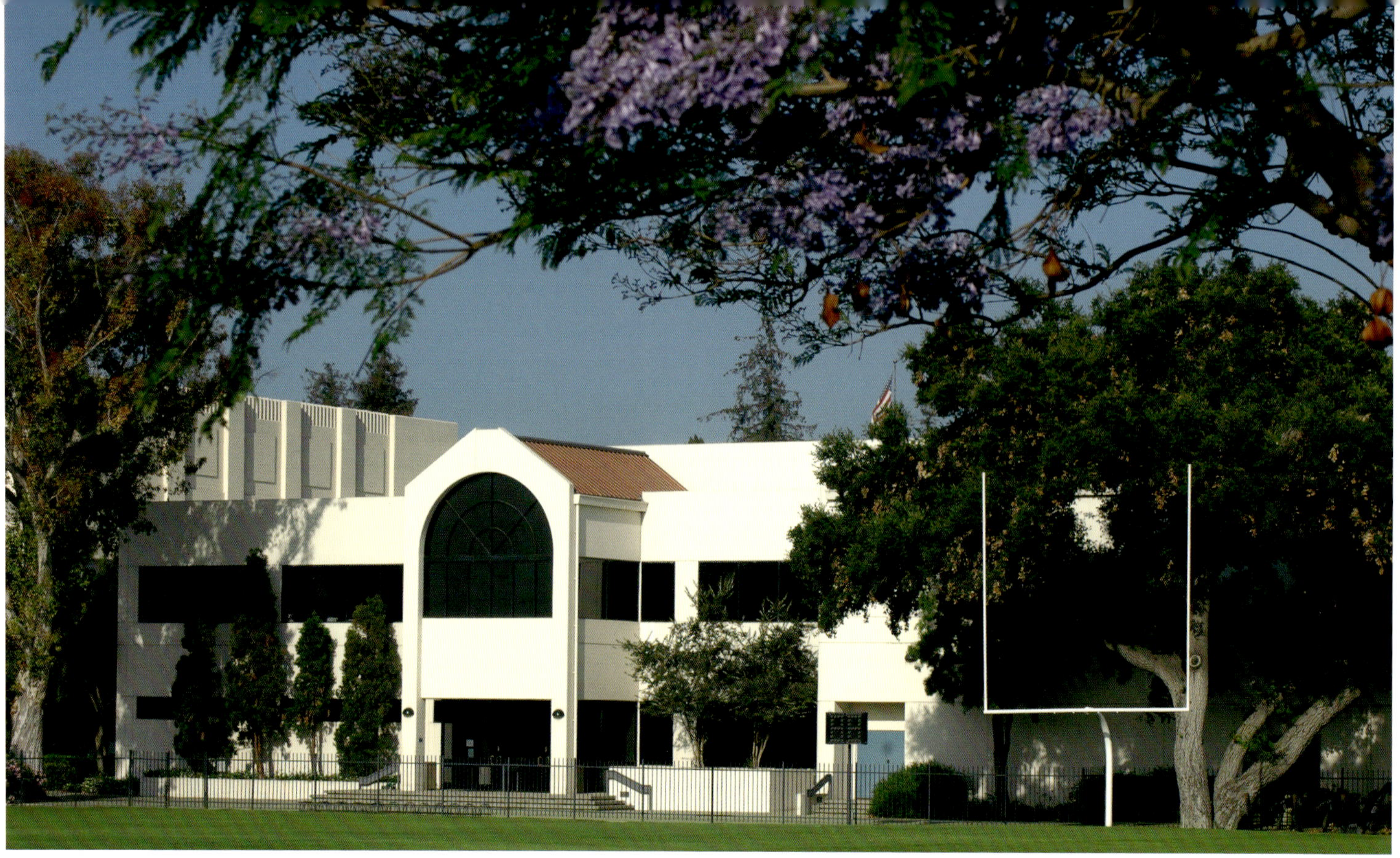

RIGHT *Liliore G. Rains Center for Sport and Recreation*

Mark Wood

BELOW *Strehle Track*

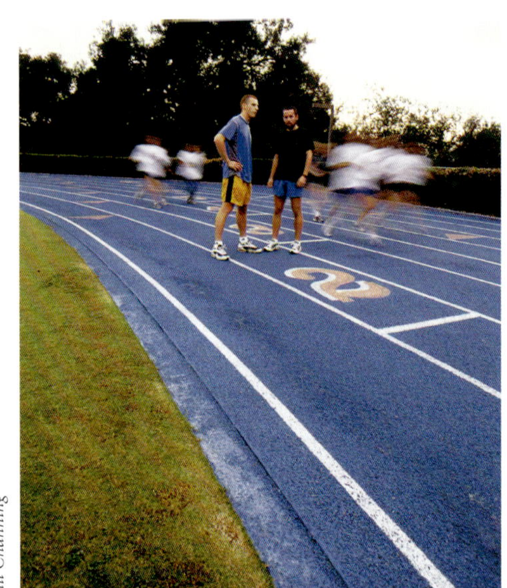

Phil Channing

An opportunity for campus renewal presented itself almost immediately in the form of an emergency. As Alexander recalls:

> *My first campus-related crisis came in early December 1969, when, after the Choir's Christmas concert, an engineering report commissioned to consider the seismic stability of Bridges Hall of Music came back bearing the devastating news that, in the professional opinion of the engineers, the building was unsafe in a moderate earthquake. This unexpected result required us to close Little Bridges with the Christmas wreath still hanging forlornly on the organ case in the abandoned auditorium.*[1]

The Trustees immediately approved a massive, nationwide fundraising campaign that ultimately netted more than $900,000 from alumni and friends of the College—funds designated either for restoration or, if necessary, for a new building. After a thorough study of the options, the decision was made to preserve and upgrade the building, a conclusion for which we can be grateful. Aside from the removal of a tower, the exterior remained visibly unchanged, its graceful original design intact, a fact celebrated when the hall reopened with a series of concerts honoring donors in February 1972. The complex of factors involved in such decisions does not, of course, always result in preservation. During President Alexander's tenure, three older structures—The Claremont Inn, Holmes Hall, and Renwick (Memorial) Gymnasium—were lost, the first replaced by an equally significant historical structure (Seaver House), the second by a new building (Alexander Hall) modeled closely on its predecessor, the last by the Liliore G. Rains Center for Sport and Recreation. Taken together, these three instances represent well the range of difficult decisions that fall to college presidents in regard to the campuses for which they are responsible.

The years of David Alexander's presidency coincided with the growth of a nationwide historic preservation movement. Launched by the passage of the National Historic Preservation Act of 1966 and enhanced by renewed concern for architectural heritage inspired by the celebration of the country's 1976 Bicentennial, it grew rapidly in extent and effectiveness, ultimately producing thousands of regional preservation organizations. The growing concern for the architectural heritage of Pomona's campus, as well as for its continued development, reflected this national context.

David Alexander remembers mixed feelings upon seeing the campus for the first time:

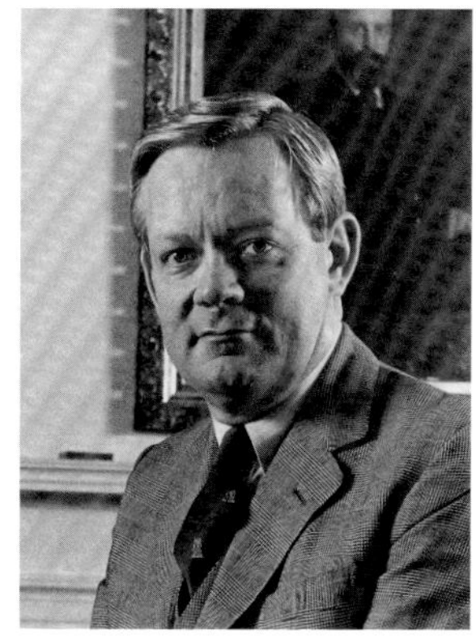

President David Alexander

> *My first recollection of the campus is not an entirely happy one. Catharine and I were on campus for interviews with the trustees; we were incognito, of course, because that was the way of presidential searches in those days. I vividly remember standing in front of Holmes Hall, which to anyone's unromantic eye was a sad ruin in 1969. Pearsons Hall, across College Avenue, did not inspire much confidence in its modernity either. These impressions fell heavily on me: much had been done on the campus recently, and the Seaver Science Center was spectacular. Southwestern at Memphis was engaged in the construction of a new science center, but I was impressed by the Seaver buildings, the laboratories, and especially the lavish provision of state-of-the-art equipment. The new computer in the Seaver Chemistry Building was one of the best in any liberal arts college at the time. The Carnegie Building was in the process of being renovated. Oldenborg Center drew feelings of envy from me as to both facility and program.*

Along with new buildings (Thatcher Music Building), additions (Edmunds Union), and renovations (Carnegie, The President's House) already under way or scheduled when Alexander arrived, others were called for (Pearsons, Crookshank), and two buildings were in desperate need of attention: Renwick/Memorial Gymnasium and Holmes Hall "...still stood in their wooden dilapidation." As is so often the case, it is the difficult issues that require the greatest effort and that one remembers most clearly:

> *I confess I fretted about structures, such as Holmes Hall and Renwick ("Woodpecker Haven"), the women's gymnasium, which was in poor shape. These buildings were among those scheduled for reconstruction and improvement... but it took quite a long time to deal with Renwick, and almost my entire tenure of 22 years to solve the problem of Holmes Hall.* (See Chapters I and III.)

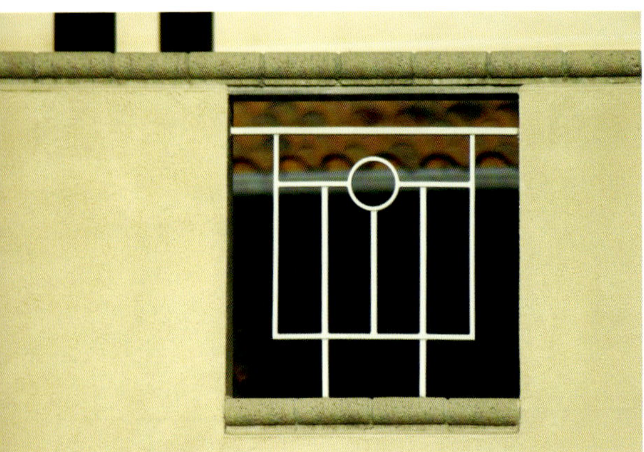

Mark Wood

Seaver Theatre

The length of Alexander's presidency was impressive at a time when the average term of office for American college presidents had fallen to six years, and the College prospered under his leadership. In 1969–70, the endowment stood at $24 million; by 1990 it had reached $296 million, the Centennial Campaign alone having raised $134 million. During the same period, the value of the College's assets rose from $71 million to $450 million. Pomona thrived equally in terms of the quality of its faculty and students. With SAT scores and GPAs steadily rising, and a student body increasingly broad in diversity and national representation, Pomona joined the top-tier of the country's liberal arts colleges, a position it continues to occupy.

Pomona's new and significantly transformed buildings touched every aspect of College life—administrative (Seaver House and Alexander Hall), academic (Thille Botany, Mudd Library), residential (Frank Dining Hall, Lawry Court and Walton Commons, Lyon Court)—including physical education facilities (Pauley Tennis Courts; Strehle Track "in its blue livery," as Alexander comments; Rains Center; Merritt Field; Haldeman Pool) and others central to its public and academic role (Seaver Theatre, Bridges Hall of Music). In design, the new structures were both respectful of historical context (a particular priority in the case of Alexander Hall) and innovative in meeting functional demands. Taken together, they demonstrate the extent of the impact the physical campus exerts on the nature and quality of the experience they frame.

Of the recent history of the Pomona campus, David Alexander comments: "Wilson Lyon left a legacy of concern for the health and beauty of the campus and its facilities. Peter Stanley's leadership gave the campus spectacular new facilities, and David Oxtoby's young presidency will be remembered for extraordinarily interesting and important construction." While college presidents are most often remembered for the new buildings that marked their tenure, Alexander reminds us that "one is not to forget the constant need for clean-up, paint-up, and fix-up. A campus is a living being that suffers from aging and use, and perhaps even neglect." Far less glamorous than new buildings, maintenance and regular upgrading of existing structures, along with careful planning for future development are, nonetheless, crucial. As Alexander notes, "I was in office long enough that every building, I think, was renovated at least once, and several residence halls more than once. When I left we were in the planning phase for an administration building and a social sciences building (Hahn), and the fate of the College Avenue houses was being decided." One of the innovations of Alexander's administration was, as he describes it, "a comprehensive and regularly updated manual for the implementation of the major campus plan prepared under the guidance of Richard Dober and Associates. These updates were reported from time to time (for example, in my annual reports), but under Peter Stanley the practice of regular public reporting on campus projects was instituted, so that the many projects for the care of the College's extensive and complex campus could be seen in context." Reflecting the College's increasing, and increasingly evident, concern for its buildings and grounds, administrative decisions such as these are at the heart of the campus environment we enjoy. ■

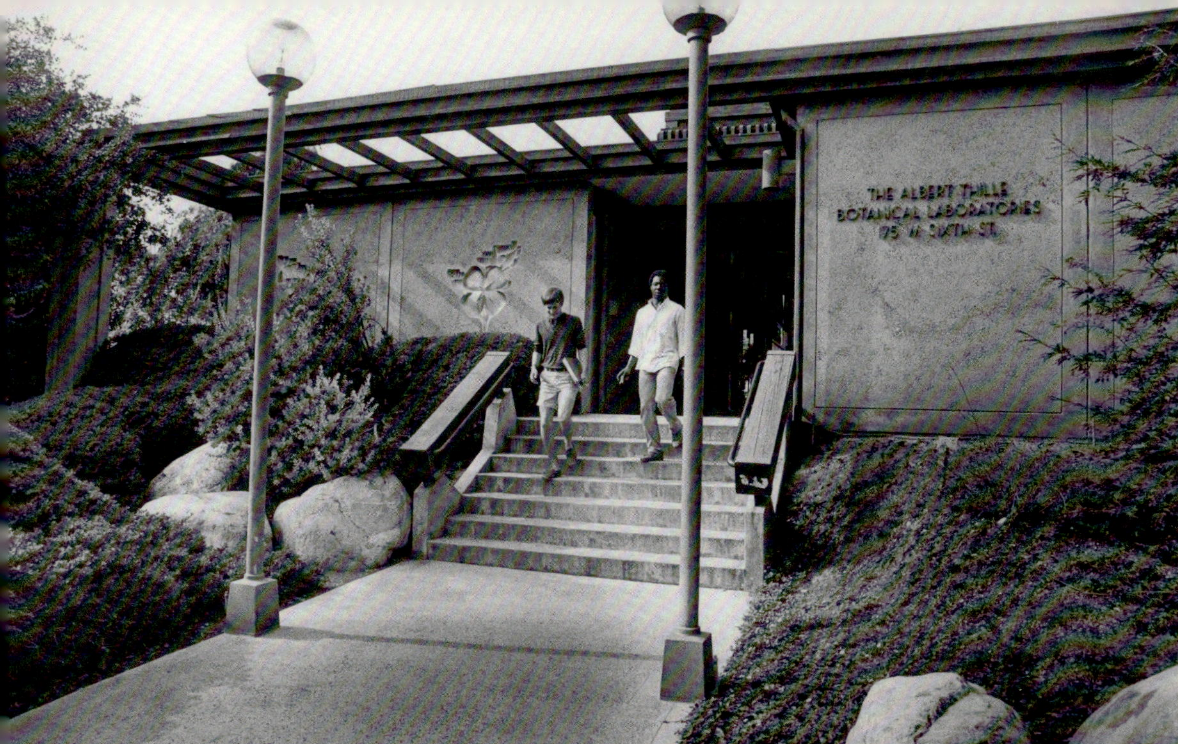

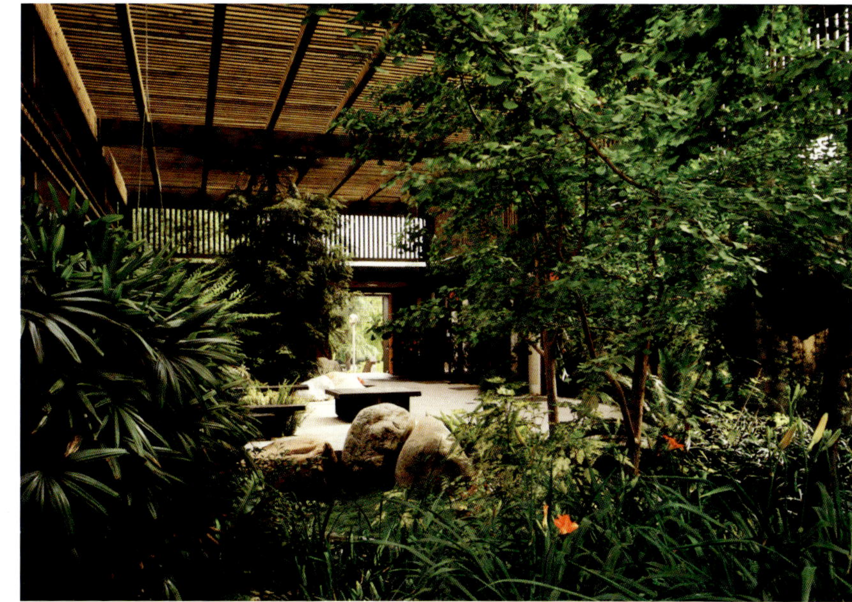

Albert Thille Botany Building

Thille Botany building came about in part through an elaborate shift of department locations in 1974. Botany and other "living sciences" had been housed in Crookshank Hall but were moved to make room for the English Department, which, in turn had been moved from Holmes Hall to free space for administrative offices. A gift from the Thille Foundation, established by citrus rancher Albert Thille, had originally been designated for a new wing on Seaver Laboratory for Biology and Geology (Seaver South). Instead, however, the donation was split, with funding going toward a new music building (Thatcher) and making possible a new building for botany.

The 12,261-square-foot building housed classrooms, seminar rooms, labs and offices, all of which opened onto an interior greenhouse-atrium, covered by a lath roof, and including a stream with fish and frogs, pools, and, in the center, a redwood tree planted by Edwin Phillips and botanist Lyman Benson. Two "phytotrons"—laboratories comprising a series of chambers in which light, temperature, and humidity could be controlled—permitted experimental work on the effects of environmental change on plant life; three "wet labs" served physiology-ecology, general botany, and bio-chemistry and micro techniques. The complex also contained a taxonomy laboratory with a "working herbarium" containing 300,000 dried plant specimens and considered one of the most important in the American West; the herbarium, like the library, was jointly administered by Rancho Santa Ana Botanic Gardens. The Thille Botany Building received an award of merit from the Pasadena chapter of the American Institute of Architects in 1977.

Thille was also home to several works of public art—a wall sculpture given in 1976 by its creator, Linas Naujokaitis, and a group of students, faculty and alumni calling themselves the "Botany Gang"; and two cast stone "sunken reliefs," based on botanical specimens, by local sculptor John Edward Svenson. The latter, which adorned the façade facing Sixth Street, were recently reinstalled at the entrance to the Rancho Santa Ana Botanic Garden. ■

Albert Thille Botany Building

BUILT 1976; dedicated March 14, 1976
LOCATION 175 West Sixth Street at Harvard Avenue
ARCHITECT Everett Tozier (Tozier and Abbott, Claremont), with Professor Edwin Phillips
PURPOSE Botany
MATERIALS wood frame
COST $800,000 (approx.)
DONORS Thille Foundation ($290,000); estate of John P. and Magdalena Dexter
NAMED FOR Albert Thille
DEMOLISHED 2004, to make way for Richard C. Seaver Biology Building

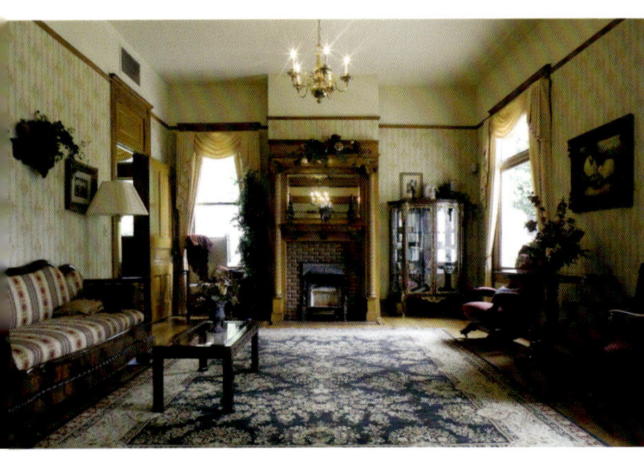

Henry Cabala

ABOVE *Seaver House, interior*

BELOW *Seaver House in transit from Pomona to Claremont, September 1979*

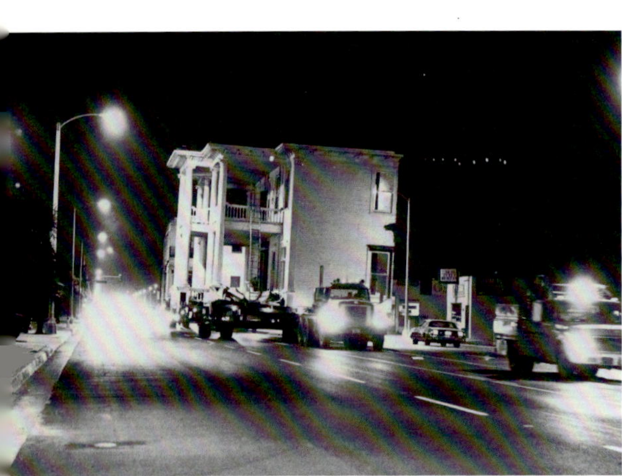

Seaver House

The Seaver House, built in Pomona in 1900 by Carlton and Estella Seaver, was home to their six children, all of whom graduated from Pomona and many of whom have, over the years and in a variety of ways, significantly affected the development and life of the College. The handsome Classical Revival home was given to the College in 1979 after the death of Nila Seaver, youngest of the six, and moved to the campus site formerly occupied by the Claremont Inn (see Chapter 1). Dedicated in 1980, it has, appropriately enough, served since then as the center of alumni affairs.

The house originally occupied a large site on then-residential East Holt Avenue, one lot east of Garey Avenue. Early photographs show it to have been rather grander and more imposing than its neighbors (themselves substantial) and also the most purely classical in design. A two-story frame dwelling with brick foundation walls and chimneys and a shingle roof, it boasted interiors finished in white oak and yellow pine. The house served as a gathering place for the Seaver children (Georgia '04; Frank Roger '05; Byron Dick '08; Homer Carlton '11; Marguerite '14; Nila '19) and their Pomona friends who often spent the night on the then-fashionable sleeping porches (one each for boys and girls). Their mother Estella, a gracious hostess fond of large parties, established a Shakespeare Club that presented plays annually in the house's ample back yard. Interestingly, audiences were limited to women, as it was assumed that men would not take the performances seriously; on one occasion, however, one of the actresses' husbands appeared in women's dress and, though suspected by some, was not discovered until the play's end, at which time he vanished. The front yard was graced by an enormous magnolia tree, said to be the largest in the state; at Christmas, it was festooned with lights and the house's many windows were adorned with candles.

Relocation

The move of the 175-ton Seaver House from Pomona to Claremont, a distance of 10 miles, requiring 20 hours, a nine-man team and the cooperation of numerous utilities workers responsible for lifting or removing overhead wires, took place on the nights of September 11 and 12, 1979. A remarkable feat of engineering, the relocation also provided an occasion witnessed, and remembered to this day, by many. Because of its size, the house was cut in two (and its roof removed). To minimize traffic congestion and because of the distance involved, the relocation took place over the course of two nights; during the intervening day, the divided structure, suddenly ungainly in appearance, rested at the Pomona Fairgrounds. The building arrived in Claremont at 4 a.m. on September 12 accompanied by College officials, members of the Seaver family, and a veritable parade of curious onlookers, many on bicycles and roller skates.

In ensuing years, Seaver House has benefited from historically sensitive renovations designed to enhance functionality and accessibility while also retaining the original character of the grand old structure. On its north side, Richardson Garden, a discreetly enclosed and carefully landscaped space also flanked by The President's House, serves as a reception area for a variety of alumni and other College events and is home to three works of sculpture by former members of the faculty. ■

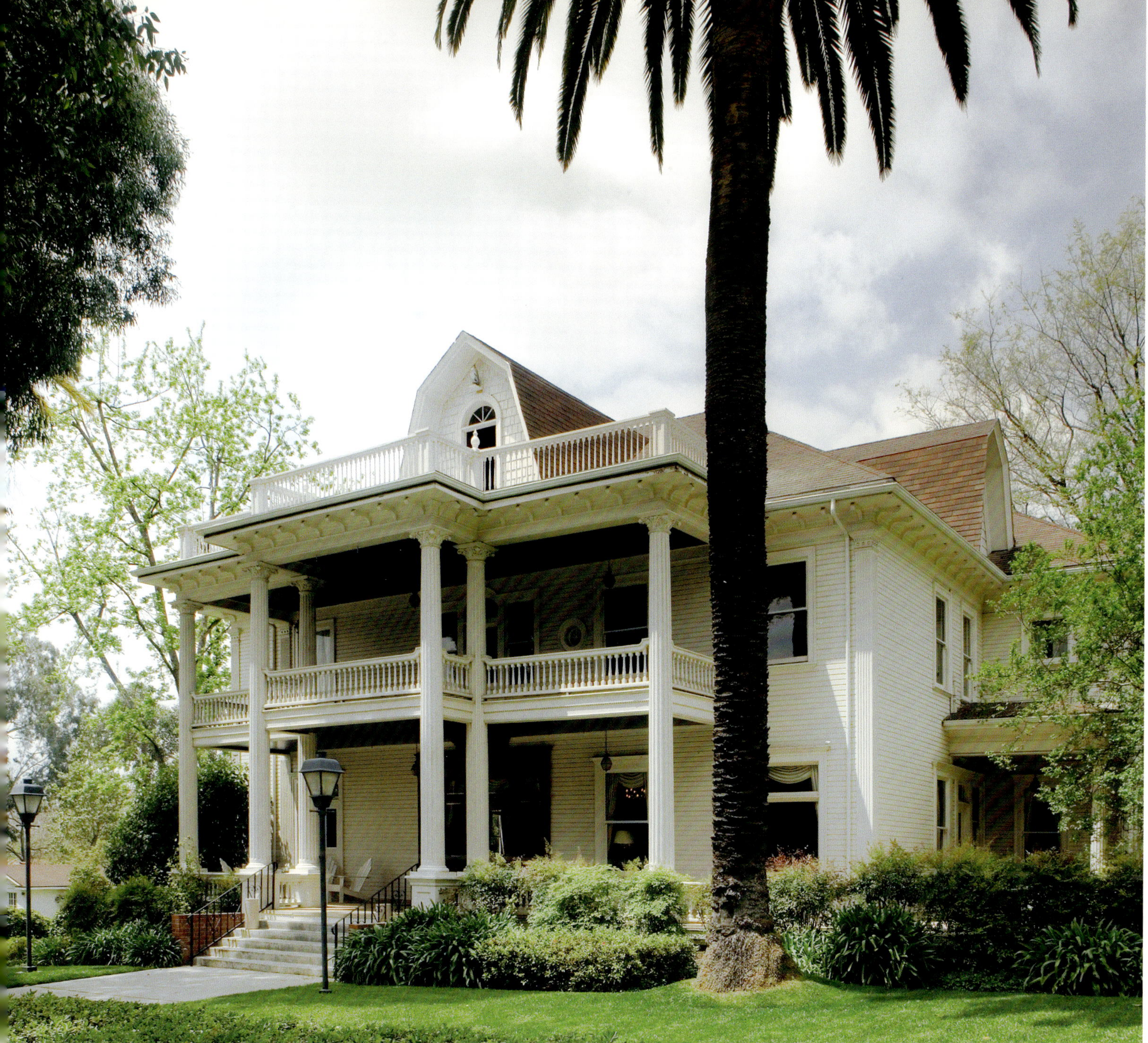

Henry Cabala

Seaver House

BUILT 1900

ARCHITECT Henry Hanson

ORIGINAL LOCATION East Holt Avenue near Garey Avenue, Pomona

CURRENT LOCATION 305 North College Avenue at Bonita Avenue, Claremont

MATERIALS wood frame on brick foundation

COST approximately $7,500

DONORS The late Nila Seaver '19, members of the Seaver Family, and anonymous donors

RELOCATED 1979; dedicated April 19, 1980

RECONSTRUCTION ARCHITECTS Theodore Criley and Fred McDowell, Claremont

OVERLEAF *Richardson Garden; located between Seaver House and The President's House; in foreground, Norm Hines '61,* First Principle, *1982, granite sculpture, gift of Karl Benjamin; in background, Enrique Martínez Celaya's* Constellation (Permanence), *2001, gift of the artist in honor of Peter W. Stanley*

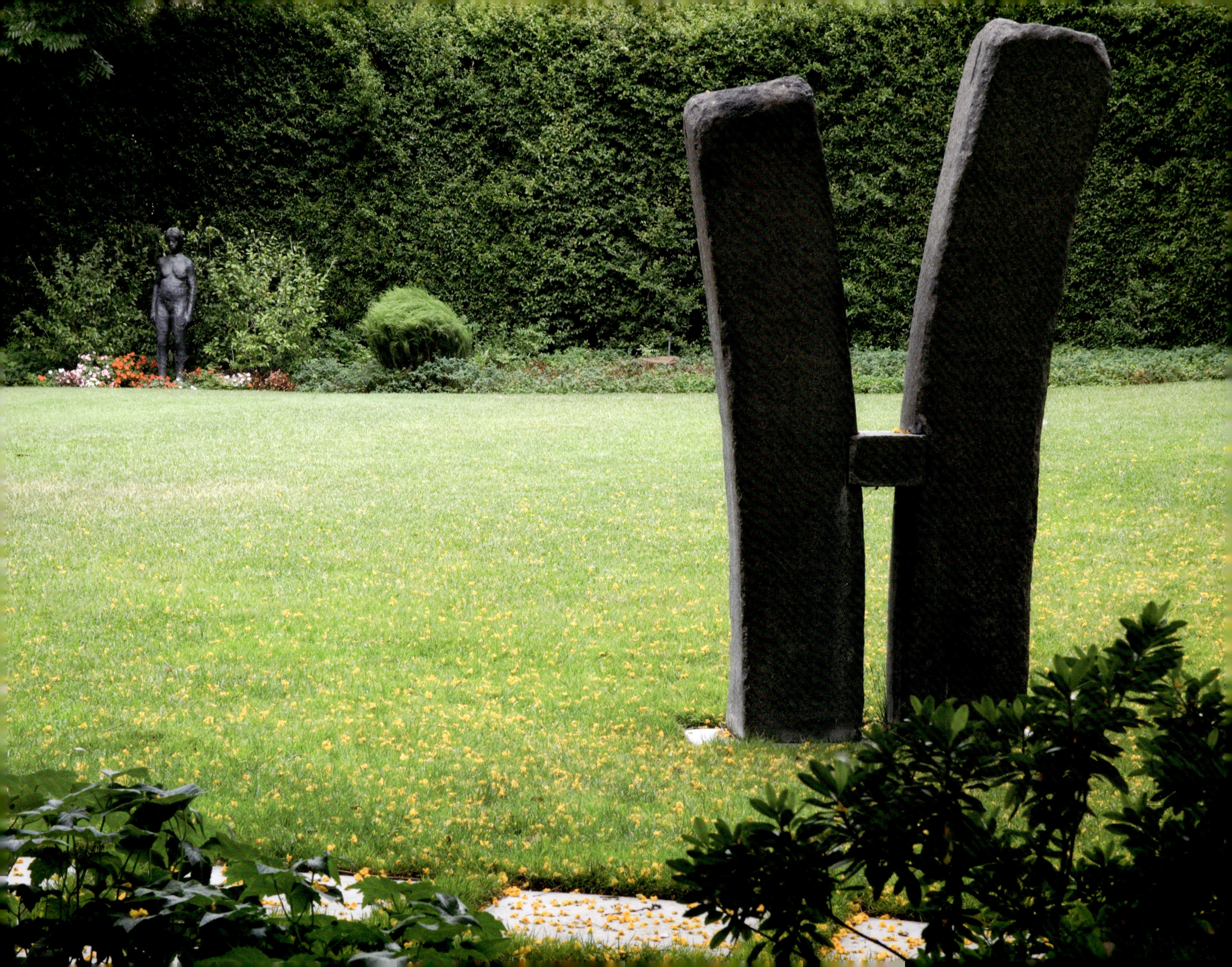

Lawry Court / Walton Commons

Lawry Court, first known as East Court, opened in 1980. Renamed to honor donor Rolla Lawry in 1988, it consists of three three-story residential towers encompassing a total of 18,200 square feet; each floor contains eight single rooms surrounding lounge and bathroom facilities. Adjacent is the Jean B. Walton Commons, named for the emerita dean of women and vice president for student affairs and containing meeting rooms and a lounge. The design of Lawry Court and its commons reflects Pomona's commitment to residential life as a significant part of the educational experience. In 1995, the Office of Campus Life designated the second and third floors of Lawry C Tower "substance free" in response to student requests for a living space free of alcohol and smoke. The residence was renovated in 2002. ■

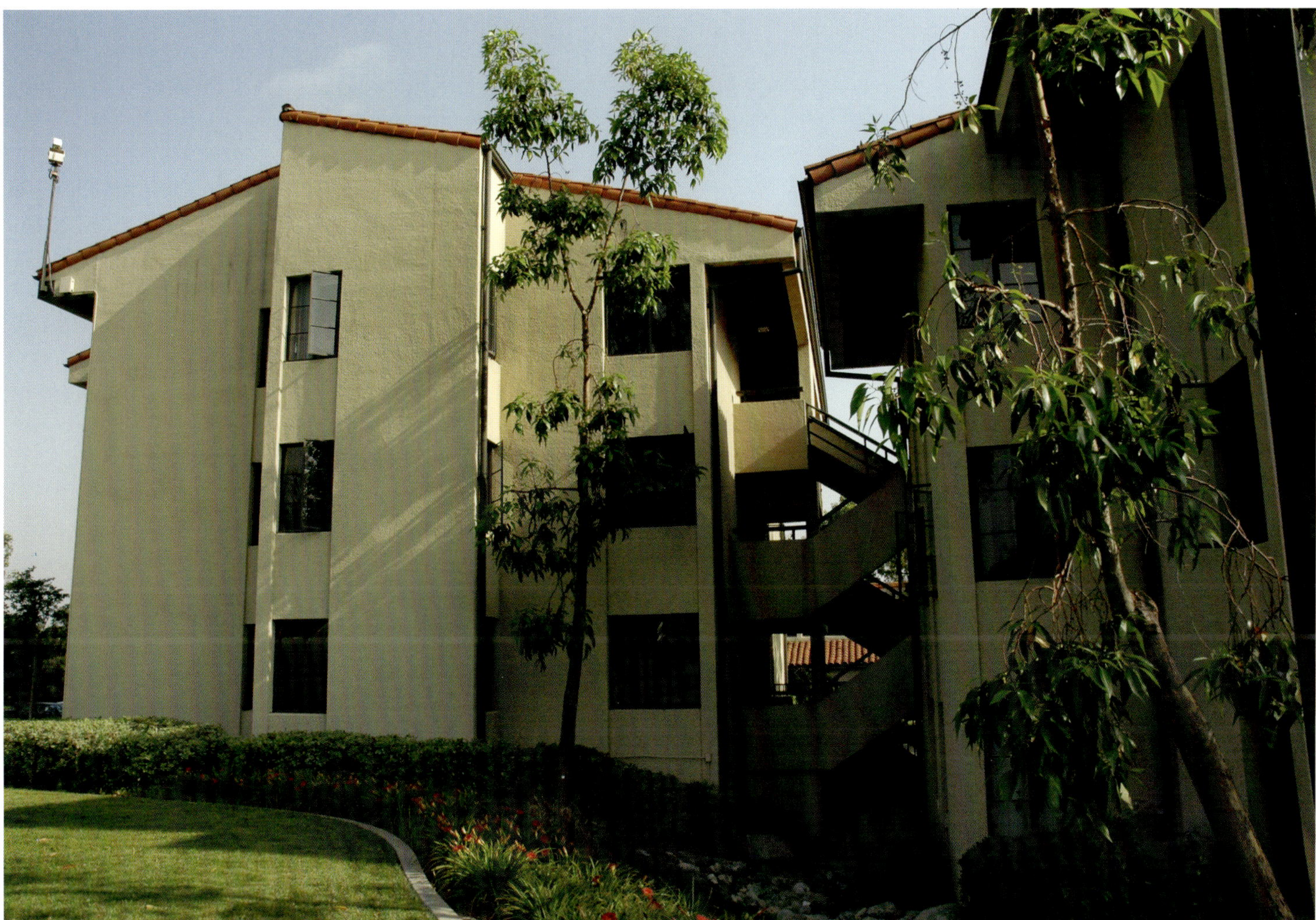

Mark Wood

Henry Cabala

Lawry Court / Walton Commons

BUILT 1980
ARCHITECT Neptune and Thomas Associates, Pasadena
LOCATION 365–395 East Sixth Street
MATERIALS reinforced concrete
PURPOSE dormitories
NAMED FOR Rolla Lawry, donor, and Jean B. Walton, vice president for student affairs and dean of women 1949–79

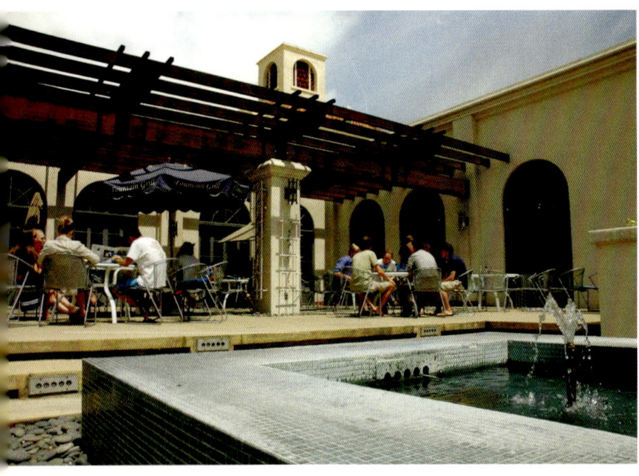

Carlos Puma

Richard N. and Mary Alice Frank Dining Hall

Richard N. and Mary Alice Frank Dining Hall

BUILT 1982; groundbreaking August 29, 1981; dedicated October 23, 1982
LOCATION 260 East Bonita Avenue (east of Mudd-Blaisdell Residence Hall)
ARCHITECT Calvin Straub, Scottsdale, Arizona; with Willis K. Hutchason, Pasadena
MATERIALS reinforced concrete, tile roof
COST approximately $1.4 million
DONORS/NAMED FOR Trustee Richard N. Frank '46, 1973–, and Mary Alice Bentley Frank '47

Frank Dining Hall was the cornerstone of a complex of projects proposed in the College's Centennial Plan that was adopted in 1978. Announced in July 1980 and completed two years later, it replaced two smaller dining rooms—Harwood (built 1931) and Gibson (1949). The site was selected in part out of a desire to create a new center of student life on the south campus. The building was designed to seat 460 in large and small groups and including outside tables in settings intended to promote social interaction. The 19,600-square-foot Frank Hall joined Frary Hall and Oldenborg Center as the College's dining facilities, and the hope was that it would help link north and south campuses. The family of Richard N. Frank '46, trustee 1973–, and Mary Alice Bentley Frank '47 has long been associated with Pomona College. Their interest in sponsoring a dining facility was a natural outgrowth of Richard Frank's experience in the food industry. At the time the building was constructed, he was president and CEO of Lawry Foods, Inc., a large and highly successful business originally based on the production of a seasoning salt concocted by his father, Lawrence L. Frank, for use in the family restaurants; Richard Frank ultimately expanded the company to include over 100 specialty food products.

The architecture and landscaping of Frank Hall were inspired by innovative design approaches developed at what was then known as Lawry's California Center (now the Los Angeles River Center and Gardens) a twelve-and-a-half–acre complex of corporate headquarters, gift shops, restaurants, and manufacturing operations located at the confluence of the Arroyo Seco and the Los Angeles River, where the Golden State and Pasadena freeways intersect. Although the arched colonnades, cloistered courtyards and lush gardens of Lawry's Center resembled an historic Spanish-style estate more than a corporate headquarters and manufacturing facility, it was up-to-date in functional detail. Likewise, Frank Hall was constructed with attention to energy conservation: the skylight around the central tower reduced the amount of electricity needed; large windows offered natural ventilation and heating; and hot water was provided by solar technology.

Inside, low ceilings, carpeted floors, and a number of separate dining areas all served to control noise levels. The hall's food service ("scramble") area was larger than at Frary but employed the same "scatter system" that was deemed more efficient than the single-line cafeteria. Frank Hall's enclosed outdoor dining areas were designed to encourage students to confine their meals to designated areas and to prevent the migration of dishes and cutlery throughout campus. The building's interior was the work of Mary Alice Frank, a design professional, who was also involved at the time in the restoration of the historic Seaver House. Among the many amenities she provided were works of art, including paintings by Professor Karl Benjamin and Cathy Segaul '82, and a ceramic mural by Professor John Fassbinder for the fountain in the entrance plaza.

In addition to construction funds, the Frank family established a trust to support maintenance of the building for its first 28 years. Frank Hall won the City of Claremont's architectural commission award for new construction in 1983, and a special citation from the Claremont Chamber of Commerce the following year. ■

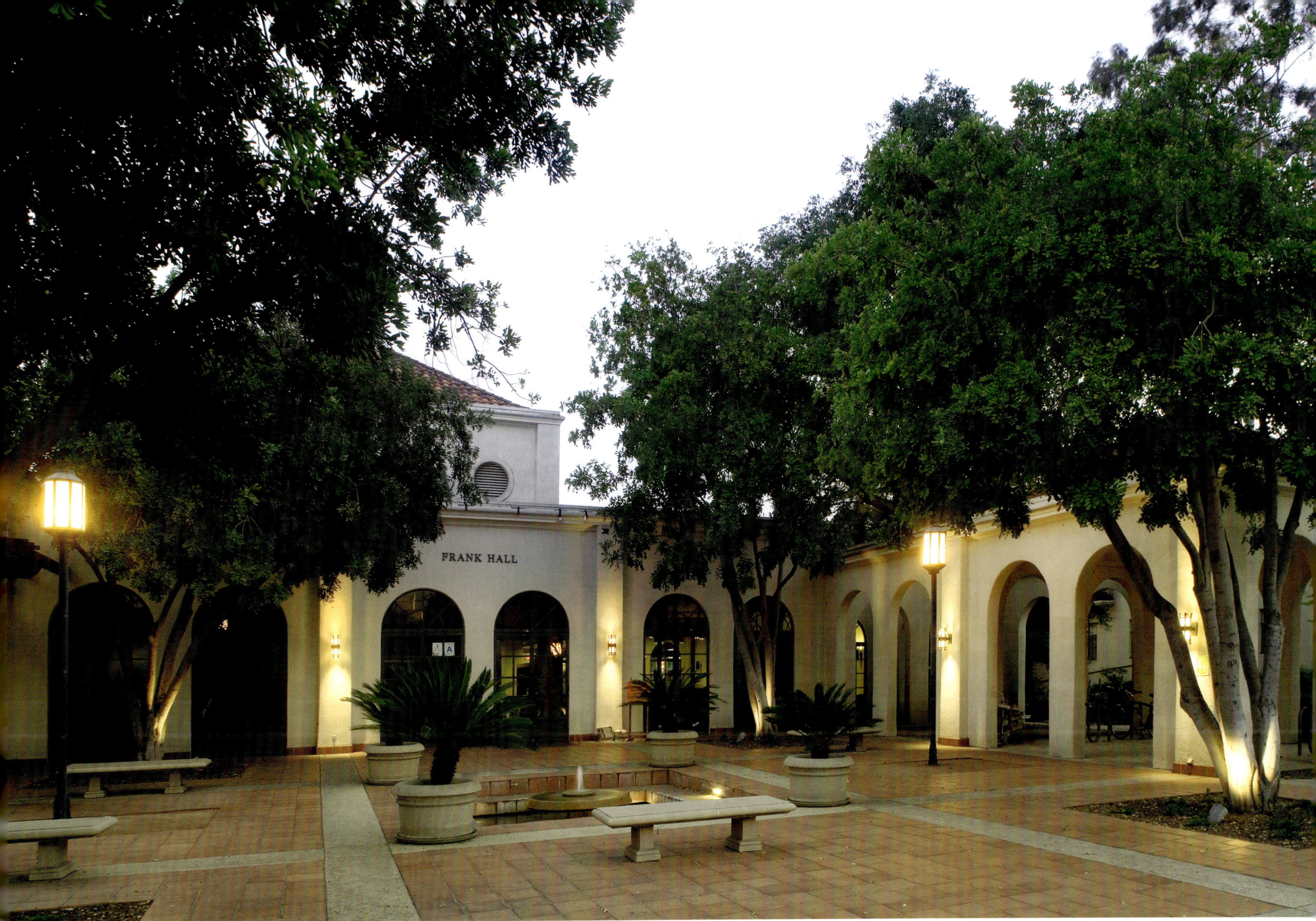

Henry Cabala

Seeley G. Mudd Science Library

BUILT 1983; dedicated April 16, 1983
LOCATION 640 North College Avenue (southeast corner College Avenue and Seventh Street)
ARCHITECT Howard Morgridge, Los Angeles
MATERIALS reinforced concrete, tile roof
COST $3.1 million
DONORS Seeley G. Mudd Fund, $1.5 million; James Irvine Foundation, $1 million; Booth Ferris Foundation, $100,000; Keck Foundation, $300,000; and a contribution from the Lluella Morey Murphey Foundation
NAMED FOR Seeley G. Mudd, trustee 1930–68

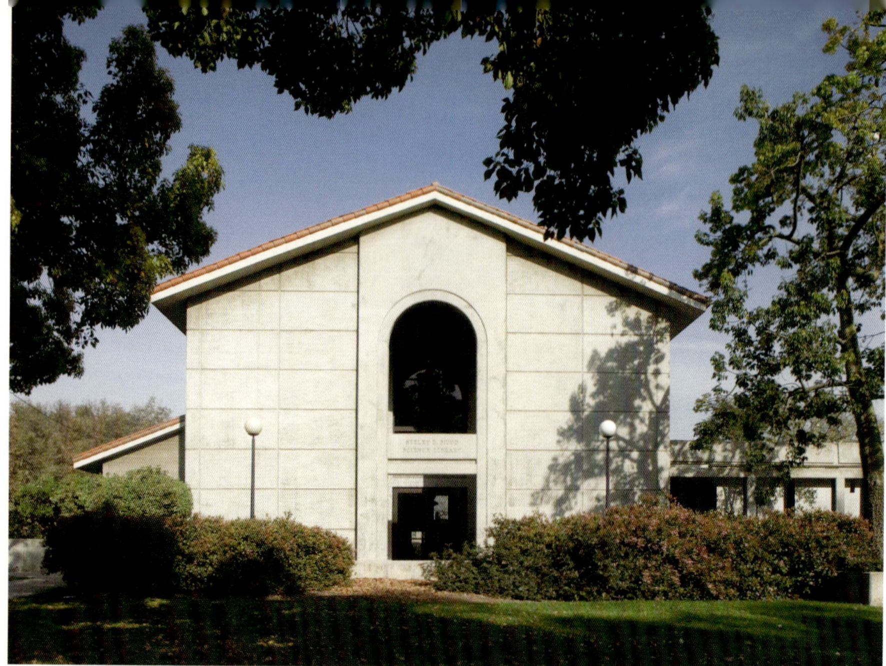

Henry Cabala

Seeley G. Mudd Science Library

The College's Centennial Plan, adopted in 1978 with a target completion date of 1987, the College's 100th birthday, had established a fund-raising goal of $80,000,000; of this, $30,000,000 was to be earmarked for construction and renovation. A new science library was one of the highest priorities.

Mudd Library replaced six separate departmental science libraries then on campus, serving Biology, Botany, Chemistry, Geology, Mathematics, and Physics/Astronomy. The need for a centralized library for the sciences was based on the projection that those currently in use would outgrow available space within five years. The new facility was designed to accommodate the 80,000 books and periodicals already in departmental collections and to provide room for 40,000 more. Centralization also provided a more efficient and cost-effective single catalogue system for all science materials, with acquisitions, cataloguing and other technical services to be provided by Honnold Library of The Claremont Colleges. The wheelchair accessible facility offered 150 seats in four different furnishing configurations, study alcoves, computer catalogue terminal, Microtest readers, photocopy machines, electronic security systems, study and meeting rooms, and a lounge.

Seeley G. Mudd, M.D., was the son of Seeley W. Mudd, the founder of Cyprus Mines Corporation and a trustee of the College from 1914–29. A long-time resident of Los Angeles and member of Pomona's board of trustees, he specified that his estate should be used to create a fund for construction of buildings at leading private universities or colleges; accordingly, a total of $42 million was donated to over 30 institutions concentrated in California but also including Harvard, Yale, Princeton, and M.I.T. Mudd himself was an honors graduate of Harvard Medical School (1924). He had spent 17 years engaged in radiation and x-ray therapy research at Caltech, had served as dean of the USC School of Medicine, and, in addition to Pomona, was a trustee of the Carnegie Institution, Washington, D.C.; the University of Southern California; Stanford University; and Caltech. Pomona's Della Mulock Mudd Hall, 1947, was named for his mother. Mudd's gift for the science library attracted additional contributions from the James Irvine, Booth-Ferris, and Keck foundations. An additional gift of $1,500,000 from the Seeley G. Mudd Fund, Los Angeles, supported the purchase of a new IBM 4341 mainframe computer.

The reinforced-concrete structure, topped by a Mission tile roof, matched that of the neighboring science buildings. Mudd Library is distinguished, however, by five cathedral-like arches spanning the main floor and mezzanine. The arched window facing College Avenue houses a sculpture by Professor Norm Hines '61 titled *Lunar Libration* (1983), a gift of the Chapman Family. ■

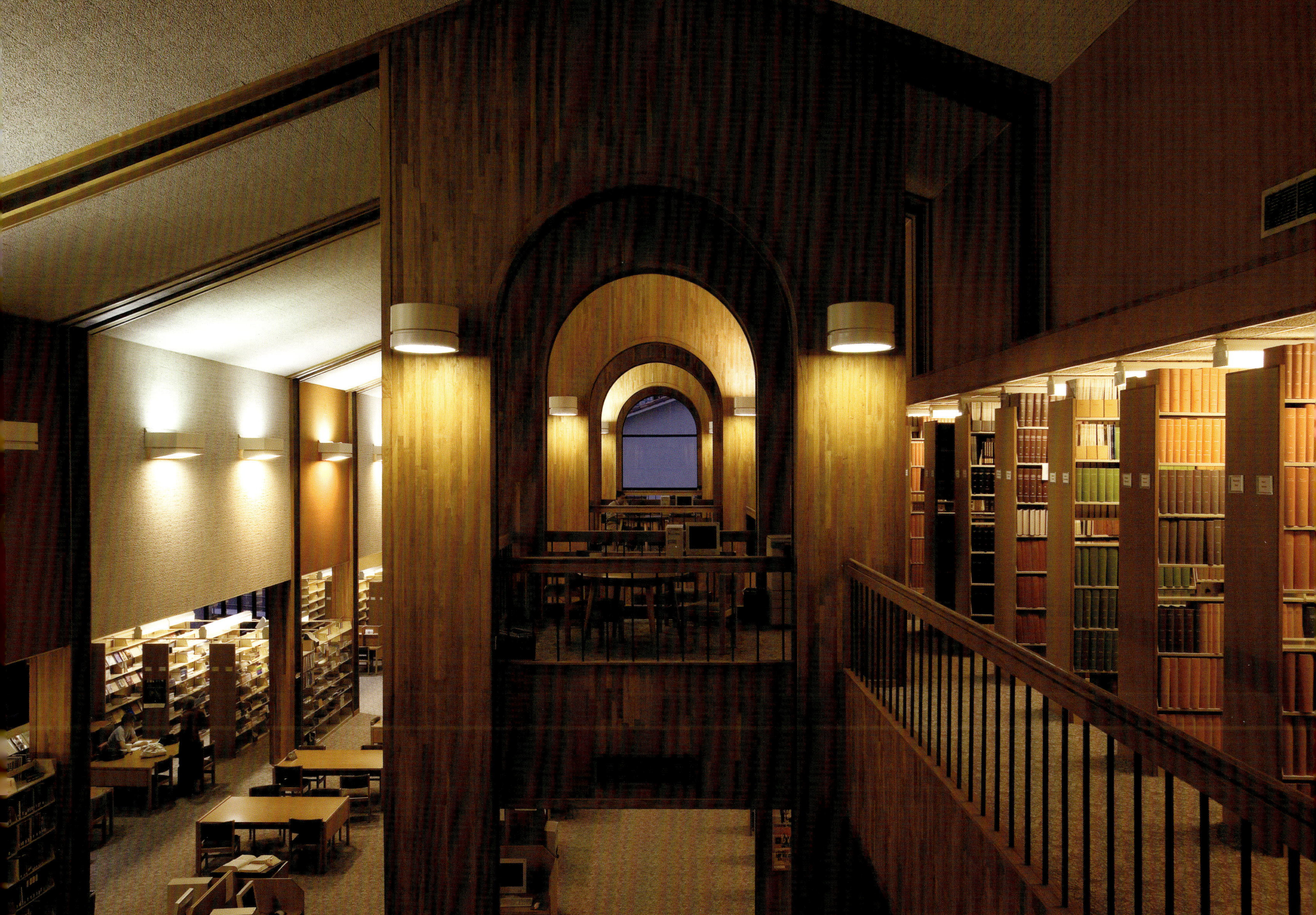

Henry Cabala

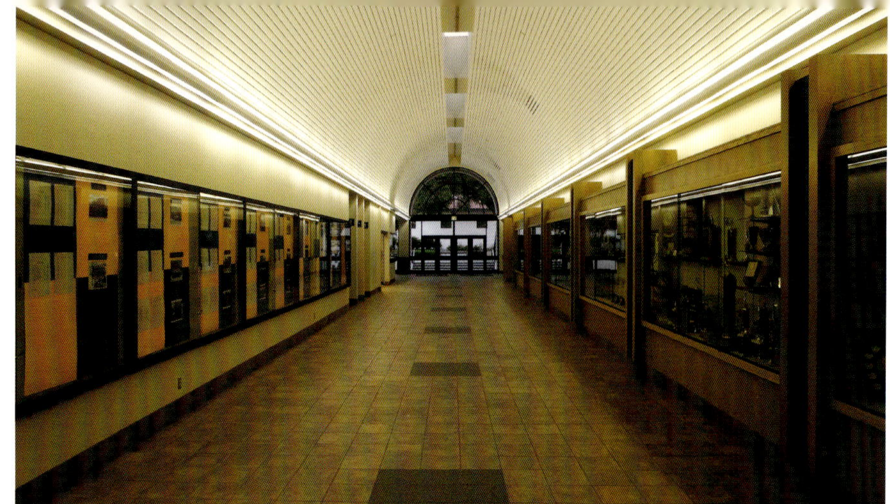

Henry Cabala

Phil Channing

ABOVE *Haldeman Pool*

ABOVE RIGHT *Liliore Green Rains Center, interior*

Liliore Green Rains Center for Sport and Recreation

In 1986, Pomona College was notified that it was to receive a gift of over $40,000,000, the largest in its history. Nearly as remarkable as the sum was the fact that it came as a complete surprise from a donor no one on campus appeared to have known. Similar astonishing disclosures were received elsewhere—Caltech, Stanford, Loyola Marymount, the Hospital of the Good Samaritan in Los Angeles, and The Menninger Foundation in Topeka, Kansas, all found themselves named in the will of Liliore Green Rains, who had died in November 1985 leaving a total of over $250,000,000 to be divided equally among the six institutions.

Liliore Rains had lived in a mansion situated on four and a half acres on Doheny Road in Beverly Hills (the house was sold to Merv Griffin after her death). Active in philanthropy but often preferring anonymity, she had been president of a charitable organization known as Colleagues, had chaired the Los Angeles Council of Girl Scouts, and sat on the boards of the Los Angeles Orphanage Guild and the National Urban League. Her father, Burton E. Green, had co-founded Beldridge Oil Co., which was later purchased by Shell Oil, and had also been a real estate developer in Beverly Hills. Her late husband, Judge William M. Rains, had attended Loyola Law School, to which she had donated a library in his name. Her only connection with Pomona College was a nephew who had attended. Despite her many good works and an active social life in the 1950s and '60s, Mrs. Rains was, in her later years, reclusive and described as "enigmatic."

Pomona's first response to the Rains bequest was to raise faculty salaries; the second was to make plans for a new physical education facility. The new complex essentially wrapped itself around Memorial Gymnasium, which was refurbished and parts of which—the floor and walls of the basketball court, for example—were preserved. To the structure was added a second gymnasium named for Robert T. Voelkel, vice-president and dean of the college 1975–86, who had strongly supported the College's athletic programs; Voelkel Gymnasium, home to the Pomona-Pitzer men's and women's basketball teams, was equipped with electronic scoreboards and motorized bleachers for 1,200 spectators. Three practice courts, along with the remodeled Memorial Gym, made possible simultaneous scheduling of intramural, recreational, and intercollegiate sports. The approximately 86,000-square-foot, wheelchair accessible center also included a state-of-the-art weight and training room; four racquetball and two squash courts (gift of Loma Sessions in honor of her husband T.J. Sessions); a library and conference room (Nancy and James L. Burke, Jr. Room); three locker rooms; space for physical therapy; a multipurpose room (Albert H. MacLeod Room) for dance and aerobics; and faculty and administrators' offices. At the time, Pomona's athletics and recreation program included 15 intercollegiate, 13 intramural, and countless recreational sports activities; its facilities included The Robert Strehle Track, named for the long-time coach of the track team and donated by H. Russell Smith '36 (1986); the Pauley Tennis Courts, gift of Mrs. William Pauley Pagen and

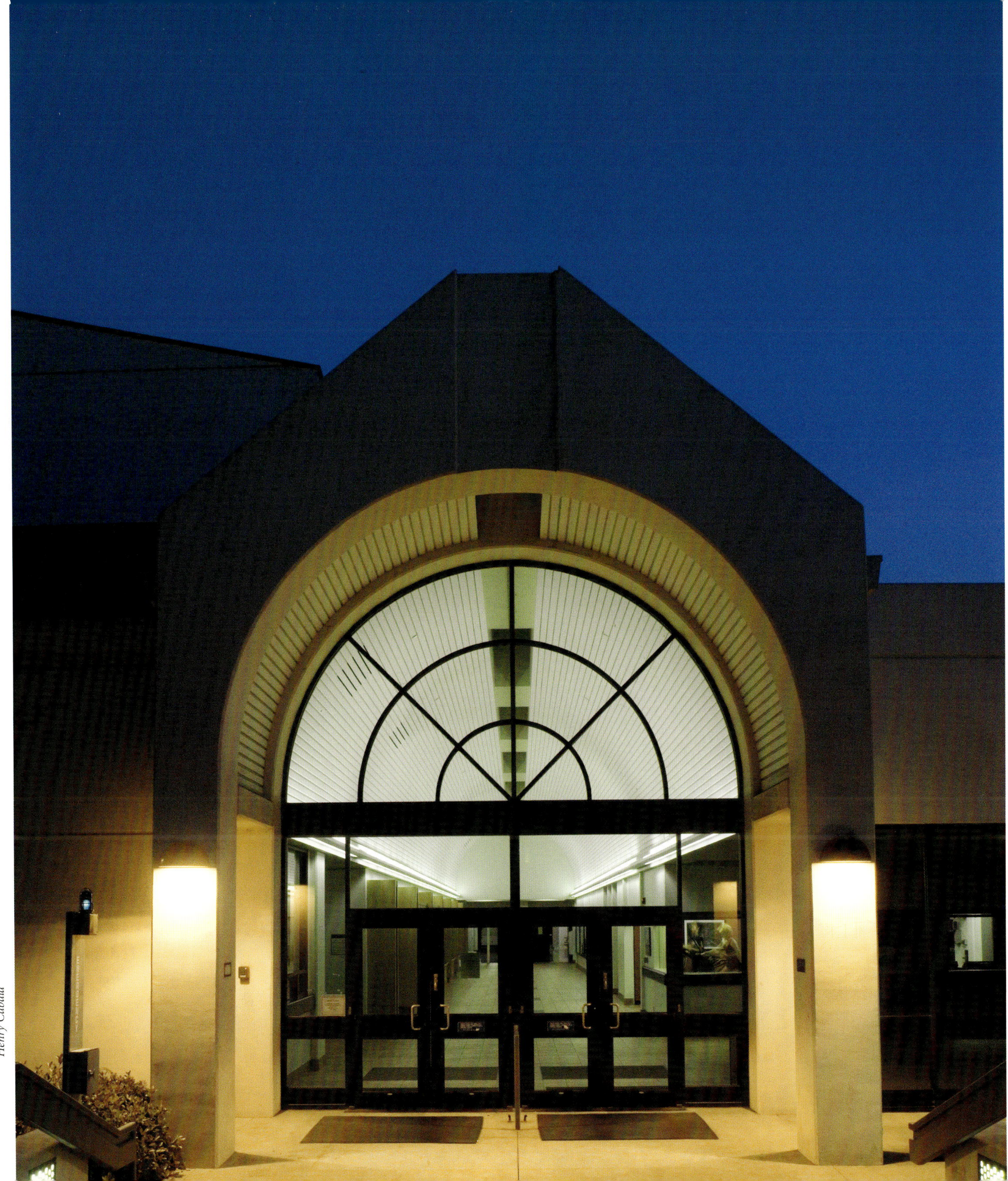

Henry Cabala

Liliore Green Rains Center for Sport and Recreation

BUILT 1989; dedicated April 8, 1989

LOCATION 220 East Sixth Street (east of Smiley Hall)

ARCHITECT Parkin Architects

MATERIALS reinforced concrete

COST $8,895,000

DONOR/NAMED FOR Liliore Green Rains

The Edward W. Pauley Foundation (1986); and Merritt Field, named for legendary football coach Earl "Fuzz" Merritt '25 (1991). At the dedication of Rains Center on April 8, 1989 (Alumni Weekend), President Alexander noted that the facility represented Pomona's commitment to the well-being and physical development, as well as the intellectual growth, of all its students.

The war memorial plaques that had been a prominent feature of the original Memorial Gymnasium found a place in the new Rains Center, in addition to two works of art added later: in the interior stairwell, a steel wall sculpture titled *Four Players*, 1999, by R. Bret Price '72, the gift of James F. and Rea (Raymond) Ludke '63, parents of Jamie Ludke '98; and, outside the building on its west side, a stainless steel and granite sculpture, *In the Spirit of Excellence*, 1989, the work of Professor Norm Hines '61, donated by Trustee Ranney E. Draper '60 and his family in honor of his father Ranney C. Draper '25.

During the summer of 1991, a new $3.1 million swimming pool, given by and named for Henry F. Haldeman, was added east of Rains Center, adjacent to Alumni Field, which was also refurbished at the time. Haldeman pool was dedicated on November 24, 1991. ■

BELOW LEFT *Merritt Field*
BELOW RIGHT *in foreground, stainless steel and granite sculpture* In the Spirit of Excellence, *1989, by Norm Hines '61, gift of Ranney E. Draper '60 and the Draper family in honor of Ranney C. Draper '25*

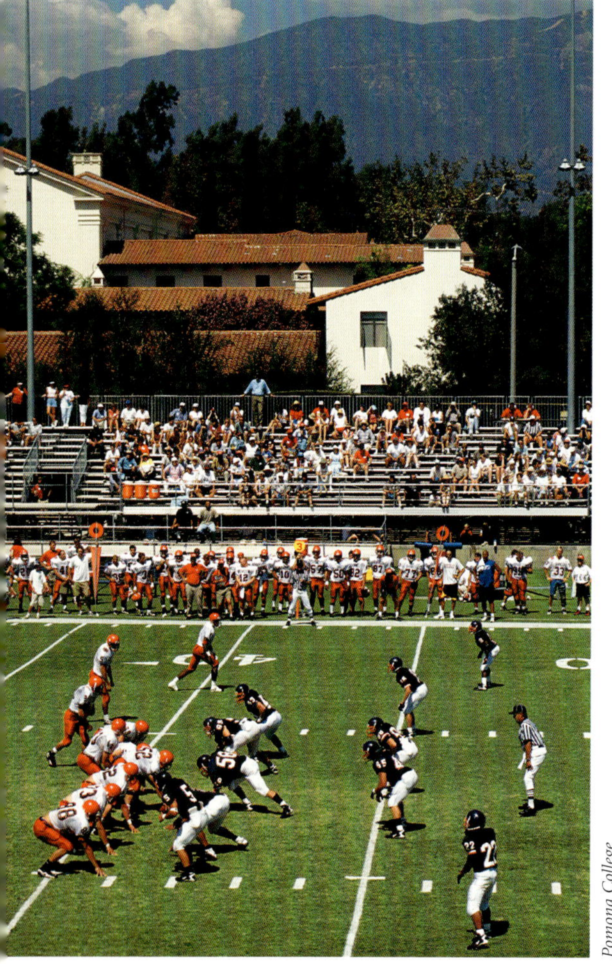

Pomona College

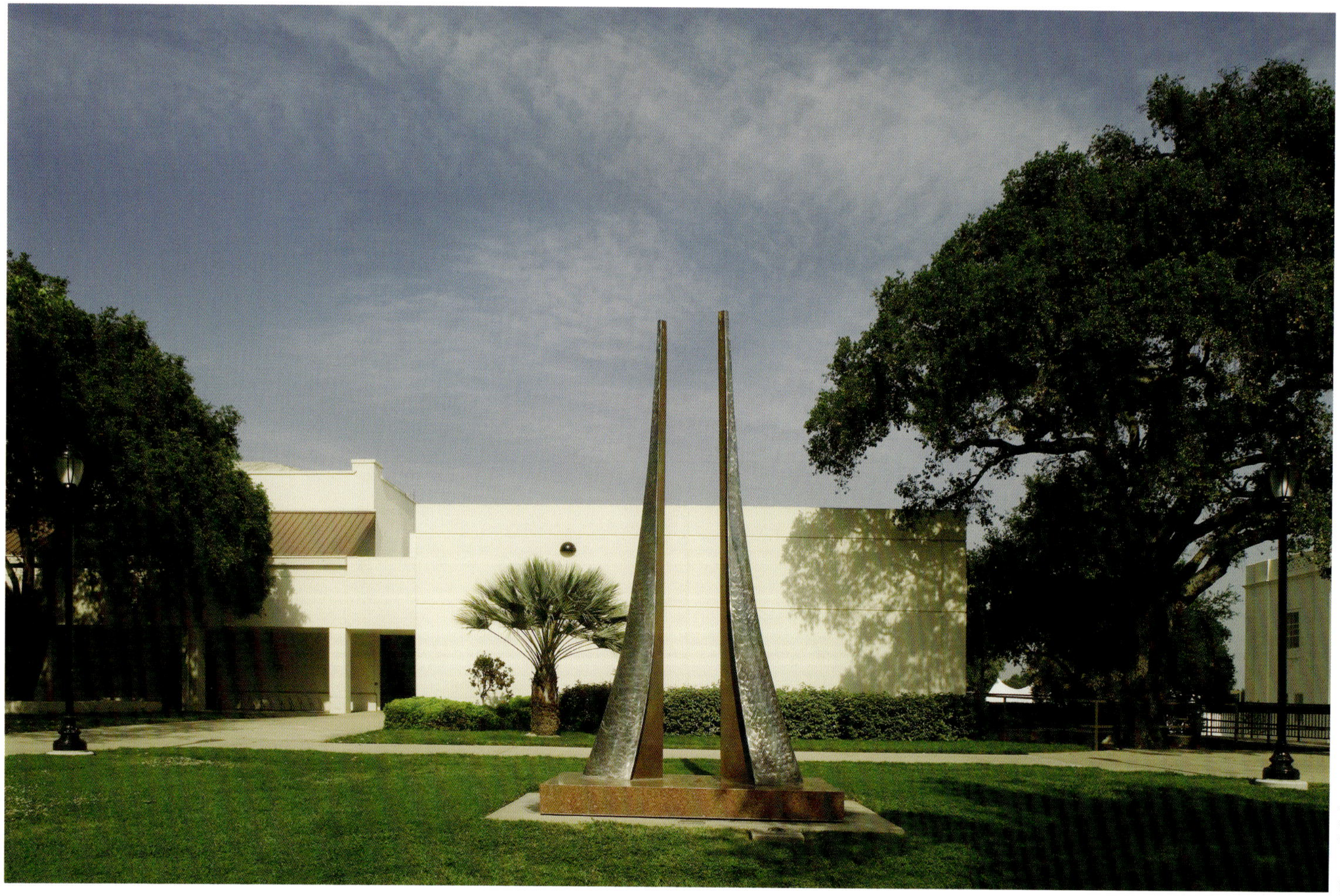

Henry Cabala

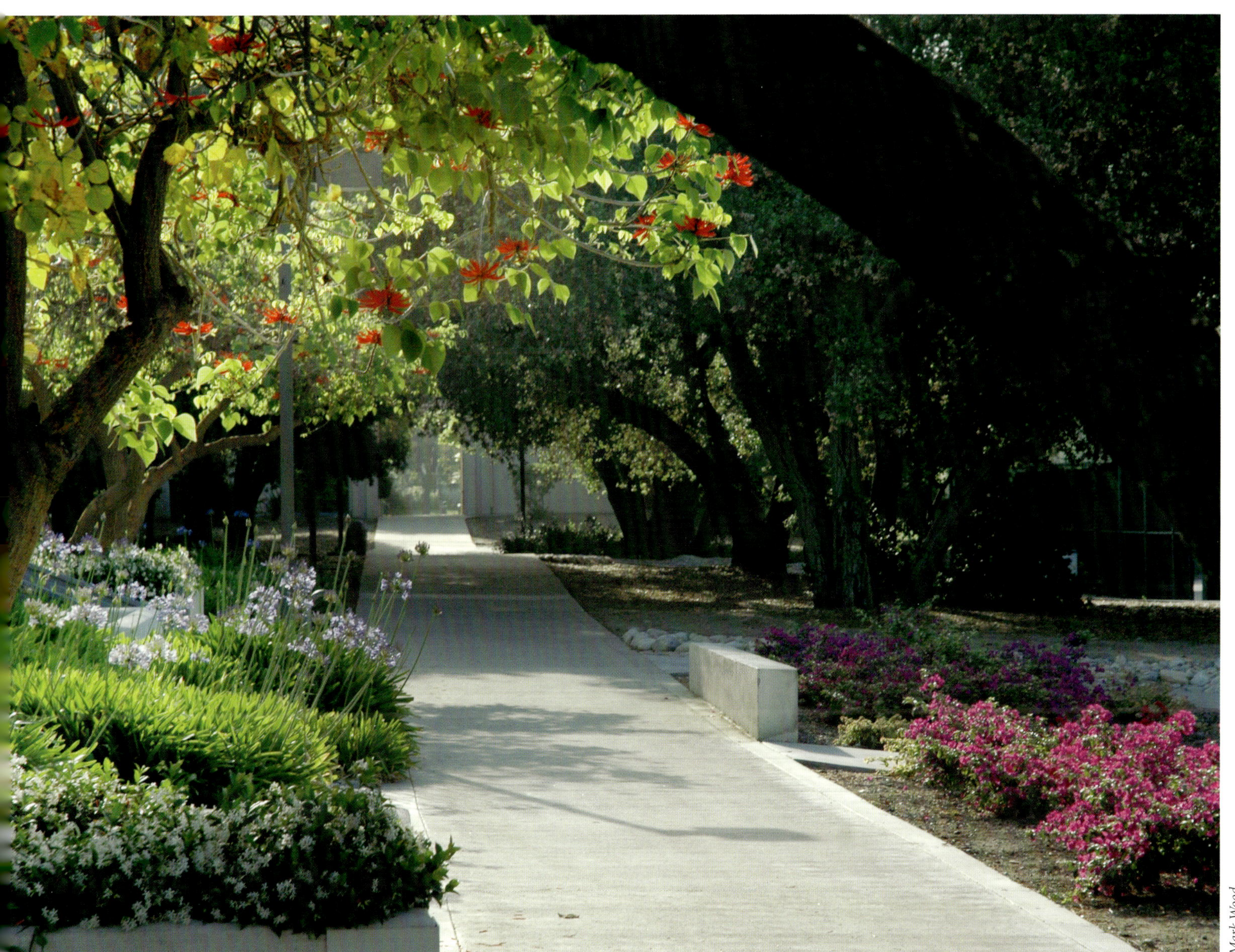

Mark Wood

Draper Walk and Plaza

BUILT 1989; dedicated August 31, 1989
PRESIDENT IN OFFICE David Alexander
LOCATION Extending from east end of Stover Walk to Mills Avenue
DONOR Ranney E. Draper '60, trustee 1984–
NAMED FOR Ranney C. Draper '25, president of Alumni Association, trustee 1957–95, attorney and civic leader

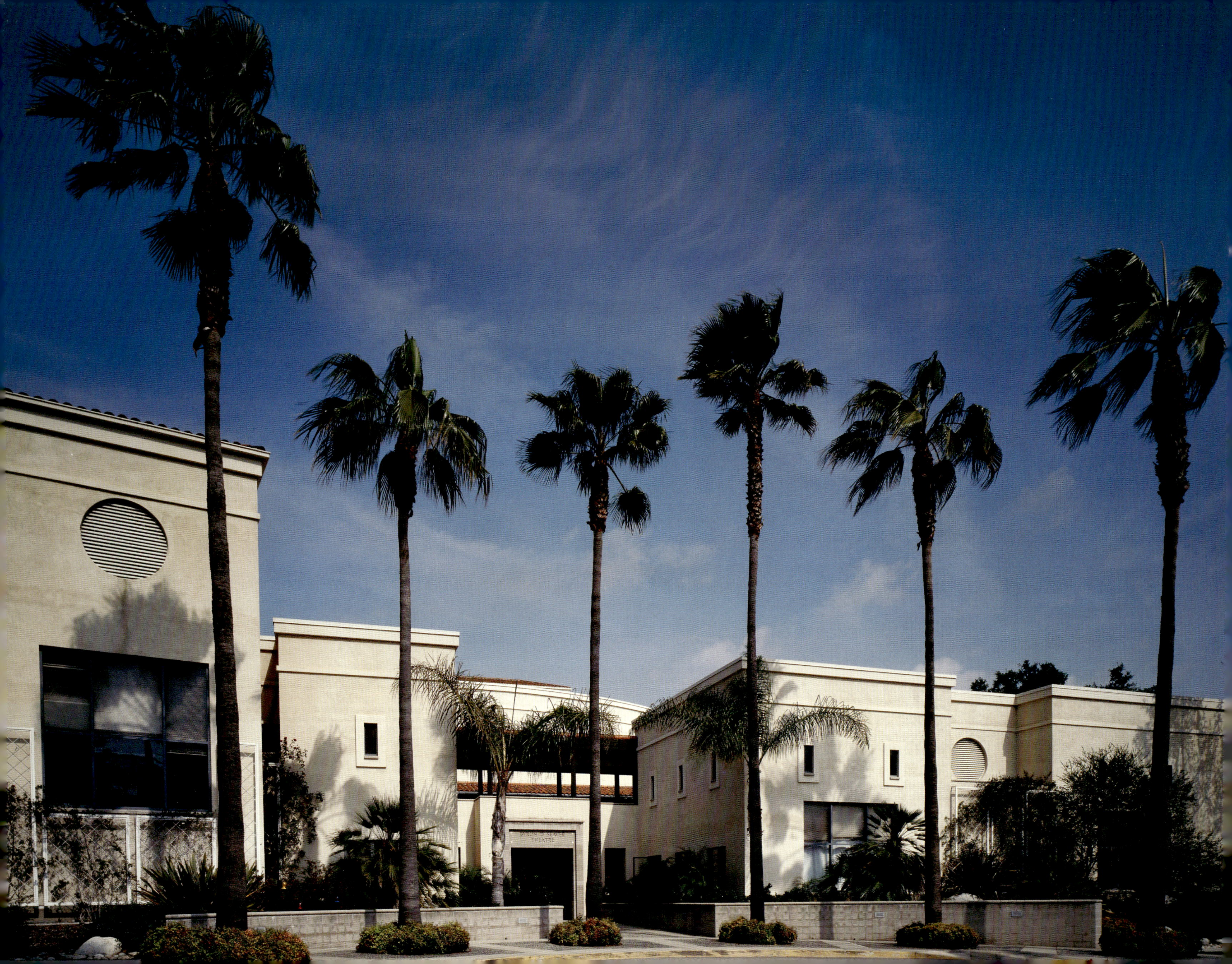
THEATRE

Mark Wood

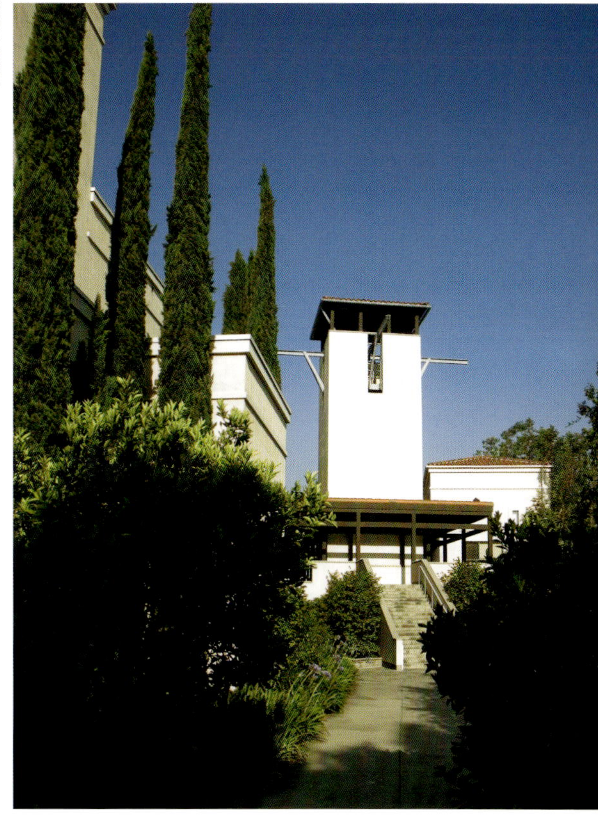

Byron Dick Seaver Memorial Theatre

A dedicated theatre building on the Pomona campus was badly needed. Holmes Hall (see Chapter 1), which had housed performances for many years, had become increasingly inadequate to the task; it was closed to use in 1987 and demolished three years later. At the time Seaver Theatre was constructed, department offices were in a converted private home on Seventh Street and performances were held in Garrison Theatre (Tenth Street at Dartmouth Avenue) that then belonged to Claremont University Center but was later purchased by Scripps College. The ambitious project was announced in 1987 but not begun until 1989 when the College received a $9.6 million donation from Richard C. Seaver '43 in honor of his father, Byron Dick Seaver '08, for whom the building was ultimately named. An attorney in Los Angeles, Byron Dick Seaver was the third child of Carlton and Estella Seaver, whose home, relocated to Claremont from its original site in Pomona, now houses the College's alumni office.

Constructed on a large lot east of Oldenborg Center and Frank Hall, the new 64,348-square-foot theatre blended academic and public functions in classrooms intended for performance and a theatre designed for teaching. The principal auditorium, which seats 340, was planned to enable audience-actor integration with runways, overhead galleries, and adaptable caliper stages for flexibility. The 52,000-square-foot building houses a hundred-seat "black box" theatre, individual studios, scene and costume shops, a library, and faculty offices arranged around a courtyard, enhancing their accessibility. The building's signature tower functions both as marquee—banners are flown when performances are scheduled—and a public elevator. In 1989, the building's design by the architectural firm BOOR/A, Portland, Oregon, which had designed other performing arts centers, won a citation from the American Institute of Architects for an "unbuilt project"; in 1995, the finished building received an award of merit from the U.S. Institute for Theatre Technology, which noted its handsome courtyard and flexible, non-intimidating teaching spaces inside and out.

The variety of theatrical forms that Seaver Theatre was carefully designed to accommodate included, importantly, Kabuki, a traditional form of Japanese popular theatre. That Pomona College offers Kabuki instruction as well as a regular schedule of traditional western theatre performances is due to Professor Leonard Pronko, who joined the faculty in 1957 and was chair of his department at the time Seaver Theatre was built. Pronko, the first non-Japanese ever to complete the Kabuki Training Program at the National Theatre of Japan, was awarded the Order of the Sacred Treasure by the Japanese Government in 1986.

Fittingly, the gala opening of the Seaver Theatre in March 1991 was celebrated with Kabuki performances, including the traditional *The Demon's Claw*, and an original Kabuki "Western" titled *Revenge at Spider Mountain* by Leonard Pronko, first produced in 1977 to mark the 25th anniversary of Kabuki at Pomona College. ■

OVERLEAF *Seaver Theatre, courtyard*

Henry Cabala

Byron Dick Seaver Memorial Theatre

BUILT 1990; dedicated November 3, 1990
LOCATION 300 East Bonita Avenue (eastern terminus of Bonita Avenue)
ARCHITECT BOOR/A (Stanley Boles of Broom, Oringdulph, O'Toole, Rudolf, Boles & Associates)
MATERIALS reinforced concrete, stucco, tile roof
DONOR Richard C. Seaver '43, trustee 1974–
NAMED FOR Byron Dick Seaver '08
COST $9.9 million

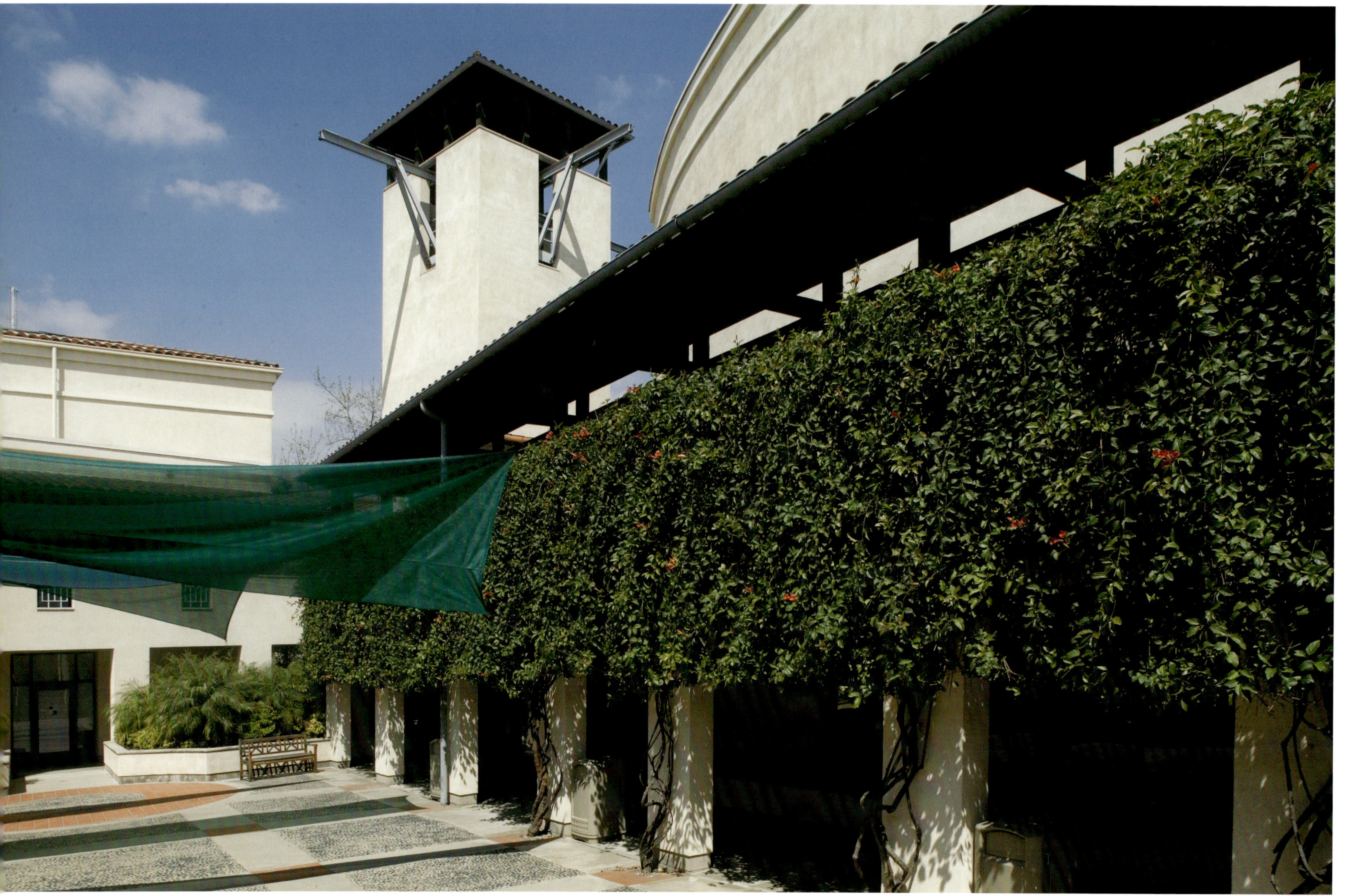

Henry Cabala

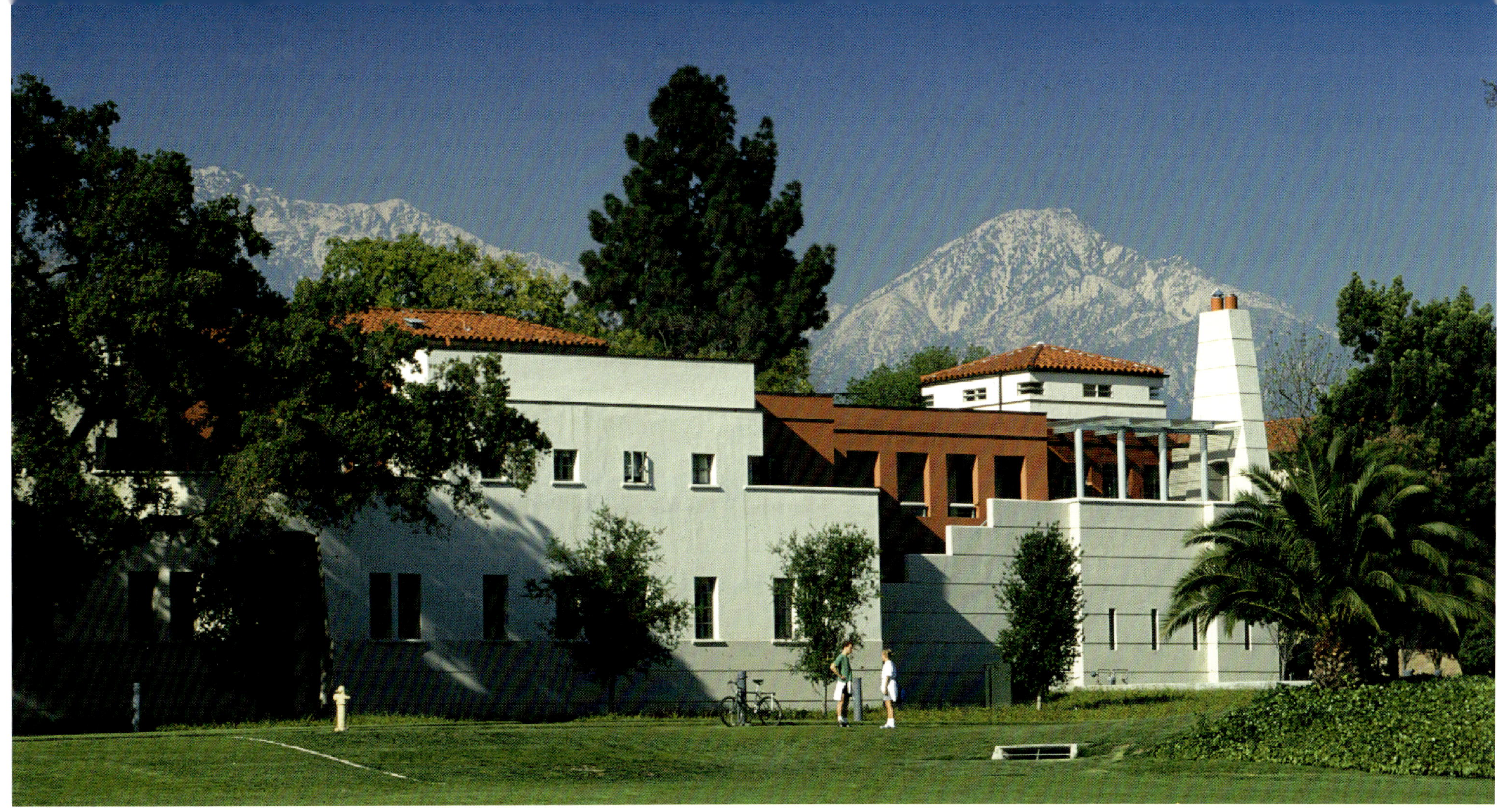

E. Wilson Lyon Court

> *The fundamental problem of our times is very easy to state. It is a matter of human beings learning to live together decently and in peace. Our best guarantee of its fulfillment is the necessity of its accomplishment.*
> —E. WILSON LYON, SEPTEMBER 13, 1945 (quoted in dedication program September 6, 1990)

Lyon Court, which opened in 1990, was named in honor of Pomona's sixth president who had believed fervently in the importance of congenial housing. The new residence, encompassing a total of 24,238 square feet, replaced Olney Dining Hall, which had been made redundant by the construction of Frank Hall, and completed the south side of Harwood Court. Renovated in 1998 and again in 2004, Lyon Court consists of one-room doubles and houses primarily first-year students. ■

Lyon Court

BUILT 1990; dedicated September 6, 1990
LOCATION 173 East Second Street
PURPOSE dormitory
ARCHITECT Peter de Bretteville
MATERIALS reinforced concrete
NAMED FOR E. Wilson Lyon, president 1941–69

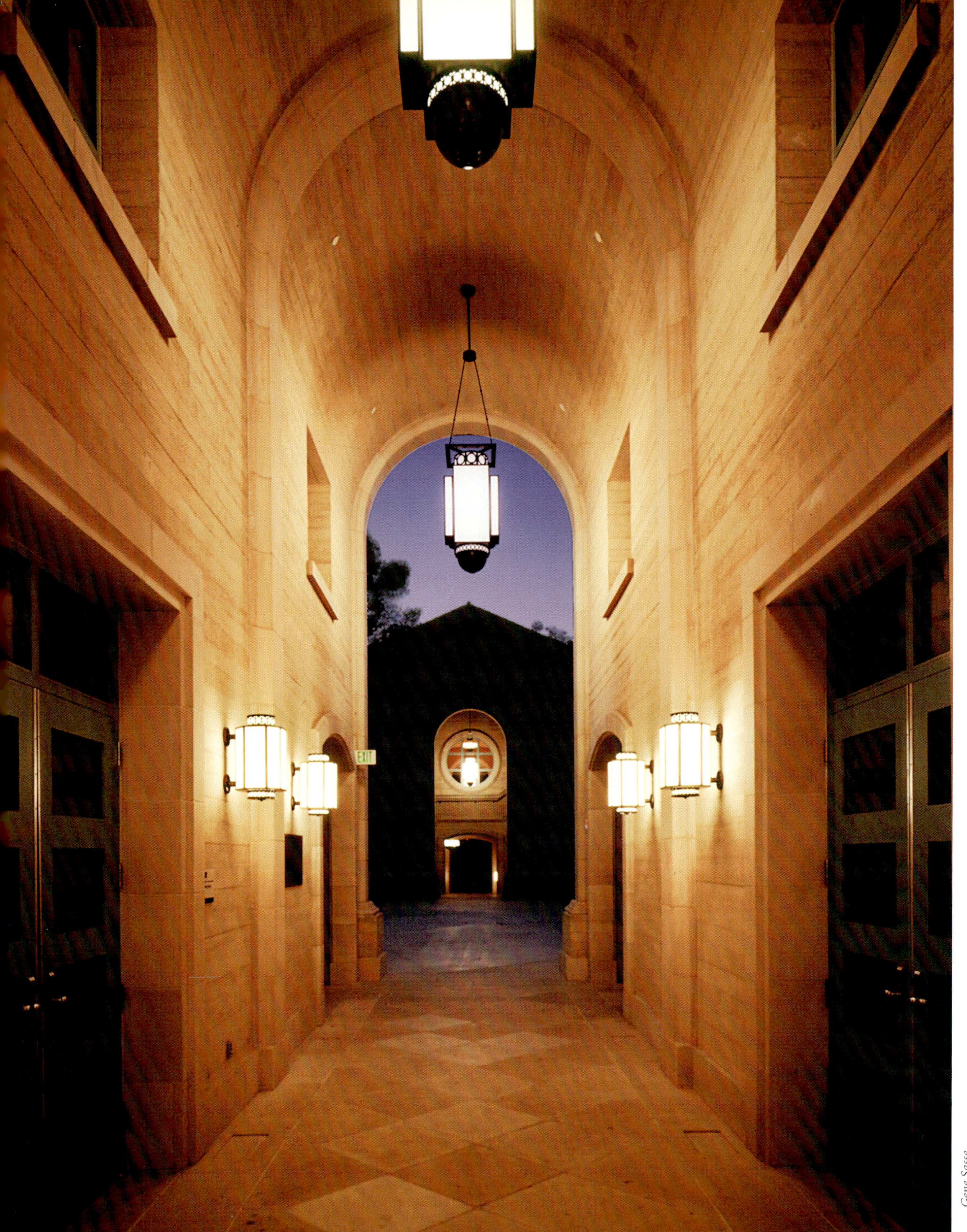

Gene Sasse

CHAPTER VI *A* SECOND MILLENNIUM 1991–

Smith Campus Center

A Second Millennium, 1991–

PRESIDENTS PETER STANLEY
and DAVID OXTOBY

The campus gives shape to the College, and the College gives meaning to the campus. Both embody the same creative tension. Their historical roots provide a really powerful sense of place.—PETER STANLEY[1]

THE PERIOD OF PRESIDENT PETER STANLEY'S TENURE was remarkable for the significance of the new buildings constructed and, equally, for the number, quality, and extent of renovations of older structures. That Pomona's campus today bears a closer relationship to its historical roots than has been the case for many years is a tribute to the sensitivity with which new buildings have been designed and older ones restored to former glory while, at the same time, being upgraded to meet contemporary needs.

Peter W. Stanley came to Pomona College from The Ford Foundation, where he had been director of the education and culture programs for the past seven years. Inaugurated in 1991 as the College's eighth president, Stanley was, from the outset, sensitive to the role of the physical campus, an awareness that reflected, in part, the concern for heritage and regional identity fundamental to the ongoing nationwide historic preservation movement. In his inaugural address, Stanley noted the need for a campus center and pledged to see this goal realized. Dedicated in 1999, the Smith Campus Center was the most ambitious of the three important new building projects of Stanley's tenure (the others being the Hahn and Andrew buildings) and one whose impact on the daily life of the Pomona community is particularly significant. Equally important, the building has, through its design, recaptured the spirit of Myron Hunt's 1908 campus plan, opening north-south axes across Marston Quadrangle to Mabel Shaw Bridges Hall of Music and Sumner Hall, and creating an east-west corridor from Mason Hall to Rains Center.

The Campus Center project was enormous in scope—physically, programmatically, financially, and in terms of planning, a contentious process that he admits may have been intensified by his insistence that the building "belong to everyone, not just be a student union."

My sense of Pomona was that it suffered greatly from the lack of a space where people of all descriptions—faculty, students, staff, visitors, of every political and cultural persuasion—regularly crossed paths and had the opportunity to engage each other. I didn't want the campus center to become one more gated community, one more cul-de-sac, to which one of the constituencies could retreat and avoid this sort of engagement. The result was that everyone weighed in with their aspirations and their fears. The resulting building, which I've always found visually stunning, never quite freed itself from this planning quagmire. It remains to be seen whether the renovations in 2006 can solve the programming problem without sacrificing too much of its architectural elegance.

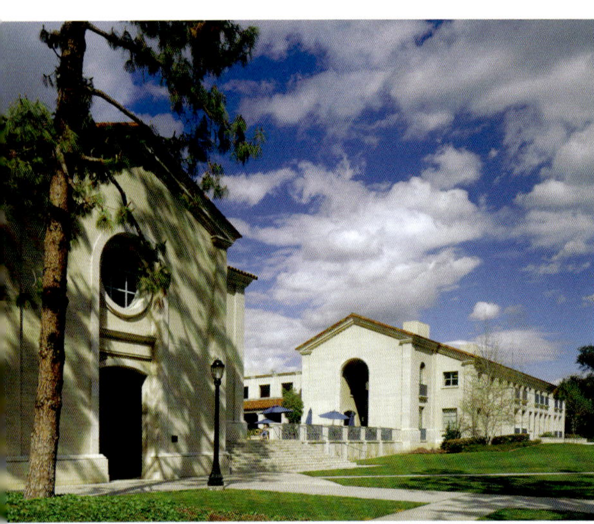

Henry Cabala

H. Russell and Jeanne Smith Campus Center

As significant to the Pomona campus as the new buildings constructed during Stanley's tenure were, the renovations of several of the College's oldest and architecturally most significant buildings were equally so. Undergoing complete renovations were Sumner Hall (1993), the newly named Sontag Greek Theatre (1997), Carnegie (1998), Mabel Shaw Bridges Hall of Music (2001), and Pearsons (2003) and Crookshank (2004) halls. Renovation, in these cases, meant meeting the seemingly contradictory goals of restoring as many of the structures' original features as possible while also bringing each up to date in terms of safety, access, and technology. John Giboney, Director of Campus Planning from 1982 to 1999, cites these renovation projects as among the most demanding, successful, and satisfying of his years on campus. The challenge, as Stanley explains, lay in the mutually exclusive goals of those most concerned:

Little Bridges was (along with Carnegie) the signature building of the campus. The renovation occurred simultaneously with the installation of a magnificent new organ. The challenge was to strengthen the building structurally, make it more accessible, correct some inadvertent mistakes from earlier renovations, and improve its already-admirable acoustics. No one wanted to risk compromising the building in the process. There were two camps, each animated by their love of the existing building. Members of the Music Department, who use the building, assigned highest priority to making it more functional and more accessible. Others, whom we might call originalists by analogy to current judicial discussions, resisted adaptations that might compromise the integrity of the original plan and wanted to take the opportunity to restore features of the building, such as ornamentation, that had been lost over the years. The problem was that both camps wanted what was best, and that there was no middle ground on which they could agree. Fortunately, only the exterior was at issue. The renovation of the interior was entirely to the good. In the end, I concluded that we were at risk of loving Little Bridges to death: that the emotions attached to the building had as much to do with the way it was used as with the way it looked, that the building was there to serve the music and the community, and that sensitive adaptation was inherent in the notion of a living tradition. The resulting enlargement was modest in scale and was carried out with such care that the building remains both beautiful and beloved.

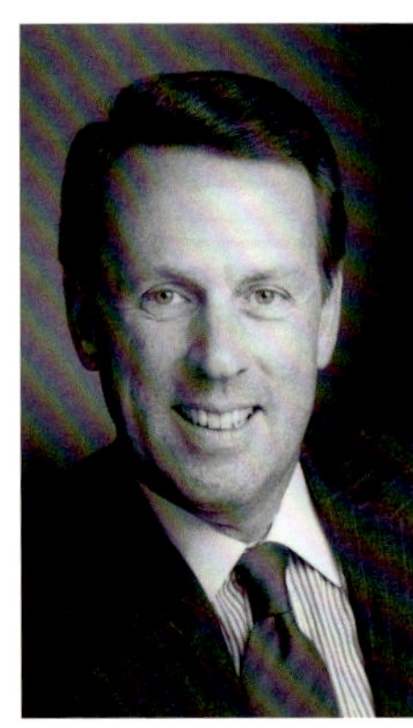

President Peter W. Stanley

The growth of the campus during this period was closely tied to that of the endowment, which doubled between 1996 and 2002, ultimately exceeding $1 billion. This unprecedented increase was due in great part to The Campaign for Pomona

College, endorsed in 1995. When formally launched in 1997, more than a third of the ultimate goal of $150 million was already in hand; by 2002, the campaign concluded 37 percent above its initial goal, having raised over $206 million and significantly met every program objective. A similarly impressive record was set in terms of applications for admission, which had reached new highs in each of the five preceding years, as had the levels of academic achievement of those admitted.

New and renovated classroom buildings reflected, as they enhanced, the College's curriculum as it underwent important changes during this period. The relocation of the Pacific Basin Institute from Santa Barbara to the Pomona campus in 1997, and the introduction in 1998 of the Intercollegiate Asian American Studies Program, consolidated ongoing efforts to intensify Pacific Rim studies. In 2000, a new major in Cognitive Science was added to the curriculum as part of the Department of Linguistics and Cognitive Science that, as Stanley remarked, served to position the College at the forefront of the study of "the nature of mind and thought...that will only grow in importance as our century unfolds." The discipline moved into its new home, the newly completed Edmunds Building, in the spring of 2007.

As president, Peter Stanley was sensitive to the fact that change on a campus is as necessary as it is inevitable, and, equally, to the difficult questions that have to be addressed along the way:

> *...because this is, after all, California, the College has change in its genes. In California, either a tradition is a living tradition, amenable to change, or it dies. And so just as the College introduces new subjects into the curriculum and new faces into the faculty and the student body, the campus' architecture, landscaping, and patterns of use continually evolve. The College can't be a museum, and neither can the campus. But careless or opportunistic change to the campus would waste one of our greatest assets. Because at the end of the day, the College's identity and integrity are expressed visually in the shape and character of its house.*
>
> *During my time at the College, we dealt with all the classic issues that test the hypothesis that the tension between tradition and change can be productive. Nobody ever says, "I'd like to put up a cheap, ugly building or pave over this little corner of paradise." And almost no one ever says, "You can't materially change anything that's here now or add anything that wouldn't have been designed by Myron Hunt or Ralph Cornell." But what do you do about the constantly increasing need to facilitate movement and provide parking for cars? How do you arrange lighting, route pedestrian traffic and balance the need for open campus borders that are also secure? How can you adapt historic structures to technology and also increase their accessibility? How aggressively "green" should the College be, and at what cost to other values? How adventurous should we be about enlarging the architectural vocabulary and adding new styles of buildings? To me, these were deeply personal questions. They weren't just about stewardship or policy.*

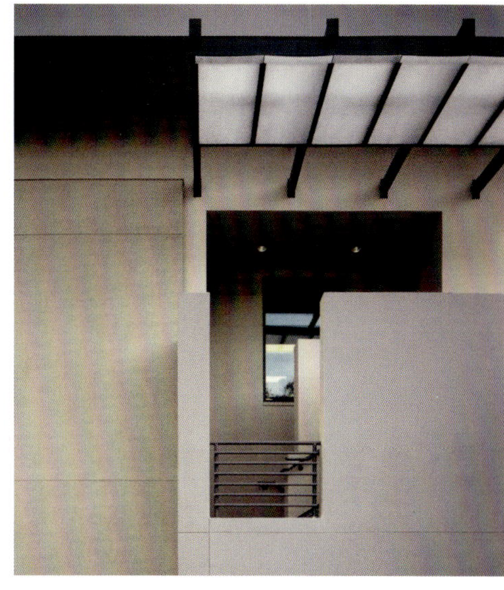

Gene Sasse

Andrew Science Building

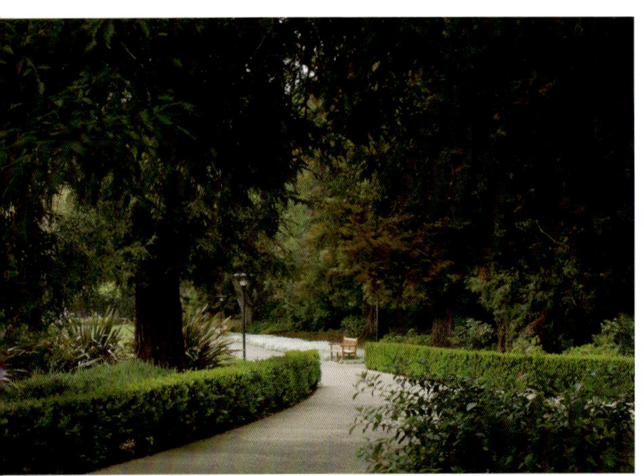

Path in Marston Quadrangle

Stanley made it a point to walk the campus both by day and by night many times a week. These ramblings enhanced his awareness of the campus as a whole and his recognition of the significance of its open spaces, such as Marston Quadrangle.

> *Marston Quad is one of the great public spaces of Southern California. But it is curiously empty of people much of the time. One reason for this is that it's a little too large. Another is that Southern California is not an Italian hill town: people don't flock to the public square to act out their lives. As a result, Marston Quad sometimes seems a sort of atavism, and well-meaning people regularly try to appropriate it in one way or another. My thought was that the Quad was so central to Pomona's identity that we ought not to let it get chipped away. Because once we lost the idea that this public space belonged to everyone, that could never be recovered. The idea of the commons is difficult to sustain in California. Instead, I thought, we ought to renew the plantings and the lawn, repave the walks, light it better: in a word, honor it. This involved some challenges to tradition.... There used to be very large, thick, tall hedges bordering the walks at the east end of the Quad. They were sacred in some quarters. But they were also dangerous, because they blocked light and sight lines. Women, in particular, said that they did not feel safe there at night; but I knew this myself from having walked there in the dark many times. So we tore out those hedges and opened up the sight lines. And, what do you know: the new, opened sight lines framed Big Bridges even better than the hedges had. The space is, I believe, still lightly used. But on a balmy afternoon when it is filled with sunbathers, Frisbee-throwers, the occasional musician, and little clusters of people engaged in conversations, it is as close as the Inland Empire is ever going to get to having a town square.*

Stanley concludes:

> *If there is a theme that runs through (my thinking about the campus) it is about public space and public purpose. One of the major contributions of small, residential colleges is to bring widely diverse people together and cause them to engage each other in ways that create a learning environment. The campus is the theatre where that occurs.*

In 2001, President Stanley announced his intention to retire at the end of the 2002–03 academic year, and the search for his successor began. Two years later, David Oxtoby was named by the Board as the ninth president of Pomona College.

President David W. Oxtoby

David Oxtoby came to Pomona from the University of Chicago where he had served as dean of physical sciences for the previous eight years. A theoretical chemist of international reputation, he was only the second Pomona president trained in science—Pomona's fifth president, Charles K. Edmunds, 1928–41, was a physicist and engineer—and the first chemist. His interests were, however, broad, extending to mathematics, music, languages, and theatre.

The history of President Oxtoby's tenure has, of course, only begun, but in terms of the development of the campus, it is off to an auspicious start. His first year in office saw the completion of an extensive and historically sensitive renovation of Crookshank Hall and the new Richard C. Seaver Biology Building (2004); in 2005, ground was broken for the Lincoln and Edmunds buildings. As this book goes to press, a major renovation of Mason Hall is under way.

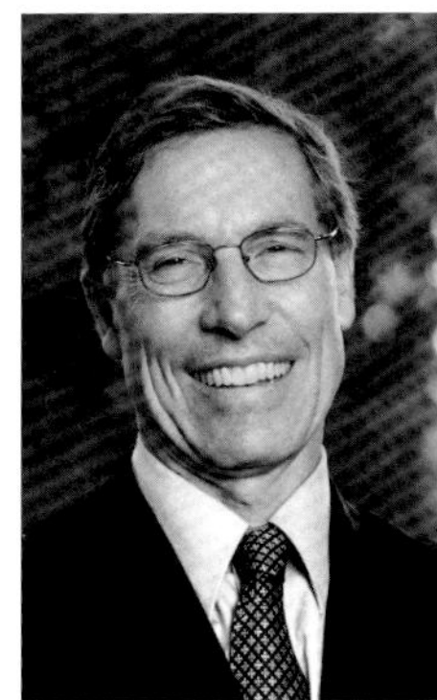

President David W. Oxtoby

The Seaver Biology and the Lincoln and Edmunds buildings were, as Oxtoby noted, part of a multi-year effort to bring Pomona's science facilities back to the cutting edge in fields that have evolved significantly over the years:

> *The nature of science teaching has changed dramatically since the three buildings that made up the original Seaver Science Center were built in the 1950s and 1960s. In all fields, we have moved from large, lecture-based classes toward smaller, discussion and group-oriented classes. Most importantly, we have encouraged our students to become involved in collaborative research with faculty early in their college careers, since that is what stimulates students to become scientists. The Seaver Biology Building was designed with this model of research-based teaching in mind, just as the Lincoln and Edmunds buildings have been designed to expand our student-research opportunities in other fields, ranging from psychology and computer science to neuroscience and environmental analysis.* [2]

As a new cycle of strategic planning gets under way to identify the opportunities and challenges of the coming decade, Oxtoby expects the College to set new priorities for the campus as well.

> *As we plan for the decade ahead, we will no doubt shift our emphasis to other areas where changes in the world and new academic opportunities now call for changes in bricks and mortar. The choices we make in the years to come will be guided by the kind of thoughtful long-term planning Pomona College is known for. It will also be informed by the core principle that our students and faculty in every field—from the arts and humanities to the social and natural sciences—deserve the finest space in which to work, so that they can develop their talents to the fullest.*[3] ■

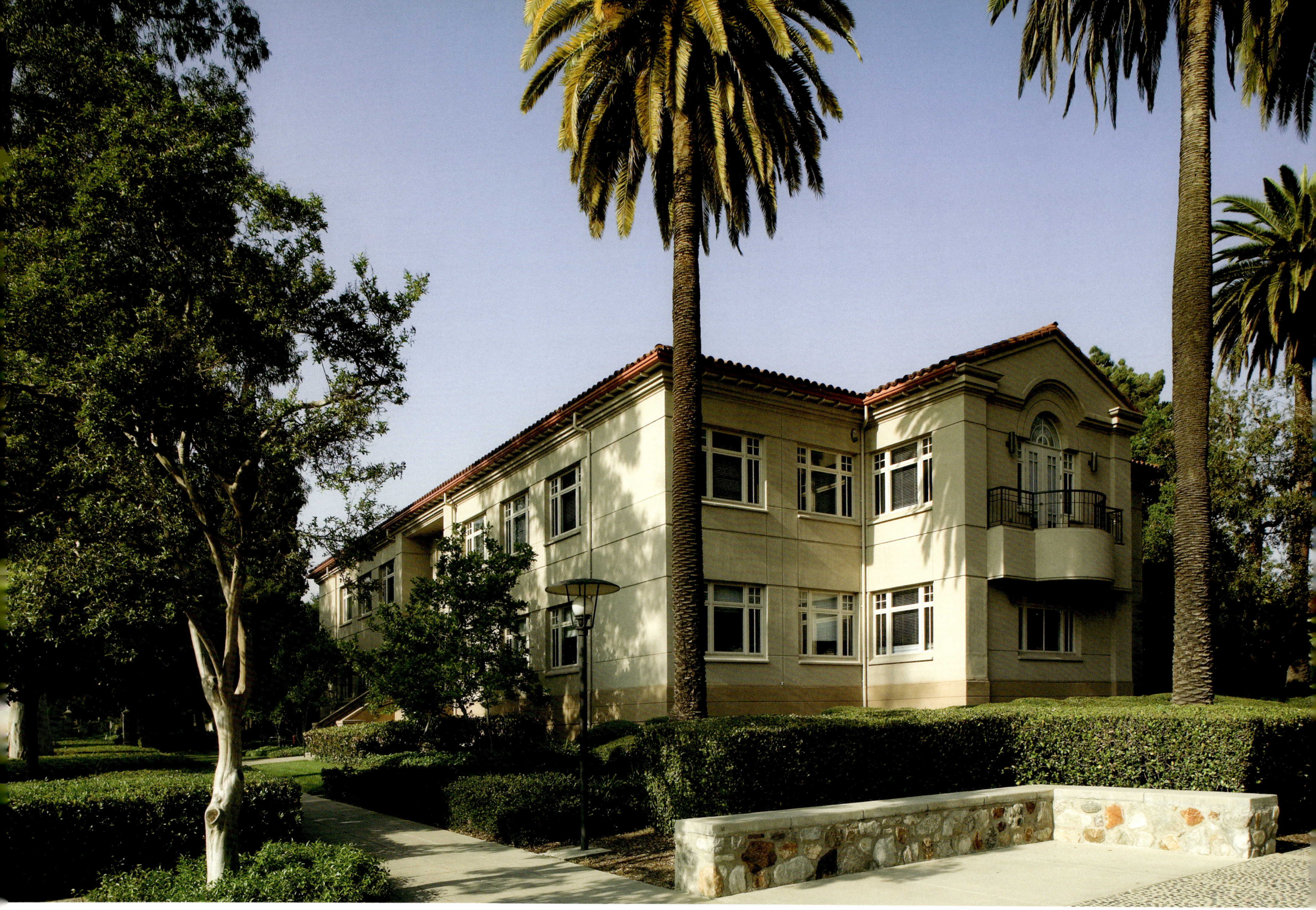

Henry Cabala

David Alexander Hall of Administration

Over the years, the College's administrative offices have been housed in a number of buildings—Sumner Hall, in its original location (1888); Holmes Hall (1893); Pearsons Hall (1898); Carnegie (president's office, 1908); and the relocated Sumner Hall (1923). As the College grew, it became impossible to centralize administrative functions under one roof, and a new administration building was one of the chief goals of the Centennial Campaign.

When ground was broken for the new structure at the corner of Sixth Street and College Avenue in 1990, the building that had occupied that site for nearly a century—venerable Holmes Hall—was gone but not forgotten. Declared unsafe and impractical to renovate, Pomona's first dedicated academic building had been demolished, but its memory left a mark on the new building, which was designed to fit Holmes Hall's basic footprint (except for the one-story wing housing the Business Office) and to echo the tile and stucco appearance Holmes had presented to the world since its 1916 renovation. Likewise, many of Alexander Hall's exterior details (entry steps, window patterns, sizes, and shapes) derived from Holmes, as did its traditionally appointed interior that includes chair rails, baseboards, paneling, and a central staircase whose metalwork detail and wooden banister mirror the one that served its predecessor.

Christened the David Alexander Hall of Administration, the building honors President Alexander's 22-year tenure, which had concluded the year before the new building's dedication. ■

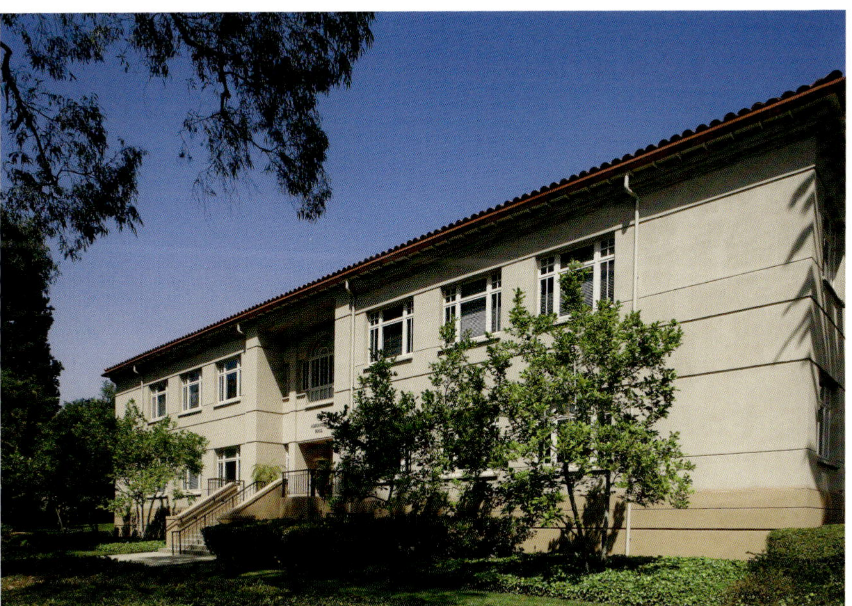

Henry Cabala

David Alexander Hall of Administration

BUILT 1991; dedicated in 1992
PRESIDENT IN OFFICE Peter W. Stanley
LOCATION 550 North College Avenue
PURPOSE Administrative offices and meeting rooms
ARCHITECT Julie Maser (Hoover Associates)
MATERIALS steel frame and drivit, tile roof
COST $6,300,000
DONORS The Weingart Foundation, trustees, friends, and other donors
NAMED FOR David Alexander, seventh president of Pomona College (1969–1991)

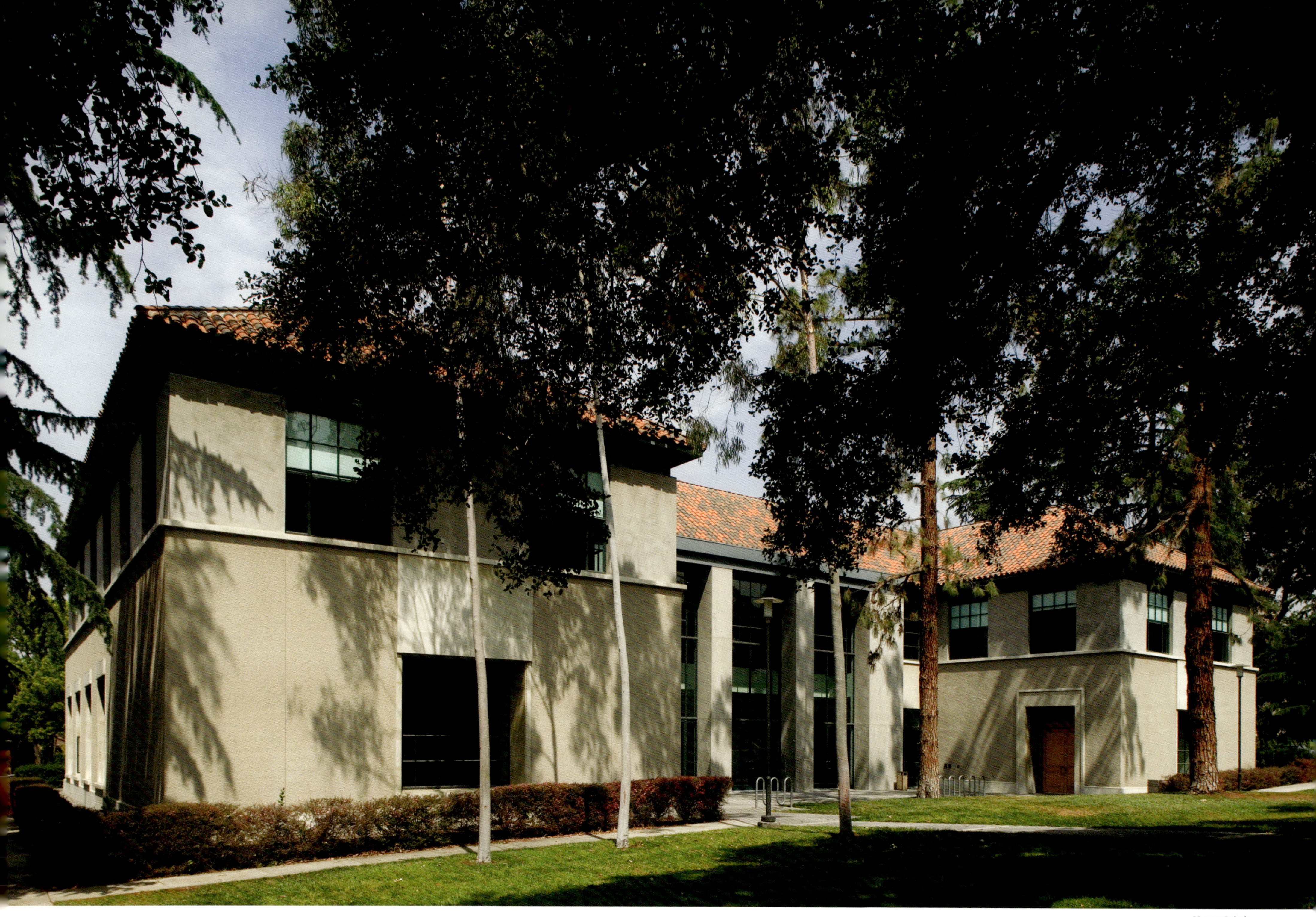

Henry Cabala

Edwin F. and Margaret Hahn Building

In the late 80s, during the Centennial Campaign, Edwin '24 and Margaret Hahn approached President Alexander about making a gift to the College, indicating they wished it to be major and to address a pressing need. At the time, the first priority was also the most expensive—a building for the social sciences that would relieve overcrowded Carnegie Building, provide space for conferences and symposia increasingly needed by Sociology/Anthropology, Politics, Economics, and Public Policy Analysis, and complete the western quadrangle of the College—in Alexander's words "thereby fulfilling the Master Plan developed by the internationally renowned architect Myron Hunt, and his partner Elmer Grey, in 1908." When the Hahns' gift for the building was made in 1990, no one imagined how long and arduous a process was in store.

The College's claim to the undeveloped lot behind Carnegie, where the new building was to be constructed, was disputed by the City of Claremont, which claimed that when the land was acquired from the Pacific Land Improvement Company in 1893 it was agreed that it would remain a public park. Environmental concerns were also expressed, particularly concerning the removal of trees. The ensuing legal battles, which began in 1990, extended for six years and included challenges by a citizens' group. Ultimately, the courts ruled in the College's favor, clearing the way for construction. In deference to community concerns, the building's height was reduced from three stories to two, its setback from Harvard Avenue increased to 30 feet, and a number of unhealthy trees were replaced by 40 new ones. In a related agreement in 1997, the City acquired from the College Leonard A. Shelton Park, at the corner of Harvard and Bonita avenues.

When completed, the 27,600-square-foot Hahn building contained technologically up-to-date classrooms and offices, a large first floor hall for lectures and conferences, and a computer lab. At the dedication in October 1997, it was noted that the need for additional space for Sociology and Anthropology, which had been introduced into the curriculum in 1956, had grown more acute as the social sciences had gained popularity. In addition to Sociology and Anthropology, Hahn now houses the Pacific Basin Institute, which is dedicated to education in Asia-Pacific affairs, and its Jigsaw Archives, a comprehensive video library that includes the Institute's award-winning *The Pacific Century.*

In April 1998, the building was awarded the City of Claremont's Architectural Commission award for Excellence in Design. Its completion was followed by the renovation of Carnegie so that, together, the two provided a state-of-the-art instructional center for Politics, Economics, Sociology/Anthropology, and Public Policy Analysis. The two buildings are also physically related: Hahn includes chilled water and air conditioning for Carnegie. ■

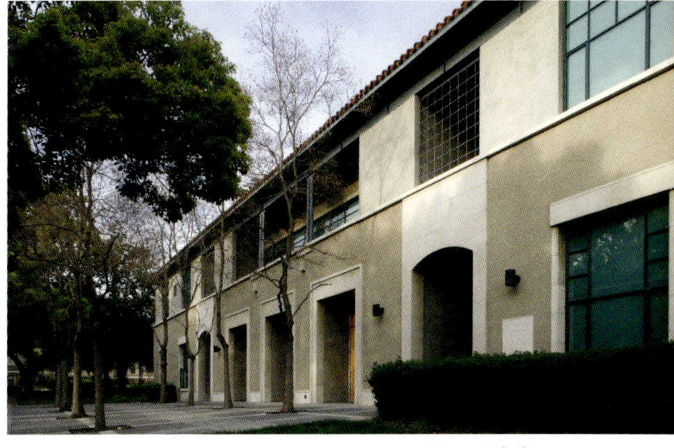

Henry Cabala

Edwin F. and Margaret Hahn Building

BUILT 1997; dedicated October 17, 1997
PRESIDENT IN OFFICE Peter W. Stanley
LOCATION 420 North Harvard Avenue (between Fourth Street and Harrison Avenue)
PURPOSE Sociology, Anthropology
ARCHITECT Scott Kelsey, Anshen and Allen, Los Angeles
MATERIALS reinforced concrete, tile roof
COST $7,400,000
DONORS/NAMED FOR Edwin Franklin Hahn '24 and Margaret Hahn

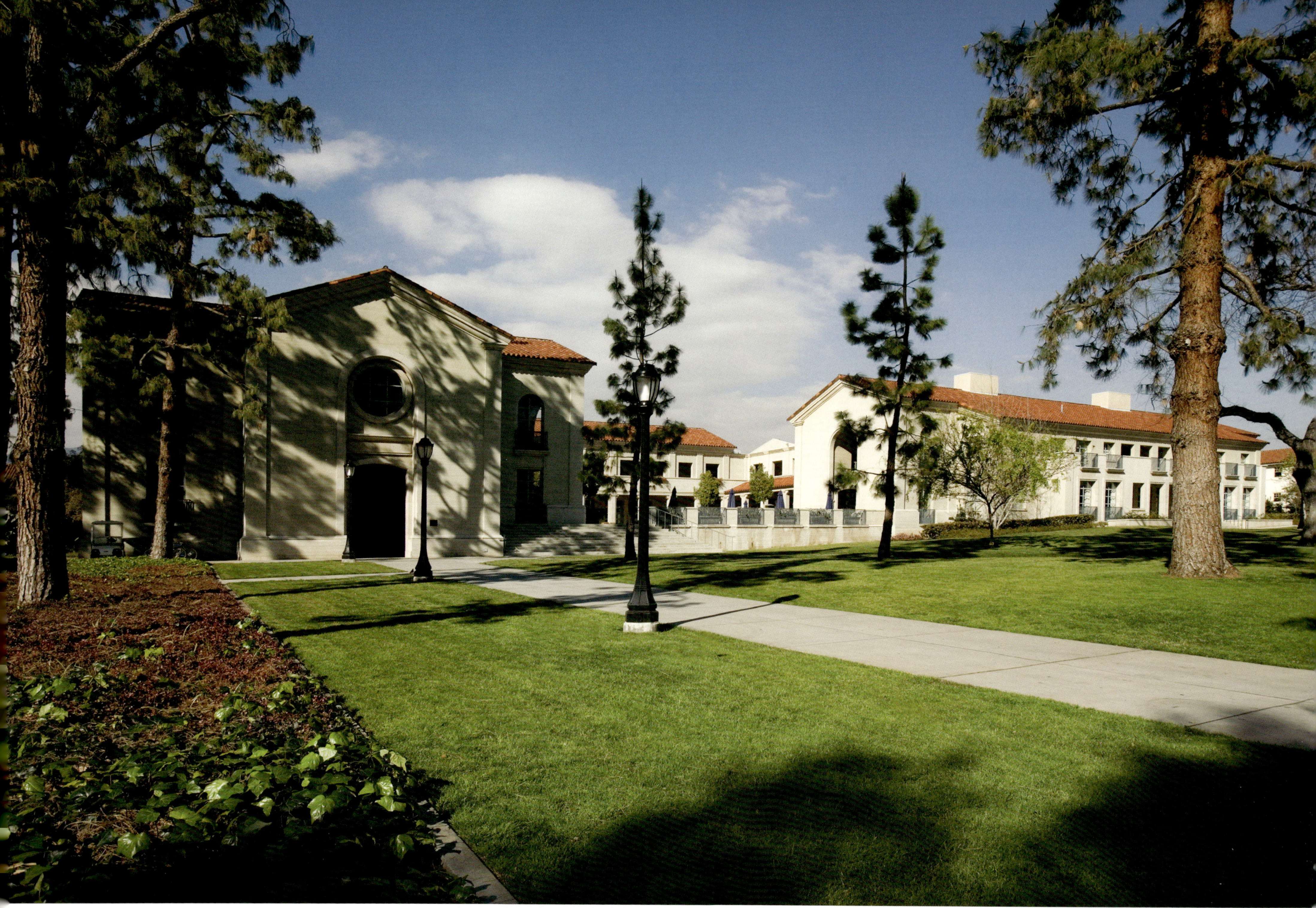

Henry Cabala

H. Russell and Jeanne Smith Campus Center

Two parts Spanish cathedral and one part Greek agora, the new Smith Campus Center is a big and sophisticated work of architecture, a handsome building that seeks to redefine both the campus itself and the routines and rhythms of campus life. Borrowing freely from a range of architectural traditions, the Smith Center is easily Pomona's most important structure of recent years. —Lawrence Biemiller

The groundbreaking ceremony for the H. Russell and Jeanne Smith Campus Center in October 1997 fulfilled a 61-year-old dream and a campaign promise made by H. Russell Smith '36 when he was president of the Associated Students of Pomona College in his senior year. A longtime member of the Board of Trustees, which he chaired from 1969 to 1988, Smith never forgot his pledge. A true "center" for the campus had, indeed, been needed for many years, a fact noted by President Peter Stanley when he took office in 1991. Stanley was concerned about the tendency of students, faculty, and staff to isolate themselves in dormitories and offices, in part, he believed, because the campus lacked a focal point, a hub where they could congregate as part of their daily routines.

The Campus Center commission, which was awarded to prominent architect Robert A.M. Stern Architects of New York, was challenging, to say the least. The new building was to replace the existing Edmunds Union, both physically (except for the original ballroom, which was to be preserved) and in its function as a student center, and, at the same time, to provide something Pomona had never possessed—a hub that would serve as a logistical and symbolic center of the campus. The structure's prominent site east of Alexander Hall facing Marston Quadrangle further intensified the mandate that it be, as well, a distinguished work of architecture in its own right. In an interview with architectural historian Jayne Merkel in 2005, architect Stern noted the dilemmas he and his colleagues (project architects Graham Wyatt, Adam Anuskiewicz, and Diane Scott) had faced:

The building is not a student center. It is a campus center. That is a very important distinction and I want to emphasize that. Students may think it was only for them, but it was always the dream, going back to when Mr. Smith was an undergraduate, to have a campus center that would bring together faculty, administration, staff, alumni, and students. The problem with the brief was that although the location was excellent for a student center, and had been the site of a student center since the 1930s, it was also at the most visible intersection of the campus, where guests to the college were most likely to arrive and get their first impressions. The challenge was to create a place where students could take the last hurrahs of youth, but not out on display for arriving dignitaries.

Stern, who is also dean of the Yale School of Architecture, is noted for his careful attention to historical context, and, true to form, he conducted extensive research on the history of Pomona's campus before committing to a design. In a lecture celebrating the dedication of the building on September 18, 1999, Stern noted that his intent had been to "pick up the lost strands of [Myron] Hunt's plan of north-south

H. Russell and Jeanne Smith Campus Center

Built 1999; dedicated September 18, 1999
President in office Peter W. Stanley
Location 170 East Sixth Street
Architect Robert A.M. Stern Architects, New York
Materials reinforced concrete, tile roof, cast stone ornament
Cost $18.3 million
Donors/Named for H. Russell '36 and Jeanne Smith
Renovated 2006-07

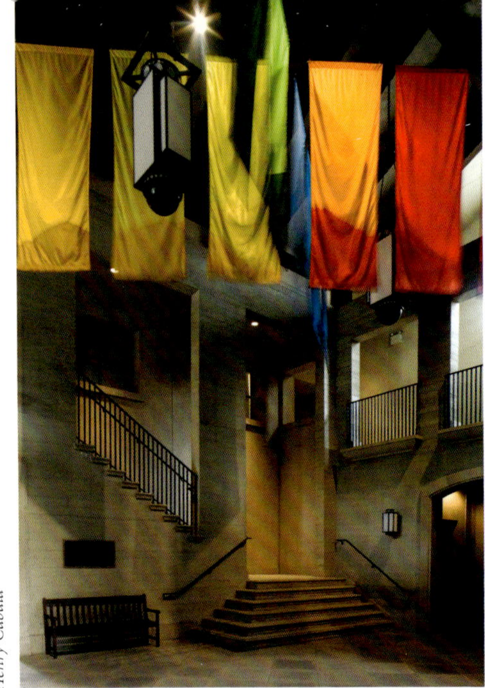
Henry Cabala

Smith Campus Center, forum

buildings and east-west arcades, and to acknowledge both his and Sumner Spaulding's (architect of the Clark campus and Frary Hall) language of pitched tile roofs, open passageways, covered arcades, and courtyards. We wanted to match the weightiness and gravity of Hunt's and Spaulding's buildings, which we believed best expressed the nature of the College and its mission."

The reference of the Campus Center to Myron Hunt's work at Pomona is perhaps most apparent in the way it echoes Bridges Hall of Music across Marston Quadrangle, two arched entries separated by 84 years and rejoined by a newly opened north-south axis crossing east-west Stover Walk. The new building is, in the words of architecture critic Lawrence Biemiller, "a direct response to Hunt's classic Beaux Arts design that aligned the principal buildings along a central axis, Marston Quadrangle." He continues: "The architectural highlight is a Greek-style colonnade of square columns supporting a second story with square windows separated by pilasters and then a perfect cornice beneath a red-tile roof.... But no description can do justice to this composition's perfect proportions, which would be at home on any classical acropolis."[1] The building consists of three two-story pavilions surrounding a large south-facing courtyard. The structure's significant bulk (65,000 square feet of new floor space, in addition to the 9,000-square-foot ballroom renovation) is minimized by its setback from Marston Quadrangle and the fact that it is designed as a series of linked pavilions. The number and variety of facilities accommodated within are indicative of the College's multiple goals for the Campus Center and the challenge it represented: the 200-seat Rose Hills Theatre, mail center, snack bar and restaurant, social and meeting rooms, offices, and, on the east, the preserved Edmunds Ballroom with a new "forum" entry. Although the budget did not allow the building's basement to be completed at the time—it is currently undergoing modifications—Stern declared himself pleased with the building.

> *I'm very happy with the Smith Campus Center, first of all for the way it fits into the campus and carries out the spirit of the original plan, and meets the complex agenda of circulation and symbol at a crucial corner of the campus. It is very effective in that way. I'm also happy with the way the building was realized as a tectonic object, with the level of quality of the exposed board-formed poured-in-place concrete walls, one of my few experiments with that material, which has been the tradition at Pomona from the very beginning. The third thing about the building that I take pleasure in is the way we were able to minimize the amount of space that required heating and cooling, treating many of the passageways as open-air loggias, arcades, and the like, which allowed us to get much more building than one might have imagined for the budget, and a finer building, one that really responds to the local climate, with its tremendous heat in the summer—the arcades stay cool—and the relatively benign winters.*

It is inevitable that buildings serving as many functions as a campus center will be required to evolve over time along with the needs of its users. Since 1999, a number of changes have been made, primarily to make the Center's spaces more inviting to students while retaining its dignity as a central campus meeting place for the entire College community. Colorful banners were hung in the two-story "forum," the Coop Fountain was outfitted with sofas and booths and extended to a patio space on the north, and further renovations of the basement, which had been left unfinished for future expansion, and other floors began in Summer 2006. ■

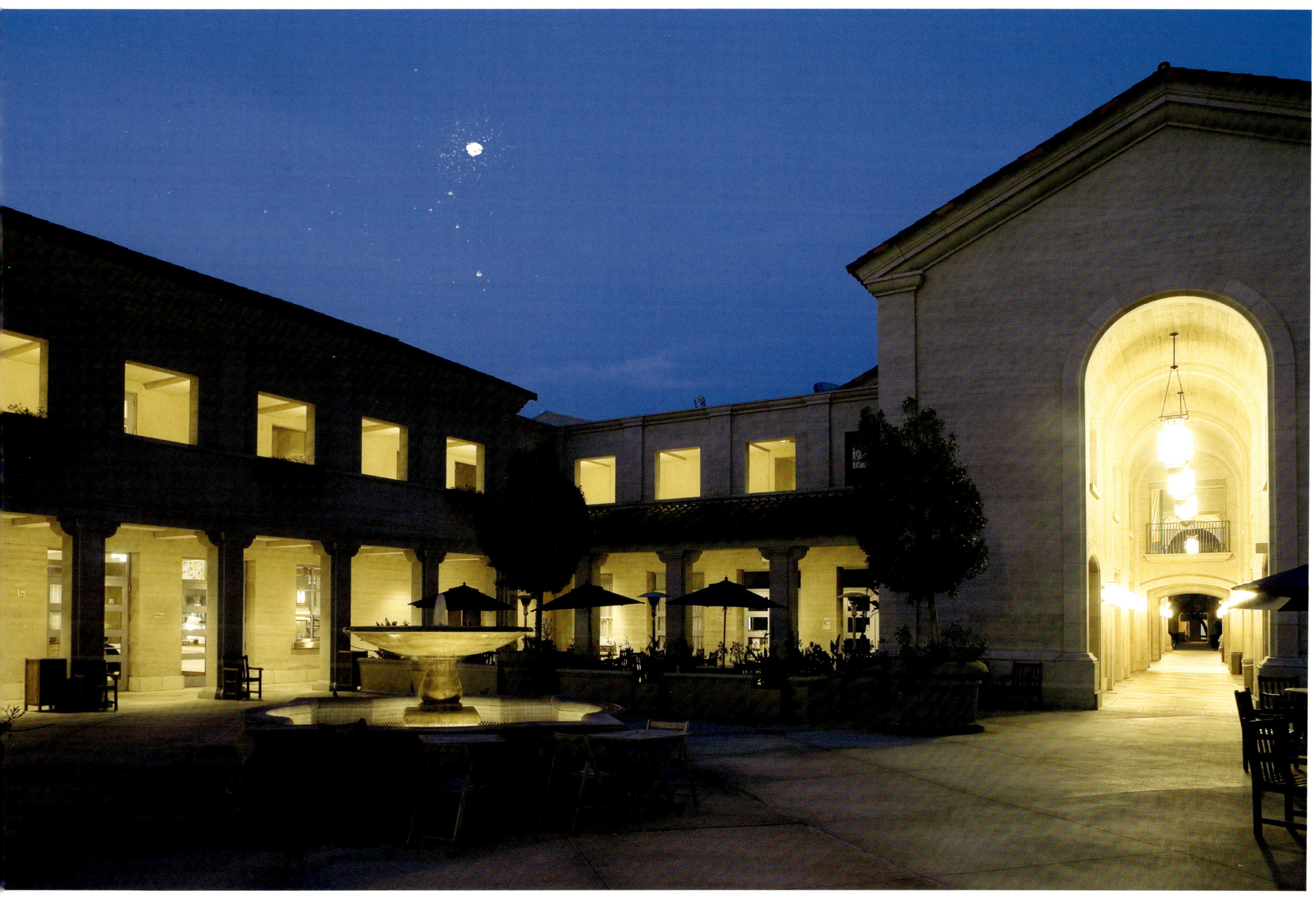

Henry Cabala

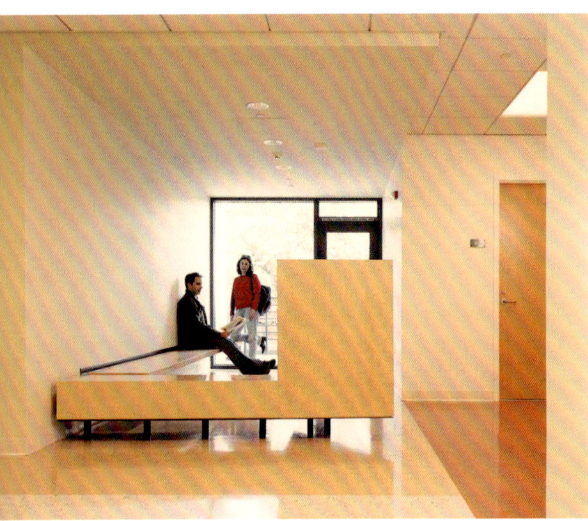

Gene Sasse

Andrew Science Building for Mathematics, Physics and Computer Science

Pomona College has always been of great importance to us since we met here, were married here, and found the shape of the rest of our lives through the liberal arts education received here. We feel our support of this building...is our way of giving back a little for all that we have received.
—EDITH ANDREW '57 AT THE DEDICATION OF THE ANDREW BUILDING, FEBRUARY 19, 2000

Andrew Science Building for Mathematics, Physics and Computer Science

BUILT 2000; dedicated February 19, 2000
PRESIDENT IN OFFICE Peter W. Stanley
LOCATION 165 East Sixth Street
PURPOSE Mathematics, Physics and Computer Science
ARCHITECT SMP/SHG (SmithGroup, Inc), Santa Monica
MATERIALS reinforced concrete, tile roof
COST $4,800,000
DONORS/NAMED FOR Edward '56 and Edith '57 (trustee 2001–) Andrew ($1,100,000 challenge grant for construction); Mr. and Mrs. Y.M. Posthuma ($150,000 to name student faculty research laboratory); Ralph M. Parsons Foundation ($500,000 for laboratory space); and other donors

In a brochure celebrating its opening, the new Andrew Science Building for Mathematics, Physics and Computer Science was referred to as "more than a building—it puts innovative teaching into concrete form." The teaching of science had, in fact, changed dramatically since the completion of the Seaver Science Center in the early 1960s, particularly in terms of an emphasis on interactive learning environments and extensive use of ever-more-sophisticated technology. Curricular developments, in combination with substantial increases in the number of science majors during the 1990s, made it imperative that Pomona's facilities be upgraded. Accordingly, The Campaign for Pomona College, launched in 1997, identified "sustaining leadership in science" as one of its principal objectives.

The five-phase science master plan, with a goal of $35,000,000, called for a complex of state-of-the-art classrooms and laboratories to support current teaching and research methods and also provide flexibility for future changes in pedagogy and research. The opening of the Andrew Building marked the completion of phase one, providing a home for computer science; high technology mathematics classrooms; an astronomy classroom with an array of projection and computer technology including connection to the Jet Propulsion Laboratory and Pomona's telescopes in Brackett Observatory and on Table Mountain; an introductory physics classroom and laboratory; and modern physics research labs.

The relationship between facilities and curriculum is always to some degree symbiotic, and, as the Andrew Building took form, science curricula were revised and updated. The focus of both was on interactivity—enabling close faculty-student research to which students would be introduced from the beginning of their studies. To accomplish this, for example, the new physics laboratory was strategically placed adjacent to the introductory physics classroom, allowing large- and small-scale student projects and experiments to be undertaken during class periods and facilitating participatory learning and problem-solving. The presence of laptop computers throughout the laboratory helps students visualize concepts and test hypotheses.

The Andrew Building, adjoining Millikan Laboratory on the east, defined a new science courtyard and, at the same time, a new image for the sciences at Pomona; the structure won a design award from the City of Claremont. As it opened in January 2000, phase two of the master plan—the renovation of Seaver North—had just begun. Again, the need was to replace aging systems and install high-tech computer capabilities, with a goal of keeping Pomona's science programs competitive. ■

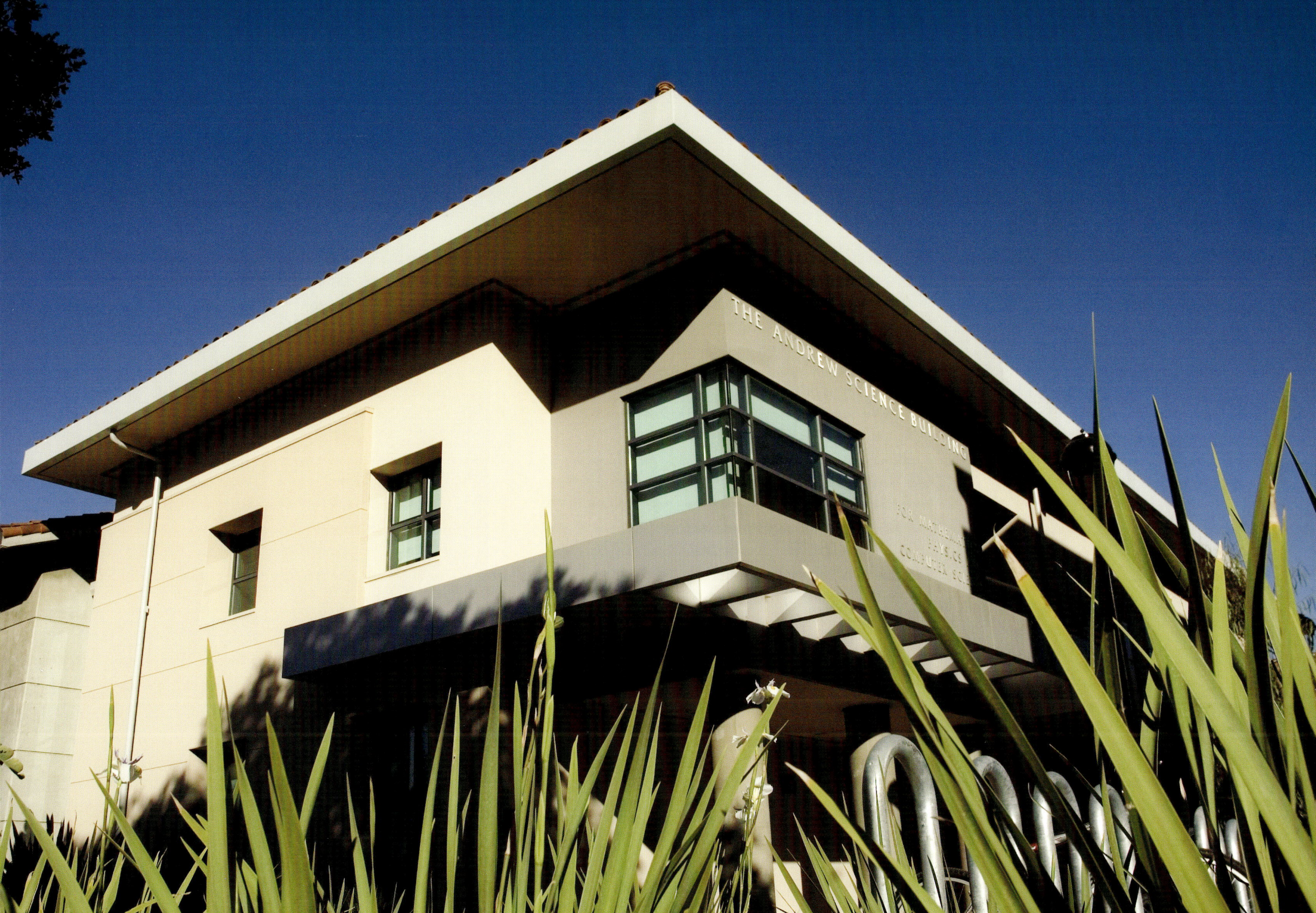

Mark Wood

Richard C. Seaver Biology Building

BUILT 2003–04 (ground-breaking ceremony September 2, 2003; opened spring 2004; dedicated February 26, 2005)
PRESIDENTS IN OFFICE Peter W. Stanley; David W. Oxtoby
LOCATION 175 West Sixth Street (northeast corner Sixth Street and Harvard Avenue)
ARCHITECT Bauer and Wiley, Architects
MATERIALS reinforced concrete, tile roof
COST $23,500,000
DONOR Estate of Frank R. Seaver '05 as distributed by the Seaver Institute
NAMED FOR Trustee Emeritus Richard C. Seaver '43, 1970–

Richard C. Seaver Biology Building

Like the Andrew Science Building, the Richard C. Seaver Biology Building, which replaced the Thille Botany Building, was the product of dramatic changes in the teaching of science and the resulting need for facilities that would serve an evolving curriculum. According to Professor David Becker, who was heavily involved in planning the new building: "Even 20 years ago, biology was largely a descriptive body of knowledge that students had to memorize. Today, students learn through experiments how something works or came to be. Courses emphasize student application of scientific inquiry, reading what's known, designing a hypothesis, doing experiments, and analyzing their own data. This all starts in the freshman year. In the 1950s, molecular biology didn't even exist."

Along with spaces designed for student-faculty collaboration, an important goal of Pomona's new, 46,270-square-foot biology building was to provide state-of-the-art research and teaching labs for genetics, cell biology, neurobiology, plant and animal physiology, and ecology. Another was to entice non-science students, and to this end, the architects designed inviting entrances and laboratories visually accessible to passers-by. If the response of Professor of English Arden Reed is indicative, this strategy is successful. Asked about the newly completed building, he replied "It makes me want to be a biologist." Anchoring the campus on its western edge, Seaver Biology will, it is hoped, infuse the campus with a sense of excitement about science. Landscaping along Sixth Street and Harvard Avenue was reconfigured to improve day-lighting and to create outdoor spaces that encourage "chance encounter and contemplation."

Appropriate to its focus, Seaver Biology is a "green building," meaning that it is both energy efficient and "friendly" to the environment. To make the building green was not inexpensive—an additional $1,260,000 was required—but well worth the investment. In 2002, the College's trustees had adopted a Statement of Environment Policy, which was reflected in the new building. As President Peter Stanley commented:

> *One of the greatest challenges of our time is to learn how to live responsibly and prudently in a finite world without diminishing the quality of our lives or constraining the scope of our aspirations. For colleges, science buildings are the ultimate test, because of their concentration of high-tech equipment, they can be terrible energy hogs. So we set out to make the new life sciences building and, eventually, the renovated Seaver South examples of how first-rate science could be done in an energy-conscious, environmentally friendly manner.... Everything that has been added to this building to promote sustainability has been proven to work. In many cases, special features are notably cost-effective over time, even in the narrowest economic terms. So extra up-front costs are also prudent investment.*

The Richard C. Seaver Biology Building is one of the only academic buildings in the state, and the first in Claremont, to be built to LEED (Leadership in Energy and Environmental Design) Green Building standards. Among the numerous features contributing to LEED status are large windows that maximize natural light; light shelves that bounce sunlight onto ceilings, which in turn direct light onto work areas; high-efficiency indoor lighting controlled by sensors; photovoltaic panels for solar energy; certified renewable wood and recycled, low-emitting construction materials; and a thermal energy storage system designed to reduce energy use during periods of peak demand.

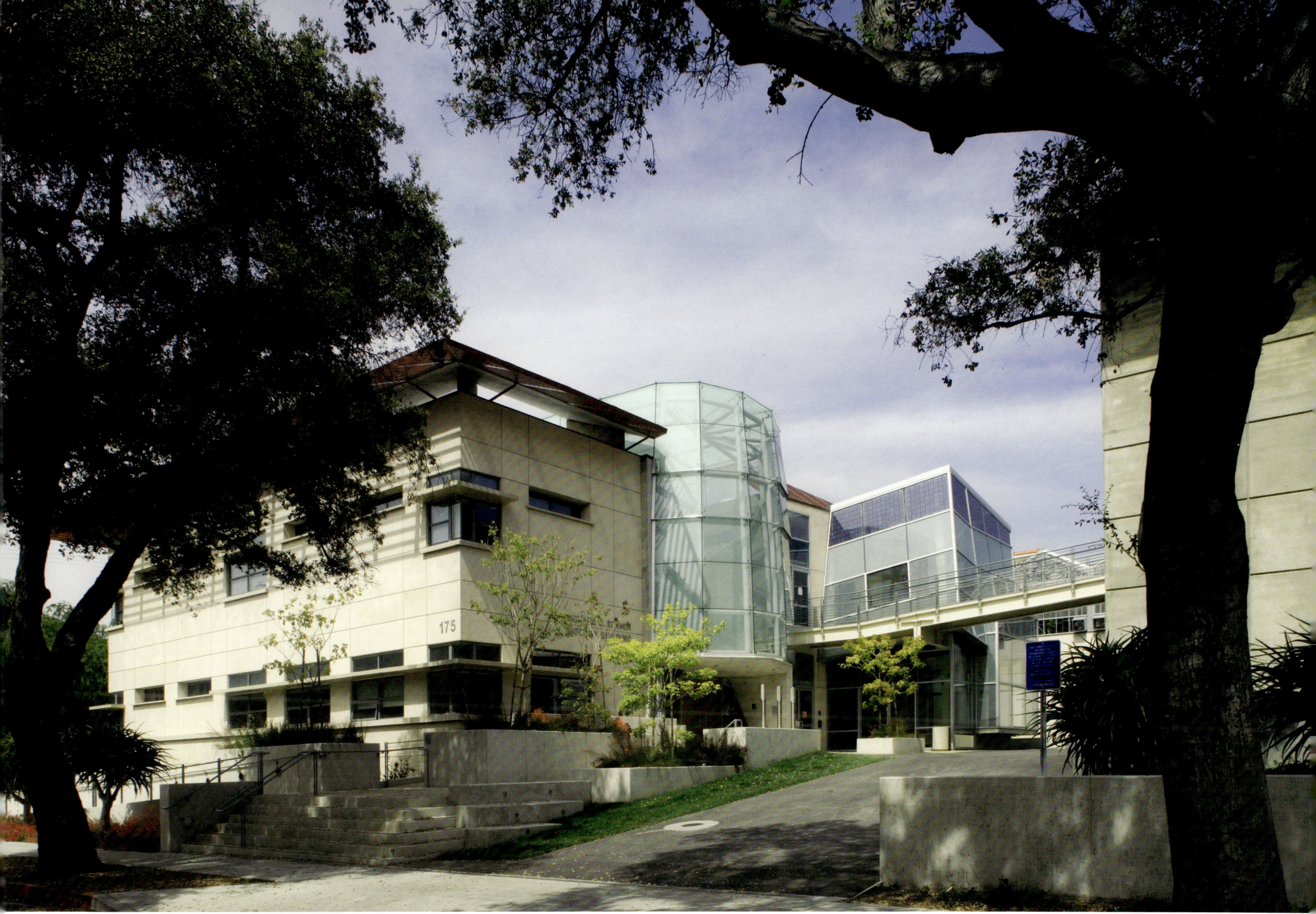

Henry Cabala

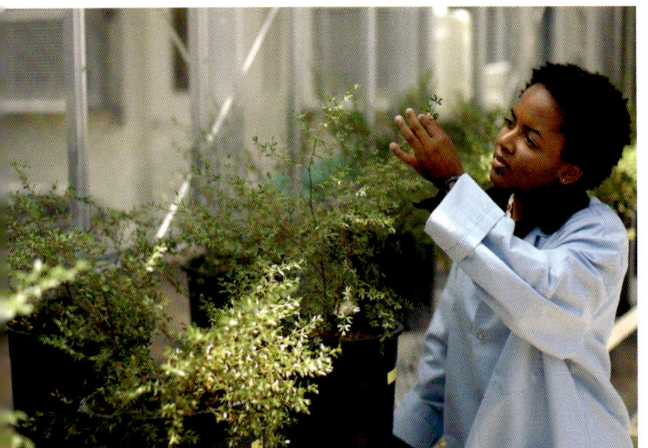

Carlos Puma

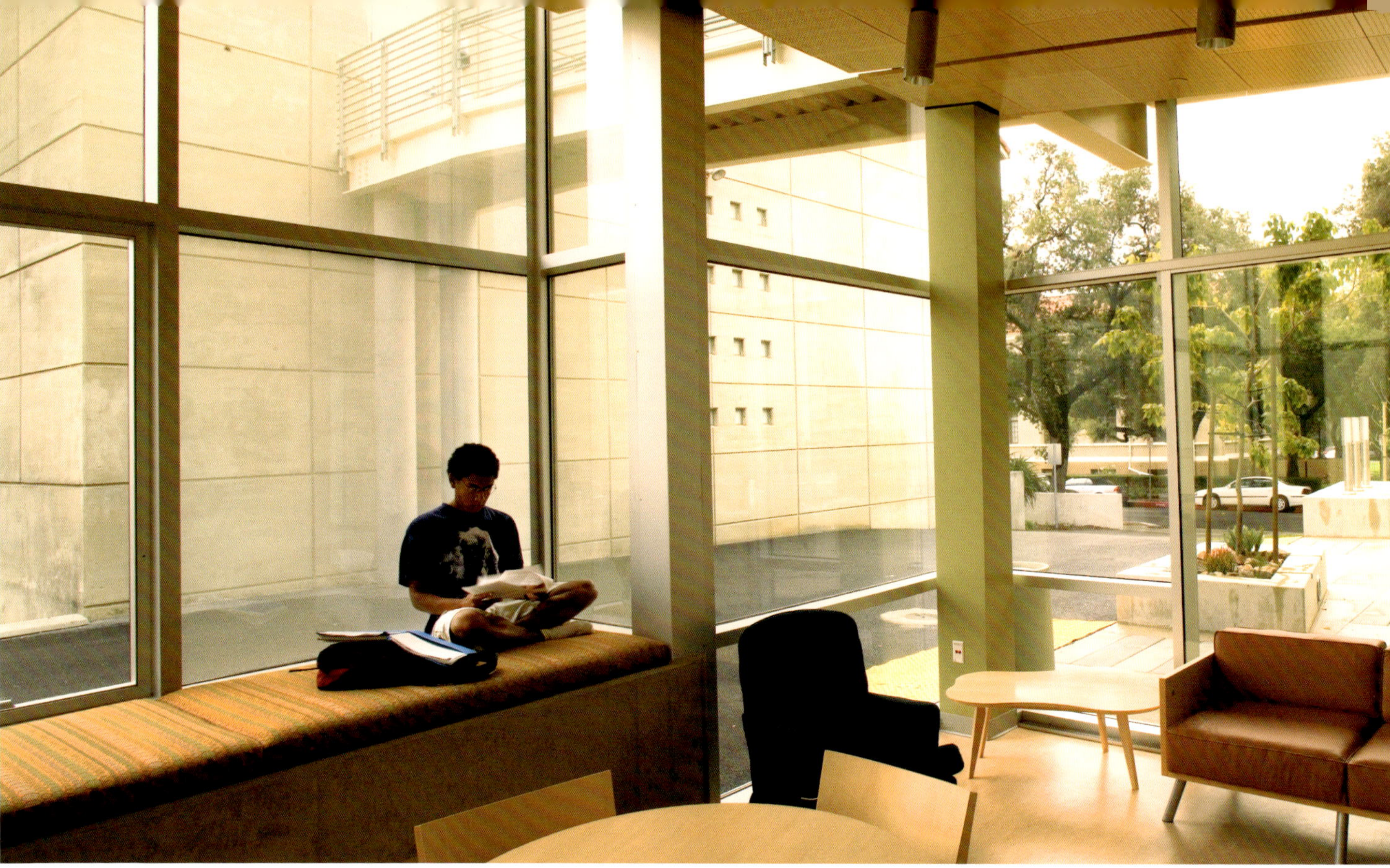

Phil Channing

ABOVE LEFT *Seaver Biology Building, greenhouse*

ABOVE RIGHT *Seaver Biology Building, lounge*

Interestingly, some of the building's innovations derive, in fact, from old ideas. These include cooling the building by blowing fans over stored ice (because it takes less cold air to cool the structure, ducts and fans can be smaller); the use of solar panels to generate electricity during daylight hours; the reduction of water consumption by means of low-flow, motion-activated faucets and toilets; and porous blocks in the parking area to allow rain to soak through to the soil rather than run off.

The resulting building exceeds California energy-saving design codes by 10 percent, saving an estimated $75,000 per year. The effort to attain silver certification by the United States Green Building Council places the Seaver building in the top five percent of all academic laboratory buildings in the country in terms of energy-conscious design. This seems appropriate given that Pomona sends a higher percentage of its science graduates to Ph.D. study than almost any other American college or university; at the time of the building's dedication, 56 undergraduate students were working with biology faculty on research projects.

As President David Oxtoby, himself a chemist, remarks:

> *The exciting part of science happens in the lab, and the new, larger research labs will allow even more students to collaborate with faculty and conduct hands-on research. That we were able to make the investment in an environmentally sound biology building is a testament to the vision and commitment of our Board and to the Seaver family, which has supported science education at Pomona for more than 50 years.* ■

J.C. Cowart Information Technology Building

Construction of a new multi-use structure began in 2004. The facility provides 130 subterranean parking spaces for Pomona College faculty, staff, and visitors. The Office of Information Technology Services (ITS) occupies a 12,000-square-foot office component. ■

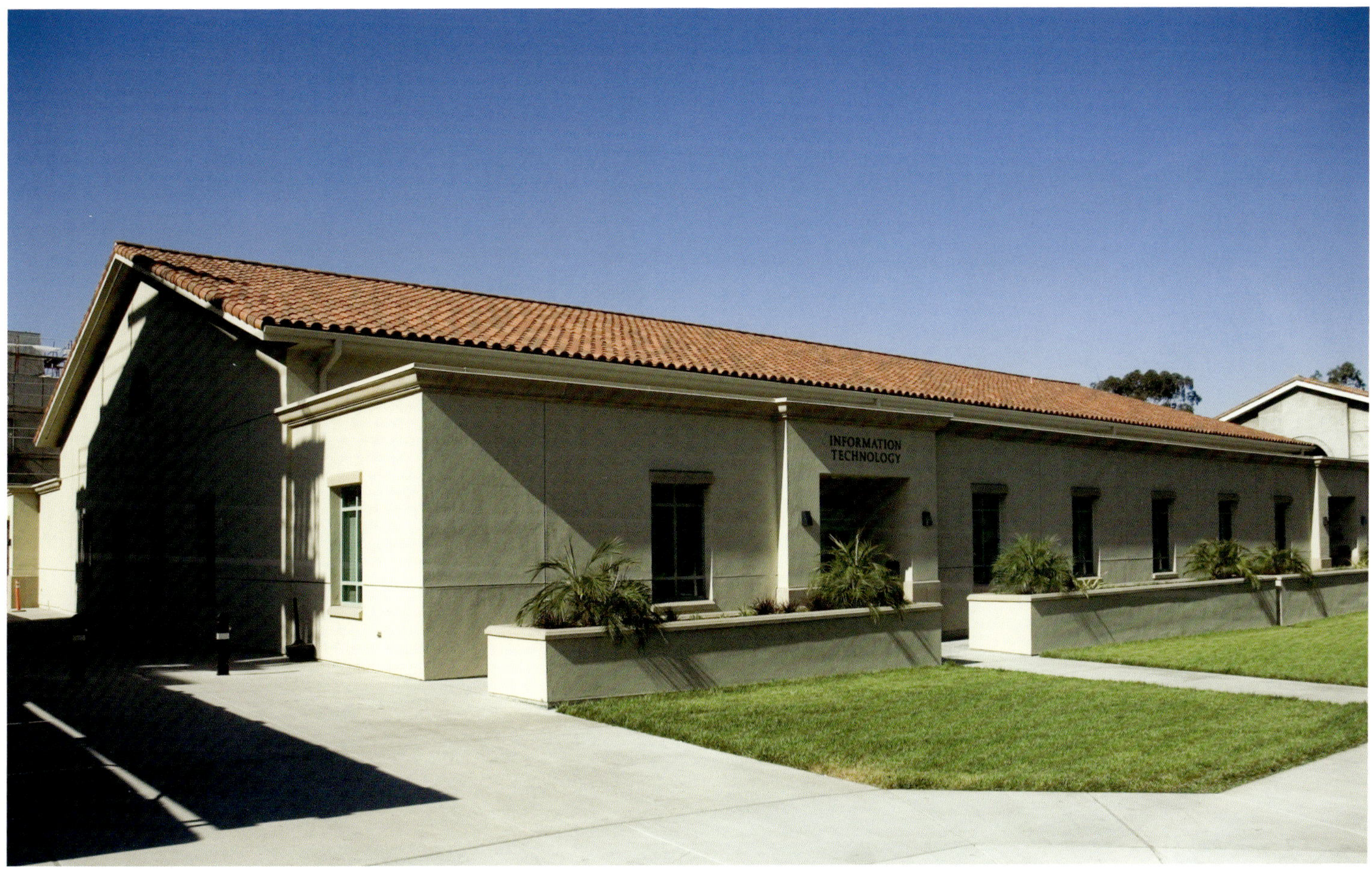

Mark Wood

J.C. Cowart Information Technology Building

BUILT 2005
PRESIDENT IN OFFICE David W. Oxtoby
LOCATION 156 East Seventh Street (on the site previously occupied by the residence of the Dean of Students)
ARCHITECT International Parking Design
COST $6.3 million
DONOR/NAMED FOR J.C. Cowart ($2.5 million)

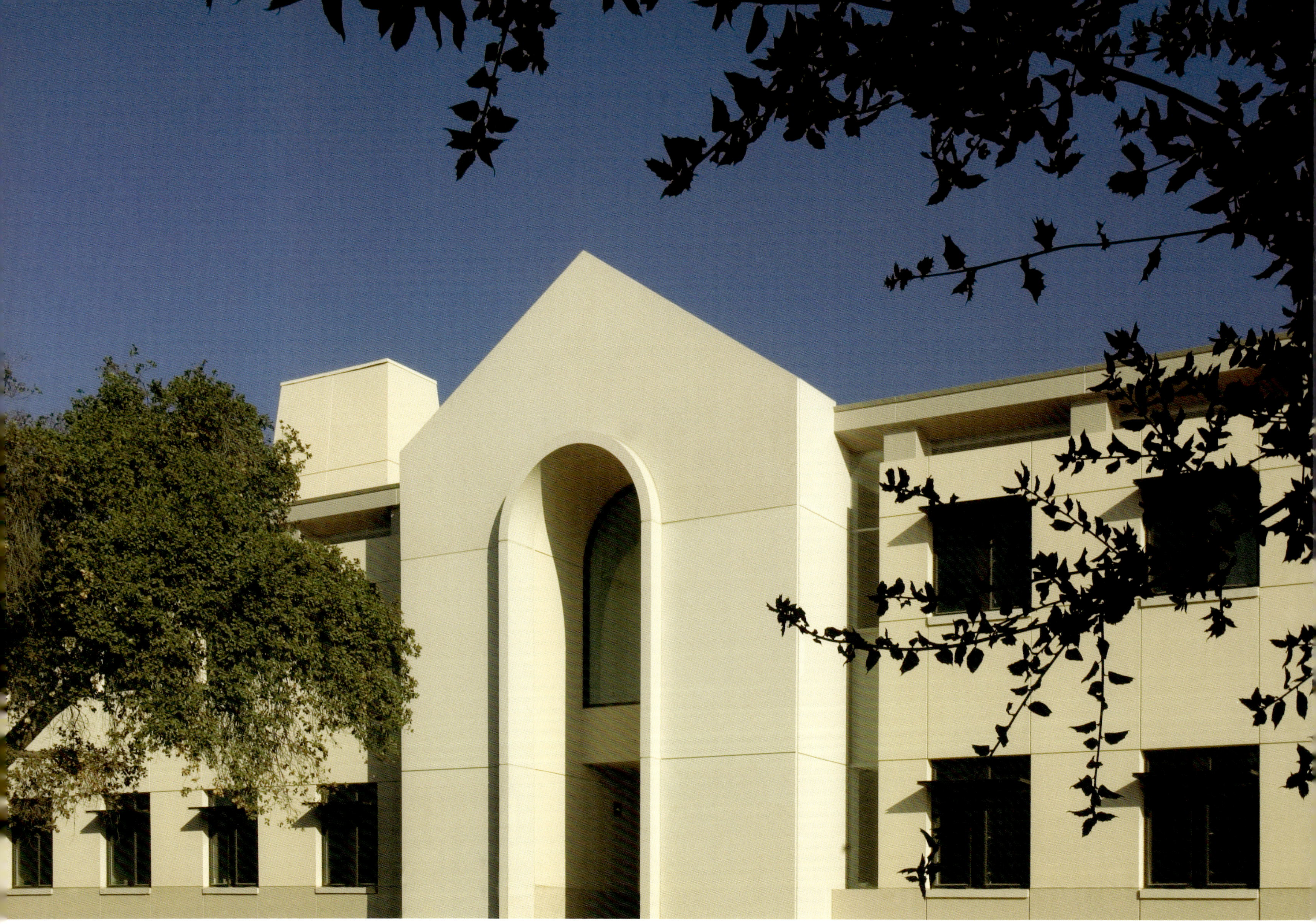

Lincoln Building (Psychology, Neuroscience; Intercollegiate departments of Asian-American, Black, Chicano/a Studies)

Edmunds Building (Computer Science, Environmental Analysis, Geology, Linguistics/Cognitive Science)

Construction of the Lincoln and Edmunds buildings, at the intersection of Sixth Street and College Way, began in May 2005. The new buildings, made possible by a lead gift of $10 million by alumna Lillian Lincoln Howell '43, have a combined 93,000 gross square feet of academic space. Occupants of the complex include Psychology/Neuroscience, Linguistics and Cognitive Science, the Intercollegiate Departments of Chicano/a Studies, Asian-American Studies, and Black Studies, Geology, Environmental Analysis, and Computer Science. The new structures incorporate a host of sustainable design features intended to produce significant annual reductions in the amount of electricity and water consumed and to result in a LEED Silver certification.

Planned for the central courtyard—envisaged as an informal classroom, site for receptions, and area for repose and contemplation—is a site-specific installation by noted artist James Turrell '65. Titled *Pomona Skyspace*, the work reflects Turrell's preoccupation with space, light, and the awareness of perceptual boundaries: "It is about how you confront space," he says. "It is about seeing that you are seeing." What better celebration of the place that is Pomona College? ■

Lincoln Building
Edmunds Building

BUILT 2006-07, dedicated March 2007
PRESIDENT IN OFFICE David W. Oxtoby
LOCATION Sixth Street and College Way
ARCHITECTS DMJM Architects, Los Angeles
PROJECTED COST $40 million
DONORS Lillian Lincoln Howell '43 (gift of $10 million); Ranney E. Draper '60; Stewart R. Smith '68; Fletcher Jones Foundation; Kenneth T. and Eileen L. Norris Foundation; Ralph M. Parsons Foundation
NAMED FOR John C. Lincoln and Lincoln C. Howell (Mrs. Howell's father and son); President Charles K. Edmunds (1928–41)

James Turrell

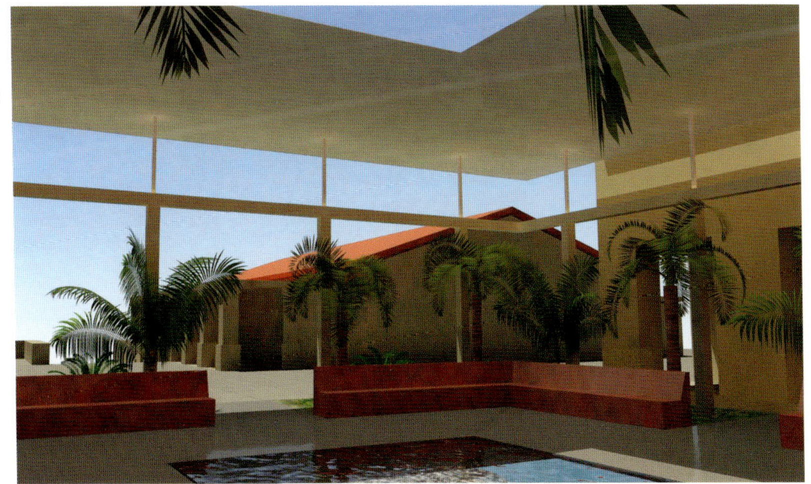

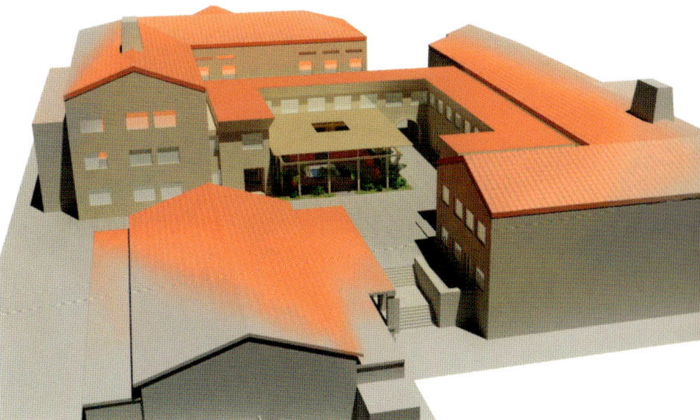

James Turrell

RIGHT *James Turrell '65, proposal for* Pomona Skyspace, *2007, and Lincoln and Edmunds buildings models*

OPPOSITE *Edmunds Building*

Mark Wood

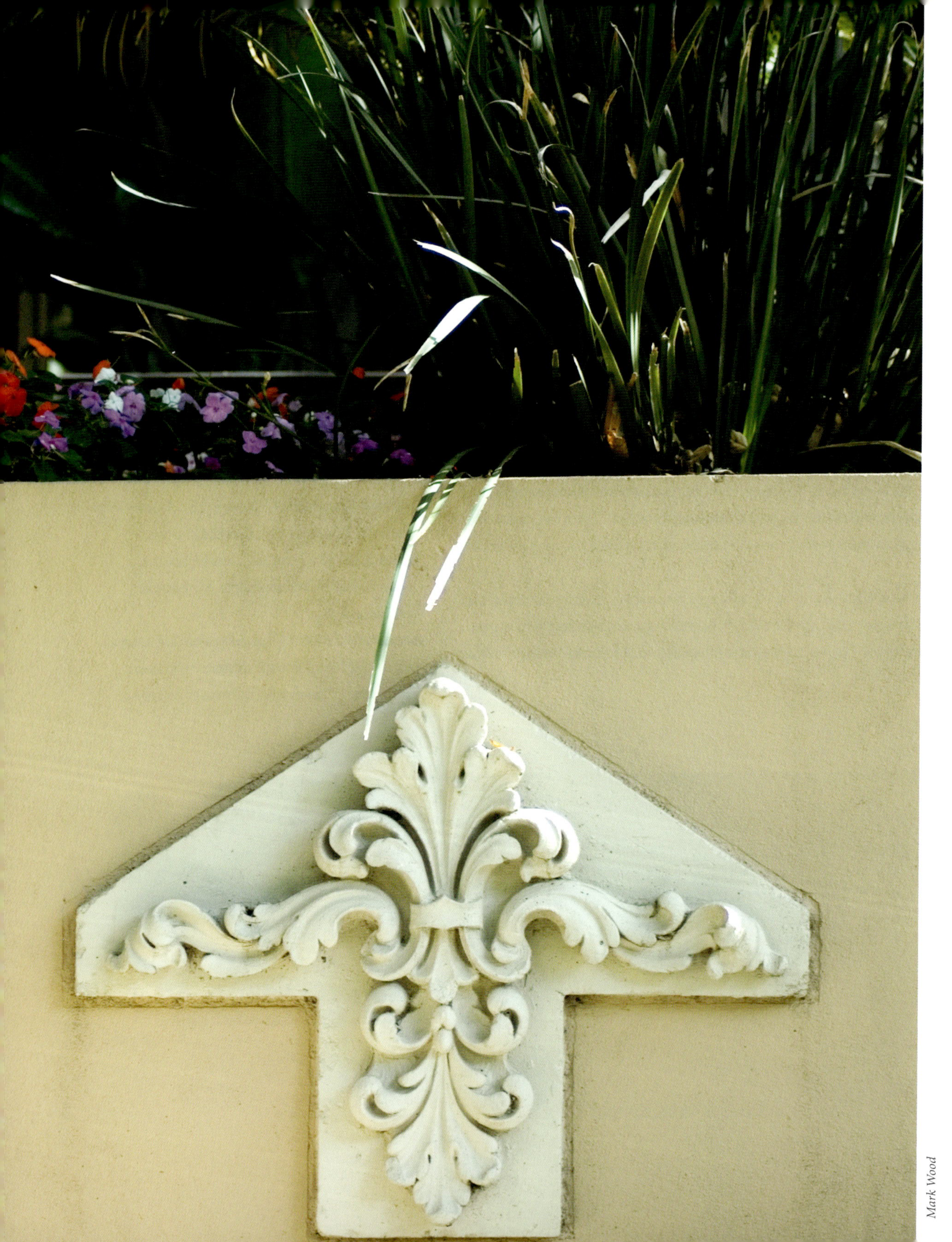

Mark Wood

POSTSCRIPT

Architectural ornament from Holmes Hall, preserved in a courtyard outside Alexander Hall

Dusty Sage to Urban Oasis: Reflections on a Place

When I call to mind a sense of the place that is the Pomona College campus, I conjure up an image that may be mythical. I recall the specter of two professors, in the 1890s, toiling down College Avenue in a horse-drawn cart. In the back of their wagon are small saplings of eucalyptus that they are planting on either side of a dusty track on the edge of the American desert. In anchoring these young trees they took the long view, creating a "past for the future," a link to our time, a handsome avenue that engages, and indeed frames our memories of Claremont.

For these now ancient trees help us form our associations with the place, this extraordinary oasis in what was then wilderness. It was not a "city on a hill" in the Bostonian sense, but a college with Puritan ties set on an alluvial plain of sagebrush, oak, chaparral and scattered arroyo stones. Now many of those trees on College Avenue are massive and the mud track that initially covered the saplings in dust is today a grand avenue with arroyo stones split to form the distinctive old curbing. Many of the trees have survived, sentinels along the corridor of memory. They are, in fact, both guideposts and props, framing memories like photographs and also furnishing these images with an evolving sense of scale as the vegetation and architecture have changed. Did you know that there was once an oak in the middle of College Avenue near the College Gate? Did you know there was once a charming Arts and Crafts inn with porches looking out toward these trees on the Avenue where the Claremont community met?

I can remember the quadrangle behind Pearsons and Crookshank when it was a dusty track and the space across College Way from Walker and Clark dormitories when it was a weed-filled lot. The campus grows greener in each successive generation. The massive plantings of "mock orange" (*Pittosporum Tibira*) along College Avenue, powerful in their geometry, reinforce the tree corridor with great elongated rectangles of shining foliage. The vast sweep of lawn on Marston Quadrangle, with its scalloped edging of sycamores, and the more recent delight of its iris shoals, define a place of contemplative beauty, shaping another passage of memories of student courtships in sycamore shadows on soft Southland nights.

But, perhaps in the way a small bamboo cage containing a chirping cricket can remind a Japanese family in a crowded apartment of the forest that used to edge the city, the luxuriant parkland on the Pomona campus can serve to anesthetize us to the larger loss of Eden, the environmental destruction of so much of the splendor of Southern California that surrounds us. It was the promise of that Eden that brought so many of the early settlers from New England to this Southland region, now decimated by shopping malls, roads and housing tracts. They were spurred on by the siren calls of Charles Fletcher Lummis in

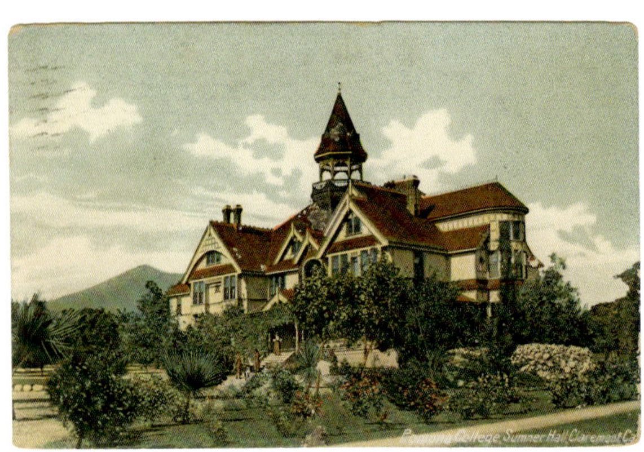

Sumner Hall, ca. 1894, postcard

his *Land of Sunshine* magazine, and the pictures of the citrus groves on the labels of fruit crates that the early agronomists shipped "back east," as my mother, a native Angeleno born in 1911, would say.

Those lemon groves that surrounded the College shape the memories of my own family. My mother and father both took the train in the 1920s from Los Angeles to Claremont through the acres of citrus that defined the garden cities of the San Gabriel and Pomona valleys. Later our family took the automobile in the 1950s when I went to the campus to watch Saturday Sagehen football games with my father. He was a star athlete in high school, who was so injured in the freshman-sophomore pole rush, an archaic and now forgotten campus initiation ritual, that he could not play football in his freshman year. Later, he was so strapped in the next Depression year that he worked in those groves instead of playing on the Pomona fields.

I remember watching those orange trees dart in and out of our windshield as the moving car sped through the diminishing farmscape before the I-10 was built—that concrete juggernaut that forever changed this landscape. The upright Victorian farmhouses, wrapped in their gingerbread-festooned porches, sitting so primly in their groves, abandoned, like ravished matriarchs pushed aside by a mass of low-slung plaster ranchettes that followed the freeway.

And then a third generation came to Pomona, my daughter, passionate organic farmer and environmental policy advocate, who took Amtrak and then the Metrolink, on some of the old Pacific Electric tracks, to Claremont in the year 2000. First journeying across the country from her boarding school in green New Hampshire to the vast smoggy morass of the Los Angeles basin, she then traveled from Union Station to Claremont, thanks now to restored service and a renovation of the handsome station to greet her, in itself a long preservation battle. No doubt she was the first of her class to use that commuter train. Even though the groves are gone and the transit users are commuters, she was an eager advocate for a future America with limits to sprawl and respect for mass transit.

But, when I was a student here in the early sixties, one could still smell the perfume of the orange and lemon groves. There were still grandmothers of students who lived in Arts and Crafts bungalows embedded in those groves who would invite one for tea in the afternoon or something stronger in the gathering twilight and reminisce about the days when they took the stagecoach to Yosemite, as mine did.

There was a greenbelt between Foothill Boulevard (the historic Route 66) and the foothills of Mount Baldy in those days. When my father was here in the Depression years he could work "smudging" the pots to keep those trees warm on cold frosty mornings. Those groves plaited with eucalyptus and palm-lined roads formed a rich agricultural tapestry that defined the very word "Pomona" for they gave the word its context (though I suspect that most of the members of my class, if polled in 1963, would not have known Pomona was the Roman goddess of the orchard, despite their exposure to Professor Harry Carroll's classical history course in our freshman year). They thought Pomona was merely the place name of the adjacent town—even then dying as malls evicted the citrus groves and farmland beyond it and shuttered part of the main street—which then tried to reinvent itself as a mall. Now, thankfully, people are living again on Pomona's main street as they did a century ago.

The "Smudge Pot" coffee house and night club was our reminder of those early years and vitalized the basement of the old Coop, a student project in my senior year, 1963. The Smudge included students from Claremont Men's College and Scripps as well in a joint endeavor that involved fashioning walls with egg crates, spotting the three rooms we created out of a dusty and cavernous basement with actual smudge pots, the oil burning stoves that warmed the trees. We recovered these from a warehouse in Pomona, painted them a glossy black, surrounded them with islands of large smooth Mexican beach pebbles discovered during an Easter break on the Ensenada shoreline, and lit them with red lightbulbs that sent shafts of an eerie roseate glow up their stacks. They provided an instant atmosphere for the folk and jazz singers and musicians who played at the club for some 20 years.

One hopes now that the expanded basement space in the Smith Campus Center will re-awaken this function and perhaps recover the name as well. This must be an increasingly quaint "place maker" as tighter air pollution laws made the pots extinct, and many of the groves that supported them were bulldozed for homes north of Foothill Boulevard.

Indeed, there has been so much change in the larger landscape beyond the Pomona campus that it is harder for today's students to find themselves in space and time beyond those elongated eucalyptus columns. Now there is a national student body, some 60 percent coming from outside California and the links to the gentry of the Southland recede before the meritocracy of a nationally recognized school. How will they know that, in the sprawl of shopping centers and suburban ranchettes there are, buried still, early adobe ranchos like Palomares, arts and crafts buildings like the Pitzer House and scattered farm structures crafted from the native boulders? Even Mount Baldy is less of a presence unless one arrives in the brilliant sunshine after a rain-washed February week to see a snowy outline in the distance. Do we even remember it was a student ritual to climb it in the 1920s?

So the bronze map in the foyer of the Smith Campus Center was designed to serve as an anchor, holding the images of that larger framing landscape, renewing and informing administrators who come from afar and students who may know little about Southern California when they arrive beyond the perception that it is a warm and friendly place, a young puppy of a region. Ah, the conceit of that title, "Inland Empire." Never heard that growing up. Harrumph. The bronze relief depicts a cultural landscape before "empire." Are we less provincial now?

Certainly, the creation of the Smith Campus Center has recovered some of the sophisticated design vocabulary and design relationships of the College plan and given it a renewed coherency. The circulation system that landscape architect Ralph Cornell '14 brilliantly conceived is recovered in its connecting pattern of walkways linking the buildings that run parallel to the Quad. The massing of simplified forms and modified Spanish Colonial style of the Smith Center calls to mind the quality of the better buildings on campus—Little Bridges, Frary Hall, the Clark dormitories—compatible yet distinctive. Out of that commitment to create a new Campus Center, which replaced the brutalist annex to Edmunds Union of the 1970s, one hopes will come a stronger community feeling reinforced by this firmer physical sense of place.

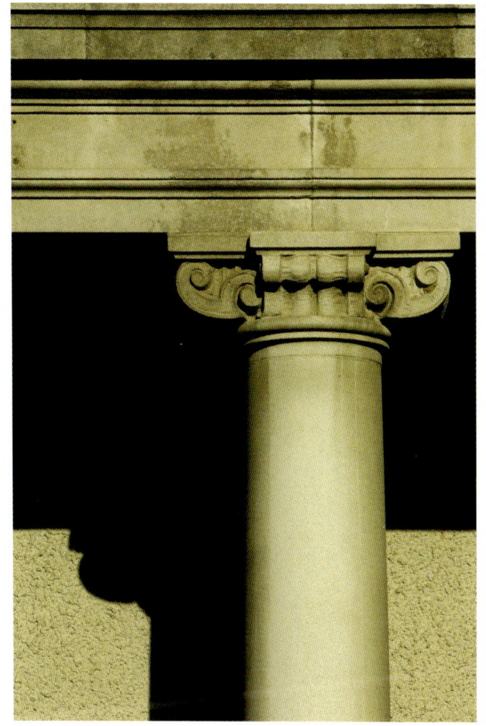
Mark Wood

Bridges Hall of Music, Lebus Court

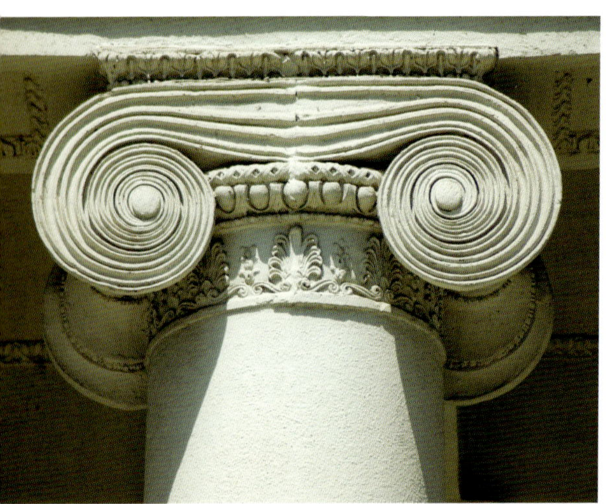

Mark Wood

Carnegie Building

I am glad they kept the old ballroom and hope there will be more dances, but then I believe in a certain social structure that gracious architecture can sometimes nurture. Indeed, why not have one dorm where the gracious living of my student days—with afternoon tea, silver, flowers, and paintings on the walls—is offered as an option, a real example of diversity, instead of allowing the forlorn dorm parlors to become annexes to student bedrooms?

Indeed, is it too much to hope that acknowledging the unity of architectural style might be of even greater value at a time of increased cultural diversity on the American campus? Unity of design in one place offers an alternative to the hodgepodge of styles that has configured so many American campuses in the past decades as each architect has sought to create building identity from a tabula rasa rather than acknowledge the value of context and the civility of compatible styles in conversation with one another.

As to that larger and ever more diverse world beyond the campus, we can be grateful that President David Oxtoby has brought a programmed response to the need for awareness beyond the gates, providing a way for students to visit the cultural institutions of the larger landscape in a Pomona van and encouraging students to visit 47 destinations in the Southland before they graduate. Those destinations, one hopes, will form deeper associations and give students some larger, rooted connection to this complicated place, this lost Eden of Southern California so full of museums, cultural centers, musical offerings and outstanding gardens.

Most of my generation of students never wandered beyond their pasture of required courses to experience the metropolitan reality that grows more exciting each year. Indeed, it was a struggle to bring reality in; when I presented a docket of speakers to come to the College in 1962, I had to evoke the canon of free speech to obtain approval from a faculty committee that only wanted other academics to visit, not communists, John Birchers, Black Muslims and former drug addicts, whom I sought and eventually succeeded in bringing to campus.

How can Pomona grow deeper than the roots of its eucalyptus-lined avenue? And how can it nurture its collective memory and use the recall of place associations as it continues creating new building fabric and nourishing community life? This is the challenge now, and it will take attentiveness to the processes of architectural planning and community-building. Small, crafted elements like gates, benches and lighting can help accomplish this by recovering the narrative traditions of earlier wall paintings, and new buildings can support the work of artists and craftsmen. The organic farm in the Wash that has involved so many students from all of the colleges in the past four years may point the way to a bringing together of building and planting that creates a sense of community, engaging local residents and school children as well. It is the larger strategy of place-making that Pomona now needs to reinforce as it recovers its connections to its own estimable past and increases its commitment to the region beyond the oasis of Claremont, where the word "Eden" still beautifully applies and the eucalyptus continue to frame the view. ■ —Ronald Lee Fleming

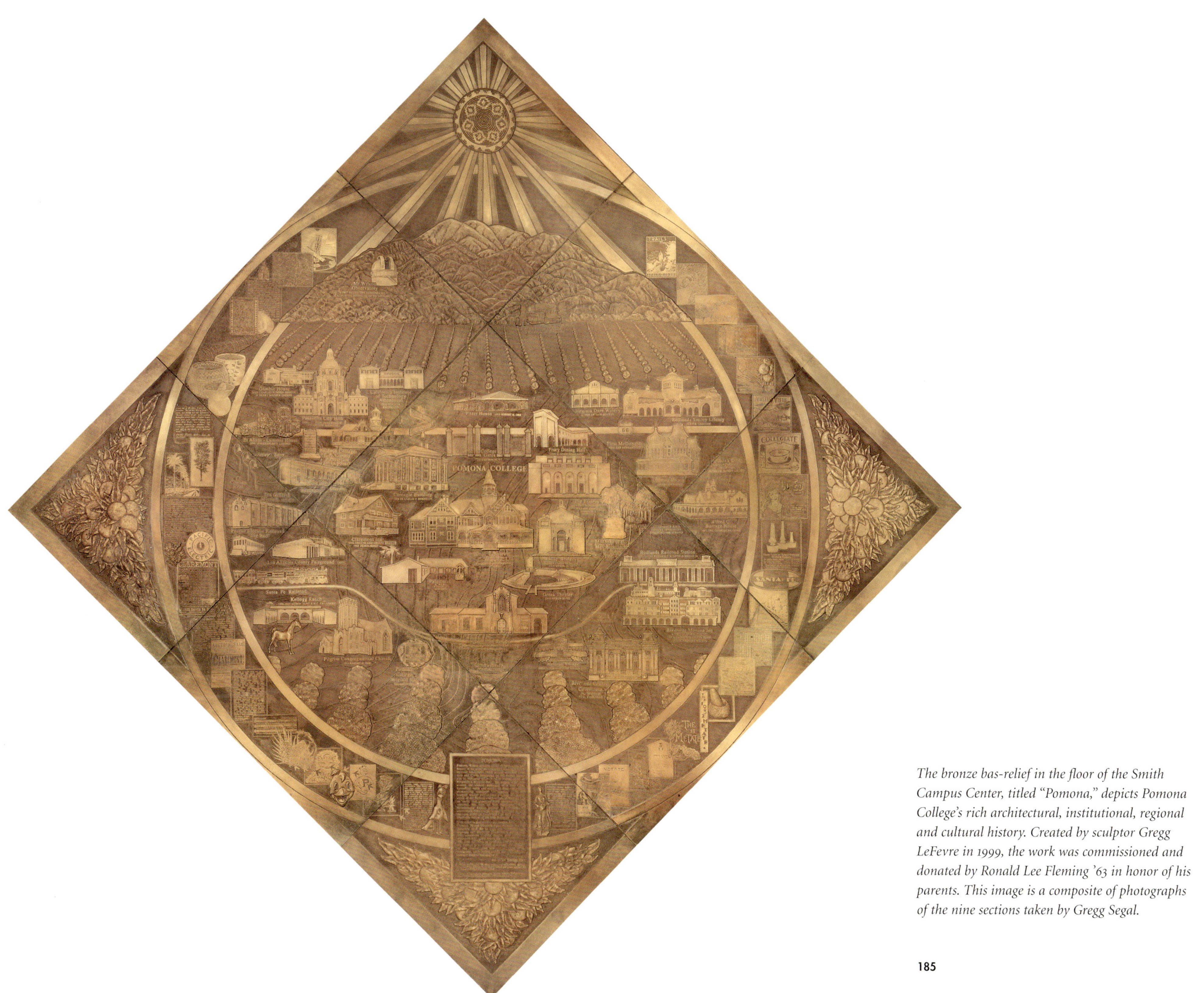

The bronze bas-relief in the floor of the Smith Campus Center, titled "Pomona," depicts Pomona College's rich architectural, institutional, regional and cultural history. Created by sculptor Gregg LeFevre in 1999, the work was commissioned and donated by Ronald Lee Fleming '63 in honor of his parents. This image is a composite of photographs of the nine sections taken by Gregg Segal.

NOTES

I. The Early Years

Introduction

1. Paul Venable Turner, *Campus: An American Planning Tradition* (New York: The Architectural History Foundation; Cambridge, Massachusetts: MIT Press, 1990), 54.
2. E. Wilson Lyon, *The History of Pomona College: 1887–1969* (Claremont: Pomona College, 1977), 41.
3. Charles Burt Sumner, *The Story of Pomona College* (Boston: The Pilgrim Press, 1914), 85.
4. Sumner, 149.
5. Sumner, 150.
6. Sumner, 247–49.
7. Turner, 9.
8. Turner, 6.
9. Turner, 8.
10. Turner, 101.

Buildings

1. Carolyn Lyon, taped conversation with John Lyon, 30 September 2005.
2. John Lyon, addendum to taped conversation with Carolyn Lyon, 30 September 2005.
3. Carolyn Lyon, taped conversation with Elizabeth Lyon Webb, 10–17 July 2005.
4. E-mail to author, October 2005.
5. Although it was recognized as early as the 1920s that Carnegie was inadequate to serve as Pomona's library, it was not until 1945, during the tenure of President E. Wilson Lyon, that a central library for the associated colleges was proposed. The building was made possible by the bequest of William Honnold, a trustee of Pomona and member of the founding board of The Claremont Colleges (established in 1925), who died in 1950. Construction on Honnold Library began in 1951, and the building was dedicated and began operations the following year. Of the 230,000 books and 146,600 documents moved to the new structure, more than half were from Pomona (Lyon, 441–45).

II. Myron Hunt at Pomona College

Introduction

1. *This essay is dedicated to the memory of Professors Phoebe Stanton (Johns Hopkins University) and William Jordy (Brown University), two beloved mentors, scholars and teachers, who introduced me to art history and modern architecture.*

Buildings

1. Donald M. Pattison, *Pomona College Magazine*, Spring 2001.
2. Lyon 152.

III. Consolidation and Growth

Introduction

1. Frank P. Brackett, *Granite and Sagebrush* (Los Angeles: The Ward Ritchie Press, 1944), 121.
2. Brackett, 121–22.
3. Brackett, 137.
4. Brackett, 128.
5. Lyon, 236.
6. Lyon, 264.

Buildings

1. *Pomona Today*, Autumn 1982.
2. David Alexander, e-mail to author, November 14, 2005.
3. Lyon 199–200.
4. Caroline Potter, "Eden in Bright Sunlight," *Pomona College Magazine,* Fall 2002, 14.
5. Robert A.M. Stern, *Dedication of the Smith Campus Center, September 18, 1999* (Claremont: Pomona College, 2000) 13.
6. Lyon, 274.
7. Lyon, 197.
8. Lyon, 536.
9. An employee of the Oakland Public Library in the years following World War I, Ena H. Thompson had helped install new library systems for the State of California. She was an avid reader, firmly persuaded of the values to be found in studying the Classics. In 1977, she expressed this love of great literature through funding the English Department's Ena H. Thompson Library and Reading Room in Crookshank Hall. In 1979, she endowed the George Erving Thompson Memorial Professorship in Government, with the expressed hope of inspiring "the students of Pomona College to good citizenship and worthy character to the honor of the College." Soon thereafter, she funded the Ena H. Thompson Lectureship in History, which brings an eminent guest lecturer to the campus each year. In 1981, Mrs. Thompson was awarded posthumously the Trustees' Medal of Merit.
10. David Scott, "Orozco's *Prometheus*: Recapitulation, Transition, Innovation," *College Art Journal*, XVII, no. 1, 1957, 2.
11. Lyon, 270.
12. Lyon, 330.
13. Carolyn Lyon, taped conversation with Elizabeth Lyon Webb, July 2005.

IV. The Lyon Years

Introduction

1. Turner, 251.
2. Turner, 264.
3. Carolyn Lyon, taped conversation with John Lyon, 30 September 2005.

Buildings

1. Lyon, 439.
2. Lyon, 487.
3. Lyon, 523.
4. *The Student Life*, December 9, 1965.
5. *Pomona Today*, April 1970.

V. From Regional to National

Introduction

1. President Alexander's reflections cited here derive from an e-mail to the author, November 14, 2005.

VI. A Second Millennium

Introduction

1. All comments attributed to Peter Stanley in this chapter derive from an e-mail to the author, October 2005.
2. David Oxtoby, *The Pomona College Annual Report of the President, 2004–05.*
3. Oxtoby, *Report.*

Buildings

1. *Pomona College Magazine*, Spring 2000.

SELECTED BIBLIOGRAPHY

Lawrence Biemiller, "The Center of the Campus," *Pomona College Magazine*, Spring 2000, 36–43.

Frank P. Brackett, *Granite and Sagebrush*. Los Angeles: The Ward Ritchie Press, 1944.

Susan Doubilet, "Smith Campus Center, Pomona College, Claremont, California," *Architectural Record*, August 2000, 142–45.

Thomas A. Gaines, *The Campus as Work of Art*. Westport, Connecticut: Praeger, 1991.

David Gebhard and Robert Winter, *Los Angeles: An Architectural Guide*. Salt Lake City: Gibbs Smith, 1994.

Marjorie L. Harth, *Art at Pomona 1887–1987: A Centennial Celebration*. Claremont: Pomona College, 1988.

_______________, *José Clemente Orozco: Prometheus*. Claremont: Pomona College, 2000.

_______________, "Genesis Revisited," *Pomona College Today*, Fall 1997, unpaginated insert.

Myron Hunt & Elmer Grey, Architects, Los Angeles, supplement to *Pomona College Bulletin*, November 21, 1908, vol. 5, no. 4, unpaginated. Special Collections, Honnold Library, Claremont Colleges.

William H. Jordy and William H. Pierson, Jr., *American Buildings and Their Architects*. Garden City, NY: Doubleday, 1970.

E. Wilson Lyon, *The History of Pomona College: 1887–1969*. Claremont: Pomona College, 1977.

Leo Marx, *The Machine in the Garden: Technology and the Pastoral Idea in America*. New York: Oxford University Press, 1964.

Jayne Merkel, "Postgraduate Studies: Smith Campus Center, Pomona College, Claremont California," *Architectural Record Review* (supplement to *Architectural Record* magazine), April 2005, 17–24.

Lewis Mumford, *The Brown Decades: A Study of the Arts in America, 1865–1895*. New York: Harcourt, Brace & Co., 1931.

Stefanos Polyzoides and Peter de Bretteville, "Myron Hunt as Architect of the Public Realm," *Myron Hunt, 1868–1952: The Search for A Regional Architecture* (exhibition catalogue). Pasadena: Baxter Art Gallery, California Institute of Technology, 1984.

John Ruskin, *The Seven Lamps of Architecture*. New York: E. P. Dutton & Co., 1921.

Vincent Scully, *American Architecture and Urbanism*. New York: Praeger, 1969.

_______________, *The Shingle Style: Architectural Theory and Design from Richardson to the Origins of Wright*. New Haven: Yale University Press, 1955.

Phoebe B. Stanton, *The Gothic Revival and American Church Architecture, An Episode in Taste, 1840–1856*. Baltimore: Johns Hopkins University Press, 1968.

Kevin Starr, *Americans and the California Dream, 1850–1915*. New York: Oxford University Press, 1973.

Robert A.M. Stern, *Dedication of the Smith Campus Center, September 18, 1999*. Claremont: Pomona College, 2000.

Charles Burt Sumner, *The Story of Pomona College*. Boston: The Pilgrim Press, 1914.

Paul Venable Turner, *Campus: An American Planning Tradition*. New York: The Architectural History Foundation; Cambridge, Massachusetts: MIT Press, 1990.

Alan Trachtenberg, *The Incorporation of America: Culture and Society in the Gilded Age*. New York: Hill & Wang, 1982.

Frederick Jackson Turner, *The Frontier in American History*. New York: A. Holt & Co., 1920.

Robert Winter, *The California Bungalow*, foreword by David Gebhard, *California Architecture and Architects*, no. 1. Los Angeles: Hennessey & Ingalls, 1980.

Robert Winter, *Myron Hunt at Occidental College*. Los Angeles: Occidental College, 1986.

Judy Wright, *Claremont: A Pictorial History*. Claremont: Claremont Historic Resources Center, 1980.

_______________, Revised Edition, 1999.

Romy Wylie, *Caltech's Architectural Heritage: From Spanish Tile to Modern Stone*. Glendale, California: Balcony Press, 2000.

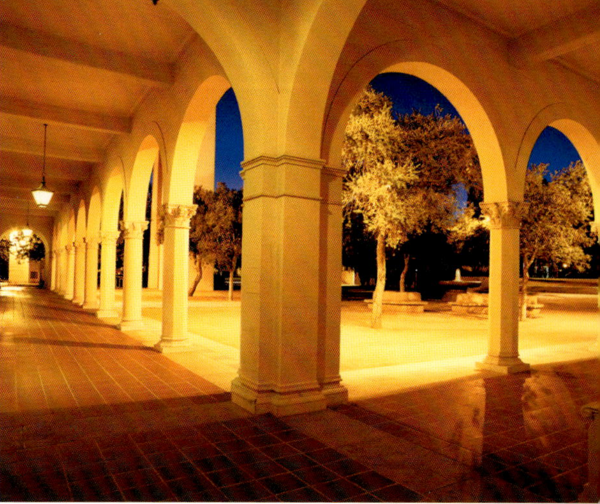

Gene Sasse

Eli P. Clark Men's Dormitory

INDEX

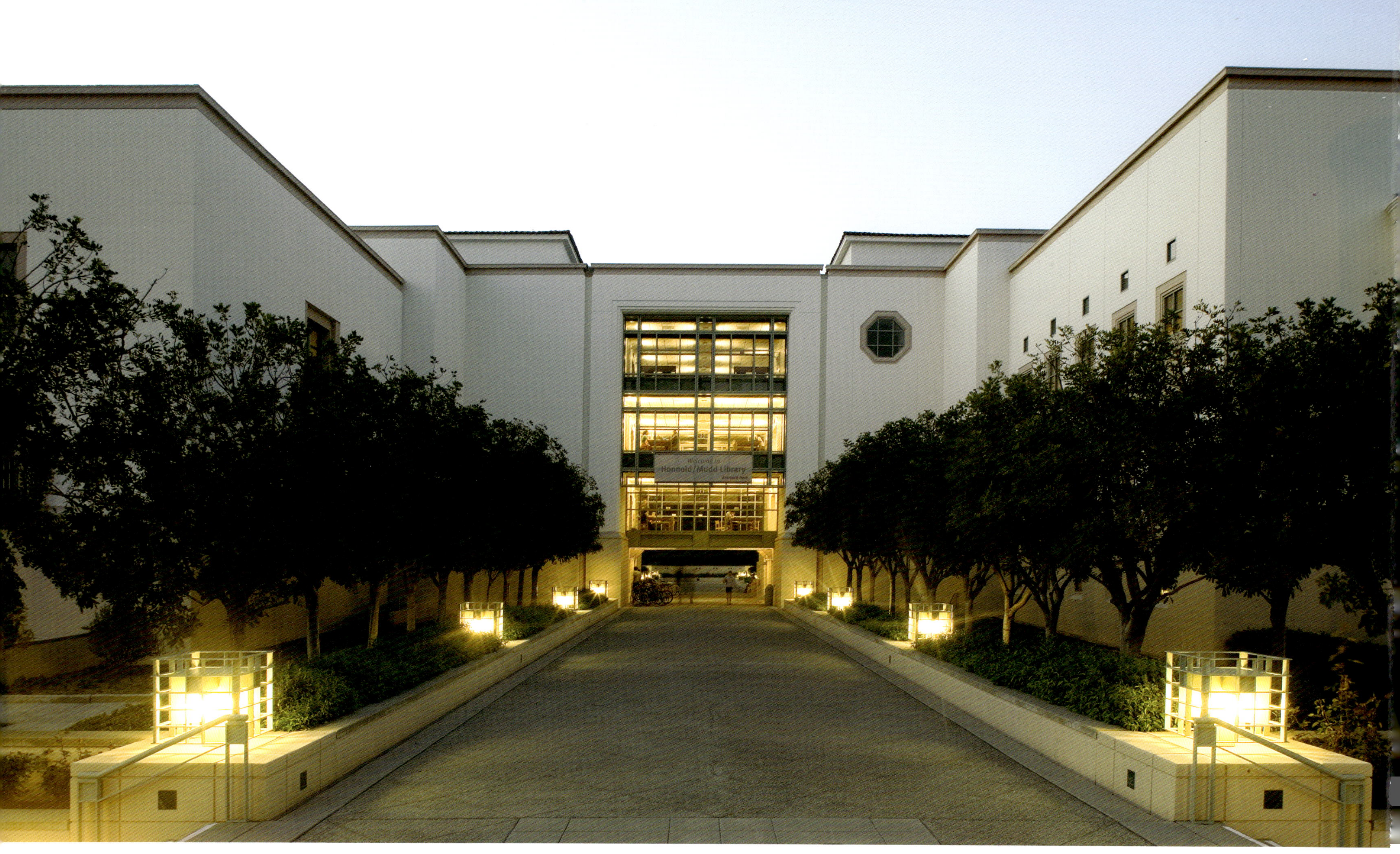

Henry Cabala

Honnold Library of The Claremont Colleges

About the Author

Marjorie L. Harth is Emerita Professor and Director, Pomona College Museum of Art. A graduate of Smith College and The University of Michigan, she served as director of the Galleries of The Claremont Colleges (1981–1993) and the Pomona College Museum of Art (1993–2004) while also teaching regular museum studies seminars. Her recent research has focused on museum ethics, particularly the dilemmas facing institutions responsible for indigenous collections. A frequent contributor to *Pomona College Magazine*, she is the author of a number of articles and exhibition catalogues, and two books: *Art at Pomona: 1887–1987*, and *José Clemente Orozco: Prometheus*.

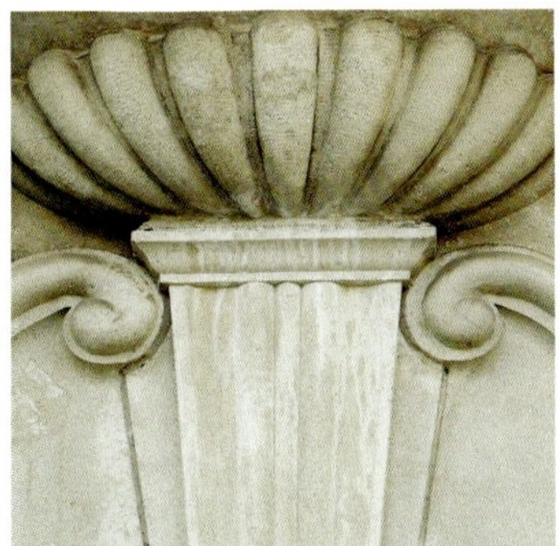

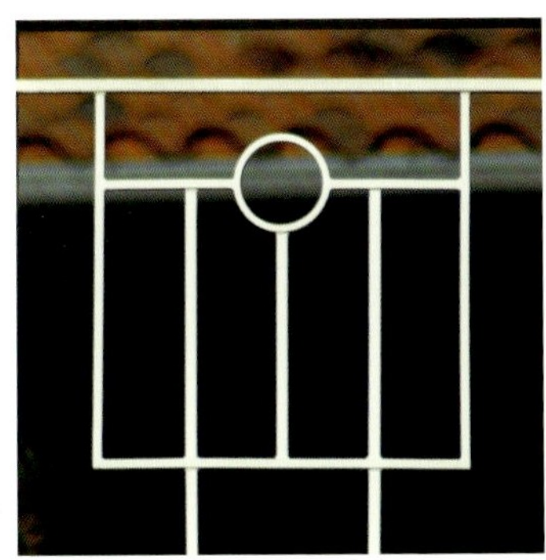

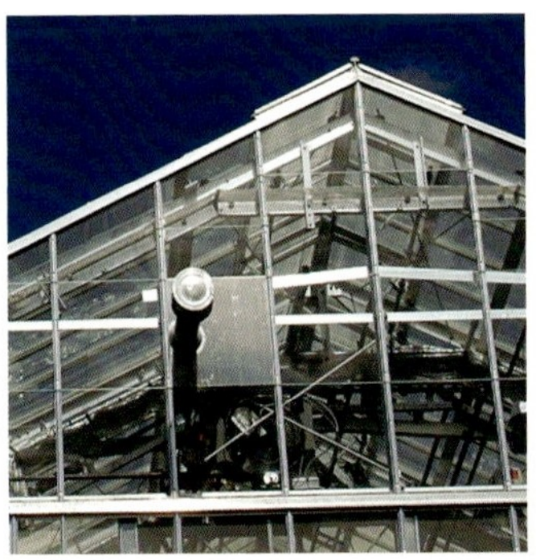

Contributors

Ronald Lee Fleming '63, A.I.C.P., is an urban planner, preservation advocate, environmental educator, and the author of several books on community character. A self-styled "venture" philanthropist, he lives in Cambridge, Massachusetts, and gardens in Newport, Rhode Island. He is a fourth generation Angeleno who has returned to his New England roots but carries a torch for Southern California that still casts for him an elegiac light.

George L. Gorse, Viola Horton Professor of Art History, has been a member of the Pomona College faculty since 1980. A specialist in the history of Renaissance and Baroque art, architecture, and urbanism, he has published widely, focusing particularly on the city of Genoa. Equally knowledgeable about modern American architecture, his many courses include a first-year seminar on the Pomona College campus.

Verlyn Klinkenborg '74 was the 2005 Pomona College Moseley Writing Fellow and returns regularly to teach on campus. A native of Iowa, he now lives on a small farm in upstate New York. An acclaimed writer, he is the author of *Making Hay*, *The Last Fine Time*, *The Rural Life*, and, most recently, *Timothy; Or, Notes of an Abject Reptile*. He is a member of the editorial board of *The New York Times*.